MAXIMINUS THRAX

MAXIMINUS THRAX

FROM COMMON SOLDIER TO EMPEROR OF ROME

PAUL N PEARSON

Skyhorse Publishing

Copyright © 2016 Paul N. Pearson

First published in Great Britain in 2016 by Pen & Sword Military, an imprint of
Pen & Sword Books Ltd

First Skyhorse Publishing edition 2017

Skyhorse Publishing books may be purchased in bulk at special discounts for
sales promotion, corporate gifts, fund-raising, or educational purposes. Special
editions can also be created to specifications. For details, contact the Special
Sales Department, Skyhorse Publishing, 307 West 36th Street, 11th Floor, New
York, NY 10018 or info@skyhorsepublishing.com.

Skyhorse® and Skyhorse Publishing® are registered trademarks of Skyhorse
Publishing, Inc.®, a Delaware corporation.

Visit our website at www.skyhorsepublishing.com.

10 9 8 7 6 5 4 3 2 1

Library of Congress Cataloging-in-Publication Data is available on file.

Cover design by Dominic Allen
Cover photo: Bust of Maximinus Thrax in the Capitoline Museum, Rome.
Photograph copyright of Paul N. Pearson.

Print ISBN: 978-1-5107-0863-1
Ebook ISBN: 978-1-5107-0875-4

Printed in the United States of America

Contents

Acknowledgements

I am very grateful to historian and author Harry Sidebottom for taking the time to read the manuscript and discussing various points of interest. Any remaining errors are mine, as is my interpretation of the historical sources. I would like to thank Roy and Lesley Adkins for fostering my interest in archaeology and Roman history at the Beddington villa excavation back in the early 1980s and, more recently, for sound advice on publishing; and Philip Sidnell, Daniel Mersey and Matt Jones for seeing the manuscript through the process at Pen and Sword. Christian Roemer took pity on my lack of German during the tour of the Harzhorn and was then kind enough to read an early draft. I thank Ian Haynes for interesting discussions and a memorable visit to the excavations underneath San Giovanni in Laterano. Lyman and Patricia Gurney have been very helpful regarding text analysis of the *Augustan History*. Francesca Boldrighini of the National Museum in Rome was very patient with my queries. The British School in Rome supported my research with their excellent library facilities and helpful staff. I am also very grateful to my family, who have endured my enthusiasms over the last few years.

List of Illustrations

1.1. A page from the oldest surviving manuscript of the *Augustan History* in which the life of Maximinus begins *(reproduced with permission of the Biblioteca Apostolica Vaticana in Rome)*.

2.1. The dynasty of Septimius Severus. Note that both Elagabalus and Severus Alexander claimed Caracalla as their natural father *(coins with the permission of CNG coins)*.

3.1. Geta, the boy prince, c. 200 CE *(CNG coins)*.

3.2. Septimius Severus, 196 CE, with an imposing bodyguard *(CNG coins)*.

3.3. Tombstone naming the troop of Julius Maximinus of the *equites singulares*, c. 200 CE.

3.4. Mosaic floor and part of a surviving wall of the *palaestra* (exercise space) attached to the bathhouse of the imperial horseguard in Rome *(photograph by the author with permission, Vatican museums)*.

4.1. Julia Mamaea, 230 CE.

4.2. Severus Alexander goes to war *(profectio)*, 231 CE.

4.3. Severus Alexander, 232 CE.

4.4. Ardashir, Persian king of kings, c. 230 CE *(all coins with permission of CNG coins)*.

4.5. Boiler boy: Persian armoured horseman, third century graffito from Dura Europos.

5.1. The walls of Dura Europos and the palace of the *dux ripae* overlooking the Euphrates *(www.colorado.edu)*.

5.2. Restored Roman-style temple at the Armenian Royal Fortress at Garni, Armenia *(author photograph)*.

5.3. The harsh Armenian terrain traversed by the Roman army invading Persian Medea *(author photograph)*.

6.1. The Album of Canusium with the name of Petronius Magnus erased from the first column. Modified from Salway (2000).

6.2. Maximinus addresses the troops (*adlocutio*): from his first issue of coins, 235 CE (*CNG coins*).

6.3. The Harzhorn in Germany (arrows show line of ancient trackway and Roman assault) (*author photograph*).

7.1. Distribution of finds on the Harzhorn ridge (*arch.rwth–aachen.de*).

7.2. Roman horseshoe (*Thorsten Schwarz, Wikimedia Commons*).

7.3. Roman ballista bolts (*Braunschweigisches Landesmuseum, Wikimedia Commons*).

7.4. The Harzhorn battlefield: the Romans attacked up this slope (*author photograph*).

8.1. Germanic spearpoint from the Harzhorn (*Thorsten Schwarz, Wikimedia Commons*).

8.2. Roman *dolabra* (axe head) inscribed LEG IIII S A, Harzhorn region (*Martin Oppermann, Wikimedia Commons*).

8.3. Victory coinage (VICTORIA GERMANICA), 235-6 CE (*CNG coins*).

9.1. The imperial family: Maximinus Augustus, the divine Paulina (reverse: ascending to the heavens on a peacock) and Maximus Caesar, Prince of Youth (PRINCIPII IVVENTVTIS) (*coins with the permission of CNG coins*).

10.1. The amphitheatre at Thysdrus (El Djem) attributed to the elder Gordian (*Jerzystrzelecki, Wikimedia Commons*).

10.2. Coin of Gordian I advertising the Security of the Two Emperors, and Gordian II (*CNG coins*).

10.3. The forum of Aquileia, Italy (*author photograph*).

11.1. Foundations of hastily built defences, Aquileia, 238 CE. This was originally the river dock front. Semicircular towers, probably mounting artillery, were added either side of the steps down to the river (*author photograph*).

11.2. Roman crossing point of the river Sontius (Isonzo), Italy, at low water before the spate (*author photograph*).

12.1. Pupienus: *fathers of the senate*.

12.2. Balbinus: *mutual faith of the emperors*.

Introduction

This book is centred on the life of an extraordinary individual, the Roman emperor Maximinus Thrax ('the Thracian'), but my wider ambition is to use the subject to explore the much neglected history of the early third century in the west and especially the troubled 230s of the Common Era. This was an extraordinary period of struggle and upheaval when the Roman Empire was at its greatest extent and arguably the height of its power but began to face the might of a resurgent Persian Empire in the east. The events related here are every bit as dramatic and the cast of players just as rich as the better-known periods of Roman history of the first centuries BCE and CE, but the deeds and names of the principal characters have hardly permeated modern consciousness: we have all heard of Caesar, Caligula and Nero but who has heard of Severus Alexander, the three Gordians, or of Maximinus Thrax?

The reason for this may be an anomaly of more recent history. The teaching of classical Latin from the Enlightenment onward has focused overwhelmingly on a few great authors from the so-called 'golden age' of Latin literature which runs from Cicero to Ovid, that is, writers who lived and wrote a few decades either side of Year 1 (there being no Year 0). Knowledge of this literature and its historical context, with the ancient Greek classics, was long at the core of what was considered a good education throughout Europe. In contrast, writers and historians from later in antiquity have tended to be disparaged or ignored, mainly because their use of language evolved away from the perceived gold standard or they used Greek in a Roman context. So while the earlier period of Roman history has become a core part of 'general knowledge' which educated people might be expected to know something about, the later period has not.[1]

This makes the third and fourth centuries particularly fascinating for the general reader interested in knowing more about history: an inquirer of the twenty-first century might very well learn of consequential events of that period for the first time and be surprised and delighted afresh by knowledge of globally significant happenings. Moreover the events have many modern-day parallels and ironies for our own civilization which may be passing its high water mark.

I came across Maximinus while reading the first volume of Gibbon's majestic *Decline and Fall of the Roman Empire*. It struck me as the most exciting sequence of events in that book and something of a fulcrum in Gibbon's account, and I wondered why our modern culture has forgotten the story. I decided to fill the gap, and the process of discovery has taken me through a series of topics from the wondrous archaeology of Roman Mesopotamia, sadly under great threat at the time of writing, to studies of ancient eclipses, early Christianity, Roman statuary and even eighteenth-century theatre. The project was already underway in 2009 when the Internet first started to register news of stunning archaeological finds being made on a wooded ridge near the Saxon Plain of Germany which, it slowly became clear, relate directly to the Thracian's story. With the work nearly done, I read the excellent published PhD thesis of Karen Haegemans on the reign of Maximinus which provides the perfect entry point for anyone interested in accessing the full literature on Maximinus and his times.[2]

Although I am an academic by trade, my intention here is not scholarly research but to tell an entertaining story from the past to interested people. As an avid consumer of the ignoble genre of 'popular' history, I especially enjoy narrative accounts, that is, learning of unfolding events without too much forewarning of the ultimate outcome. The historian upon whose work much of this book rests would have understood this. He wrote in Greek and his name is Herodian (not to be confused with the so-called 'father of history' Herodotus, who wrote six centuries earlier). History in the ancient world was always about the delight and drama of the telling and hearing, not just the dry facts, although it was also supposed to be accurate and verifiable. Narrative history has surprising twists and turns, soaring episodes and uncomfortable bumps. It relates to that most human of impulses, the telling of stories round the campfire. Most modern historical research, in contrast, focuses on facts and analysis and tends to be written for other academics, and professional historians often recoil from what has been called "the fear of narrating battle-history, or the history of events".[3] But narrative history has one great strength that we neglect at our peril: it allows us to consider the human response to moments of crisis, uncertainty, risk and decision, and to reflect on how things came to pass and what might have been different had other decisions been made.

We know very little about Herodian the man. The general view is that he was from the east of the empire, possibly the great city of Antioch, and was a minor functionary in the Roman civil service. An older idea that he may have been a much more important personage – a senator – has gone out of fashion although the reasons for that are not clear to me. He is sometimes criticized in comparison to other historians from a more classical age and especially his part-contemporary, Cassius Dio.[4] I think that is unfair. Herodian was an eyewitness to extraordinary events that would otherwise be unknown and, as he tells us, "I had a personal share in some of these events during my imperial and public service." Unfortunately he does not tell us which parts of his story he witnessed, although we can make some informed guesses. Nor did he tell us what his role in the imperial service was. But we should recall his words, penned in Greek around the year 245:

> My policy has been not to accept any second-hand information which has not been checked and corroborated. I have collected the evidence for my work with every attention to accuracy, limiting it to what falls within the recent memory of my readers. But I believe that future generations too will derive some pleasure from the knowledge of events which are important and compressed within a brief span of time.
>
> Herodian, *History of the Empire*: I.I.3[5]

We are just the latest of Herodian's future generations to benefit from his industry. I have felt real pleasure reading his account which forms the backbone of my own narrative. I encourage anyone interested in knowing more about the events described herein to do so as well. There are, of course, many other historical sources of greater or lesser reliability which will be introduced in due course.

Prologue

Winter was turning to spring in the year 194 and west was battling east. Lucius Septimius Severus, legitimate emperor of Rome in the eyes of the senate, was camped out with his army near the city of Perinthus in the province of Thrace. He was engaged in civil war with Caius Pescennius Niger who also claimed to be emperor and controlled most of the eastern provinces including Egypt, which ordinarily provided much of Rome's grain. That winter, Severus's army had slog-marched its way overland from the eternal city, swelling along the way with detachments from the Danube legions and fresh levies of local recruits.[1]

In ancient warfare there was a distinct campaigning season which began in the spring and ended in the autumn. The reason for this was not that some kind of chivalrous truce broke out each year, but that the baggage animals that carried all the equipment needed grazing. With the stalks still ripening and the army unable to move long distances except by the main highways and supply lines, Severus proclaimed a set of military games to be held on the *nones* of *Martius* (7th March). The excuse: a birthday celebration for his young son, the most noble prince Publius Septimius Geta. The boy was five years old with chubby cheeks and curly dark hair. Events included running, wrestling, horsemanship and no doubt other martial arts. The finest soldiers competed for silver medals and athletic glory. The occasion, which is described in an ancient document called the *Augustan History*,[2] breaks some of the stereotypes of ancient Rome: it does not involve fights to the death between condemned criminals nor is there mass slaughter of wild animals. Instead it sounds much more like a medieval tournament.

And like any tale of Robin Hood, the games had an unlikely star. He was a young man of barbarian stock from the interior of the province, drawn to the legions hoping to enlist. As such he was typical of the auxiliary recruits that did most of the fighting for Rome. What made him stand out from the crowd – literally – was his freakish physique. He was enormously tall, with exaggerated (but handsome) manly features and possessed awesome brute strength. To the astonishment and delight of the crowd, this man could pull fully laden wagons by himself, tear apart green saplings and smash rocks with his bare hands.

Today he might compete in Olympic shotput or sumo wrestling, or win fame as a TV strongman. In ancient Rome, perhaps even more so than now, he was a born celebrity.

We can imagine that the raucous comrades of the muscular giant were desperate for him to take part in the wrestling, especially if bets were being taken. The problem was that the games were not open to ordinary citizens. Despite this, goaded by his friends, the Thracian directly approached the emperor and publicly begged an opportunity to compete. Such audacity could have been interpreted as insolence and might have earned severe punishment or worse. The supplicant spoke in "almost pure Thracian"[3] rather than Latin, but he was able to make himself understood through interpreters.

The emperor Severus, a wiry little fellow with a trademark ragged forked beard, was renowned for quick and sound decision-making. Casting his penetrating gaze over the petitioner, he reflected on the dilemma. The Romans, of course, loved a spectacle, none more than himself, but anyone could guess that this man was likely to be unbeatable. Those he would defeat would include army officers who could hardly be humiliated by a civilian, still less a barbarian, in front of their men and emperor. So, stroking his beard (if we may be allowed to interject some modern imagination), Severus announced a kind of side-show to the main event. He invited challengers from the common soldiers, those burly back-stagers engaged in supplying the army and setting up the show, to take on the giant. For these men there was little to lose other than pride, and much to gain – a chance of appearing heroic in front of the emperor and perhaps receiving some reward. By the day's end, no fewer than sixteen challengers had been vanquished in succession. Severus handed the Thracian a set of silver trinkets and ordered him to enlist in the Roman army.

And so the story might have ended, except that the next day the big man once again attracted the emperor's attention, this time by behaving uproariously with his friends "in a barbarian manner" somewhere in the crowd. Fortunately, Severus was in a playful mood and announced that he wanted to see if he could run as well as wrestle. So, instructing him to follow, he began cantering up and down the parade ground. The new recruit had to obey such an order, direct from the emperor, to complete exhaustion. No doubt the crowd cheered him on as he trailed behind the emperor's fine horse, increasingly out of breath. After many circuits, Severus turned to ask him if he was still prepared to wrestle, which of course he was. The largest men in the crowd were ordered to come forward. Once again the giant proved unbeatable, and after seven new challengers were wrestled to the dust, the delighted emperor called a halt to proceedings. At the closing ceremony he declared the Thracian champion of the games, awarded him a collar of gold, and earmarked him for his personal bodyguard.

A gold collar (in Latin, *torquis*) was a great honour, generally a mark of bravery, and a soldier who earned it was henceforth known as a *torquatus* and would receive double pay, or at least different allowances. The Thracian recruit became something of a celebrity and, we are told, a particular favourite of the emperor himself. Tall tales circulated: some compared his physique to the legendary Greek wrestler Milo of Croton, and others, with even more enthusiasm, to the demigod Hercules. Men said he was eight feet and six inches in height. He would eat forty, some said sixty, pounds of meat a day and could drink a 'Capitoline amphora' of wine in one sitting (which was 26 litres, so perhaps we are entitled to conclude that this was an ancient saying for drinking a lot). He sweated pints at a time and, even less charmingly, he could loosen a horse's teeth with his fist, which one at least hopes refers to an enemy charger in battle and not some peaceful beast of the fields.[4]

Although we do not know his Thracian birth name, we do know that like many other provincials he became known by a Roman one: Caius Julius Verus Maximinus. Incredible as it may seem, this circus strongman was destined to become emperor of Rome. Known to history as Maximinus Thrax, this is the story of his life and times and the upheavals he put in motion that some have argued marked the beginning of the end for classical civilization.[5]

Maximinus's Giantism, and a note about Sources

Maximinus, it seems, really was a giant of a man. The most reliable of the ancient authors, Herodian, who may have seen him in person many times, says he was "of such frightening appearance and colossal size that there is no obvious comparison to be drawn with any of the best-trained Greek athletes or warrior elite of the barbarians".[6] Moreover the written works are supplemented by coins and inscriptions and other archaeological evidence. The coins of this period had reached a high stage of artistic excellence and the engravers aimed for a genuine likeness of the emperor. Statues survive, and they show a big and powerful individual with a very heavy brow, prominent nose and jaw and penetrating gaze. Other Roman emperors were not depicted like this: balding, corpulent individuals were more usual.[7]

This opens up interesting areas of speculation. From the Thracian's reported physical features, a Chicago professor of neurology, Harold Klawans, proposed a diagnosis of acromegaly.[8] This is a condition involving excessive growth hormone that causes heavy muscular and skeletal development that becomes apparent after puberty and, if untreated, can result in giantism. It is often, although not exclusively, caused by a benign tumour on the pituitary gland. Acromegaly is rare, but not excessively so, affecting about one person in 20,000, and it would have been a feature of ancient life as well as modern (indeed more so, because nowadays it is usually treated with surgery).

In more recent times, several men with this condition have made their way to fame by playing to the crowds as professional boxers, wrestlers and horror actors. Here are some examples, most of them over seven feet tall, with imaginative nicknames and stories reminiscent of the Thracian: Rondo Hatton (1894–1946), Hollywood B-movie horror star who played the 'Hoxton Creeper' in *Sherlock Holmes and the Pearl of Death* (1944); Primo Carnera (1906–1967), 'The Ambling Alp', world heavyweight boxing champion; Richard Kiel (1940–2014), starred as 'Jaws' in *The Spy who Loved Me* (1977); Carol Struyken (1948–), starred as 'Lurch' in *The Addams Family* movies; André Rousimoff (1946–1993), French professional wrestler, starred as 'Fezzik' in *The Princess Bride* (1987); Nikolai Valuev (1973–), 'The Beast from the East', world heavyweight boxing champion, star of the movie *Stone Head* (2008) and now Russian parliamentarian; and Paul Randall Wright (1972–), professional smackdown wrestler and actor, starred as 'Walter Krunk' in *Knucklehead* (2010).[9] When we consider that a Roman 'foot' was a little less than the modern measurement and no doubt inconsistently applied,[10] even the reported height of Maximinus seems to come within the bounds of possibility, although it would also be strange indeed if there was no exaggeration in the telling.

When such outlandish claims are made, the easier path for the historian is to dismiss them as invention, but perhaps this particular ancient story could be true in essence. As we shall see, giantism provides Maximinus with a plausible early career, which has some independent corroboration, and it can also help with deeply puzzling aspects of his image as depicted on the coinage and statuary. We also should remember that for all those who confidently claimed that tales of Richard III of England's 'crookback' were mere Tudor propaganda, the unlikely discovery of the king's skeleton finally told otherwise.[11]

Be that as it may, it would be disingenuous to embark on the story of Maximinus and his times without offering a huge caveat. The unfortunate truth is that third-century history must be approached with a sense of extreme caution regarding the likely veracity of the ancient texts, and unfortunately the aforementioned story of Maximinus at the military games is from the most unreliable of them all. The historical sources are reviewed in the first appendix but the salient facts are as follows.

Evidence of what happened comes to us either from archaeology, including artifacts, papyri and inscriptions, or from ancient books. Surviving historical sources are of variable quality and reliability and they are complexly interlinked.

What they have in common is that they are not the originals: they all come to us via Byzantine or Carolingian manuscripts, often after multiple copying and frequently heavy editing and alteration. Many of the works are obviously incomplete and some are just fragments quoted in other works, possibly not in the right order. Even so, the texts are rich and detailed. Historians have worked hard to determine how they are related and the likely content of lost works that later authors have evidently drawn from and sometimes refer to directly.

The most important work on Maximinus and his times is Herodian's *History of the Empire from the Death of Marcus Aurelius*,[12] a detailed, structured narrative in Greek that survives virtually intact. Also of great use in setting the scene is the *Roman History* of Cassius Dio, a senior senator and twice consul, but unfortunately it only extends to the beginning of our period. Most of the other ancient works add relatively minor details, although sometimes they are important and enlightening ones.

The great exception to this is a large and complex work known as the *Augustan History* (in Latin, *Historia Augusta*). This is a compendium of lives (*vitae*) of emperors and claimants to the throne, many of which are dedicated to the emperors Diocletian (reigned 284–305) and Constantine (reigned 307–337), and so were apparently written in the late third to early fourth century. The lives appear under the names of six authors: Aelius Spartianus, Julius Capitolinus, Vulcacius Gallicanus, Aelius Lampridius, Trebellius Pollio and Flavius Vopiscus. Gallicanus is distinguished by the title *vir clarissimus*, which means 'illustrious man', denoting a senator. These men are known collectively as the 'writers of the *Augustan History*' (*scriptores historiae augustae*), but none of them is otherwise known. The main period dealt with in this book is covered by Lampridius and Capitolinus although all of them chip in with something of interest for our story.

All scholars agree that the collection is notoriously unreliable and contains a great deal of error and quite a lot of false or obviously fabricated content: fake imperial letters, wild gossip and miraculous omens abound. The problem is that it also contains potentially useful and correct information that would otherwise be lost to us. There are several instances where unique information from it has been independently corroborated by inscriptional or archaeological evidence.[13] We know that for our period of interest the *Augustan History* made great use of Herodian (which is easy to detect, as we have the original with which to compare it), as well as a lost work attributed to the Athenian statesman Publius Herennius Dexippus and, very likely, at least one other fairly reliable lost source. When one compares passages derived from Herodian with the original, the general sense is one of reasonable accuracy plus embellishment, wherein the embellishment could be miscellaneous information from other sources (a scholar writing at that time would have been steeped in information now lost to us), or fabrication for effect, or, of course, both.

Particularly intriguing are many references in the *Augustan History* to a work by Junius Cordus (sometimes given as Aelius Cordus) on the lives of the emperors. These references usually contain trivial gossipy details relating to their supposed dietary preferences, unlikely deeds and various salacious details, seemingly in emulation of the more flighty parts of Suetonius's famous work on the first *Twelve Caesars* of Rome. The cautious–sceptical twentieth-century consensus was that the history of Cordus, like some other supposed works referred to only occasionally in the *Augustan History*, was a fictional invention. Hence he was a vehicle for the frequent padding out of the accounts when real information was lacking. Amusingly, Cordus is often contradicted by the *scriptores* when being cited, and in more than one place he is censured for being superficial and a poor historian.[14] Other scholars have taken the view that a work by Cordus really did exist in antiquity, although it was prone to invention and wild exaggeration. Resolving this question seems very difficult despite the entrenched views on offer.[15] A point in Cordus's favour is that references to him begin and end abruptly with two reigns, as opposed to being distributed randomly throughout the many lives, which is consistent with a work that only covered a subset of the emperors dealt with in the *Augustan History*. I am prepared to peep over the parapet and state that I think it is more likely than not that a work by Cordus actually existed, although it contained very little of historical worth.

The dubious status of Cordus is, however, a minor issue in comparison to a thesis first proposed by Hermann Dessau in the late nineteenth century that the entire *Augustan History* is an elaborate fraud written by just a single author at a significantly later date than it claims. Hence Lampridius, Capitolinus and their colleagues never existed! The reasons for suspecting this are complex, but include the obviously fictitious nature of certain sections; textual analysis; consideration of events, customs and personal names that seem to make sense only from a late fourth-century perspective; logical inconsistencies; and several slips of information that seem out of place or could not have been known to Diocletian and Constantine's historians. What we do know is that the *Augustan History* must have been completed by 485 CE because it was cited at that time. If it is indeed by a single person, it is a very entertaining deception because one of the 'authors' refers to some of the others.[16]

Dessau's bombshell ignited a great scholarly debate, particularly among German classicists, some of whom supported and extended the idea while others flatly repudiated it. Still others adopted a middle ground, acknowledging that the stylistic similarity of the *scriptores* is down to a common model (the imperial biographies of Suetonius), or that they all borrow extensively from a lost work, or that they could have been extensively edited and augmented at a later date – the great Nobel prize-winning historian of the ancient world, Theodor Mommsen, was one such. All this was most ably summarized in 1922 by David Magie, who broadly followed Mommsen's line when the standard English translation of the *Augustan History* was issued.[17] But Dessau's original view grew dominant through the twentieth century through the weighty support of top scholars, especially the charismatic Ronald Syme of Oxford, a New Zealander by birth, who wrote two influential books on the subject. Syme's books are themselves oddities: works of great distinction delivered in an idiosyncratic and didactic style that, to put it mildly, scarcely encourages dissent. His pupil, T. D. Barnes, went so far as to state "I hold Dessau's disproof of the *Historia Augusta*'s pretensions to be irrefragable, and there is no point in wasting more space"; and as another remarked, following Syme's contributions, "defenders of the ostensible date and multiple authorship appear to have capitulated, retired or fallen silent".[18] One can hardly blame them given Syme's combination of virtuoso erudition and the irascible tone and accusations of credulity that he directed at those who were wont to accept the *Augustan History* more at face value.

The kind of classical education that allowed previous generations of scholars to engage in recondite disputation on the style and content of fourth and fifth century Latin is increasingly a thing of the past. A more modern development has been the application of statistical analysis of words, phrases and text structure using computational algorithms (a discipline known as 'stylometry'). The first application of this method in the 1970s supported the idea of single authorship and was enthusiastically welcomed by Syme himself before his death. However that pioneering work was subsequently criticized on methodological grounds and much more sophisticated treatments published in 1998 came emphatically to the opposite conclusion. Analysis of the linguistic content and style of the writer, using the full panoply of stylometric methods available at that time, not only upheld the likelihood of multiple authorship, specifically rejecting the idea that there is a single main author, but it was also been found that the individual lives or *vitae* may have been attributed to the correct range of authors all along! Or, to be precise, there is evidence that the thirty *vitae* divide between six distinct styles of writing which account unequally for between one and nine *vitae* each, and that those six styles correspond to the six names that head all of the respective documents. But because we have no independent writings by the authors to compare them with, we cannot (of course) confirm that 'Aelius Lampridius' or any other named individual wrote a particular group of the lives.

The implications of this result, if verified, are very far-reaching because they provide strong support for the general authenticity of the collection which had been pretty much written off in the twentieth century by Syme and his followers. It is much more difficult to imagine a set of six fraudsters working together to a general plan than it is a single scribe of nefarious purpose penning the entire work in secret under a series of pseudonyms. Despite this development, or perhaps because of it, the great debate seems to have almost died; the Dessau/Syme view remains the orthodoxy, and with one prominent exception (a thoughtful essay by Daniël den Hengst from 2002) the stylometric studies have almost never been cited except by a very few other stylometricians. Twenty-first century historians of the later Roman Empire, it seems, might be guilty of having their collective heads in the sand.[19] Further investigation of the stylometric case seems warranted.

Syme (1971, p. 189), in his inimical fashion, specifically sanctioned against using the *Augustan History* to flesh out the story of the Thracian as "sheer aberration". Here we will proceed, cautiously, to do what he warned us not to do, so as to preserve the sense of narrative in the ancient documents and allow the reader some discretion in the matter. Arguments about the historical sources aside, what we can be confident of is that Maximinus, a relatively obscure individual of extraordinary physique, came to prominence in Rome, and we can wonder: how did that happen?

Chapter I

Nurs'd in Blood and War

Origins

None of the early sources gives a date for Maximinus's birth but according to the late antiquity writer Zonoras it was in 172 or 173 CE, which would fit the facts. Herodian says that he was from "one of the semi-barbarous tribes" of innermost Thrace where he was a shepherd boy in a small village. Characteristically, the *Augustan History* gives more details:

He was born in a village in Thrace bordering on the barbarians, indeed of a barbarian father and mother, the one, men say, being of the Goths, the other of the Alans. At any rate, they say that his father's name was Micca, his mother Ababa. And in his early years Maximinus himself freely disclosed these names; later, however, when he came to the throne, he had them concealed, lest it should seem that the emperor on both sides was sprung of barbarian stock.[1]

It also adds the colourful detail that in his youth he was leader of a gang of bandits.

Thrace (if taken in the broad geographic terms implied in this account which includes the outlying province of Moesia Inferior) was a central cog in the Roman Empire that today is centred on Bulgaria. It is varied territory: low-lying and fertile tracts fringe the Black Sea and the basin of the lower Danube but the outer districts are mountainous and subject to extremes of weather. This was the land that had been invaded in the fifth century BCE by Darius and Xerxes, kings of Persia, on their way to attack Athens and Sparta, and later by Alexander the Great heading in the other direction. Thracia, later a client kingdom of Rome, was finally incorporated into the empire as a province in 45 CE. It remained an important buffer zone, but in a north-south sense, protecting the civilized riches of the Mediterranean from the nomadic barbarians of the northern steppes. Its capital was Byzantium (later Constantinople and now Istanbul) on the Bosporus: even then an opulent and well-connected city. Byzantium owed most of its wealth to water-borne trade, however, rather than the more meagre products of the provincial interior.[2]

Thracian civilization is very ancient indeed. The earliest worked gold in the world has been discovered in the graves of its forgotten kings, older even than the gold of the pharaohs. Despite this, to the ancient Greeks the Thracians were the original 'barbarians' (the phrase possibly means 'the bearded ones') and anti-Thracian prejudice ran strong down to Roman times. Rome had fought some of its earliest wars against Thrace in the fourth century BCE, and not always with success. One relic of this history was that one of the standard gladiators in the Roman arena was the fearsome 'Thrax', equipped with a vicious short-curved blade and a small shield, who was generally pitted against a more heavily armoured but less nimble opponent.

Not all gladiators who played the Thrax actually came from Thrace but one who did was the most famous of them all: Spartacus, leader of the great slave revolt of 73–71 BCE that rocked the Roman world and even threatened Rome herself. In the end, Spartacus lost his revolution to massive state power and brutality. But the trail of devastation he caused can hardly have improved the image of Thracian strongmen in the eyes of the Romans. The stereotype of the brutish, ignorant, Thracian muscle-man even propagates into modern times.[3]

North of Thrace, along the Black Sea coast, the land opens out onto the steppes of central Asia. This vast and relatively flat area was home to a kaleidoscope of semi-nomadic peoples including the Scythians, Goths, Getae, Dacians, Carpi, Alans and Roxolani. In the twentieth century, when mechanized armies tried to control the expanse, it was discovered that the tactics of sea power were necessary because territory cannot be 'held' in endless tracts of waving grass any more than they can on the ocean. The expansionist Romans, who could only project their military might with blade and point, also discovered that the area could not be occupied, civilized or even controlled. The problem then reduced to one of keeping the steppe barbarians out.

The Alans, the tribe supposedly on Maximinus's maternal side, were a people of the grass and marsh between the Don and Volga. According to the Roman historian Ammianus Marcellinus they lived a completely nomadic existence with no fixed dwellings, and survived principally by hunting and raiding. For religion they worshipped a sword stuck in the ground wherever camp was pitched. The women and children performed all the domestic tasks while the men trained exclusively for warfare, especially mounted archery. For an Alan warrior there was no more contemptible fate than to die peacefully in old age. Interestingly, the Alans are about equally well attested in ancient

Chinese sources as in Roman. Both civilizations admired their skills as mounted archers and used a phonetically similar name for the tribe.[4]

The Goths on the other hand were a western Germanic tribe that according to their own rich oral history (written down much later), once inhabited the shores of the Baltic in northern Europe which includes 'Gothland' in modern Sweden. They migrated southeast to the lands bordering the northern shore of the Black Sea which then became their homeland. This might seem an unlikely trek but archaeological evidence has provided solid support for it: there is a continuity and movement of material cultures extending across the neck of Europe in the first two centuries CE that corresponds to the migration of the Goths.[5] Their final movement seems to have been in the late second century, during upheavals at the time of Rome's so-called Marcomannic wars in the reign of Marcus Aurelius (161–180 CE). This brought them up against the Alans in the east and the Roman province of Dacia in the west, with the Roman controlled Danubian plain to the south. Their new homeland seems to have suited them. Numbers increased dramatically in the third century, so much so that eventually the press of humanity along the imperial border would prove a major problem, especially when the fierce Goths and Alans were disrupted by the arrival of the even fiercer Huns from across the steppe.

Some modern historians, in defiance of all the ancient texts, contradict the notion that Maximinus was of part-barbarian extraction. The tales are dismissed as propaganda, but without any positive evidence that it is so. Of course they may be right, but it seems telling that Maximinus never honoured his parents posthumously as was the normal way for Roman emperors on founding a new dynasty, nor did he conspicuously enrich his home town, wherever that was, so perhaps it is true that he was ashamed of his origins. The story about Micca and Ababa comes from our least reliable source, the *Augustan History*, and even there it is treated as hearsay. But the names have given historians something to consider. It has been argued that they are plausibly Gothic and Alanic in their etymology, and so these people may have truly existed. Alternatively, it has been suggested that the names are a joke or riddle by the author of the *Augustan History*, inspired by the Greek word for 'semi-barbarian' as used by Herodian (πмст з Ку з Ку шх, which transliterates as 'mixo-barbaros' and sounds a bit like Micca-Ababa). It has also been pointed out that the Goths are not thought to have moved into the Roman frontier region until several decades after Maximinus's birth, only becoming a significant force in the later third century and into the fourth, supporting the view that the claim is an anachronism from the time the *Augustan History* was supposedly concocted. On the other hand, more recent archaeological evidence suggests that close contact between Goths and Romans in the Danube sector began earlier than was previously thought.[6]

Even the story that Maximinus had been a brigand is not entirely implausible. Herodian says he came from a mountainous district. For centuries the upland regions of Thrace had been under the effective control of outlaws. Normally it was just too expensive and difficult to pacify these areas, but occasionally the Roman war machine would move in, hungry for recruits. No doubt that was a dangerous undertaking. Evidence for just such a recruiting drive comes from a marble column at the sanctuary dedicated to Asklepios (god of healing) and the gods of Thrace near the modern village of Baktun (or Baktoun) in Bulgaria. The inscription is dedicated by a man named Aurelius Dionysodorus in thanks for divine aid for fulfilling his task of rounding up brigands for the army. It dates from the late second or early third centuries, and so is plausibly related to Severus's campaign against Niger.[7]

So there is nothing inherently improbable about Maximinus being of humble origin in Thrace, which was an undeniable ethnic mixing zone on the edge of the empire. Here the great river cuts through a major continental divide at the gorge of the Iron Gates before flowing into a wide horseshoe-plain bound by the Transylvanian Alps in the north and Balkan Mountains in the south. Following the treaties drawn up at the end of the Marcomannic Wars, the Romans claimed dominion over both banks and all riverine traffic, and they fortified the south especially with a line of legionary bases, auxiliary stations and watchtowers. The northern half of the basin (now the Romanian side), although nominally in barbarian territory, was culturally, climatically and geographically as one with the south and the Romans were probably not fussy as to the origin of their recruits so long as they were prepared to subject themselves to the required discipline and training and to swear a binding oath of allegiance to the emperor. Here then, in the hills overlooking the plain of the lower Danube, is the likely homeland of Maximinus Thrax.

Imperium

What kind of world was Maximinus born in to? At the close of the second century the Roman state and culture was presiding over and melding with an enormous and relatively stable empire that stretched from what is now Egypt to England and Syria to Spain (Map 1). For hundreds of years the aristocracy had been obsessed with the idea that to conquer and subjugate foreign enemies was proof of their personal virtue. The great consul-generals of the Republic and, later, the dynastic emperors, had effected a series of military expansions that had turned an obscure town in Italy beset by local wars into the greatest

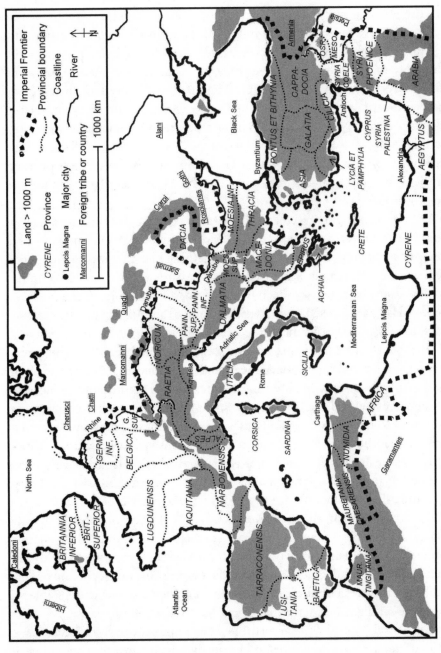

Map 1. Sketch map of the Roman empire in the early third century, based on Birley (1988).

metropolis in history and capital of the known (to them) world. If we are to search for reasons for how this came to pass, two factors come to the fore. First, Roman pride did not accept defeat or subjugation, so they would fight on when others would sue for peace. This was proved beyond doubt in the war of annihilation against Carthage in the third and second centuries BCE that first propelled the city state onto the world stage.[8] Second, and perhaps more admirably to modern eyes, they did not just conquer and destroy; from the earliest days they built and developed. Their famous road system, bureaucracy and organization swiftly followed their many victories, nurturing an ordered monetary economy, peace, law and infrastructure in conquered territory. Or, if all those things were already in place as they were in much of the east, then the Romans were comfortable with overlordship, and were seemingly tolerant, on the whole, of racial and religious diversity as long as that tolerance was reciprocated.

Arguably the height of Roman genius was to perceive that endless expansion must inevitably bring collapse. The first of the emperors, known by his honorific name Augustus which meant something like 'the revered one' (ruled BCE 27–CE 14), famously advised his successors against further conquest although they did not always heed this wisdom.[9] One prominent emperor who did was Hadrian (ruled 117–138 CE). Possibly from his personal experience as a staff officer in the distant and seemingly unwinnable Mesopotamian wars of his predecessor, Hadrian seems to have appreciated that the problems of communication and supply made the permanent subjugation of lands far from the transport hub of the Mediterranean impossible. So instead of seeking glory in campaigns beyond the frontiers, he spent much of his relatively long reign on tour, restoring provinces and cities, adjudicating disputes and designing new fortified boundaries. One such frontier famously runs across Britain separating the Romanized area (now England and Wales) from the wild tribes of Caledonia: a second 'Hadrian's wall' runs through the desert of Libya, separating the Roman province from the nomadic peoples of the Sahara.[10]

The area of Roman rule (*imperium*) was always loosely defined, in that the Romans never accepted equals and projected their power beyond all the nominal borders.[11] Distant lands were referred to as barbarian territory, or *barbaricum*: places of fear and adventure. Because the empire covered such a huge area, and long-distance communications travelled no faster than a galloping horse or a swift-sailing galley, its management required a delicate balance between strong central control and powerful local autonomy. To achieve this, it was divided into series of provinces, each of which had a governor appointed in Rome for a fixed period. Provincial governors were responsible for security, justice and regional development. Within each province were cities, towns and villages, each of which knew its place in the grand scheme and had its own administration drawn from the local elite. The people took great pride in their cities, commonly attributing their wealth and success to local gods whom passing travellers were expected to honour.

Security was guaranteed by the Roman army, which set the standard (literally as well as metaphorically) for subsequent professional armies in its organization and efficiency. In the early third century it was still divided into a number of self-sufficient units called legions, each of which had everything necessary to fight a smallish war in its own right. But the legions only accounted for about half the fighting strength: there were also large numbers of additional units called auxiliary cohorts which were often locally drafted. Just as in the civil administration, senior military appointments were temporary. An aristocratic career typically involved a string of military, religious and civil appointments in many provinces as well as periods at Rome itself. The mobility and exclusivity of the ruling class was a key factor for maintaining the overall cohesion of the empire.

Supreme power was concentrated in the office of *augustus*, rightful heir of the deified first emperor.[12] The office of *augustus* is generally translated now as emperor. This position was held for life. It was nominally conferred by the senate but in practice it was passed down through imperial dynasties to natural or adopted sons while the senate enthusiastically applauded the choice. A junior office that was used for the heir apparent, if there was one, was that of *caesar* (a title that the emperor also held by right). At times there were two *augusti* (father and son, for example), or even three, but it was usually clear who was senior partner. The emperor's wife (or sometimes, mother) often held the equivalent female title of *augusta*, but the term was honorific and she did not possess the formal powers of an emperor, although several 'empresses' wielded real power behind the scenes, especially, as we shall see, in our period of interest.

The emperors and their families were regarded as being a small step from divine. After death they were formally deified – literally made into gods – by solemn ritual, and would be worshipped ever after in temples of the imperial cult across the empire. That was providing, of course, their reputation withstood the transfer of power. In contrast, the legacy of disgraced rulers or other prominent individuals was subject to a degrading ritual called *damnatio memoriae* (damning to the memory), in which all their statues and other images were smashed and their names chiselled out of public inscriptions.

The emperor's adjudication was the highest court of the empire, which meant that he had to decide complex legal questions, whether in person or through some deputy. He was also expected to lead the combined legions in times of war. On the occasion of a major campaign or battle the emperor would be formally invested with the office of *imperator* or commander-in-chief of the armed forces, by the senate (the English word 'emperor' derives from this). The imperial power was also bestowed for the first time on his accession to the supreme office of *augustus*. A more regular title awarded to the emperor was the *tribunicia potestate*, or tribunician power. This ancient office was supposed to give the bearer special responsibilities for looking after the needs of the ordinary people, the plebeians. It was awarded annually thereafter and is used to date the years of an emperor's reign on coins and inscriptions. As a special honour the emperor might at some point be conferred with the title *pater patriae*, father of the fatherland. He was also inaugurated as the highest priest of the state religions, *pontifex maximus*; literally the great bridge builder, insofar as priests were supposed to bridge the real world with the divine: a title of deep religious significance that continues to be held with pride by the pope in Rome despite its emphatically non-Christian origin.

Although it was close to being a monarchy, the constitution had developed from a republican system of government that had operated for hundreds of years in the centuries BCE, the glorious history of which was universally honoured by the ruling classes. The senate, a kind of parliament of the senior aristocracy, was a remnant of this system, and through it the top positions in government were allocated. Augustus himself and subsequent emperors acknowledged that their power derived from, and was wielded on behalf of, the senate and people of Rome (in Latin, *senatus populusque romanus*, or S.P.Q.R., as frequently seen in the backdrops of Hollywood epics), a conceit that meant they were not kings but first citizens (*principes*). Highest of the senatorial offices was *consul*, of whom two were appointed at the start of each year.[13] Such had been the case since the earliest days of the republic and the passing years themselves were remembered by the names of the two consuls rather than some more convenient numbering system. The consuls and ex-consuls were the most senior of the senators; usually the emperor himself would take the office in his first year (if he had not done so already) and occasionally thereafter. Other top appointments included *quaestor*, *praetor* and *aedile*, and a man of senior senatorial rank could aspire to pass through such ordered posts during his public career, which was known as the *cursus honorum* (and roughly translates as the 'honourable path'). His progress depended much on complex ties of obligation, bribery and patronage which seem to us very corrupt but were regarded as normal politics by the ancient Romans; as, evidently, by some more recent ones too. The tradition usually worked smoothly even during times of political turmoil, lending the system real resilience.

The senatorial order was restricted to extremely wealthy men, although they were not necessarily men of ancient noble lineage in that it was possible to move into the senatorial order as a 'new man'. Below this was wider nobility called the equestrian order, the *equites* (who are sometimes referred to as 'knights'), who might also follow a *cursus honorum* of their own but generally through lesser appointments in civilian and military life. Alternatively, an equestrian gentleman might pursue wealth through holdings in agriculture or industries such as shipping, building, pottery, metalwork or mining. The equestrian class provided the backbone of the system and, like the senators, a highly exclusive list of their membership was maintained in Rome. One of the biggest changes that was affecting the Roman social structure in our period of interest was that equestrian provincials were becoming ever more powerful and influential as senior military commanders, taking positions that in previous centuries had been the sole preserve of the senatorial class.[14]

Below the formal aristocracy there was a large and varied set of free men who strove to better their lot within the empire and who could themselves become vastly rich. More often than not the free citizens were poor peasants. Initially the empire had applied a firm legal distinction between Roman citizens – those men from Rome itself and its Latin environs – and all the rest, but citizenship gradually expanded to take in the elites of the provinces and in 212 CE the emperor Caracalla extended it to all free men of the empire.[15]

At the bottom of the social pile were the masses of slaves: people born to servitude or captured from distant lands with little hope of a better life. A minority had relatively easy livings in rich estates or in the entourages of great and famous men; the more miserable ones spent their long days and short lives in servitude, prostitution, working the land, down mines or chipping rocks in the baking heat to provide aggregates for road surfaces – and countless other such jobs. Slaves could hope to be set free and for their children to thrive as free citizens. But driven by fear, ambition or bitterness, young slaves often became bandits or pirates. Hence the countryside and seaways across large districts of the empire were never safe, and brutal punishments were inflicted on runaways when they were caught.

On the whole the rural economy worked by barter as it always had done, but for hundreds of years coinage had been a means of exchange for expensive deals, especially in the more civilized eastern part of the empire. A cartload of rock or wood could be bought in kind but if you wanted to create something substantial, money was required. This filtered down from the top, mainly through military pay. It was issued in gold, silver and bronze, a system common in the ancient world and which lives on at least in appearance in modern currencies. The Roman coinage was underpinned by its precious metal content which guaranteed very low inflation because the coins themselves had intrinsic worth and were not mere tokens.[16] It meant that protecting productive mines such as those in Dacia (modern Romania), Sardinia and Spain was a priority for the empire. In our period of interest, the bulk of the currency was minted in Rome but many cities in the east of the empire were allowed to manufacture their own local bronze coinage. These diverse and interesting pieces usually have Greek script and the emperor's bust on the obverse side and local gods and legends on the reverse.

Because the first emperor Augustus never formally abolished the Republican constitution, the bureaucracy of the empire was very complex and remained divided between emperor and the senate. The coinage provides a good example of this: gold and silver were controlled by the emperor but bronze was issued by the senate, even though there was a supposedly fixed rate of exchange between them (which a given merchant might or might not accept, depending on the quality of the coins). Some of the provinces were controlled by the senate and others, generally the more outlying ones where the armies were concentrated, directly by the emperor himself. In reality the power of the senate had been in long-term decline and senators often lived in fear of the emperor who wielded arbitrary and absolute power above them as individuals, if not collectively. Treason or suspected disloyalty was frequently followed by executions and ruthless purges of senior figures, in which wealth and property were forfeited to the state. Unsurprisingly, trumped-up charges were common in some reigns.

The emperor could earn the loyalty of his subjects through respect for his wise rule and military victories or he could demand it with menaces. This meant that less well established rulers tended to rely heavily on the army, both their own imperial (so-called praetorian, or 'palace') guard in Rome and the legions distributed around the empire. If this loyalty could not be earned through virtuous leadership, it could be bought with donatives (money handouts) which were ritually paired with oaths of allegiance to the emperor. But if a weak emperor lost the support of the military, it could very often signal a brutal end.

Severus

At the beginning of the third century the emperor was a man in his early fifties called Lucius Septimius Severus whom we have already met in the context of military games in which Maximinus supposedly first came to prominence. The workings of Roman bureaucracy and imperial power-play are well illustrated by this man's advancement and the events that led him to supreme office. We will take his career as the starting point for our narrative.

Severus was born in 146 CE into a wealthy noble family in the city of Lepcis Magna in the province of Africa (modern Libya). His ancestry was part Italian and part Berber Libyan.[17] A surviving image show him with distinctly darker skin than his Syrian wife, leading to modern debates about whether he qualifies as a 'black emperor', which may tell us more about our own attitudes to race than the ancients'. As a young man he travelled to Rome and was admitted to the senatorial rank, which was denoted by a broad purple stripe on his toga, and he embarked on his *cursus honorum*. He took a range of offices of increasing seniority while his performance was monitored and his reputation evolved. From possibly being in charge of road maintenance in Rome, he probably spent a time as a court advocate, and then took successive jobs as the high office of *quaestor*, which included legal duties and supervising the public finances. When his cousin became governor of Africa, Severus was offered the senior military command there, which both illustrates the power of patronage and shows how easy it was to switch from civil to military posts. Then, in 191, he obtained a vital posting: appointment by the emperor Commodus to the governorship of Upper Pannonia. This was a key frontier province beside the Danube spanning parts of modern-day Austria and Hungary, and was home to several legionary bases distributed along the south bank. This command indicates that the emperor trusted Severus's loyalty emphatically because it made him one of the most powerful men in the empire. For his part, Severus, it seems, found himself at home among the rough and ready soldiers along the Danube.

For almost a century the Romans had become accustomed to strength, wisdom and stability flowing downward from the man at the top – this was the legacy of Trajan, Hadrian, Antoninus Pius and Commodus's father, the philosopher-emperor Marcus Aurelius. The days of mad and bad emperors like Caligula and Nero seemed to have been banished to history. Hence it must have been very troubling that Commodus preferred the grand gladiatorial spectaculars of the Colosseum to the sober business of just rule and careful military strategy that the empire demanded. As his credibility declined over the years he curried favour with the troops and increased their pay, for which he had to debase the silver coinage and so initiated financial problems for the empire as a whole. In the last years of his reign, Commodus was apparently suffering from a severe psychotic illness. He renamed the city of Rome after himself as *colonia commodiana*, while the twelve months of the year were renamed according to his personal names and fancied titles: *amazonius, invictus, pius, felix, lucius, aelius, aurelius, commodus, augustus, hercules, romanus, exsuperatorius*. He began to identify himself with the strongman Hercules and ordered his own image to be portrayed on the coinage in the hero's garb as 'Hercules of the Romans', clothed in the skin of the Nemean lion. He would dress like this at public events and, wielding the gnarly club of his hero, bludgeon condemned men to death.[18]

The ancient sources tell us that Severus was ambitious and superstitious and had long aspired to rule the empire.[19] Such hopes must have seemed very far-fetched for most of his life, until, to near-universal relief, Commodus was assassinated, bringing to an end the great dynasty that had held power for nearly a century. The man elected by the senate to replace him as *augustus*, Publius Helvius Pertinax, was widely respected as a just and wise general and administrator, including by Severus. But Pertinax quickly made himself unpopular by trying to roll back some of Commodus's policies too quickly, and especially by attempting to check the power of the praetorian guard which had flourished under Commodus's excesses. Pertinax was slain by the praetorians after just 86 days in power.

Total chaos ensued, as has been relayed to us by Cassius Dio, an invaluable eyewitness from the senatorial class and later twice consul. He tells us that after some deliberation the praetorians offered the throne to the highest bidder, which not only emphasized their brute strength over the senate's legislative power but also was widely seen as demeaning the sanctity of the supreme office. The winner of this unorthodox auction was a necessarily very wealthy man called Marcus Didius Julianus who offered the praetorians a breathtaking 25,000 sestertii (or 250 gold pieces) each for the imperial throne. The day's pay for an ordinary soldier was, perhaps, 10 sestertii, and the paper strength of the Guard was 16,000 men. Although the real number of praetorians was no doubt much less than this, it was still a huge bribe. Julianus must have calculated that the massive outlay would, in time, bring in a hefty return.[20]

In fear of the praetorians, who were at that time riotously celebrating their windfall, the senate had no option but to acquiesce to this arrangement, so Julianus was formally conferred with the titles of *caesar* and *augustus* and invested with imperial and tribunician powers. Julianus had to issue much new coinage to pay the troops what had been promised. His coinage proclaiming *concordia militum* ('the unity of the army') was a sure sign that there was a problem in that area. The new emperor and the praetorian guard that had rashly backed him began to realize that real power in the empire was not to be found in the city, but on the frontier.

As usual on the accession of a new ruler, senatorial messengers were dispatched across the empire, carrying the news to the provincial governors. But instead of inspiring celebration and shows of loyalty, all they brought with them was consternation and outrage. The whole sorry spectacle was too much for many, including Severus and his hardened legions on the upper Danube. Severus was proclaimed *imperator* and *augustus* by his troops at the legionary base of Carnutum in modern-day Austria. This was an illegal act that made him and everyone involved an enemy of the state, but it was well calculated. He marched on Rome at the head of an impressive army drawn from about 15 legions all along the Rhine–Danube frontier (the Moesian legions especially could be relied on because they were commanded by Severus's brother).[21]

We know from Cassius Dio that as the army converged on the capital the situation became very tense. Military power in Rome resided in the elite praetorian guard and the so-called urban cohorts (a kind of police force under the command of the city prefect). Julianus attempted to negotiate with the approaching contender and, as his options diminished, even offered joint rule, but was soon deserted by the troops and deposed by the senate.[22] He ended up being slain in the echoing marbled halls of an empty imperial palace.

The immediate problem for Severus was to assert control in the capital and especially to neutralize the power of the praetorian guard whom he rightly blamed for Pertinax's death. What followed was a breathtaking piece of power-play. The entire guard was ordered to assemble – unarmed – to salute their new emperor and hear his address. Presumably these very well-paid soldiers were hoping to get away with the crime of murdering Pertinax and replacing him with the rich Julianus, having, in their eyes, atoned for it by deserting Julianus at the end. But Severus quietly had his fully armed Danubians surround the elite troops, and after delivering a monumental dressing-down, he ordered them all to be stripped of their ranks and marks of distinction and dismissed from the service. The tension of the scene became extreme. Sparing the men their lives, Severus told them to vacate Rome as private individuals and never to return, on pain of death. To replace the guard he would conscript a new set of praetorians from his own army.

The disgrace of the praetorians was marked by one of those poignant scenes that somehow typifies ancient Rome. Cassius Dio tells us that during the forced disbandment, the mounted troop among the guards were ordered to give up their horses to be led away, but one horse in particular refused to leave his master and kept returning to him, neighing loudly. When this attracted the attention of the crowd, the soldier requested a sword, killed his faithful horse, and then killed himself. Dio remarked that "it seemed to those that watched that the horse, too, was glad to die".[23]

The Black and White Wars

Severus had restored the empire's dignity, and the senate gladly (on the whole) accepted his seizure of power. The new emperor styled himself as the avenger of Pertinax, for whom he demanded a belated state funeral and deification. He also briefly added 'Pertinax' to his own name as his (posthumously) adopted son, so that the rationale of his legitimacy was clear to all. But although he did not have to battle for Italy, he did face a rival claimant in the east: the governor of Syria named Caius Pescennius Niger (the epithet means 'black') whose troops had proclaimed him emperor for much the same reason as had Severus's men. In the preceding months, Niger had mobilized the eastern armies and sent messengers to the senate demanding the throne, but these had been intercepted by Severus. While it seems in retrospect that diplomacy might have resolved the situation, Severus chose to have Niger declared an outlaw of the state and set out to defeat the eastern legions in battle.

In so doing he had to tread carefully because there were also strong forces in the west of the empire under the control of the respected governor of Britain, Decimus Clodius Septimius Albinus (whose name means 'white'). There seems to have been some frantic diplomacy between Severus and Albinus during the march on Rome and the upshot was that Albinus agreed to support Severus in return for receiving the subordinate title *caesar* and being named heir to the throne. As Severus set out for the east, Albinus's appointment as *caesar* was enthusiastically confirmed in Rome and the two men shared the consulship. But watching from the sidelines, Albinus must have known that Severus had sons of his own and was not likely to honour this commitment in the long run, so he chose to stay with his legions in fortress Britain, awaiting the outcome of the power struggle. The death of Severus in battle would have been ideal for him.

The war against Niger was to be a bitter fight with several major engagements, but in the end Severus (through his general Anullinus) was victorious at a great set-piece battle at Issus in Cilicia. This was precisely the same field of battle on which Alexander of Macedon had defeated Darius of Persia in an even more titanic east–west struggle over half a millennium before. Like Darius, Niger was attempting to prevent the opposing forces descending onto the plain of Issus from the mountain pass to the north. The decisive moment of the second Battle of Issus came when a large Severan cavalry detachment managed to evade and outflank the opposing forces and attacked them in the rear, fortuitously (or divinely, it was claimed) aided by a heavy thunderstorm in the faces of the defenders. The forces of Niger dissolved in rout and many were cut down in their flight; Niger fled the scene but was captured and killed at Antioch. One small detail we know of this battle is that at one point Anullinus had his troops adopt a *testudo* or tortoise formation of interlocking shields while under intense missile attack.[24]

Despite this success, the new emperor's position was still precarious and he had made many enemies. Although he was a very distinguished senator and general, he was still something of an outsider to Rome – an African with dark skin and a Punic accent – and that must have seemed strange to the conservative men of the city. Sensing that internal unity comes through fighting a foreign foe, Severus next launched a sharp campaign against satellite powers of the entirely independent Parthian empire to the east, ostensibly as punishment for supporting Niger. Commanded by the emperor in person, the move culminated in annexation of the kingdoms of Osrhoene and Adiabene on the east bank of the Euphrates and the submission of the Arabs of upper Mesopotamia. Severus was awarded a personal triumph and the title *parthicus adiabenicus* and *parthicus arabicus*.

But he was not one to rest on his laurels. To the dismay of many in the senate and the publicly expressed mood of the people of Rome,[25] Severus showed his ruthless streak by immediately turning on Albinus, accusing him of treachery, but not before sending assassins. Perhaps expecting this development, Albinus survived the attempt on his life and, with no other option, had himself declared *augustus* and hence a direct challenger to the imperial throne. Albinus boldly crossed the English Channel (*oceanus britannicus*) and invaded Gaul, routing a Severan army composed mainly of units from the Rhine that was sent to intercept him. His victory (in 196 CE) won him a substantial breathing space, whereupon he installed his court at Lugdunum (Lyons) and consolidated his power base throughout Britain, Gaul and Spain for over a year. This enabled him to bring great wealth and, importantly, new troop levies to the fight. Early the following year, Severus in person led a second army against Albinus, this time relying heavily on his favoured Danubian units. When battle came, outside Lugdunum, it is said that the two armies were about equally matched with 150,000 fighting men on each side. While that may be an exaggeration there is no doubt it was one of the greatest battles of the imperial era. Once again the decisive moment was a Severan cavalry attack. Albinus was defeated and either killed himself on the field of battle or was executed. Severus is reported to have ritually ridden over the dead man's body. Then, the following year, he attacked Parthia again, this time the main empire, looting the capital Ctesiphon and taking the title *parthicus maximimus* before retiring behind a new forward line on the Euphrates.

And so we come to the year 200 CE (or, as the Romans saw it, the year of the consulship of Titus Claudius Severus Proculus and Caius Aufidius Victorinus). Severus was undisputed master of the Roman world, largely thanks to the loyalty and professionalism of his core units from the Danubian frontier and especially their cavalry. In many ways the civil wars had been a bloody repeat of the convulsion that had followed the death of Nero and the end of the Julio-Claudian dynasty over a hundred years earlier. But with all opposition crushed and with his own dynasty secure through his two young sons, Antoninus (who was raised to the rank of *augustus* despite being just ten years old) and Geta (given the title *caesar*), and with an intelligent and respected wife to advise him (Julia Domna, a Syrian lady of impeccable nobility), Severus's position was finally unchallenged.

Chapter II

Cursus Maximini

Tiro

Maximinus rose from obscurity to hold a senior position in the army. As a non-citizen he could not have held public office except in the military. If we accept the story that he was selected for the imperial bodyguard at the time of the civil war against Niger, he would still have undergone a prolonged period of training. As the *Augustan History* put it, Severus ordered the regional commanding officer to "take him in hand and school him in Roman discipline".[1] Thus he would have started out in the local army, as indeed Herodian clearly stated.

The army was always hungry for young male recruits of the right type who first had to pass a strict medical examination. The military manual of Vegetius tells us that "there are in men, as well as in horses and dogs, certain signs by which their virtues may be discovered. The young soldier, therefore, ought to have a lively eye, should carry his head erect, his chest should be broad, his shoulders muscular and brawny, his fingers long, his arms strong, his waist small, his shape easy, his legs and feet rather nervous than fleshy".[2] From this account one can almost imagine the stern eye of the recruiting officers pacing the lines, poking at pigeon chests. For a man like Maximinus the physical examination would not have been a problem.

The language of the army was Latin, supplemented by Greek in the east, which stamped a degree of uniformity on the forces and prevented a polyglot cacophony from developing. It was normal for provincial recruits to take a Roman name on enlistment, although they might continue to be known by their real name also.[3] Why the Thracian chose Caius Julius Verus Maximinus (if indeed he had not been born with it, as the revisionist historians prefer) we do not know. An outside possibility is that it may be related to his tribal name: if his father was indeed a Goth called Micca, that could be the word for 'big' in Gothic. Maximinus means something like 'from small to big' in Latin, and he later named his son Maximus ('big'). Alternatively he might have had a patron of that name[4] or possibly there was no particular reason. Troopers would obviously have to adopt different names from one another, so they might simply have picked ones they liked.

Basic training was hard and brutal. According to Vegetius "the Romans owed the conquest of the world to no other cause than continual military training, exact observance of discipline in the camps and unwearied cultivation of the other arts of war". All recruits learned to march long distances using the 'military step', make fortified camps, swim so that they could traverse rivers and swamps, and handle a wide range of weapons. The cavalry were trained in advanced horsemanship and how to execute a range of evolutions in troop formation under the orders of their squad commander (*decurion*). Man and beast would have to stay calm in the din of battle and, critically, the cavalrymen would have to know amid the smoke and dust when to pursue and when to regroup. They trained on open ground and rough country alike. New recruits were issued with their much coveted armour, boots and clothing which were expected to be kept in tip-top condition: "Nothing does so much honour to the abilities of the commanding officer as the appearance and discipline of the soldiers, when their apparel is neat and clean, their arms bright and in good order and when they perform their exercises and evolutions with dexterity." The Roman army was a spit-and-polish outfit, especially, doubtless, the elite and ceremonial unit that Maximinus was supposedly destined for.

Boot camp was tough and living quarters very cramped, but for those who could endure it the main attractions of joining up were comradeship, regular pay, food and medical attention, plus the eventual promise of Roman citizenship and the possibility of seeing the world. There were few other options of excitement in the life of an ambitious peasant. Social mobility was extremely limited in the empire except in the army where promotion through the ranks was assured, or at least possible, for a brave, obedient and diligent man, and each step would come with an increase in pay and privileges. Entry into the army may also have liberated men who came from relatively low–status tribal families from the bonds and hierarchies of their own societies.[5] Marriage was not allowed but *de facto* marriage was commonplace, and indeed it was to be formally permitted for soldiers around the time of Maximinus's enlistment.

The taller, stronger recruits were typically enlisted in the cavalry, with higher pay and prestige. The sources agree that Maximinus was one such. If there is any truth in his Alanic ancestry, he may have been born to the saddle. It is most likely he was initially enrolled into an auxiliary cavalry unit, or *ala* (literally, a wing, because cavalry were deployed on the flanks in pitched battles). An *ala* was a relatively small company of about 500 men commanded by an equestrian officer, the *praefectus alae* (prefect of the wing). It was divided into troops (*turmae*) of 32, that most divisible number, each under the commanded of a *decurion*. The *ala* as a single unit or its constituent troops could easily be moved from one sub-command to another and they were often used for policing or garrison duties.[6]

The military mark, which may have been a tattoo on the hands (historians debate the point), was considered a badge of honour that had to be earned. It signified the transition from mere recruit (*tiro*) to soldier. Vegetius was adamant that it was necessary first to determine if a man was really fit for service in his strength, capacity to learn and obey, and in courage, "for many, though promising enough in appearance, are found very unfit upon trial". To be made a Roman soldier was a mark of passage and the bearer would be held in respect and comradeship for the rest of his life. Similar selection processes and rites of enlistment are central to modern recruitment practices around the world. On being admitted to the army, a solemn and binding oath of loyalty to the emperor (the *sacramentum*) was made: more than once it was referred to by Rome's historians as the secret of the empire's success. It included the soldier's vow on no account to abandon his fellows through flight or fear and never to leave his allotted station except to pick up a weapon, strike an enemy or save a citizen.[7]

As a ranker, Maximinus would have learned the inner ways of the army, including all the superstitions, cheats and scams of the lower ranks and most importantly what motivated the men, invaluable experience for his later career as a commander. Exactly what the Romans thought of their giant recruit can only be guessed at… where to find a big enough horse may have been the first problem.

Stipator Corporis

On completion of his training the Thracian was posted to the imperial palace in Rome to take his place among the imperial bodyguard (*stipatores corporis*) by order of the emperor himself, at least according to the story in the *Augustan History*. Indeed it was standard practice for emperors to have a physically imposing bodyguard, so the story is plausible. The emperor Caligula had used Thracian gladiators for his personal protection; we hear of the emperor Nero ordering one of his bodyguards who was standing nearby "because of his great size" to overpower a disgraced prefect; Trajan is depicted on his victory column in Rome accompanied by guards "of staggering size". Bodyguards were chosen from the imperial horseguard (*equites singulares augusti*) which Severus expanded from 1,000 to 2,000 men. This elite regiment had favoured Danubians for generations, even more so now under Severus, so this is very likely the army unit that Maximinus would have been assigned to.

The horseguard had its barracks on the Caelian Hill, a short clatter to the imperial palace and the centre of Rome. The increase in numbers under

Severus meant that a new barracks block was hastily constructed there around this time, next to the old one that had been built a century before. The horseguard was drawn from the best and bravest fighting troops of the empire. There was a strict height requirement: according to one historian they were "taller than most modern European royal guards", which must have been especially impressive in ancient Rome where the population was relatively short. It also helped if they were handsome in appearance, and Maximinus is described as such.[8]

Like modern guards regiments, the *equites singulares augusti* doubled as an elite fighting unit and a ceremonial one. In peacetime they rode out each morning to their training fields to the east of the city where they practised incessantly with a wide range of weapons including lances, javelins, crossbows and slings. This allowed for maximum versatility for deployment in battle where their job was to protect the emperor and act as a strategic reserve. Another crucial role was to accompany a commander in parleys with the enemy:

> If the field marshal goes to see the enemy commander face to face, to make or receive some proposal, he should choose as an escort the strongest and finest-looking of the younger soldiers, stalwart, handsome, and tall men, decked out with magnificent armour ...For often the whole is judged to be the same as the part one sees, and a field marshal does not decide what to do from reports he has heard, but in fear of what he has seen.
>
> Onasander, quoted in Speidel, 1994b, p. 120.

Indeed they were expected to be spectacularly turned out at all times with gleaming metalwork and richly embroidered red capes and belts (so much so that a good cavalry cape exceeded the price of a fine horse).[9] They rode stallions, similarly bedecked of course, to be all the more imposing and because stallions were more likely to kick and bite in battle. Their drill was expected to be immaculate and was frequently watched by the emperor. Parade (or sports) armour was worn for ceremonial occasions, including gold and silver trappings and, sometimes, fearful bronze masks with ethereal, neutral expressions. Personal fitness and strength were paramount, not least because the men were expected to be able to mount in a single vault and lead their horse over jumps in full armour with weapons. Detachments of the horseguard would also escort the emperor through the crowded streets of the capital, clearing the way with boots and cudgels, and watching the crowds with menacing eyes whenever he appeared in public.

Rome was probably the largest city in the world at that time, with over a million inhabitants,[10] so what a country boy like Maximinus would have thought of it can scarce be imagined. Multi-storey building was the norm, sprawling across district upon district around the major roads and the famous seven hills. In the centre there were great public buildings such as the forum, racetrack (Circus Maximus) and stadium (Colosseum), not to mention many splendid public spaces and temples. The commercial hub of the city was also in the centre, including great market places and quayside trading districts. But Rome was old, overcrowded and difficult to negotiate, with wealthy districts crammed up against ghettos and virtual no-go areas even for the city police. Soldiers about their daily duties would inevitably come into contact with the wealthy elite who were famous for extreme snobbery. The young Maximinus may very well have learned to despise the rich and refined senatorial order during his time in Rome, as the *Augustan History* implies. It says he was scorned even by the slaves of the nobles, who would refuse admittance to their mansions. The sophisticated Greek senator Cassius Dio described the Danubian troops that Severus brought to the capital as "a throng of motley soldiers most savage in appearance, most terrifying in speech, and most boorish in conversation": it is almost as if the two men met.[11]

The emperor was also an outsider and relied not so much on refined politicking in the capital but upon his own fearsome military reputation and that of his fanatically loyal troops. After the disgrace of the praetorians the new guard became dominated by foreigners – Pannonians, Illyricans, Thracians and others – much to the disgust and fear of the people of the city. In this context it is not difficult to imagine the imposing figure of Maximinus at the emperor's shoulder, towering over quaking petitioners as they were admitted to the imperial presence. We are told that by having Severus's ear, he "could obtain from the emperor anything he wanted" and in his days in the palace Maximinus "became famous among the soldiers, well liked by the tribunes [that is, the commanding officers], and admired by his comrades".[12]

Decurion

Posting to the camp of the horseguard was highly prized throughout the empire and the best troopers from all units aspired to it. Once there, promotion was very fast. After just three years a recruit could expect to be commanding his own *turma* (squad) as decurion, and in a few more years he could be fast-tracked to centurion and potentially posted back to his legion in that exalted rank, many years earlier than would have otherwise been possible. This practice is a well-attested career route from inscriptions, and the to-and-fro of elite soldiers from the provinces to Rome helped raise standards and personal loyalty to the emperor on the frontiers. While in Rome the chosen men were very well housed. A huge aqueduct delivered copious sweet water to the Caelian barracks (necessary for the horses, of course) and the air was comparatively fresh. Unsurprisingly, as the men were very well paid, the city's best bars and most exclusive brothels could be found in the streets around.[13]

Most historians regard the whole story of Maximinus's enlistment in the guard as an invention of the *Augustan History*, but a piece of potentially corroborating evidence has come to light (see Plate 3). In the graveyard of the imperial horseguard there is a monument to a fallen trooper called Titus Aurelius Claudianus which reads:

D(IS) M(ANIBVS)
T. AVRELIO CLAVDIANO
EQ(VTI) SING(VLARI) AVG(VSTI), TVR(MA) IVLI
MAXIMINI, NAT(IONE) SVRVS,
V(IXIT) A(NNOS) XXX, M(ILITAVIT) A(NNOS) X.
M. VLP(IVS) TIBERINVS,
SIGNIFER, HER(ES) EIVS,
AMICO OPTIMO
B(ENE) M(ERENTI) C(VRAVIT)

(Sacred to the spirits of the dead, Titus Aurelius Claudianus, of the emperor's horseguard and squad of Julius Maximinus, Syrian by nationality, lived for 30 years, served for ten years in the army; Marcus Ulpius Tiberinus, standard bearer, set this up, his best friend, well deserving).

The historian Michael Speidel, who wrote the definitive study of the monuments of the horseguard, has suggested that this squad commander was none other than the future emperor.[14] The names Julius and Maximinus are fairly common, but no other man with that combination is known to have served in the guard, and the dating of the tombstone on stylistic grounds is about right for around 200 CE when Maximinus would have been in Rome. As a decurion, Maximinus would have had responsibility for his *turma*, its training and appearance, especially for "obliging them to keep their cuirasses, lances and helmets always bright and in good order", as Vegetius says. Each squad was allocated its own comfortable barracks unit with a cellar and sunny verandah. Maximinus, by now quite experienced, would have learnt the habit of command and the necessity of being respected and obeyed.

The emperor's bodyguards figure in a story from this period, although with no known link to Maximinus. The second most powerful man in Rome at the time was the praetorian prefect Gaius Fulvius Plautianus, cousin and long-term friend of the emperor. As a mark of special favour, his young daughter Plautilla was married to the prince Antoninus when he reached the age of 14 in 202. However Antoninus grew to hate his young bride and eventually Plautianus formed a plot against the emperor, sending a tribune to murder both Severus and Antoninus and have himself proclaimed emperor in their place. But the tribune revealed the plot to the emperor and agreed to send for Plautianus under the pretence that the deed had been carried out. When Plautianus entered the imperial quarters, Severus ordered him to be seized by "some of the younger members of his personal bodyguard".[15] Plautianus protested his innocence but in the struggle Antoninus spotted that he was wearing a breastplate under his clothes. That was taken as clear evidence of guilt, so Plautianus was killed on the spot by the guards. (Plautilla, by the way, was banished and later murdered on the orders of her ex-husband.)

Centurion

Eventually, it seems, the emperor appreciated that Maximinus was more than the average knucklehead, perhaps recognizing the intelligence, industry and capacity for command that is so evident from his later career, because we are also told that he "helped Maximinus to advancement in the service", which presumably means that at some point he was reassigned to one of the regular legions, probably with the rank of centurion. If so it would most likely have been one of the Danubian legions in the area of his birth. He was probably formally admitted to the citizenship of Rome on attaining the centurionship.[16] By then he would have been about 35 years old, extremely well-connected and well trained in the art of war.

The empire had been pacified by Severus's conquests, just as the propaganda claimed, and the first decade of the third century was marked by relative peace and prosperity. But as Antoninus and Geta, the two young princes, grew through adolescence in the luxurious palaces of Rome, their childhood squabbles morphed into a more intense rivalry and became a worry to their parents whose grand plan was that they would inherit the empire jointly in a spirit of benign cooperation. Ten years after the victory at Lugdunum, Antoninus was 19 years old. Geta was less than a year younger, not so ostentatious as his brother and long used to bearing the less exalted title of *caesar* to his brother's *augustus*, although he was not necessarily reconciled to the fact.

Then, around 207, the military situation in far-flung Britannia began to deteriorate alarmingly. The province had always had its security problems, necessitating the permanent posting of no fewer than three full legions and their associated auxiliaries, a military presence that was out of all proportion to the economic significance of the island. The endemic threats were raiders from north of the great wall, from what is now Scotland, and from Hibernia (Ireland) across the sea where proud and wholly independent kingdoms flourished.

The governor at this time was Lucius Alfenus Senecio, a Numidian by birth, who had previously governed one of the Syrian provinces (which nicely illustrates the mobility of the upper classes at this stage of history). He had been waging war against a tribe known as the Maeatae in eastern Scotland, evidently with some success because a victory monument naming him is known from near the wall.[17] Cassius Dio provides corroboration by noting significant victories in Britain during the reign of Severus. However, the enemy had not been subdued, and the fighting seems to have led to a combination or alliance of the two main northern tribes, the Caledonae and Maeatae, in full-scale war against the troops based on the island. Herodian says that they rose up "laying waste to the countryside, carrying off plunder and wrecking almost everything". Whether this devastation was north or south of the wall he does not indicate, but recent archaeological evidence points to a large refugee camp just south of the wall at Vindolanda dating from about this time, perhaps indicating displacement of the population from the more Romanized zone of central and southern Scotland. At this point Senecio appealed to the emperor for reinforcements and even proposed that the great warrior-emperor himself might lead an invincible expedition to chastise the northern tribes. All this could have been so much shadow-play: the unstated strategic aim, as the well-connected Dio tells us directly, which had been on the drawing-boards of Roman staff officers for years, was to complete the conquest of this troubled island once and for all. Then, of course, the legionary presence could be permanently scaled down making the island less of a drain on the Treasury and less likely to spawn rebel armies.[18] The invasion and conquest of Hibernia (Ireland) would then be the obvious next step.

Although he is reputed to have foreseen his own death in Britain through signs and portents, Severus saw the merits of leading the campaign in person. The historical sources suggest that one motive for the war was that his fractious sons both needed to be removed from the luxuries of Rome and gain military experience and reputations to match his own.[19] An even more fundamental reason for the enormous outlay was that the Roman military machine required frequent war to maintain efficiency. This was not just a question of the morale and discipline of the fighting troops. The supply chain of armaments and equipment and the complex logistics of war needed to be tested in battle. As there was negotiated peace with Parthia, the simple question was: who else could be attacked? Accordingly, the Caledonian expedition was to be a major event involving many new troops brought into the island, including the core of the new imperial guard (along with the *equites singulares augusti*) and detachments from the Danubian legions[20] and with a vast imperial treasury, the distributed coins of which frequently turn up in British fields to this day. We can never know if Maximinus was among the guards units or Danubian troops moved to Britain in 208, but if he was one of the emperor's hand-picked men, it seems likely.

The local garrison referred to their uncivilized foe as *brittunculi* (little Britons).[21] Conquering them may have appeared fairly simple on a map (and contrary to some reports, the Romans did use maps): it was not an especially large area to control in imperial terms and, being hemmed in by the ocean, there was nowhere for the barbarians to run. With the greatest warrior-emperor in history (Severus himself) in command and the full resources of the empire behind the campaign, victory seemed assured. But the tacticians in sunny Rome may not have fully appreciated that the Scottish terrain is extraordinarily harsh, with mountainous expanses in the interior, boggy tracts in the low ground and atrocious weather possible even in summer (although Herodian's bald statement that "most of Britain is marshland" seems unfair). An army might well clear a glen of its inhabitants, only to see the population filter over the high ground to a more remote recess. In the event, the campaign dragged on for several seasons, with the high command spending winter interludes in the relatively more civilized locale of Roman Eboracum (York).

Archaeological evidence shows that the Romans advanced systematically up the east coast of Scotland beyond what is now Aberdeen, building a string of forts as they went. But the tribes refused to array themselves in battle formation and instead mounted a ferocious guerrilla war in the dismal swamps. The squaddies quickly learned to choose death over being captured. According to Cassius Dio, 50,000 troops died in this fighting. But at the same time the tribes knew they could not win either, and eventually there was some kind of negotiated peace. The Roman army evacuated all its forward positions while Severus, and both sons, claimed victory and the coveted title of *britannicus maximus*, as advertised prominently on the coinage for all the empire to celebrate.

Despite the propaganda the Romans seem to have decided that the north of Britain could not in fact be pacified or more probably that it was not worth the effort, just as Domitian and then Antoninus Pius had concluded 140 and 60 years before. At some point a strategic decision was made to re-fortify Hadrian's wall and abandon all of Scotland once again to the *status quo ante*.[22] The disappointment was, for Severus, underlined by his failing health and an odd occasion where, it seemed to all those present, his son Antoninus drew his sword and was actually about to stab the old man in the back, his courage failing him at the last moment. It did not matter: on 4th February 211 the emperor weakened dramatically in the imperial headquarters at York. Summoning his sons to his deathbed he famously urged them to "be harmonious, enrich the soldiers, and scorn all other men."

Primus Pilus

As Severus had willed, Antoninus and Geta were formally joint emperors, but the prospect appealed to neither. We can, perhaps, understand Geta's reticence on the matter as Antoninus has gone down in history as one of the cruellest tyrants ever to wear the imperial purple, for which distinction there is a lot of competition. Perhaps it was because it was rumoured he was visited in his dreams by the mad emperor Commodus. Even today some of his deeds have the power to shock: how, after endless machinations he succeeded in having his brother, the co-emperor Geta, murdered by a squad of centurions as Geta took shelter in their mother's arms (another possible role for Maximinus, although it is much more likely our man was serving with the legions at this time); how he had an old lady (the noble sister of an earlier emperor, no less) executed because she dared to comfort his own weeping mother on the occasion of this fratricide; how he had four of Rome's most sacred priestesses, the Vestal Virgins, buried alive for allegedly breaking their vows of chastity, one of them with none other than himself; and how after a joyful welcome to the great city of Alexandria he ordered the massacre of all the young men on the grounds that some had previously ridiculed him (over 20,000 died, according to Cassius Dio, although the figure is almost impossible to believe; in Herodian's account, dead and wounded alike were cast into mass graves and the Nile ran red with blood). The paranoid emperor was becoming known by his nickname Caracalla, the name for a style of cloak worn by the Gauls; it is by this name that he is generally known to history to distinguish him from others called Antoninus and as such we will call him from now on. According to Herodian, his trademark cloak was embroidered with silver and he sometimes wore a blond wig to appear all the more barbarian. Dio also relates that Caracalla sometimes indulged in luxurious living "even to the point of keeping his chin wholly bare".[23]

Despite these signs of maniac depravity, the sources agree that he was popular with the military whom he lavished with donatives and also accompanied in the field, ostentatiously sharing quarters and rations with the soldiers and marching alongside them, even eating from the same wooden spoons. Such deeds hint at cultivation of the army in the face of criticism from the citizens and nobility. Caracalla also raised army pay even beyond the level authorized by his father, partly to counter his unpopularity after murdering his brother. To help finance this, he introduced a new silver coin, the double-denarius, a beautiful, broad-flanned piece, somewhat in the Persian taste which was, nevertheless, not twice the weight of the single denomination and so is thought to have caused more inflation in the economy. That the coin is a double is indicated by the fact that instead of a wreath, the emperor wears the seven-rayed solar crown.[24] This crown looks like something from a Christmas cracker but was, nevertheless, the forerunner of the headgear so prized by medieval kings. The coin is known today as the *antoninianus* after the emperor, although strangely, we do not know what it was called in ancient times. Caracalla's portrait is that of an arrogant, glaring young man, which takes on a slightly comic aspect in the knowledge he was of very diminutive stature.

The *Augustan History* tells us that Maximinus, now entering middle age, held various military honours under Caracalla and served for a long time as centurion. It was normal for a centurion to serve in a variety of graded posts within that rank, transferring from legion to legion as opportunities for advancement arose. Caracalla campaigned in Dacia early in his reign as sole emperor, with a fair chance that Maximinus was once again in action in one of the Danubian legions. Although the war has received little attention from historians and is barely mentioned by the contemporaneous chronicler Cassius Dio or the *Augustan History*, there is evidence that it was more than just a local problem. The Roman province of Dacia had been conquered by the emperor Trajan a century earlier in a brutal war that involved the massacre of most of its inhabitants. Trajan's column, which still stands in Rome, is monument to this genocidal victory. Dacia was rich in precious metals that were used to underpin the Roman currency. But almost a hundred years on, the area was still not peaceful, hence invasion by a barbarian tribe called the Carpi from across its eastern border necessitated a response in 214 CE, allegedly led by Caracalla himself working out of the town of Porolissum (the splendid remains of which can be seen today near Zalău in Romania). The invading Carpi were successfully beaten back, and although the occasion was evidently not deemed notable enough for Caracalla to claim a formal triumph, he did claim *imperium* for the third time.

It seems possible that Maximinus distinguished himself in this fighting and was promoted to senior centurion, or *primus pilus* (which means 'first spear'), an exalted rank in which he allegedly served for several years under Caracalla.[25] This was the highest that an ordinary soldier might normally aspire to, being leader of the first (and largest) cohort of a legion. It was also a very well-paid position. The *primus pilus* had a vital role as military adviser to the commanding officer. If we remember that the staff officers were often men of senatorial rank who in their careers had to turn their talents not just to military matters but also to all aspects of government, law, engineering and oratory, it is clear that the *primus pilus* was central in any legion and, if he proved competent, would have fostered patronage with very senior men. To have progressed to such a position (and at a comparatively young age for that rank) Maximinus would have needed more than just heaps of muscle and a talent for drinking gallons of wine: he would have needed intelligence, diligence and bravery. His later career and the comments of all his biographers, even those antagonistic towards him, demonstrate these personal attributes beyond doubt.

In his early years Caracalla was keen to advertise his military title *britannicus maximus* ('greatest victor in Britain'), but there must have been those who knew the facts and regarded the claim as symbolic, if not absurd. As his popularity declined, he decided on an eastern war in emulation of his father. He may have reasoned that the coffers of Parthian Ctesiphon would be ripe for the picking again, but he decided to gain his victory by guile rather than outright conquest as his father had done. The essence of the plan, as narrated independently by Cassius Dio and Herodian, is so treacherous as to make one blush even now. Caracalla proposed alliance with the Parthian king Artabanus V, who was then engaged in civil war with his brother Vologaeses. To cement the deal he offered his hand to a Parthian princess, daughter of Artabanus, and the marriage would confirm a grand treaty in which both empires would formally agree military aid against all their respective enemies including Vologaeses (which must have seemed a good offer as Rome had no obvious enemies at the time, unless, that is, the Parthians fancied taking a shot at the distant Caledonians). The offer was initially rejected, but according to the version told by Herodian it was subsequently repeated and accepted, leading to a great peace conference and elaborate betrothal ceremony inside Parthian territory, probably at the city of Arbela (Irbil in the Kurdish area of modern Iraq).

Herodian, who might well have been there, describes the scene beautifully. For history buffs it is reminiscent of the 'field of cloth of gold' summit between England and France in 1520, with both sides seeking to trump the other in ostentation and opulence. The entire population of Arbela was bedecked in garlands of flowers, dressed in gold and richly dyed clothes, dancing to flutes and pipes to the beat of drums which was "their favourite form of dancing on occasions when they have taken quite a lot to drink".[26] With everyone craning their necks and waiting for the grand arrival of the emperor of Rome in state, Caracalla withdrew from the scene and the Roman army fell upon their hosts with vicious intent. Artabanus escaped the massacre with his bodyguard and a few retainers while everyone else, unarmed and with little to protect them but their flowing silks, was savagely cut down. The fate of the princess is unknown. As the Roman army retreated in good order, they burned and pillaged everything in their path and took as many captives as possible.

The massacre has several parallels in ancient history but it would be wrong to suppose that it did not offend the moral code of the ancients. Herodian, for one, was outraged. He contemptuously recorded how the senate, despite being aware of the facts, awarded Caracalla the title of *parthicus maximus* and full triumphal honours out of fear and flattery, remarking that such dishonourable deeds could not be kept secret even by an emperor.

At some point around this time Maximinus married a woman called Caecilia Paulina, of whom we know extraordinarily little. Her name Caecilia is ancient and aristocratic, although she may equally have been descended from a freed slave of that family. We are told, rather charmingly, that the giant could wear her bracelet as a ring on his finger. Paulina bore Maximinus a son called Maximus or, to give him his full name, Caius Julius Verus Maximus, and possibly other children as well (a daughter is mentioned in one of the later historical sources).[27]

Mercator

Caracalla's reputation continued to slide until one day, 8 April 217 CE, while still on the march in the east, he went to relieve himself behind a bush and was killed in the act, probably on the orders of the praetorian prefect Marcus Opelius Macrinus. The story goes that Macrinus had discovered, from his routine reading of the imperial correspondence, that he was about to be denounced and arrested for treason, giving him little option except to act fast to save his own skin. He skillfully arranged the assassination without directly implicating himself and, being second in command of the army, was made emperor on the spot. The troops saluted him and eventually he was legitimized by the senate in Rome, whereupon Caracalla's mother, the aged matriarch Julia Domna (wife of Septimius Severus), killed herself by starvation.[28] Many citizens of the empire no doubt rejoiced in the end of a cruel tyrant but less so elements of the army, which had prospered very well under the Severan dynasty.

The now wealthy and distinguished officer Caius Julius Verus Maximinus, a military man through and through, owed everything to Severus and his son, Caracalla. So, according to the *Augustan History*, he resigned from the army in disgust and retired as a private citizen to the land of his birth. Here he acquired an estate and began trading across the Danube with the barbarian tribes (Goths and Alans) to whom he was related. The story is plausible; it would have been normal for him to retire at this age, and Thracians in particular are known to have frequently returned to their homeland after military service. The contrary winds of a new dynasty (Macrinus proclaimed his son Diadumenian first as *caesar*, then co-*augustus*) would have seen close associates of the previous regime dissolve away.[29]

At this point in our story we may imagine the 40-something celebrity soldier and ex-commander as an entrepreneur on the lower Danube. The details of trans-frontier trade have been studied intensively.[30] The empire exported luxury items like pottery, brooches, bronze ornaments, glassware and wine. Weapons, especially the high-quality Roman short sword, were also in huge demand beyond the frontier, as were silver and gold coins, although more as prestige goods rather than exchangeable currency except among the merchants themselves. The return flow involved the raw materials of the ancient world: slaves, animals, hides and furs, timber and textiles and even the wagons that transported them (apparently they were not worth sending back). There was also a lively amber route originating in the lands around the Baltic, where Eocene amber continues to be washed up in large quantities to the present day. The lower Danube was one of the great gateways in and out of the empire and a man like Maximinus with powerful local and imperial connections could have profited greatly from the trade. With a young family about him, it is tempting to think that these were the happiest days of his life.

But things were to change once again as in less than a year Macrinus found himself facing a serious military revolt. This began with *legio III gallica* stationed near the city of Emesa in Syria (now the city of Homs, recently, tragically, devastated by civil war), and rapidly spread through the disaffected army. The Emesa garrison was persuaded by a local noblewoman, Julia Maesa (sister to the deceased empress Julia Domna), to recognize her grandson Varius Avitus Bassianus as emperor. Maesa told the soldiers that the youth, who was only about 15 years old, was Caracalla's illegitimate son. Avitus adopted Caracalla's hyper-noble name Marcus Aurelius Antoninus to support this dubious link to the previous imperial family. Maesa also promised the soldiers large sums of money to support the rebellion. The old dynasty, or at least a branch of it, was striking back. It was a very female coup, and what followed was a high point of matronly power in the empire.

Macrinus, who was not far away at Antioch, sent a force to crush the revolt but catastrophically for him some of his soldiers defected to the rebels. Before he could bring more troops into the area the reinforced rebel army marched out to do battle outside Antioch. The set-piece engagement went badly for Macrinus because his army fought with little spirit and, as the engagement intensified, more of the troops changed sides. Seeing this, he ran from the scene, and when his absence became known his army simply ceased fighting under offer of a general amnesty. The young Avitus/Antoninus, instructed by his grandmother Maesa, sent a letter to the senate demanding that his claim to imperial power and his dubious pedigree be legitimized, and with strong army support the senate had little choice but to agree. Macrinus and his son were hunted down and executed, and Maesa and Avitus made their way to Rome.

Praefectus Alae

Long-suffering Rome had recently experienced the deranged eccentricities of a variety of young emperors including Commodus and Caracalla, and might reasonably have expected the law of averages to reassert itself. But as any statistician will tell you, the law of averages doesn't work like that.

We should remember that in the centuries BCE, Rome and its armies had smashed their way eastward into an all-round superior collection of civilizations. Philosophy, art, architecture, religion: these were all areas that the conquered lands prided themselves with (although in fairness we must allow the Romans the discovery of concrete). The east also possessed an aristocratic class that could easily be incorporated into the empire. So long as the local civic pride and gods decreed it, the Romans easily assimilated a great constellation of eastern cities as part of the civilized world. The Greek areas kept their language and alphabet, and life continued as normal except in a state of *pax romana* rather than constant inter-city warfare, with their economies enhanced by the empire's wider connections across the entire Mediterranean.

But now a barely pubescent eastern noble and, it so happens, religious zealot, was commander of the Roman empire and all its forces. The youth must have been received with no small degree of excitement, interest and scepticism by the people of Rome. Avitus's home city of Emesa was famously home to the temple of the sun god El Gabal (which, from the Arabic, still recognizable today, literally means Man of the Mountain) and Avitus was hereditary chief priest of this cult, a role which he took very seriously. The temple housed a giant and peculiar black stone which, it was said, had fallen from the sky in former times. Its description suggests a meteorite, one of many that had been, and still are, found in the desert. In fact it was not the only such stone to be worshipped in the east; they are collectively known as baetyls. The pampered boy identified with this god, and on being made emperor he ordered the baetyl to be transported in state to Rome and the procession was recorded on some of his coins. As well as the holy meteorite the new emperor brought other exotic eastern ways to the capital, dressing exclusively in fine silks and necklaces and appearing in public with rouge on his cheeks and painted eyes. It is by the name of his sun god, Elagabalus (an Arabic–Latin hybrid) or Heliogabalus (a

Greek–Arabic–Latin hybrid) that he is chiefly known to history, although he did not use the name himself.

The *Augustan History* tells us that Maximinus decided to rejoin the army now that the house of Severus was (theoretically) restored, and sought an audience with the young emperor. If such a meeting took place it must have been in Rome. The interview was not a success. Maximinus was disgusted by the behaviour and lewd speech of the 13-year-old, who wanted to know, specifically and numerically, whether his conquests of women matched that of his opponents in the wrestling ring. Maximinus, who as far as we know was a dutiful husband, was by now quite probably doubting that the boy on the throne could really be a grandson of Severus, and once again resolved to retire to his estate. At this point some of the imperial advisers intervened, and managed to persuade him to accept a senior military command. The reasons for them doing this, we are told, was that he was already a celebrity, regarded as the "bravest man of his time", and widely identified by the people with heroes like Hercules, Achilles and Ajax. Bringing such a man back to the army would have been perfect publicity for the new regime and for raising the emperor's standing among the common troops. Moreover it fits with what we know of the political situation at that time. The coinage was pumping out the message of *fides militum*, or faith of the army, and *concordia militum*, concord of the army.

The Byzantine historian Zosimus tells us Maximinus held, at one time, the rank of *praefectus alae*, that is, commanding officer of an auxiliary cavalry regiment. This was an equestrian position; in other words it entailed the equivalent of a knighthood, or being admitted to the equestrian order. It may well be that ennoblement was the price demanded by Maximinus for his return to the army. Such a move for a distinguished commoner was not unprecedented; other deserving soldiers, since at least the days of Claudius, had broken through from *primus pilus* into equestrian rank and senior command. Moreover the reign of Elagabalus was later criticized for its lax attitude to maintaining exclusivity among the ranks of the nobility. For Maximinus, being knighted would have been a major step because further senior military appointments would suddenly have become open to him, with previously undreamt of prospects of career advancement.

Tribunatus

Although Maximinus was persuaded to give his public support to the new regime, we are told that subsequent to this first audience he did everything he could to avoid meeting the boy emperor, even to the extent of feigning illness on royal occasions.[31] The story, if it is true (and it hardly fits with his image, which suggests that it might be), is interesting because it indicates that he was a known personality. Meanwhile, his meteoric career continued. The post of cavalry prefect was evidently followed by the tribuneship (the rank of *tribunatus*, equivalent to a modern general) during the reign of Elagabalus. This entailed leading the legion on the battlefield, of course, but day to day activities were largely bureaucratic. One ancient source describes the duties thus:

> The tribunes' task is to keep the troops in the fort, to lead them out for training, to get the keys of the gates, to go round the guards from time to time, to be there when the soldiers get their rations, to check the food, to keep the quartermasters from cheating, to punish crimes within their purview, to be often at headquarters, to hear the quarrels of the men, and to inspect the sick quarters.
>
> Aemilius Macer, quoted in Speidel, 1994b, p. 95.

Meanwhile, as Maximinus buckled down to such tasks, the boy emperor could not be controlled by his mother or grandmother and his reign was marked by a glut of religious fanaticism, cruelty and bloodshed. Elagabalus increasingly identified himself with the sun god, as is evident on his coin issues, and the ancient sources give descriptions of exotic religious ceremonies and festivals. He built a giant temple complex to El Gabal on the Palatine Hill in the centre of the city (the *elagabalium*), in which the top god (that is, himself) was joined by his eastern consorts Astarte and Atargatis. This seems to have been justified as a fusion of religions, by which El Gabal, Astarte and Atargatis were identified with the ancient Roman 'Capitoline triad' of Jupiter, Juno and Minerva whose temples were on the adjacent Capitoline Hill. But it difficult to imagine that the Roman people would have seen all this as anything other than competition for the state religion, especially when the emperor then refused to officiate at the traditional new year rites at Rome's most sacred temple, that of Jupiter Optimus Maximus on the Capitoline, and delegated the job to a city functionary.

In the following years Elagabalus took several wives but divorced them in succession. One of these, Julia Aquilia Severa, was an acting Vestal Virgin: to wed her was a deeply sacrilegious act to the traditional Roman religion. The emperor excused it by appealing to his own divine, eastern, status. Despite this, the ancient sources agree that Elagabalus was by nature a lover of men and was trying to distract from this by taking wives in an ostentatious manner. It became widely known that he had male consorts; one was a charioteer called Heirocles, another an athlete named Zoticus, both of whom he is reported to have ceremonially married. According to Cassius Dio, Elagabalus referred to himself at one time as the 'Queen of Heirocles' and offered money to any surgeon who could equip him with female genitalia. All this shocked the Victorians, but modern writers have identified him as transgender transsexual and within the normal range of human sexuality as now understood.[32]

The ancients may have been less understanding and the *Augustan History* lists many more extraordinary stories relating to Elagabalus's deviant extravagance. Still in his teens, he is supposed to have built palaces for single use, which he navigated in a chariot drawn by naked women. He would order dishes such as flamingo brains and nightingale tongues, or concoctions made from 10,000 mice or 1,000 weasels which his guests would eat from spoons inscribed (as if it was a childrens' party) with a chance take-home gift that could range from ten pounds of gold to ten dead flies. He fed geese to his hunting dogs and parrots to his lions and then let the ferocious animals loose in the guest apartments as the inhabitants slept, causing death and injury, and on one occasion he suffocated a party of diners in an enclosed room with a trap-door ceiling by means of endless cascades of flowers. To what extent such stories (and there are many more of them) reflect historical truth or should be regarded as rhetorical flourishes by historians extemporising on a theme, the reader can make their own judgement.[33]

With unlimited power but no restraint the refined adolescent became unpopular with just about everyone including the army high command, who became disgusted by his antics. So in an attempt to boost the regime's popularity, the emperor's grandmother Julia Maesa (still the real power behind the throne) persuaded Elagabalus to appoint his more respectable younger cousin as *caesar*. This was done with great solemnity. But the move backfired because the guard soon took to the sensible, even likeable lad, and saw the merits of doing away with Elagabalus and his weak mother Julia Soaemias (one of Maesa's daughters) and proclaiming as emperor his more sensible cousin in his place. The end was brutal, short and efficient. It was March 222.

Chapter III

Regime Change

A New Alexander

Born Gessius Bassianus Alexianus, the new emperor was only 13. He had been given the name Marcus Aurelius Severus Alexander on adopting the rank of *caesar* the year before. The first three parts of the name continued the ruse of claiming to be related by male descent to the royal house of Septimius Severus (who, it should be noted, had himself appropriated the name of the beloved emperor Marcus Aurelius); like his cousin he also claimed to be an illegitimate son of Caracalla (Marcus Aurelius Antoninus). (See Plate 2 for the genealogy). Changing the name Alexianus to Alexander, although a transliteration, was an even bolder piece of propaganda on behalf of his handlers, as it recalled the Macedonian king Alexander the Great, foremost of all the conquering heroes. It would be a hard image to live up to.

The empress Julia Maesa was by now an old lady and presumably disconsolate after the murder of her eldest daughter and grandson, and was probably sidelined by the praetorians on pain of death. The real power behind Alexander's throne was to be his mother, Julia Mamaea, who took the title of *augusta* on his accession. With firm control over everything that her son did and the willpower to match, by careful steps she became arguably the most powerful woman of all time up to that point. We can imagine that she was determined not to suffer the same fate as her recently slaughtered sister, so surviving the first few months was the initial challenge, but she also had to plan for the longer term. Accordingly she was vigilant not to allow corrupting influences into the palace[1] and instead ensured that Alexander was provided with the highest standard of education in both Latin and Greek that Rome could supply. She busied the boy with legal work so that he could grow into his responsibilities and learn the business of governing on the job. She also removed all previous senior advisers from public office including the palace eunuchs so favoured by Elagabalus. In their place she appointed a cabinet of advisers: 16 senior senators known for their good sense and probity who would report to her. She recalled from banishment the famous jurist and most formidable intellectual of the day, Gnaeus Domitius Annius Ulpianus (known and revered in legal history as Ulpian and regarded, perhaps a little anachronistically, as a pioneer of human rights[2]) and appointed him praetorian prefect, which in this time of peace made him a sort of prime minister. The cult of the sun god Elagabalus was expelled from the city and the old religion of Rome was restored. The visible symbol of this was the re-dedication of the *elagabalium* to Jupiter Ultor (the avenger) and the quiet return of the sacred meteorite to the east. Aside from suppression of elagabalism there was a new spirit of religious freedom in the city: even Jews and Christians, normally rated the most corrosive of religious fanatics because of their intolerance to other gods, were now to be permitted to worship openly.

Meanwhile Alexander, or rather his mother and advisers, set about restoring the social strata of Rome that had been undermined by the previous lax regime. In the words of the *Augustan History* the senate was 'purified', as were the equestrian order and the lists of the thirty tribes of free citizens. Presumably this meant the expulsion of undesirables who had been promoted by Elagabalus, although that would not include useful people like Maximinus. It was decreed that henceforth, new senators would only be promoted with the support of the existing senate. But the principal challenge faced by the regime was to curb the power of the army and in particular the praetorian guard in Rome which had resurfaced as a major political force following its total replacement by Septimius Severus. This was an elite army within the army, deeply conservative and proud of its history, reputation and higher pay. The praetorians had disposed of Elagabalus and, if not controlled or appeased, might do the same to the new emperor at any time. Although the murder of Elagabalus and his mother might have been seen as reasonable by many, the imperial family can hardly have been enthusiastic about it.

After some deliberation, Ulpian started to cut back on the privileges of the guard and even had some senior men executed, probably on charges of corruption. Since he has gone down in history as a famous jurist and one of the founders of the Roman legal system, we can probably assume that these were not simply show trials. The late historian Zosimus names Flavius and Chrestus as two of those who opposed Ulpian at this time and it has been suggested that they were also praetorian prefects but junior to Ulpian.[3] The policy backfired disastrously: the sentences led to rioting by the guard and there was actual fighting between the praetorians and the citizens in the streets of Rome lasting three whole days according to one source. The praetorians even threatened the people with arson, a blood-curdling ultimatum in such a dense and crowded wooden city. Further details of these tumultuous events are, unfortunately, lost to us, but we do know that the civil disturbances (in 223 or 224) ended with

Ulpian's violent death even as he sought safety with Alexander and Mamaea in the imperial palace. The man deemed responsible for Ulpian's death was made governor of Egypt, perhaps to pacify the guard, but from there he was arrested and taken to Crete for execution. These were power struggles at the highest level, but the regime survived.

Gradually Rome started to feel the benefits of sensible government after a long interlude of transient or worse than eccentric rulers. The grain and oil supply to the city was improved and, in what is Ulpian's real legacy, the legal system was restored and strengthened. It was inherited by medieval Europe and still influences us today.[4] A new set of taxes was applied to craft goods (the *Augustan History* specifies new taxes on trousers, linen, fur, locks and jewellery), bringing in money to fund public works. A building programme in the capital began with the restoration of the great Flavian amphitheatre (the famous Colosseum), which had been in disuse for some years following lightning damage. Its re-inauguration was celebrated on a special issue of coinage in 223.[5] Other great public buildings including the Circus Maximus and the old Theatre of Marcellus were also given a makeover. A few years later came the grand opening of a huge new aqueduct, the *aqua alexandrina* (water of Alexander) which supplied a renovated public bathing complex, the Alexandrian baths (*thermae alexandrianae*) and possessed a pool so impressive as to be nicknamed "the ocean". Alexander was himself keen on swimming, it was said. This aqueduct, parts of which survive today, brought fresh waters from upland springs about 11 miles to the east of the city.[6] The new water source also fed a succession of more humble pumps and fountains across the city that also bore the emperor's name. The basic equation was that the more clean water that flowed in to the city, the more dirty water was flushed out, helping to improve the public health situation.

Rome's facelift was not all functional. Its great history was celebrated anew by the dedication of colossal statues of the previous emperors, with bronze plaques listing their achievements and titles (of course, the dedication was just to those who had been deified by the senate; the disgraced, mad, defeated and murdered were naturally omitted). In this way the eastern imperial family of dubious legitimacy overtly identified itself with the city's great past. According to the *Augustan History*, Alexander was then able to lower general tax rates to stimulate the economy and improve the coinage, and he actively supported art, science and literature. That the coinage was improved can be objectively demonstrated: the silver content stabilized and the regime never issued the infamous lightweight double-denarius that had been used by Caracalla to fund his military handouts (and which had also been issued by Macrinus and Elagabalus). Restoring the silver standard must have been challenging, and meanwhile the big bold bronze sestertius continued to be hammered out in huge quantities with no diminution in their weight or quality. Remarkable as it seems today, the currency of a century before circulated more or less interchangeably with the latest issues.

Vir Clarissimus

Herodian's abbreviated account of Maximinus's career is that he "progressed through all the ranks in the army and was given charge of legions and commands over provinces". Reconstructing his senior military career under Alexander has taxed historians; it requires ingenious interpretation of the ancient sources but at least, from now on, more glimpses of the man himself or the offices he may have held occasionally crop up in inscriptions. His first governmental posting may have been in Mauretania Tingitana (modern Morocco). There, at Aquae Dacicae (modern Sidi Kacem) near the ancient city of Volubilis (now a UNESCO World Heritage Site, with its magnificent colonnades and mosaics) a dedicatory inscription to Julia Mamaea has turned up, from around the year 221–223, erected by the fourth cohort of Gauls under "C(aio) I(vlio) Maximino v(iro) e(gregio) (p)raes(ide) pro legato". It has been noted that several ex-commanders of the imperial horseguard proceeded to this post of *praeses pro legato* in Mauretania (essentially, provincial governor), probably because it required skill in training and commanding cavalry forces. The local military was dominated by specialist lancers who had the speed and mobility to protect the borders from marauders from the south and, as we shall see, Mauretanian light cavalry were also posted to other parts of the empire when required. Hence the inscription is further corroboration, if not actual proof, of the career pathway outlined in the oft-despised *Augustan History*. The title *vir egregius* (outstanding man), first heard of in the time of Marcus Aurelius, denotes a man of equestrian rank, and the governorship of Mauretania was indeed usually an equestrian position.[7]

Maximinus may have been made governor of Mauretania Tingitana in the last year of Elagabalus (221), returning to Rome shortly after Alexander was confirmed in his offices. The *Augustan History* says there was much rejoicing when he publicly backed the new regime, and moreover that the new emperor elevated him to the senatorial rank. The phrase he is supposed to have used for Maximinus is "the tribune to whom I have given the broad stripe".[8] A broad purple stripe on the toga was the mark of a senator, and it came with the rarefied title *vir clarissimus* (most illustrious man). Around this time, Mamaea set up a military council composed of "men of proved reputations for maintaining discipline and waging wars". We do not know if Maximinus was one such adviser, but if he was as prominent by this time as implied by the *Augustan History* it would at least seem possible. It was even decreed that historians were to be consulted if military action was being contemplated, which shows a level of wisdom sometimes not even encountered today.

Also according to the *Augustan History*, Maximinus was then given command of a newly conscripted 'fourth legion'. It is a peculiarity of the Roman legionary system that, under certain circumstances, whole legions could be conscripted in one draft and, eventually, retire together. Alexander is supposed to have said, in his speech celebrating the occasion, that Maximinus's task was to train the raw recruits and produce 'many Maximini' for Rome (as the name Maximinus literally means 'from small to large', this could be some kind of pun). If the story is not wholly fictitious, the fourth legion is probably *legio IIII flavia felix* in upper Moesia.[9] It might indicate that problems on the Danube frontier required the trusted and steady hand of a famous soldier and friend of the regime. Moreover there is other evidence of Maximinus being in the Balkans in Alexander's reign. Based on clues in one of the later historical sources it is thought that he may have been promoted into the military high command with the post of *praefectus civitatium moesiae et trebelliae* – a kind of military governorship of the lower Danubian frontier provinces (the area of his birth).[10] Perhaps his knowledge of the tribes and fluency in the local language was considered a great asset.

Protection of the Danube and the neighbouring provinces of Upper and Lower Moesia was entrusted to four legions. *Legio XI claudia* was based at Durostorum (modern Silistra in Bulgaria) on the lower reaches of the river as it approached the Black Sea coast. Upstream were *legio I italica* based at Novae (Svishtov, Bulgaria), *legio VII claudia* at Viminacium (near Kostolac, Serbia) and supposedly Maximinus's own command, *legio IIII flavia felix* at Singidunum (Belgrade, Serbia; where, unusually, the modern city grid is a direct overlay of the Roman plan). The epithets of these great and proud legions reflect some aspect of their history and helped distinguish them from other units that might have the same number. For example, *flavia felix* (from the command of which Maximinus may have been elevated) means the lucky Flavian legion; it was originally enlisted by the emperor Vespasian late in the first century, whose *nomen* was Flavius. Each legion had its own emblem: for *legio XI* it was Neptune, presumably because its base was near the sea; for *legio VII* the bull; for *legio I* the boar; for *legio IIII* the lion. All this helped create pride in the unit just as it does in modern army divisions. With such a sweeping command of the Danube sector, Maximinus would by now have been one of the most senior generals in the Roman army.

A Royal Wedding

In 225 Alexander turned 16 and by now his coins show him sporting a tufty beard. He was a bright lad, gaining a reputation for intellect beyond his age[11] and in particular an excellent memory. Mamaea now arranged for him to be married to a beautiful aristocratic girl of the same age called Sallustia Barbia Orbiana, daughter of the senator Seius Herennius Sallustius Barbius who might possibly have been given the rank of *caesar* at the same time[12] pending the birth of an heir. The people rejoiced, and the glorious event provided a huge boost to Alexander's popularity in Rome and across the empire. The celebrations were widely commemorated on the coinage of the day and by all accounts the young couple found themselves perfectly matched.

But what followed is sadly reminiscent of the tale of Snow White and the evil queen. As *augusta* and consort to the emperor, the girl Orbiana now outranked Mamaea as the senior lady of the empire, not to mention in youth and beauty and the love of her son (Mamaea's coins show a rather plain woman with a beaky nose, whereas Orbiana looks altogether more appealing; and there is a curvaceous statue of the goddess Venus in the Louvre that is supposed to be in her likeness). However there were no regular issues of coins in Orbiana's name and Mamaea continued her hold over one of the six departments of the mint.[13] Clearly Mamaea still regarded herself as the real ruler of the empire and became increasingly jealous of the girl empress and, we are told, began to insult her and act cruelly towards her in public. After a couple of years of this treatment, Orbiana's father plotted with the guard to neutralize Mamaea in some way. Exactly what he was attempting to achieve is difficult to establish; Herodian says his charges were against Mamaea only, and not the emperor, and so were not necessarily treasonable, which seems a very tolerant attitude.[14] Whatever it was, the plot backfired and Sallustius was exposed and denounced to Mamaea who handed him over for execution. Orbiana was banished to Libya, at which point she disappears from history. Banishment was very often a prelude to murder as had happened most recently to Caracalla's teenage wife Plautilla, although one cannot help hoping this was not the case with Orbiana considering her much more sensible husband and the generally more enlightened regime. It seems curious that Alexander did not intervene on his young wife's behalf: we can assume either that he had his own reasons to suspect her complicity in the plot or he was too frightened of his overbearing mother (as Herodian alleged). If Alexander ever married again, and the sources disagree on this, his wife or wives were never commemorated on the coinage.

In terms of publicity, the sorry saga of Orbiana had rebounded, especially on Mamaea; and Alexander, although still young, did not come out of it looking especially decisive either. But good government and peace continued and the empire flourished. Alexander matured from a mere boy to a handsome young man, his development showing itself on his coinage year on year. Eventually, in 230, he celebrated the tenth year of his elevation as *caesar* and ninth as *augustus*. The occasion was marked by a distribution of money and a solemn renewal of the formal vows of loyalty from the troops. His was already the longest reign since Septimius Severus and promised great things. According to later tradition, Alexander was by nature just, kind, generous and considerate; and his contemporaries, too, described him as humane and benevolent. Now in his early twenties, his position was unchallenged and, we are told, he was loved by the people: something that had not been claimed of any emperor for decades (certainly not of Septimius Severus, who had ruled by fear). A Golden Age seemed to be dawning. But at this time a new 'Beast from the East' emerged: one whose rise would have profound consequences for the future of Rome and provide a stern martial test for the young emperor and his top generals.

A New Xerxes

The Roman empire was (in its eyes) surrounded by barbarians: semi-savage tribes inhabiting far-flung forests and mountains, and there were many tales of human sacrifice and other shocking practices from beyond the borders. The Romans recognized external kingdoms when it suited them, exchanging embassies and gifts, but the diplomacy was never conducted in any sense as equals. The one partial exception to this was the great Persian empire to the east which, the Romans well knew, boasted civilized roots much older than their own, although that did not stop them calling the inhabitants barbarians. In the sixth century BCE, when Rome was an insignificant town in central Italy, Persia was the greatest of all the world powers. The pharaohs of Egypt trembled at the mention of their kings. Its zenith was the time of the so-called Achaemenid dynasty, which included famous leaders such as Cambyses, Cyrus, Darius and Xerxes. But as every Roman and Greek knew, the westward expansion of mighty Persia had ultimately been checked by the heroes of Marathon and Thermopylae. And then, subsequently and astonishingly, the whole Persian empire had been conquered by Alexander of Macedon in the fourth century BCE. West had triumphed over east.

In fact Alexander's conquests hardly outlived him and the area he despoiled quickly fragmented into a number of sub-units under his generals and their successors. These included, most notably, the Ptolemies in Egypt and the so-called Seleucid dynasty centred on Babylon in Mesopotamia, named after the general Seleucus who took over the eastern part of the old Persian empire.

Greek influence spread into Asia through the following century (which is therefore called the Hellenistic age) and Greek-speaking peoples migrated into many new cities in the east, even as far as Kandahar in modern Afghanistan. Inevitably, cultures fused and eventually the Seleucid dynasty itself was swept away by a revolution from a region known as Parthia (an area now in northeastern Iran). The revolt was led by the first of the Parthian kings, Arsaces I. It was these Parthians (or Arsacids as they are sometimes known) who eventually came into direct contact with the expanding Roman empire in the first century BCE, leading to an uneasy line of demarcation along the upper Euphrates.

The rulers of the Parthians styled themselves as 'kings of kings' but they also acknowledged their Seleucid forebears. Their political system was, in essence, an overlordship, guaranteed by central strength and peripheral fear. The local magnates (satraps) would organize local taxation and could muster troops in times of war and they were also expected to offer their allegiance to the overlord. As in the Roman empire, a large proportion of the population worked the land, but there were also many cities and towns distributed in three main areas: fertile lower Mesopotamia; along the northern shore of the Persian gulf; and along the silk road that snaked its way eastward to the north of the Iranian plateau. There were many ethnic groups within the empire, from Arabs in the west to Persians and Indians in the east. A substantial Greek-speaking population was concentrated in certain towns. The mix of religions was just as complex. Many towns and regions had their own deities, some of which dated back to the dawn of civilization. Some of them were 'identified' with the Greek gods and goddesses of the Hellenistic period. Judaism was well established in the west following the 'Babylonian captivity' and Buddhism in the east. Then, in the early centuries CE, the strange new cults of Mithras, Cybele and Jesus Christ added to the mix. There was also a strong substratum of Zoroastrianism, a conservative religion that had been the official faith of the ancient Achaemeneids. This was based on the teaching of the semi-legendary prophet Zoroaster of (possibly) the sixth century BCE. The supreme god of Zoroastrianism was Ahura Mazda who was worshipped at fire altars.[15]

By the first century BCE the entire eastern Mediterranean had been subjugated by Pompey Magnus 'the Great' using a masterful medley of conquest, manoeuvre and diplomacy.[16] After that, the Parthians were the only remaining power that could conceivably meet the Romans on equal terms on the battlefield or match their wealth in gold. The two empires traded freely but the Romans eyed the evident riches of the Parthian cities, and many senior Romans considered the fame that would be theirs if they could conquer significant tracts of the Parthian empire.

The border between the empires was much too long and desolate to be policed by either side and for a long while it was undefended in force.[17] Upper Mesopotamia was a jigsaw of petty kingdoms around fortified towns that were largely independent but aligned themselves with either Rome or Parthia depending on which was in the ascendancy. Conveniently, in its upper reaches, the Euphrates runs in a roughly north-south direction and so this became the notional border between east and west; there was even an occasional 'summit' conference between the Roman and Parthian leadership on the river's banks. The Roman zone initially included all the Province of Syria up to the west bank, while the Parthians claimed ascendancy over the kingdom of Osrhoene on the eastern side. Further down its course, however, the Euphrates turns east, so that the Roman 'west' bank became the south bank and could be followed a long way into Parthian heartland and ultimately to Ctesiphon. The political alignment of the many settlements along the river is very complicated and changed with time. A key factor for much of the second century was the presence of a third significant power in the area, the semi-autonomous kingdom of Palmyra, which stationed troops along the banks of the Euphrates to protect its caravan routes, including in Parthian-aligned towns such as Dura Europos. Despite these apparent fault lines there was not always a hostile stand-off between the three powers on the Euphrates because they were all engaged in the serious business of making money out of the silk road trade.[18] War in the area would hurt everybody.

Instead, the main geopolitical friction between the empires was focused on the northern edge of Parthian dominions and in particular the mountain kingdom of Armenia (centred on the modern country of that name). From the first century the Romans claimed Armenia as an ally and battled for influence there. The Roman policy seems to have been to increase its influence through a combination of overt friendliness and implied military pressure. The militarization began in the time of Vespasian in the late first century when the first permanent troops were stationed on the upper Euphrates.[19] Eventually several legions were garrisoned in strategic locations in the area. Ostensibly they were there to defend Roman Syria, especially the rich city of Antioch, but it was obvious that they could also be used for attack, either up into Armenia or down through Mesopotamia. The eminently practical diplomatic solution that the two empires eventually arrived at was for successive Armenian kings to be selected by the Parthians from among their own nobility but to be crowned by the incumbent Roman emperor. Both Parthians and Romans paid substantial sums of money to support the Armenian military to guard against barbarian incursions from the north. Thus it became a classic buffer state preventing friction between the two empires, just as long as both sides respected its neutrality and paid the tribute.

Neither the Euphrates nor the Tigris presented a real geographic border to the Roman empire like the Rhine and Danube did in Europe: on the map, both rivers look more like arrows aimed at the fertile alluvial lands of lower Mesopotamia with its many ancient cities. So, periodically, wars of conquest or plunder erupted, with Rome generally the aggressor. The Romans also had a permanent tactical advantage in that they could attack downstream. The first major campaign was by the emperor Trajan in 113, who annexed the Parthian capital itself, that is, the twin cities of Ctesiphon and Seleucia, but this conquest was short-lived and ended in rebellion. A second major expedition (162–165) occurred in the reign of Marcus Aurelius led by his co-emperor Lucius Verus, and two more, mentioned previously (195–197), in the reign of Septimius Severus, which culminated in the annexation of Osrhoene and the sack of Ctesiphon respectively.

Each war was a seismic shock along the western silk road and produced a new baseline in Roman–Parthian relations. Palmyra eventually came fully under Roman control and the Palmyran archers on the Euphrates were directly absorbed into the Roman army as auxiliaries[20] although an underlying spirit of national pride and independence still remained. Some of the land in northern Mesopotamia was annexed by the Romans and incorporated into a new Roman province of 'Mesopotamia' (effectively, upper Mesopotamia). This included the client kingdom of Osrhoene, previously very much in the Parthian sphere east of the upper Euphrates. Osrhoene was Arabic in culture, centred on the ancient city of Edessa (modern Urfa in eastern Turkey), and encompassed several other major fortified cities that were to be disputed territory for centuries to come.

By the early third century a new spirit of defiance was stirring in the far Persian empire to the east, including a renewed identification with the old Achaemenid empire and the Zoroastrian religion, and this was to have profound consequences on events across the Roman world. Successive Roman encroachments and plundering of Parthia seem eventually to have weakened that ancient empire to the point of collapse. A revolt from within brought to power a new regime under King (*Shah*) Ardashir I, a man from the ancient Farsi homeland of Iran. Ardashir's origins are shrouded in legend[21] but it seems he was of a noble and priestly line. Sometime around 210 he became King of the state of Istakhr (ancient Persis) under Parthian overlordship but he rebelled against the weak central authority and started to expand his own dominions. According to one story a full-scale rebellion started when Ardashir founded a town called 'the Glory of Ardashir' (now Firuzabad in Iraq) which annoyed the Parthian King of Kings, Artabanus V, enough to send armies against him.[22] There was an escalating series of battles, from which Ardashir emerged victorious, and finally Artabanus himself was killed (c. 224). Legend has it that the two kings fought hand to hand, or rather lance to lance, in the final engagement at a place called Hormizdeghan. There is a famous rock relief carving at Naqsh–i Rustam near Persepolis in modern Iran that shows Ardashir and Artabanus jousting in the style of medieval knights, with Ardashir knocking Artabanus from his mount. Whether this was history or pseudo-historical rewrite, the moment depicted on that carving was one of the great turning points of history. It signified the end of the Parthian dynasty and the start of a new phase of Persian history that became known as the Sasanian Empire (which, somewhat obscurely, takes its name from Ardashir's legendary father Sasan).

The really radical thing about Ardashir was that he denounced the entire Seleucid and Parthian royal houses of the last half millennium as illegitimate usurpers who had been installed by Alexander the Great. Instead he claimed descent from the great Achaemenid dynasty that preceded them, including Cyrus the Great and Darius. The name Ardashir is a transliteration of Artaxerxes, which had been the name of several achaemenid kings, the most important of whom, Artaxerxes II (ruled c. 404–359 BCE), had been responsible for the adoption of the Zoroastrian faith across the ancient Persian empire. The name itself originally meant 'king' and there is a suggestion that Ardashir deliberately chose it and the epithet 'the thinker' which went with it in conscious emulation of Artaxerxes II.[23] Two years after Artabanus had been slain, Ctesiphon itself was captured by his forces and the old Parthian regime and all its infrastructure was swept away or assimilated. Ardashir had himself crowned as *Shahanshah*, king of kings of Iran, effectively claiming sovereignty over all the previous Parthian territory. Some of Artabanus's sons and other supporters escaped to Armenia to the north from where they fought back, but to little avail other than creating a deep enmity between Armenia and the new Persian regime which Rome was naturally keen to exploit.

The political stance of the new regime is immediately obvious from the coinage. The Parthians, following the Seleucids before them, had issued coins with Greek text: Ardashir changed this to Persian, with the legends rendered in the Pahlavi script. The official religion of state was once again that of the ancient Achaemenids: Zoroastrianism, and worship of the all-powerful fire god Ahura-Mazda. Ardashir summoned the various sects of Zoroastrianism and ordered them to agree a single set of doctrines that would then become the one true religion of his empire (much as the Roman emperor Constantine later did for Christianity). He then claimed a divine right to rule granted by Ahura-Mazda, just as Artaxerxes, Cyrus and Xerxes had done hundreds of years before. On his coronation in 226, Ardashir solemnly lit a perpetual sacred fire, which is depicted on many of his coins and those of his successors. The new strand of Zoroastrianism also included co-worship of Anahita, a fearsome war-goddess, who also symbolized water and fertility, so important in the desert lands. This emphasis on the masculine and feminine, fire and water, also emulated the ancient religious policy of Artaxerxes II. The concept of holy water is just one of many possible influences that Zoroastrianism had on Christian ritual practices that survive today.[24]

Ardashir's seizure of power was, then, a true revolution: ethnic, religious, linguistic, economic, cultural and political. This new version of the Persian Empire was to be a much more virulent opponent for the Romans than the Parthians had ever been, mainly because Ardashir now claimed sovereignty of all the lands of his supposed Achaemenid ancestors; that is, all of Asia Minor up to the shore of the Aegean.[25] In effect, this claim negated all the Asian conquests of both Alexander of Macedon and Pompey the Great and placed a direct threat of invasion over Rome's eastern provinces including many wealthy cities. Perhaps the new Roman emperor's historic name of Alexander helped convince Ardashir to define his own great ambitions in response.

Despite these throwbacks to ancient history, Ardashir did not immediately set his sights on conquest in the west. Instead he pursued expansionist policies along his southern and eastern borders, assimilating weaker kingdoms either by force or intimidation. The list of fallen kingdoms is impressive: Sistan, Gorgan, Khorasan, Margiana, Balch, Bahrain and Mosul. By 230 he had also subjugated the western half of the distant and once mighty Kushan empire of the silk road as well as Bactria in modern Afghanistan, including the Hindu Kush and Helmand and Herat valleys, and much of what is now Pakistan as far as the Indus.[26] Reputedly, he displayed the severed heads of the many conquered kings in the great Temple of Anahita at Ishtakr.

Ardashir is reported to have been popular because of his wise rule and respect for the law. His grip on power was strengthened by his many military victories, and he was now in firm control of an enormous empire comparable in extent to Rome's. Arguably, his conquests exceeded even any of the great Roman generals including Caesar and Pompey, although it is fair to say he was mostly reuniting lands that had once been part of the ancient Persian empire. Be that as it may, the great trading caravans crossing the silk road between Chinese and Roman territory would pass through two thousand miles of Ardashir's taxable dominions.

Only then, in 230, did Ardashir turn his attention to the west. He began that spring by attacking the independent desert stronghold of Hatra (now Al-Hadr, Iraq), and then the other independent buffer states of Armenia (still a hotbed of dissident Parthian nobility) and Adiabene. These attacks met with less success than his eastern campaigns, and the near-impregnable fortress of Hatra held out despite one of its walls being breached.

To Alexander and his advisors this was a severe provocation. Their first move was to dispatch a diplomatic mission demanding in effect that Ardashir should not be carried away by over-optimism following his recent victories against minor powers, that he should remain within his own territory, and at the same time be reminded of Roman military might and the great victories achieved by successive previous Roman armies in Persia. This move recognized the legitimacy of Ardashir's regime within former Parthian lands but threatened dire retribution if Roman territory was violated or the independence of the buffer states compromised. The response was contemptuous: later that year (230) Ardashir ordered Persian forces to invade Roman Mesopotamia itself in strength, plundering the land and directly laying siege to a number of border forts and in particular the strategic city of Nisibis. Other raiding parties penetrated as far as western Syria and according to one late source there were also incursions further north, deep into Roman province of Cappadocia (central Turkey). The eastern legions were unprepared and weak and in a poor state of discipline. Ardashir's strikes met with great success and probably told him a lot about the forces he was up against.

These events were regarded with alarm and genuine fear across the Roman empire. The senator Cassius Dio is a particularly interesting witness because he had served as consul with Alexander in 229 and so was privy to the highest affairs of state. He retired in 230 to finish his life's work, the epic *Roman History*, at the very end of which are the following lines from an undated fragment, seemingly written that year, in which the past tense that had been used throughout the great work dramatically gives way to the present:

> He [Ardashir] accordingly became a source of fear to us; for he was encamped with a large army so as to threaten not only Mesopotamia but also Syria, and he boasted that he would win back everything that the ancient Persians had once held, as far as the Grecian Sea, claiming that all this was his rightful inheritance from his forefathers. The danger lies not in the fact that he seems to be of any particular consequence in himself, but rather in the fact that our armies are in such a state that some of the troops are actually joining him and others are refusing to defend themselves.
>
> Cassius Dio, *Roman History*, LXXX.3.1.

Ardashir had awakened a sleeping giant, and the stage was now set for a major war between two of the three great empires of Eurasia.[27]

Chapter IV

Duke of the Riverbank

Dura Europos

In 1920, Captain M.C. Murphy of the British Indian Army stumbled across some ruins on a steep bluff on the uncultivated, un-irrigated southwest bank of the Euphrates. It turned out to be a corner of a whole city, lost to the desert in the third century and thereafter completely forgotten, one of the gems of world archaeology. The reason for it remaining hidden so long is that from the time of the town's abandonment onward, the main line of communication had switched to the northeast bank. Countless travellers must have passed below the eroding ruins for a millennium and a half without knowing what was atop the far cliffs.[1]

Dura is near the modern-day border between Syria and Iraq, a war zone at the time of writing. It was excavated periodically through the twentieth century and the finds are extraordinary, rivalling Pompeii. Originally a Hellenistic city, then Parthian, it had been conquered by Septimius Severus and made a *colonia*. The walled enclosure is about 700 metres long by 500 metres wide and arranged in a formal grid of roads, with many private and public structures, including an amphitheatre and bath complex. Of the religious buildings, remains have been found of a synagogue, a Christian church (the oldest known anywhere in the world),[2] a crypt of Mithras, a Roman military temple and further temples dedicated to the local deities, some of whom go back to the dawn of civilization. Many of these had extraordinarily vibrant frescoes on the surviving walls that astonished Captain Murphy and were photographed in monochrome in the early twentieth century.

Dura occupied a vital strategic position on the very extremity of Roman territory, adjacent to Ardashir's Persian dominions. Accordingly, it was a garrison city, home to *cohors XX palmyrenorum* (the twentieth cohort, of Palmyrenes). It occupied a promontory with steep cliffs in front and deeply carved wadis to north and south: these natural defences were augmented with strong crenulated walls that are still impressive today. The landward side had no natural defences and so here the walls and towers are best developed.

Because of its strength, Ardashir's forces had bypassed Dura in their raids into Roman territory in 230.

The most impressive building in the city was a sumptuous palace at the north end of town with extensive marble colonnades and courtyards and commanding views along the river, ideal for monitoring traffic and making the most of whatever morning and evening breezes there might be. There is inscriptional evidence that this was the command headquarters of the *dux ripae* ('Riverbank Commander').[3] The Latin word *dux* simply means leader and had been used in an informal sense since the days of the Republic, but from the mid third century it increasingly crops up as denoting a specific senior military rank above the level of legionary tribune and was eventually to morph into the medieval title of duke and its variants. It is not clear when the post of *dux ripae* was established but given its extraordinary nature as a kind of Euphrates high command it seems quite possible that the post was created in the early 230s amid preparations for Roman retaliation against Ardashir. Moreover it seems Maximinus himself held this office because he is later quoted (by Herodian) as saying that he had been "commander of legions on the frontier banks of the river" in the Persian war, a kind of transliteration of the title *dux ripae*.[4] The Romans were about to launch a massive invasion of Persia and the famous old soldier was to play a significant role.

Profectio

In response to Ardashir's aggression in 230, Alexander organized a great army that he would lead himself. The core was his own elite praetorian guard augmented by *legio II parthica* (a special legion stationed near Rome) and a new levy of men of fighting age from across Italy. In the spring of 231, as relayed to us by Herodian, Alexander addressed these troops, who were presumably mustered on the *campus martius* (the field of Mars – god of war – a great parade ground to the north of the city centre). We should not necessarily imagine that the oration is really what was said: inserting such speeches was a common stylistic device in ancient histories which were intended to be read aloud, and the speeches enabled historians to examine points of view and provide a sense of immediacy to the narrative. The speeches also served, in passing, to display their own rhetorical ability for others to admire (history was a competitive sport in ancient Rome). However, it is also quite possible that Herodian was present in the crowd that day, and even if not we can presume the speech conveys something of the pre-war atmosphere and the attitude of the real Alexander:

The Persian Artaxerxes [that is, Ardashir][5] has slain his master Artabanus, and the Parthian empire is now Persian. Despising our arms and contemptuous of the Roman reputation, Artaxerxes is attempting to overrun and destroy our imperial possessions. I first endeavoured by letters and persuasion to check his mad greed and his lust for the property of others. But the king, with barbarian arrogance, is unwilling to remain within his own boundaries and challenges us to battle. Let us not hesitate to accept his challenge. You veterans remind yourselves of the victories which you often won over the barbarians under the leadership of Severus and my father, Caracalla. You recruits, thirsting for glory and honour, make it clear that you know how to live at peace mildly and with propriety, but make it equally clear that you turn with courage to the tasks of war when necessity demands. The barbarian is bold against the hesitant and the cowardly, but he does not stand up in like fashion to those who fight back; it is not in close-quarter combat that they battle the enemy with hope of success. Rather, they believe that whatever success they win is the result of plundering after a feigned retreat and flight. Discipline and organized battle tactics favour us, together with the fact that we have always been taught to conquer the barbarian.

Herodian, *History of the Empire* VI.3.3–7.

Amid the war fever there were solemn sacrifices at the old Temple of Mars Ultor (Mars the Avenger) in the Forum of Augustus and probably all the other great temples of the city. And then the emperor set out at the head of his troops, who filed out in their finest pomp as the senate and citizens gathered to cheer them off. The departure of the emperor at the head of an army was a highly ceremonial, formal occasion (the *profectio*), celebrated in Alexander's coinage from 231, which shows him on horseback being led forth by the winged figure of Victory (see Plate 4). From then on the output from the mint takes on a martial theme generally. Vast numbers of silver coins were issued to pay the army. One common type shows *mars vltor*, shown appropriately in armour, advancing with spear and shield. Another shows *iovi propugnatori* (Jupiter the Champion) in heroic nudity, holding an eagle in one hand, symbolizing the legions, and a thunderbolt in the other ready to throw at Rome's enemies. In some of these issues Alexander is depicted wearing a soldier's cuirass for the first time on his coinage.

Alexander transferred his administration to the great eastern city of Antioch to plan the campaign, but he himself detoured via the Rhine–Danube border provinces to lend his authority to the mustering of forces there. Crack detachments from at least six legions from that area were transferred to the east: inscriptional evidence suggests these included *legio XXX vlpia* (from

Vetera on the Rhine) and *legio VII claudia* (from Moesia Superior on the Danube). At the head of these forces, the emperor marched eastward through the province of Pontus along the shores of the Black Sea, as is evidenced by hasty road repairs made that year. Meanwhile other troops were summoned from North Africa and it is likely that some of the garrisons in Britain were also reduced at this time, either to provide troops for the campaign or to cover other areas. Indeed, Herodian tells us the whole empire was in a state of upheaval.[6] The great influx of men to the east added of course to the substantial regular and auxiliary forces who were already stationed there.

At Antioch a regime of military training commenced and manoeuvres were practised as the grand army was assembled. Preparations lasted as long as a year, which indicates how serious a threat the Roman military regarded Ardashir, notwithstanding Cassius Dio's somewhat off-hand assessment of the man himself. The complex chain of command was established, while raw recruits were turned into disciplined Roman soldiers by incessant drilling and weapons practice. This was no simple legionary army as would have been understood by a Republican consul or even Caesar or Augustus, but a much more complex war machine consisting of diverse legionary detachments and auxiliaries from across the empire that needed to be welded into an efficient fighting force.

The hour of diplomacy was not, however, quite over. Further exchanges occurred but failed to produce a resolution, with Ardashir defiantly demanding that the Romans hand over the whole of Asia to the Persians. Herodian gives us the colourful detail that this last insolent message was delivered by four hundred of Persia's most magnificent armoured cavalry. As Gibbon remarked, "such an embassy was much less an offer of negotiation than a declaration of war".[7] These Persian knights were promptly disarmed and taken captive: Alexander's failure to allow them to return arguably handed the first psychological victory to the enemy. However, because it would have been dishonourable to kill or enslave them, we are told that the cavalrymen were settled as free citizens in the province of Phrygia (now part of Turkey). How wonderful it would be if some archaeological evidence of their settlement was one day to emerge.

Preparations

Inscriptional evidence suggests that Maximinus may have been in Egypt at the beginning of 232, possibly commanding *legio II traiana* in Alexandria.[8] Elements of this legion were among the many units brought together to form the new army and it is possible that Maximinus transferred to the theatre of war with them. In any event we know much more reliably that he was appointed that year to the post of *praefectus castrorum* (camp prefect) in the province of Mesopotamia; every legion had such an officer of procurement, basically a quartermaster, who reported to the commanding officer. This may sound like a surprisingly junior post, however, legionary ranks were duplicated in the higher echelons of the senior staff, hence this appointment is better interpreted as indicating that he was given overall logistical command of all the legions, a kind of military organizer of the troubled frontier province of Mesopotamia, directly answerable to Alexander as commander-in-chief.[9] It may have been at this time that the post of *dux ripae* was established for him. As a member of the general staff he would certainly have been involved in planning the Persian campaign.

An outline account of the ensuing hostilities, with details of the Roman strategy, is given by Herodian, who was also very probably in the east at this time, travelling in the imperial service.[10] He does not give a figure for the size of Alexander's army and even if he did historians would not trust it because ancient authors habitually exaggerated numbers. If we consider that the empire was at its greatest extent and its military was near full strength after an unusually long period of peace and prosperity, and that every effort seems to have been made to assemble the largest force possible, it is reasonable to assume that it must have been one of the greatest professional armies ever assembled in antiquity. Comparison with earlier and later campaigns suggests a minimum of 100,000 fighting troops out of an empire-wide total of about 350,000 regular Roman soldiers and auxiliaries,[11] but it could have been twice that number. These men would have been supported by many more slaves, tradesmen, craftsmen, merchants, camp followers and innumerable horses and draught animals. Supplying such a force would have been a major challenge but one at least that the army was used to, if not at quite this scale.

What were the Roman war aims? With the Parthian regime having crumbled and been replaced by the relatively unknown Ardashir, they may have seen this as an historic opportunity to expand Roman influence in the east by crushing the upstart and re-installing a Parthian puppet state. Despite the fact that the *Augustan History* makes a great play of Alexander's obsession to live up to the reputation of his famous namesake, the aim of the campaign was almost certainly not permanent conquest of the east. A more limited objective may have been to repulse the Persian incursions and then locate and defeat Ardashir's main army in battle. This would open the rich lands of lower Mesopotamia for plunder. With the foe vanquished, there was even the tempting prospect of penetrating deeper into Persian territory than any Roman army in history. Pillaging and the capture of slaves would more than pay for the expedition and enrich the victorious army. Peace terms would be dictated, certainly including payment of a massive tribute and a formal revocation of any claims to Roman land. Then the frontier would be strengthened and reinforced under the emperor's supervision. Alexander would return to Rome in triumph, preferably with Ardashir in chains for public execution. Such a campaign would exceed even the eastern victories of the great warrior emperors Trajan and Septimius Severus. With the empire's eastern border secure, the triumphant young emperor could then turn to unfinished business on the Rhine–Danube frontier or possibly complete the conquest of Britannia which even Severus, his (supposed) grandfather, had failed to accomplish. So with the season of war in 232 fast approaching, there was every prospect of making the empire stronger, richer and more secure than it had ever been… if only Ardashir could be brought to battle.

But the excitement and optimism were not ubiquitous. There was a disturbing wave of unrest in the army including at least two local revolts, swiftly crushed. The historical accounts are brief and enigmatic. Herodian tells of one rebellion in Egypt, presumably following the weakening of the garrison there, in which an unnamed man attempted to seize imperial power. Cassius Dio and Syncellus describe a separate uprising in Mesopotamia, centred at Edessa in Osrhoene, in which a senior Roman commander was killed. This latter event was accompanied by widespread desertion from the army, with some men joining the forces of Ardashir. One late source, the *Epitome de Caesaribus*, gives us the enigmatic tidbit that "Taurinius, who had been made *augustus*, on account of fear, threw himself into the Euphrates" (curiously, this is the only substantive fact that it records from the reign of Alexander),[12] which may refer to this episode. Zonoras gives a similar name, 'Taurinus'. This man never controlled a mint, hence no coins exist with his name or image and nothing more is known about him. The *Augustan History* also describes an attempted mutiny in Antioch. The later writer Zosimus gives us the names 'Antoninus' and 'Uranius' as leaders of revolts around this time, but these men are not given a location and both may be cases of confusion with much later traitors to the Roman cause in the east.

It is curious that revolts should erupt during preparations for war, especially so in Antioch and Mesopotamia where the troops were beginning to flood in, in anticipation of the coming campaign. The events hint at low morale and ongoing dissatisfaction in the army and perhaps a justifiable fear of the enemy. It is possible that Maximinus, with his fearsome reputation, was brought to Mesopotamia specifically to crush the rebels at Edessa as well as prepare the ground for the great invasion.

By the start of 232, Alexander and his war council were faced with a superabundance of military power that could scarcely be concentrated on any single city because of the demand on local resources; the solution was to divide the army. Even a modern army cannot just march wherever it wants: the supply lines have to be carefully planned and then well protected as the fighting force advances. Without mechanized transport this was much more of a limitation in antiquity. The obvious routes into Mesopotamia are via the two great rivers that point to the heart of Persian territory. These would provide ready transport and, of even greater necessity, abundant water. In the end, the plan of campaign dictated three separate columns: the first would go north through the client kingdom of Armenia (a clear Roman ally since the death of Artabanus) to overrun the Persian territory of Medea (around the Kurdish area of modern Iraq); the second would go south through Mesopotamia along the Euphrates, with its objective the confluence of the rivers above the marshland bordering the Persian Gulf (the area of modern Basra); and the third and largest column, commanded by the emperor himself, would penetrate by a middle route, presumably down the Tigris (Map 2). Herodian tells us that the armies were provided with a single rendezvous point,[13] which must have been Ctesiphon or nearby (that is, the vicinity of modern Baghdad), where they would converge, secure the area and arrange for the evacuation of all the plunder.

A three-pronged assault would present the Persian king of kings with the dilemma of confronting multiple attacks while at the same time having to protect his richest cities in lower Mesopotamia. Three attack lines would give the Romans flexibility to monitor enemy moves, establish the strength and disposition of opposing forces, and then seek to entrap them using rapid pincer movements. But despite the merits of the plan, the generals would also have appreciated the potential danger of splitting the force, namely that each column might be defeated in turn by a more concentrated or manoeuvrable enemy. A great deal was therefore going to depend on accurate intelligence, decisive command and fast and coordinated movement: precisely the characteristics that the Roman army prided itself with.

Like any campaign, success would also require not underestimating the enemy. The Romans knew (or thought they knew) that their traditional Parthian foe did not normally have a large standing army to draw upon. Instead the forces were organized more along the lines of a medieval feudal system. All the young men and sometimes women were expected to fight when called up. On the king's command, the army would be assembled by the warrior nobility who themselves would form the officer class, and at the end of the campaign the soldiery would return to the land. Such an arrangement could produce very large, if rather motley, armies, containing a preponderance of mounted skirmishing troops and archers: the main problem, as the Romans saw it (and

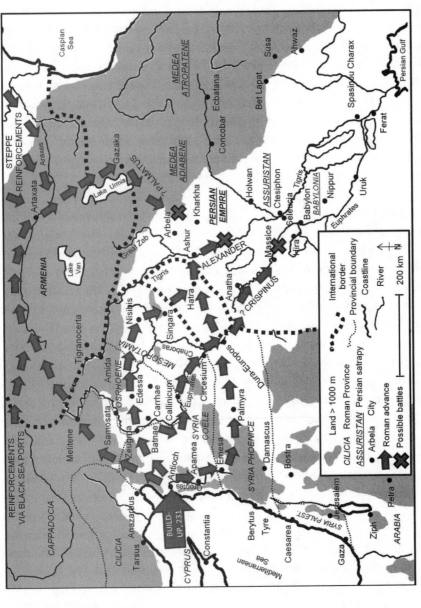

Map 2. Sketch map of the Roman/Armenian assault on Persia in 232. Tentative reconstruction based mainly on Herodian, *History of the Empire* VI.4.5–VI.5.10 and other considerations discussed in the text.

as we have seen in the emperor's speech) was to bring them to close-quarters fighting against well disciplined, well armoured professional Roman soldiers.

Cassius Dio discussed at length the tactical problems of fighting the Parthians in his *Roman History*, in a section that was written just a couple of years before Alexander's campaign. It is even possible, given the regime's supposed policy of consulting historians, that he had been given the specific brief of assessing the foe and the relevant passage is an abstract of his official report. He tells us that there were many forts and garrisons and a few cities, which included the great capital Ctesiphon, where there was a rich royal residence. Interestingly he says there was a very large Greek population, even in his own day. He describes the Parthians as being formidable in warfare "but nevertheless they have a reputation greater than their achievements" because although they had lost territory to the Romans they had never won it. And he goes on:

> The Parthians make no use of a shield, but their forces consist of mounted archers and pikemen, mostly in full armour. Their infantry is small, made up of the weaker men; but even these are all archers. They practice from boyhood, and the climate and land combine to aid both horsemanship and archery. The land, being for the most part level, is excellent for raising horses and very suitable for riding about on horseback; at any rate, even in war they lead about whole droves of horses, so that they can use different ones at different times, can ride up suddenly from a distance and also retire to a distance speedily ...They have discovered many remedies for the dearth of drinking-water and the difficulty of securing it, so that for this reason also they can easily repel the invaders of their land. Outside of the district of the Euphrates they have once or twice gained some success in pitched battles and in sudden incursions, but they cannot wage an offensive war with any nation continuously and without pause, both because they encounter entirely different condition of land and sky and because they do not lay in supplies of food or pay. Such is the Parthian state.
>
> Cassius Dio, *Roman History* XL. 15.

It is an interesting analysis by a distinguished old disciplinarian. But these traditional views do not take into account that Ardashir had spent almost a decade at war methodically disposing of the previous dynasty kingdom by kingdom and then much of the Kushan empire, hence he would have had many experienced veterans under his command, men accustomed to victory. Nor had the battles just been on the floodplains of Mesopotamia. Over the years the Persians had picked up a variety of tactics from the Romans and their other adversaries, for example in using forced marches and the regular construction of fortified camps using sandbags. Unlike the peasant levy, the core of the nobility were fully trained in the art of war. Some of the cavalry were heavily armoured (including their horses) and they fought with lances, a tactic that the Romans were unused to. The Romans were later to emulate these heavy cavalry and incorporate them into their own army, but for now it was a conspicuous tactical difference.

An evocative account of a Persian knight or *clibanarius*, as the Romans came to call them, comes from a third or fourth-century Greek novel *Aethiopica* ('Aethiopian stories') by Heliodorus of Emesa, a man who described himself as a 'descendant of the sun' and so was presumably of the Elagabalian religion of that city.[14] He tells us that men were chosen for their size and strength. They wore a helmet with a terrifying mask covering the face and had armour that was "like horny scales", consisting of overlapping (so-called 'cataphract') plates of bronze and iron, tracing each limb but not hindering movement. The horses were fenced around in the same way, with their heads tightly bound and the neck and legs plated with iron. The rider was so heavy he had to be hoisted on to his mount with ropes and pullies and "when moment of battle comes, he drives his horse with the rein, applies his spurs and goes with all his force against the enemies, looking like an iron man or like a moving image wrought with the hammer." The butt end of the long pike was secured beside the horse's thighs so that it did not give way on impact. The rider himself used his strength to supplement the blow and "through his force he destroys everyone he encounters, and with one blow he may often transfix two". Such men were not deployed as individuals – they would have been much too vulnerable – but in massed charges. This was a different concept to the mobile but lightly-armed Roman cavalry, and if not countered it might prove decisive in battle. The name *clibanarius* may be a Latin translation of a Syriac slang term for these ironclad horsemen that was in currency in the eastern Roman empire and has imaginatively been translated as 'boiler boy' (a *clibanus* was an army iron boiler or bread oven): presumably, for all their fearsome reputation, such men had a tendency to wilt in the heat.[15]

In addition to heavy cavalry, the Persians made use of scythed war chariots and armoured elephants (of the Indian variety from Ardashir's eastern dominions). How they were deployed is unknown. Judging from other ancient armies, the chariots probably ferried missile troops around the battlefield, adding an element of mobility and surprise, while the elephants were prestige units designed to intimidate the enemy, support mounted archers and, as a last resort, charge into lines of infantry and create mayhem.

The most serious defeat the Romans had suffered at the hands of the Parthians was at the Battle of Carrhae in Mesopotamia in 53 BCE, when an army led by the consul Publius Licinius Crassus had been cut off, surrounded and destroyed, and several sacred military standards had been taken. It took many years for the Romans to successfully avenge this defeat and recover their lost standards. The Temple of Mars Ultor itself had been built by Augustus in 2 BCE[16] to celebrate revenge against the Parthians, which is no doubt why the theme was once again so conspicuous in 231–232. For the Romans, it was going to be important not to let history repeat itself.

Desert Storm

The campaign was launched from Antioch in the spring of 232. The first column to depart was probably the northern army, which had the greatest distance to travel. Its commander was, possibly, a general named Junius Palmatus. After the customary sacrifices and auguries, the march began in relatively prosperous, low-lying land up to the city of Melitene in eastern Cappadocia (a distance of about 200 miles) as attested by repairs to the roads that date from this year.[17] Melitine was base of *legio XII fulminata* – the name means 'the thunderbolts' – a force that was presumably added to the column as it crossed the Euphrates into the Kingdom of Armenia.

As we have seen, Armenia was an independent power with ancient roots but Parthian in culture and now a bitter enemy of Ardashir following his revolution. But the exiled Parthian nobility stationed there would understandably have hated the Romans too, following the treachery of Caracalla at Arbela about 15 years before. Hence the military alliance with Rome must have been arranged by careful diplomatic negotiation with King Xusro the year before. Possibly Xusro or one of the exiles was promised the throne of Parthia upon victory.

Armenia controlled the land between the Black and Caspian Seas; running between these large bodies of water is a virtually impenetrable mountain range (the Caucasus), which provided a natural barrier between the civilized south (whether Armenian, Roman or Persian) and the barbarian steppes to the north. There were only three practical routes from the steppes to the south; either along the shores of the Black or Caspian Seas or through a pass in the centre of the range (now called the Darial Pass, marking the border of Russia and Georgia). The Armenians had heavily fortified these routes to keep the barbarians out, but it seems that at this time Xusro enlisted their aid, as described in the Armenian history of Agathangelos:

Now at the start of the next year, Xusrō, the king of Armenia, began to organize an army and collect a force, gathering the forces of the Albanians and the Georgians, opening the Gate of the Alans and the Pass of Čor, bringing the forces of the Honk, in order to campaign in Persian regions and attack the regions of Asorestan, as far as the gates of Ktēsiphōn.

Agathangelos, *History of the Armenians*, 19.

This quaintly Tolkeinesque passage[18] needs some explanation. The Albania referred to is not the modern country of that name but an allied kingdom to the north of Armenia bordering the Caspian Sea. The Georgians were the inhabitants of the mountain regions of Colchis and Iberia toward the Black Sea side of the Caucasus. The Gate of the Alans is the old name for the Darial Pass[19] (the Alans, recall, were reputed to be the tribe of the mother of Maximinus). The Pass of Čor is the Debend Pass at the Caspian Sea end of the range. The Honk is an ancient variant name for the Huns, fearsome warrior nomads of the steppes. Asorestan (or Assuristan) is the Armenian name for Persian Mesopotamia, and as we have seen, Ktēsiphōn (Ctesiphon) was its capital. So if the passage indeed refers to the war of 232, as seems probable[20] it implies that the north wing of the Roman army was supplemented not only by Armenians and their allies but also by 'barbarians' from the steppes who were admitted specifically to add to the mayhem. The passage even hints that this may have been the first contact between Rome and the Huns, a Mongol tribe who two hundred years later under Atilla famously laid waste to much of the western Empire. However, there is no other evidence that the Huns were present on the steppes for almost another century, so the passage is usually considered an anachronism on the part of Agathangelos or his later transcribers. If not the Huns themselves, other steppe warriors such as Alans or Sarmatians may well have been enlisted for the campaign.

Herodian gives few clues as to the route taken by the invading army, although the existing topography severely limits the options. Presumably the northern mustering point for Rome and her allies was the Armenian capital Artaxata (near Yerevan, the modern capital of Armenia). The most detailed information we have for a Roman army traversing Armenia is the campaign of Marcus Antonius (Mark Antony) in 36 BCE, which we can take as a model. The march to Artaxata was a hard slog across very rough country: Herodian describes it as an almost impossibly difficult crossing (see Plate 5).[21] The distance from Melitine to Artaxata is almost 1,000 kilometres. The mountains were only passable because it was spring, but even at this time of year the climate can be tough, with temperatures exceeding 40 degrees in daytime and approaching freezing at night. If the army covered 15 miles a day then it would have taken about six weeks just to reach Artaxata. Even then the marching was only half complete, because the soldiers would have been ordered south to cross another stretch of dry and inhospitable terrain. The target was the region known as Medea, a rich Persian province of the upper Tigris and its tributaries. The army could not of course count on surprise – there were too many spies and informers for that – but the area included great cities such as Arbela (Irbil, the site of Caracalla's previous treachery) and Karka (Kirkuk), and these were not strongly defended. The Romans knew that if Ardashir sent a strong force to counter the incursion he must simultaneously weaken the south. This was chess on a grand scale.

A month or so after the first army departed, the second (southern) column would presumably have set off from Antioch. The start point for this force was Dura Europos, likely base of Maximinus, the *dux ripae*. For the army to get to Dura there were two options, either march overland or travel down the Euphrates by barge. Those on the march would have made their way via the oasis city of Palmyra ('city of palms'). Fabled for its wealth, Palmyra had been built upon trade between the Mediterranean and the East. Like Dura, its ruins are some of the most romantic remnants of the classical world, although recently despoiled by Islamic militants at the time of writing. Palmyra had considerable semi-autonomous military power, which was necessary for security along the trade routes, especially guarding against the nomadic Arabs from the deserts of the south and east. It seems that Alexander himself passed through the city in 232; the evidence is in the form of a dedication of a statue of Julius Aurelius Zenobius, commander of Palmyrene cohorts no doubt destined for the war, as a welcome for Alexander and his general Rutilius Crispinus.[22] Crispinus had just served as governor of Syria Phoenice, and might still have held that office, but he had enjoyed a distinguished military career. We might infer, therefore, that he was in overall command of the southern column and the statue commemorates the formal transfer of command. It is interesting to find Crispinus in this context because he is to play a prominent role in later events; Zenobius is also an intriguing character, being father to the future queen Zenobia of Palmyra, famed for her courage and beauty, who was to rebel against Rome two decades later.

The presence of Alexander with the southern column at Palmyra at the beginning of the campaign is intriguing. It has been suggested that it may have been part of a ruse to mislead the enemy into thinking the main force would attack along this axis. Another explanation may be that Alexander was in the area after visiting his home city of Emesa, where he would have made sacrifices at the great temple of El Gabal, of which he was still the high priest. Although the cult had been expelled from Rome, the eastern provinces would have welcomed the emperor's public devotions and the assurance that the religion was not dishonoured in its own country. The baetyl had probably been returned to the city after the murder of Elagabalus because its temple was once again flourishing later in the century.[23]

The riverine and overland components of the southern column probably marshalled at Dura Europos under the supervision of the *dux ripae*. Roman territory extended about 50 miles downstream from this city. Beyond that tense frontier was Persian Mesopotamia, and only about 100 miles further to the south-east, the heavily defended joint cities of Seleucia and Cteisphon on the Tigris with Ardashir's palace, treasury and principal mint.

The main army was reserved for Alexander himself. This central route into Mesopotamia had been travelled by armies for hundreds, if not thousands, of years before. From Antioch the column would have crossed the Euphrates at Zeugma and moved overland to Edessa, capital of Osrhoene. Like Palmyra this city had been annexed to the Roman Empire by Severus. Also like Palmyra it had a semi-independent army to protect its trade. Interestingly, Edessa already had a thriving Christian community by this time and its king, Abgar the Great, may have been a Christian. In later centuries Edessa prided itself on its deep Christian roots and, as the religion became ascendant across the west, it claimed that an earlier King Abgar had corresponded with Jesus himself, who had reputedly sent a disciple to convert the populace.[24]

Osrhoene specialized in the training of archers, the famous *sagittae osroenae*. Good archers cannot be conscripted and trained at short notice; as Cassius Dio knew, they have to grow up with the bow, developing the right muscles and bone structure as well as advanced shooting skills from a young age. Archery had evidently been encouraged in Orshoene for generations; a contingent had fought for Septimius Severus two generations earlier.[25] On leaving the army these men had been settled back in their home town, which was granted the status of a *colonia* under Elagabalus. The pick of their sons and grandsons would then be brought up as archers ready to serve Rome; as Edward III of England is supposed to have said: if you want to train an archer, start with his grandfather. These young men, enlisted by Alexander, were to play a prominent role in the forthcoming adventures.

The idea that a particular area specialized in certain types of troops or weapons adds to the colour of ancient warfare. The Romans encouraged tribes or regions to develop specialist forces who could be deployed as auxiliary troops in distant theatres and who would add tactical options on the battlefield and potentially bamboozle an enemy. As Vegetius put it, "each nation has its own particular discipline, customs and manner of fighting... and though the legions do not place their principal dependence on them, yet they look on them as a very considerable addition to their strength." To emphasize this point, Alexander also brought into the theatre a contingent of javelin-men (part infantry, part cavalry) from the far-distant Province of Mauretania at the western end of the empire, presumably because they were adept at desert warfare. These were troops that Maximinus had commanded as governor there ten years before.[26]

An interesting glimpse of life in Edessa and the preparations for war comes from surviving fragments of a work called the *Kestoi* attributed to Sextus Julius Africanus, a Christian philosopher who is now chiefly known for being one of the first to estimate the date of Christ's birth. This work was literally dug out of the sands of Egypt along with many other papyri at a place called Oxyrhynchus, having been discarded as rubbish in the sixth century. *Kestoi* is a typically mysterious and arcane name for such a work; it means 'the Girdle' and refers to the magic girdle worn by Aphrodite that made men and gods alike fall in love with her. Africanus seems to have been something of a physician, herbalist and veterinary surgeon, but also a magician. His work, which is dedicated to Severus Alexander, includes an eclectic range of knowledge, practical advice, magic incantations and blatant (to us) fables. There is also a large component of military lore, and because of this it has even been suggested that Africanus was an army engineer. Topics range from the immensely practical – how long water should be boiled before drinking and how to provide a healthy diet for the troops – to the development of secret weapons and poisons, including chemical weapons, incendiaries and germ warfare. Examples of these include a recipe for drugging wine with poppy, henbane and asses' earwax which will put one's enemies to sleep for three days; precise instructions for the manufacture of poisoned arrows and their antidotes; and how to make spontaneously combusting goo from sulphur, rock salt, incense, sycamore sap, asphalt and a little quicklime which, when surreptitiously painted on an enemy war engine at night, would ignite in the heat of the day. It is not known to what extent these methods were deployed in the war and some may be later additions to the text dating to the sixth century, but it is interesting that this sort of thing was deemed compatible with the form of Christian theology flourishing in the east at the time.

Africanus also relates, in passing, a meeting with a fellow Christian philosopher called Bardaisan whose teachings fused Christianity with Greek Neoplatonism.[27] Bardaisan had been an archer in the king of Osrhoene's service, and had even travelled across India, but by this time was an old man. Indeed it seems that the regime of Alexander went to some lengths to understand the emerging cult of the Christians. The fourth century 'church father' Eusebius of Caesarea (a city in Palestine) tells us that a predecessor of his, a man named Origen who was the leading Christian intellectual of his day, was summoned to the court of Julia Mamaea at Antioch to explain the religion, where he remained for some time.[28]

From Edessa the route for the advancing army (as evidenced by dated roadworks) was through Roman Mesopotamia via the fortified city of Nisibis to the even greater stronghold of Singara[29] at the fringe of Roman Mesopotamia. Like Dura Europos, Singara had been given the status of a Roman *colonia* by Septimius Severus and was currently the base of *legio I parthica* (the title refers to the legion's previous victory over the Parthians, not that it was made up of Parthian troops). Also like Dura it was a heavy-duty frontier base and supply depot with a substantial civilian and mercantile economy too. Elements of the column may also have marched to Singara across the desert from Dura Europos[30] and it seems likely that the emperor himself would have done the same to join the central column, presumably being formally seen off from the gates of Dura by the *dux ripae*.

Ahead of Singara lay another diplomatic obstacle: the independent and formidable Arab oasis of Hatra that had stood as a buffer between Rome and Persian Mesopotamia for centuries. Hatra had a complex series of defensive ramparts, three deep, and was especially difficult to besiege because the abundant water in the town wells contrasted with the parched desert on all sides. Hatra had survived previous sieges of both Trajan and Septimius Severus, and would not have wanted to resign its independence. On the other hand it would have been equally opposed to being incorporated into an expanding Persian Empire and, as we have seen, it had resolutely withstood an attempted assault by Ardashir two years earlier, despite a breach in the outer walls. The Roman choice was either to conquer the city once and for all, or carefully negotiate an alliance. The latter course was taken and Hatra received a garrison of auxiliary troops from far off Morocco to man the battlements in case of a Persian counter-strike, together with a promise that its independence would be guaranteed.[31] The fact that the great Roman army did not assault Hatra as a preliminary to the campaign is evidence that permanent conquest of lower Mesopotamia was not the aim.

Beyond Hatra the logical route for this central column was to penetrate Persian Mesopotamia down the Tigris as far as Ctesiphon. But with the other two armies converging on the same area from the north and west, the prime objective for the main force was surely to find and destroy the Persian army. There were several unknowns. Would the nobility stand by Ardashir's cause when they were confronted with such a massive threat? How would the enemy show itself: In cavalry raids and guerrilla war, or as a large standing army ready to fight a pitched battle on some unidentified plain? Would the king of kings really contest this recently devastated western borderland of his empire against three separate armies when his territory (including his personal homeland) extended a vast distance beyond Roman ken to the east? Perhaps a scorched-earth retreat and later counter-attack was a better strategy.

Battle

First contact was made by the northern army, which "broke through into Medea and devastated the country, burning and plundering many settlements".[32] Ardashir personally organized a force to resist the invasion but was not able to defeat it; the reason given is that the rough terrain made cavalry movements difficult. First blood to the Romans. Then Ardashir received the alarming news of the southern Roman army sweeping down the Euphrates and closing in on Ctesiphon. He was concerned that this force had the potential of penetrating deep into unprotected territory (into the area of modern Iran, that is) so he hurried south at the head of his main army to confront it, leaving a force to harry and delay the northern column as best it could.

Initially the southern force met no resistance and made excellent progress. Its commander (who might have been Rutilius Crispinus) assumed that the main Persian army would be diverted to take on the central column and so, Herodian tells us, he became careless on the march, which presumably means he moved quickly and did not employ enough scouts. But Ardashir also moved his forces much faster than expected and managed to locate the column, cut its supply line and prepare a trap into which the Romans duly marched. Outnumbered, they were subject to missile attack from all sides and began to sustain heavy losses. Their only hope was to fortify their position and hold out for relief from the main force, but it never came. Herodian's account implies that the whittling down of the army went on for a number of increasingly desperate days until, eventually, it was destroyed.

Cassius Dio gives us the following dramatic account of a battle in which the Persians had hidden their army among woods and uneven ground and lured away the Roman cavalry by feigning retreat. As the attack developed, the Roman infantry formed a huge square for protection, but confronted by numerous mounted archers and pikemen they could not fight back:

> For if they locked shields for the purpose of avoiding the arrows by the closeness of their array, the pikemen were upon them with a rush, striking some down, and at least scattering the others; and if they extended their ranks to avoid this, they would be struck with arrows. Hereupon many died from fright at the very charge of the pikemen, and many perished hemmed

in by the horsemen. Others were knocked over by the pikes or were carried off transfixed. The missiles falling thick upon them from all sides at once struck down many by a mortal blow, rendered many useless for battle, and caused distress to all. They flew into their eyes and pierced their hands and all other parts of their bodies and, penetrating their armour, deprived them of their protection. ... Consequently it was impracticable for them to move, and impracticable to remain at rest.

Cassius Dio, *Roman History* XL.22, 23.

But this was not Alexander's army: it was Dio's account of the Battle of Carrhae in 53 BCE, so long a stain on Rome's military reputation. History *had* repeated itself. The historical details of the repeat performance are very sparse, so we must await archaeology to fill in the gaps and possibly identify the site of engagement. The battlefield must have been in Persian territory, but there is no mention in the sources that the column had reached as far as Ctesiphon, so it was probably some distance up the Euphrates from the capital near the modern towns of Fullaja and Ramadi.

Despite Herodian's account, it was probably not the whole of the southern column that was annihilated and if Rutilius Crispinus was indeed its commander we know that he lived to fight another day. Nor was the battle necessarily a prelude to total defeat. The Persians did not back up their victory with a strong counter-attack into Roman Mesopotamia and it is probable that the Romans were able to strike back effectively. Even so, it was a major setback for morale. The southern army had constituted a substantial force drawn from right across the empire: according to Herodian it was "the equal of any previous army for courage and toughness." Many of these men had been out-manouevred, surrounded, then massacred, and the enemy had been delivered the strategic initiative and a great propaganda victory.

After failing to come to the rescue of the southern column, Alexander then decided to cancel the campaign entirely and withdraw all the way to Antioch. We are not told how far into Persian territory the large central army had penetrated when this important decision was made. It presumably made some contact with the enemy and succeeded in at least some engagements because captured troops and deserters from the Persian army feature in the emperor's later campaigning. An intriguing possibility is that Maximinus, working out of Dura, had achieved just enough on the battlefield for the Romans to claim victory. Late Roman tradition[33] and Maximinus's own later propaganda claim that he distinguished himself militarily in the Persian war. But now that the southern column had been eliminated, Alexander was unwilling to risk a further decisive battle. Perhaps the old problem of confronting the Persian combined-arms tactics of missile cavalry and heavy lances with the traditional Roman mix of heavy infantry and light cavalry on the plains of Mesopotamia was becoming abundantly clear.

Accordingly, Alexander sent orders to the northern column to withdraw before it too could be picked off by Persian forces. Because Ardashir still had control of the Ctesiphon area, this army had no option but to return by the arduous mountain route from whence it had come, which was not in the original plan. With autumn now approaching, the northern wing suffered severe attrition through hypothermia and frostbite during the long and miserable slog home. Although the men could claim not to have been defeated in battle, it was an ignominious retreat for that force and Herodian says that very few of the soldiers made it back alive. Presumably most of the booty was abandoned en route or perhaps made its way to adorn barbarian hovels on the steppe.

Although Herodian acknowledged that there had been tactical victories for the Romans and roughly equal losses on both sides, he clearly regarded the campaign as a strategic defeat and blamed Alexander personally. He even accused the emperor of cowardice: "no doubt he wanted to avoid risking his own life and limb for the Roman empire." But in partial contradiction of himself, he also suggests that Alexander was restrained by his mother, Mamaea, and blamed her for womanly timidity: "She used to blunt Alexander's efforts to behave bravely by convincing him that it was other people's job to take risks for him, not his to get involved in battle."[34] This of course seems sensible to us, and also accords with later Roman thinking, which held that emperors were too important to be risked on the battlefield. Another reason for Alexander's delay may have been that he became seriously ill, as Herodian also admits. Deadly diseases were sweeping through the weakened army of the east. Be that as it may, the emperor's indisposition should not have stopped an army and Herodian records that the men were "absolutely furious" with Alexander personally for not sticking to the plan and they blamed him for failing to rescue the southern column. We can assume that the outraged men might have secretly included staff officers who had devised the plan of attack, including, perhaps, Maximinus himself.

Herodian's stinging criticisms are not echoed by all the sources however. When the dust settled, Alexander sent a dispatch to the Senate claiming victory in the war, which was no doubt published across the empire. He also issued a large donative to the troops and commissioned a special bronze medallion depicting himself, dagger in hand, trampling on two river gods representing the Euphrates and Tigris while being crowned by the personification of Victory. The needs of propaganda demanded as much. The fourth century

Latin sources, which are all sympathetic to Alexander's memory, tend to back this official view.[35] Eutropius states that Alexander defeated the Persian king with great glory. Aurelius Victor claims that he personally led an army and put the Persian king to flight. A much more detailed account is given by the *Augustan History* which goes so far as to specifically label Herodian's pessimistic version of events as contrary to state annals and as being a minority view among historians. It goes on to describe a great battle in which Alexander himself commanded the flanks, exposing himself to missile fire and performing many brave deeds with his own hands. It also correctly states, as Herodian does not, that Alexander returned to Rome in 233 and was awarded a formal triumph (for which we have numismatic evidence).[36] The *Augustan History* also includes an almost certainly bogus text that purports to be Alexander's dispatch to the senate at that time, as supposedly copied by Aelius Lampridius from the senate records, but we may read it none the less:

> First of all, there were seven hundred elephants provided with turrets and archers and great loads of arrows. Of these we captured thirty, we have left two hundred slain upon the field, and we have led eighteen in triumph. Moreover, there were scythed chariots, one thousand eight hundred in number. Of these we could have presented to your eyes two hundred, of which the horses have been slain, but since they could easily be counterfeited we have refrained from so doing. One hundred and twenty thousand of their cavalry we have routed, ten thousand of their horsemen clad in full mail, whom they call cuirassiers [cataphracts] we have slain in battle, and with their armour we have armed our own men. We have captured many of the Persians and have sold them into slavery, and we have re-conquered the lands which lie between the rivers, those of Mesopotamia I mean.
>
> *Scriptores Historiae Augustae* (Aelius Lampridius),
> *Alexander Severus* LVI. 3–6.

Assessing these conflicting ancient accounts, modern scholars have tended to view the outcome of the Persian war as a kind of score-draw with both sides having suffered considerable losses. It is true that Ardashir's incursions were halted for now: towards the end of the year it became clear that Persia was demobilizing and the bulk of Ardashir's army returned to their homelands. It may also be that a war of attrition continued between Ardashir's forces and the Roman-backed Armenians in alliance with the steppe warriors.[37] But this may be giving too much credence to the efforts of later Roman historians to gloss over what was a serious defeat against a new foe, the Persian Empire, which would be a major problem for Rome right up to their own times. The Romans would not have wanted to acknowledge that they had been bested from the beginning. Herodian, it should be remembered, may well have been in the east at the time of these events, and even in the imperial service. He had no reason to belittle Alexander, with whom he seems to have been sympathetic on the whole. He also points out that the Romans did inflict serious damage on the Persians, with about equal losses on both sides, so there is balance to his account. But perhaps the most telling fact is that contrary to the *Augustan History*, the young emperor did not take the titles *parthicus maximus* or *persicus maximus* as earlier and later emperors did on achieving military victories in the east.[38] Perhaps with so many men failing to come home from the war, the triumph in Rome was not seen as a universal success and Alexander's advisers decided not to push his claims too far.

Chapter V

Empire's Edge

Barbarian Incursions

The broad sweep of history that is the story of Rome's empire from its origin to dissolution is so grand that it has been a perennial temptation to historians, whether synthetic or narrative by temperament, to bring it within a single compass. One of the big issues that has been debated is whether Rome possessed a coherent long-term strategic vision of expansion, control and consolidation or if, instead, the empire was acquired through a series of haphazard conquests initiated by different regimes responding to circumstances with little overall planning. A related theme is whether new acquisitions were obtained by deliberate serial aggression or more as a side-effect of the constant desire to secure what was already possessed by subduing just a bit more beyond it. Similar debates exist for other great empires and entertaining as they are, there is no simple solution. Among the policy makers there was probably a surplus of vision at some times and on many other occasions, simple opportunism.[1]

Some generalizations regarding the evolution of Roman policy do appear to hold, however, as synthesized by an experienced military strategician in the 1970s.[2] For most of its history the army was surprisingly small as a proportion of the population and the Romans consistently preferred to make gains diplomatically, backed by the threat of force and the fearsome reputation of the soldiery. When fighting did occur they relied on discipline, training and equipment to deliver victory rather than force of numbers. During its expansionist phase the imperial borders were 'soft', that is, maintained through complex diplomatic ties with numerous external client kingdoms, while the legions provided defence in depth if a large-scale rebellion or invasion occurred. But as the peripheral states became fully absorbed, paying their taxes and demanding security in return, so the perimeter became progressively 'harder' with fortified frontiers that had to be manned. This process had unfolded throughout the first century in particular. It meant the army ended up mostly distributed along the periphery and the imperial defences became harder but more brittle. And as the postings of the legions and auxiliary units became permanent, so they became progressively more integrated with the communities around them. The size of the extramural settlements (*vicae*) increased, as did the frequency of local marriages on discharge, with the sons of these marriages often joining the local unit.[3] All this led to gradual divergences among the military in style, morale, and perhaps allegiance in times of civil strife. To counteract regionalism, recruits were often shifted away from their own tribal areas, but not necessarily to stations right across the empire. The linchpin of this arrangement was that security, stability, and above all pay for all the peripheral armies could only come from taxation raised by the centre.

By the third century the only truly mobile elite force in Rome consisted of the praetorian guard and imperial horseguard in combination with one special legion, *legio II parthica*, which had been set up by Septimius Severus for his Parthian war but was subsequently stationed in the Alban Hills to the east of the city beside the Appian Way. In effect these units were the true Roman army, which was supposed to provide the core for the imperial forces in general. The second Parthian legion had been Severus's backstop against civil war and was maintained by subsequent emperors in this capacity. These troops were formidable for the defence of Italy, but were not strong enough by themselves to provide a major strike force in foreign wars. It must have been obvious during the post-mortem of the Persian war that, despite the regime's best efforts, Severus Alexander had not been able to free up sufficient military power from across the empire to inflict a decisive defeat on the enemy. The most that can reasonably be claimed of the campaign was that it had weakened Ardashir's forces and temporarily put a halt to the threat of invasion from the east, returning the situation to the *status quo ante bellum*,[4] although this can hardly have been the objective of amassing such a large force. But it was not just the Persians who were weakened by the fighting. By sapping detachments from frontier legions across the empire the imperial army had inevitably been thinned everywhere else, and the potentially catastrophic effects of this soon became apparent.

As Herodian has it, Alexander, while residing in his luxurious palace at Antioch, received a message from the governors of Illyria (presumably, from the context, this means provinces such as Dalmatia, Pannonia, Noricum and Raetia) that the Germans[5] were "on the march" and had crossed both the Rhine and Danube. The phrase implies coordinated invasions over a wide area, not just a series of raids. The tribesmen had overrun garrisons on the border and were devastating cities and villages within the empire. In some places the frontier legions had lost control of the situation altogether and, according to the governors, the only remedy was for the emperor himself to bring up his forces from the east. Only in the most dire of situations would the local commanders jeopardize their reputations by pleading for imperial assistance in this way.

The Rhine–Danube line was the empire's longest border, stretching for over a thousand miles across Europe, from the North Sea to the Black Sea. It was always the most troubling frontier because of its immense length and the fact that Italy could find itself in imminent danger if the defences crumbled. Fear of barbarian invasion had been hard-wired into the Roman psyche since Rome herself had been sacked by Gauls in the fourth century BCE, at which time the invaders had to be bought off with immense quantities of gold according to the maxim *vae victis*, or "woe to the defeated". In imperial times the long frontier was thick with legionary bases, forts and blockhouses. The peoples on the northern and eastern banks of the great rivers belonged to a series of tribes, including the Cherusci, Chatti, Marcomanni, Quadi, Jazyges, Roxalani and Carpi.

Several early authors refer to the Germans as a distinct people, beginning in the fourth century BCE. In the first century BCE Julius Caesar wrote about German customs based on his contact with several tribes in the Rhine valley. Then, writing around 100 CE, the historian Publius Cornelius Tacitus gave us an especially detailed and valuable account of the German peoples in his book *Germania*. Tacitus probably knew a variety of the tribes at first hand through service in the area although for this we cannot be sure.[6] The general picture he paints is one of fairly dense population lacking urban centres: it was a landscape of villages, and even when houses were close together they always occupied their own patch of land. Caesar had said much the same, and this picture has also been supported by archaeology. The people were divided into tribal groups with strong feudal loyalties and they were ruled by a priestly elite. Their society seems to have been refreshingly democratic, at least to Tacitus's eyes, with all men having a say in policy. Clans belonged to tribes that could be united – temporarily at least – by overlords, forming substantial military alliances. Physically, the Germans were impressive to the Romans; they were strong and large-bodied, mostly fair-haired and they were ferocious in battle. They were, however, prone to indolence and inebriation from a drink little known in Italy that Tacitus describes as a liquor "made out of barley or other grain, fermented into a certain resemblance to wine".[7]

Alexander was reportedly dismayed by the news of the German invasions. The situation for the empire as a whole had become extremely dangerous. If the border defences along the Rhine and Danube collapsed even locally, innumerable warriors might flood into the empire, for them a once-in-a-generation opportunity for plunder. Groups of invading desperados could spread far and wide and then would prove very difficult to round up and repel.

But it is clear from the sources that not all the invaders were dispersing: some elements of the Germanic force were sufficiently concentrated to threaten lesser armies sent against them. This implies discipline and organization, with kings or at least warlords in command (if indeed there was a difference) and Alexander and his advisers had to face the truth that Italy itself might now be under serious threat for the first time in many decades.

Of particular concern was the morale of the Illyrian detachments that had been sent to the eastern theatre of war. Not only had they suffered considerable privations and a humiliating defeat at the hands of the Persians which, if Herodian is to be believed, they blamed on Alexander's cowardice; now they saw their homeland under direct threat because of what could be interpreted as strategic incompetence. Many of these men may have left behind wives and families for the duration of the foreign campaigning.[8] It should be remembered that Alexander had toured the Illyrian legions in person during the approach to the Persian war. Imperial authority may have been required to extract from them the better units that local commanders might have preferred to retain. That the area had been weakened to the extent of provoking multiple invasions would have reflected badly on the judgement of the emperor and his advisers. If historians had indeed been consulted in the run-up to war, as Mamaea is supposed to have decreed, then the situation should have been predicted: a similar major barbarian incursion had occurred 50 years earlier when Marcus Aurelius drained the frontier troops for his own war in the east.

Archaeological evidence for the invasions is widespread. Two forts (Zugmantel and Saalburg) on the Roman frontier line around the Taunus mountains near the legionary base at Mogontiacum (modern Mainz in Germany) were destroyed in 233–234. Zugmantel was home to an auxiliary cohort, *cohors II treverorum* (conscripted locally from the city of Augusta Treverorum [Trier], capital of the Treveri), consisting of about 200 fighting men. It was large enough to possess its own amphitheatre. Saalburg contained an even larger garrison numbering over 500 men, including both infantry and cavalry units. (This fort was spectacularly reconstructed in the early twentieth century on the orders of Kaiser Wilhelm II and now forms the centrepiece of the World Heritage site of the Roman frontier, or *limes*.) Further evidence for destruction is also known from small auxiliary forts at Butsbach, Echzell, Altenstadt, Kapersburg, Kleiner-Feldberg and Ohringen-ost.[9]

Further south, in the upper Danube sector (Roman Raetia, now shared between southern Germany, Switzerland and Austria) there was further destruction, including the auxiliary forts of Vetoniania (modern Pfunz) and Bohming in the area west of Regensburg. Excavations at Pfunz have revealed some especially poignant details of the attack. The fort was home to an elite mounted unit with the proud title *cohors I breucorum civum romanorum equitata*. The name implies that this auxiliary unit from the Breuci tribe (from the area of modern Bosnia) had been granted Roman citizenship en masse, presumably for some outstanding feat of bravery. Unfortunately the entire garrison seems to have been wiped out in a surprise attack. Soldiers outside the walls were slaughtered without their weapons. Coin hoards within the precinct indicate the frantic burial of valuables never reclaimed. A shackled miscreant in the camp gaol was killed in his chains. From these few glimpses it is likely that many other forts were attacked or put out of action at this time. The outer shell of the imperial defences had been smashed in at least two places, hundreds of miles apart. The pattern of Herodian's account plus subsequent events makes it likely that there were also major incursions along the lower Danube at the same time.

The Taunus outposts were to the east of the Rhine in an area supposedly controlled by *legio XXII primigenia* (the name means the firstborn legion because it was the first to be recruited by Caligula for his aborted British campaign). This force was based on the river at the giant legionary base of Mogontiacum, not more than one or two days' march away from the destroyed fortifications. It is one of the legions known to have supplied troops for the Persian war. Although the base at Mogontiacum was virtually impregnable, the historical accounts indicate a major tactical defeat for the thinned-out legion, which would have left the rich city of Augusta Treverorum in a threatened position, and beyond that, all of eastern Gaul. Fortunately, the potential threat had been anticipated and the city had been provided with strong walls, which was unusual for the period, and there is no evidence that it was directly attacked. But once across the Rhine, marauding bands would have had rich pickings among the many villas, farming estates and temples that were especially dense in this well-developed and prosperous part of the empire. Even the citizens of Lutetia (Paris) would have looked to the east with alarm. The depleted *legio VIII augusta* based at Strasbourg might have marched north to confront the raiders, but if it did so, it would have weakened the defences in its own sector, risking another incursion.

Alexander and his advisers must have worked hard to appraise the situation in both eastern and western theatres as messengers frantically galloped to and fro. When it became clear that Ardashir was demobilizing, even if only temporarily, a decision was made to withdraw as many troops as possible from Mesopotamia. The redeployment would obviously take time. First this necessitated adopting a more defensive disposition on the Euphrates, which, it seems, Alexander himself oversaw from Antioch. Then it meant transferring a large and varied army as quickly as possible to the west and making sure it was properly organized, trained and equipped for an entirely different theatre of war and a very contrasting kind of foe.

Alexander would have needed his most able and senior generals to accompany him to the Rhine. One of these was an equestrian officer with the impressive name Gaius Furius Sabinus Aquila Timesitheus who had been in charge of financing the eastern war[10] and was now given sweeping emergency powers for the administration of the Rhine provinces. Another was Caius Julius Verus Maximinus, who was given another extraordinary command, this time as *praefectus tironibus*. Ordinarily this title would put him in charge of military training of a legion, a position far below his station, but if as is likely it was a rank duplicated in the high command, then in effect he was made responsible for reorganizing and training the army for the new campaign. These duties may have been the same as he had performed in the run-up to the Persian war as temporary military governor of Mesopotamia, although this time he would be working alongside Timesitheus and the other provincial governors. The *Augustan History* says simply that Maximinus was made commander of the entire army (*omni exercitui praefectus*),[11] and this may not be far off the mark. It also remarks that on this appointment "everyone, everywhere was pleased – tribunes, generals, and men". It also gives us the interesting suggestion that at this time Alexander considered marrying his sister Theoclia – otherwise unknown to history – to Maximus, the only son of Maximinus, which if true would have been a singular honour. It is clear that whatever had happened in the Persian war, two of the generals at least, Maximinus and Timesitheus, must have come out of it in very good standing with the emperor.

The logistical complexity of transferring so many troops and their equipment across the empire was the sort of task at which the Romans excelled. Herodian makes it clear that Maximinus discharged his duties conscientiously, making himself very popular with the soldiers, in contrast to the emperor who, it was noticed, seemed to prefer watching chariot-racing in Antioch. When asked why he worked so hard now that he had achieved high rank and riches, Maximinus is reputed to have said "the greater I become, the harder I shall work".

A clue as to how the army was transferred come from a pair of inscriptions from near the city of Aquileia in the north-eastern corner of Italy which can now be seen in the shady cloisters of the town museum. These give Maximinus the honorific title *aquileiensium restitutor et conditor* (restorer and builder of Aquileia), indicating that troops working under him improved the roads between Aquileia and the front.[12] The city had been provided with strong walls by Marcus Aurelius many years before; the title seems to indicate that he supervised some repair work and significant new construction, perhaps barracks or other military supply buildings. From these clues it has been suggested that the eastern forces travelled by sea and disembarked near Aquileia after sailing round the eastern Mediterranean and up the Adriatic. This made sound strategic sense because on arrival they would have interposed themselves between the capital and the troubled frontier. No doubt the populace of Rome was very relieved when the forces began to arrive, shoring up the forward defences of Italy and removing any threat of barbarian invasion.

By the time the army was assembled in the west (bringing with them, incidentally, a large number of coins minted in Antioch that now appear in the archaeological record along the Rhine frontier)[13] it was already spring of 234. The situation on the Rhine and Danube may have been restored somewhat over the winter as German tribesmen retired to their homelands, dragging booty and captives. Certainly the threatened mass invasion of central Gaul had not materialized. But a reduction in the threat would not have led to a cancellation of the planned action. Roman policy was consistent over the centuries: to mete out the direst punishment for such incursions in order to deter future repeats.

Up the Line

After leaving the salubrious environs of northern Italy with its wide plains, rich estates and vineyards, the march for Maximinus's force was via snaking passes across the Julian Alps followed by a long slog through the province of Illyricum up to the great legionary base at Carnutum on the upper Danube. From there, transports would have taken them up-river into the province of Raetia (now lowland Switzerland). Roman river barges were small, shallow-draught vessels that could only take a few horses or a few score men per journey. The effort must have been wearisome in the extreme. Eventually, before the river became narrow and tumbling, the animals and men would have disembarked for another long march north. This took the great army in small detachments through the upland area between the Danube, Neckar and Rhine headwaters known as the *agri decumates* and gradually, perhaps, into lands affected by the recent barbarian incursions. According to Tacitus, writing a century before, this area was inhabited largely by riff-raff including "all the most disreputable characters from Gaul, all the penniless adventurers".[14] Perhaps he had had his pocket picked there: whether such prejudices persisted into the third century we do not know.

From the *agri decumates* Maximinus led the army into the province of Germania Superior (an area now shared between southern Germany, south-eastern France and western Switzerland). As the army marched further into the troubled zone the troops may have been shocked to see deserted districts and areas of burnt devastation – particularly as, for some, this was home.

There was no great battle to be fought, the majority of the invaders having fled, although small-scale actions might have occurred as the army restored order.

The hastily assembled army included a range of exotic auxiliary units including "a huge force" of archers from Osrhoene[15] and the well-travelled lightly armed javelin troops from Mauretania (Morocco). These elite missile troops were very effective against barbarians, we are told, because the Germans' bare heads and large build made them easy targets at long distance. But the core of the army would have been regular Roman army cohorts, including many that were originally from the Rhine and Danube areas: men increasingly hungry for revenge against the old enemy from across the rivers.[16]

The army continued its march along the imperial highway that ran parallel to the frontier west of the Rhine, probably being joined by the emperor on the way. At some point that season they crossed the great river. This was probably in the vicinity of Mogontiacum. Herodian tells us that the crossing was achieved by the construction of a pontoon bridge made by lashing boats together, a method that is well attested as a standard procedure for a Roman army. The permanent bridge at Mogontiacum may have been destroyed, by the barbarians or even by the Romans as a defensive measure, the previous year. The pontoon bridge may have been built at the same spot or, more likely, a secret crossing was attempted somewhere in the sector to achieve tactical surprise and hopefully cut off some of the marauders on the far bank. A temporary bridge could be built in a matter of days, as described for example by Julius Caesar on his invasion of Germany about 300 years earlier. A medallion minted in 235 commemorates the crossing, showing Alexander in military dress preceded by Victory with a wreath and followed by a group of heavily armed soldiers all on a bridge of boats, while the god of the Rhine wallows beneath.[17]

To the citizens of the empire this commemoration of the emperor crossing the Rhine would have implied an expedition into barbarian territory. However, as mentioned above, the area of the Taunus salient east of the river had been part of the empire for well over a century before being so recently overrun. So the medallion might have been so much empty propaganda. We do not know how far the army penetrated in 234, or how many tribesmen it was able to bring to battle, but we can be sure that there was no major victory else Alexander would have taken the time-honoured title of *germanicus* to advertise the fact. It is most likely that the enemy dispersed, while some elements fought on using guerrilla tactics, as so often happened when Roman armies crossed the frontier. The Romans may have then resorted to pillaging and burning the local villages. Despite this, it appears that the former line of the *limes* beyond the Rhine was not fully secured and after the sortie the entirety of the east bank was once again left in barbarian hands for the winter.[18]

It is unclear what other action was taken along the long frontier in 234, although we can presume that detachments of the eastern army must have been sent to stabilize the other major fracture in the imperial defences on the upper Danube and elsewhere, as security demanded. No doubt communications were upgraded all along the border zone, so the forces could respond quickly to further incursions into the empire if concentrations of the enemy were detected. Other troop readjustments east and west would have occurred throughout the winter as the difficult task of rebalancing the weight of forces across the empire was undertaken. Scouting parties (*exploratores*) would have been dispatched and spies (*arcani*) given the lucrative but perilous task of penetrating deep into barbaricum and reporting back on the attitudes of the tribes, friendly and hostile.[19]

Rhinegold

Alexander chose to overwinter at the legionary base of Mogontiacum rather than returning to Rome: a clear sign of ongoing insecurity in the area. The name of the town means 'land of Mogon', a Celtic god. The polygonal military base was already 250 years old by this time and, just like legionary bases across the empire, a straggling civilian settlement (*vicus*) had grown up around it. But unlike some of the other Roman towns in the Rhine provinces, the city seems never to have developed to any great extent, and luxuries were few. A modest theatre has been discovered by archaeologists but this seems to have been the limit of public entertainment on offer, at least of the more sophisticated kind. The main camp, one of the empire's biggest and fit for two legions, would have been bursting at the seams with billeted troops, many of them regular legionaries. Units of the eastern army and all the auxiliary troops would have been stationed in temporary encampments in the area around. Good food and suitable religious amenities for the variegated army were in short supply, and then the weather started to deteriorate.

Herodian implies that the Rhine froze that winter so it must have been exceptionally cold: the same happened just twice in the same area during the twentieth century. To collect water the men had to hack out chunks of ice with axes and mattocks and lug them back to base. The big freeze would have meant a temporary collapse in river-borne supplies just when they were most needed for the large troop concentrations: one can imagine that food and firewood became scarce in an ever-widening radius as the army tried to survive the cold snap. At the same time, German forces from over the river may have harassed the immobilized army by winter raiding, sabotage and other stratagems.[20]

In these grim conditions it is hardly surprising that discontent continued to fester. Particularly dejected must have been the large detachments of troops from Africa, now so far from their homes and in a raw winter climate that was quite outside their experience. The Africans of Mauretania traditionally fought in light tunics, not heavy furs. The largely Christian city of Edessa, home to the Osrhoenian archers, had only been formally annexed a few decades before by Septimius Severus and had recently been the scene of a serious insurrection. Most of these men would never have seen the sea, let alone have been ordered to cross it to a distant land with what many of them probably regarded as a foreign pagan army. It is even possible their presence was in part punishment for the unrest in Edessa that preceded the Persian war. No doubt fireside tales abounded of the fearsome habits of the Germans and past Roman defeats in the cold damp forests beyond the far bank, where entire armies had disappeared without a trace. Their anxiety may have been further heightened by worries about the exposed situation at home, in the knowledge that Ardashir was still undefeated.

Elements in the army also resented the continuing hold that the empress Julia Mamaea had on her son. It is quite likely that Mamaea, despite her prudent government, had never been very popular since the exile of the young empress Orbiana. She had lowered her prestige further by amassing an immense private fortune that the army would have preferred her to distribute more liberally. Stories of Mamaea's miserliness began to multiply; it was said that she had an obsession with money,[21] and according to a later tale she was so frugal that she would order her cooks to re-serve half-eaten food. Another source charges Alexander too with avarice. Just as in the Persian theatre, the empress and her entourage accompanied the army on campaign. Her caravan would have been a prominent sight in the field and no doubt she and her son took the grandest accommodation that Mogontiacum could offer that winter. But Alexander was now 27 years old and surely should have cast off his mother's influence in military matters. Some may have compared the emperor unfavourably with the real Alexander (the Great) who had conquered virtually the entire known world by the same age. It may be significant that the Rhine crossing medal, mentioned above, has the images of both Alexander and Mamaea on the obverse,[22] so the emperor was not trying to hide his mother's influence. Perhaps it was even Mamaea who commissioned it, in an attempt to improve her own image.

Exactly what damage the German incursions had inflicted on the Roman empire is difficult to assess after this great remove of time. Most likely the devastation was restricted to rural areas, including small towns and estates.

Individual groups of raiders could easily have penetrated a hundred miles or more and there would have been little mercy offered to peaceful districts. But there had been no attempt at permanent occupation by the invaders. As winter finally turned to spring, the thoughts of the Roman army turned to renewing the campaign, avenging the unprovoked attacks, and the prospect of booty. A great punitive expedition was anticipated, possibly even an attempt to annexe a new province beyond the Rhine and win glory by conquest.

But at that point Alexander decided to send out peace feelers. A mission was arranged to contact the tribal leaders, who were offered huge sums of gold in exchange for solemn and binding promises never to return to Roman territory. These chieftains presumably could hardly believe their good fortune. When the army heard of the move they were outraged: in Herodian's words they "bitterly resented this ridiculous waste of time".

The attempt to buy off the Germans must have been a difficult decision and we can only speculate as to the motive. Possibly, as the months wore on, Alexander realized that the field army was going to be very difficult to hold together for another year. Outright military victory may have seemed impossible since the Germans quite understandably refused to stand and fight. Perhaps the relatively cultivated Alexander and his mother were already sickened with the punitive measures that were standard in such instances: the indiscriminate rape, murder and devastation that were the stock in trade of a Roman army bent on revenge. Or perhaps it was simply a financial decision: it was cheaper to bribe the enemy than maintain an army large enough to crush them. But rumours that Alexander intended to discharge the legions would hardly have been popular among the men. It is also possible that the high command was getting messages that, having shown the flag in Germany, at least part of the army was needed once again in the east, intact and ready to face Persia.

The financial and logistical problems of maintaining a large field army were indeed considerable. There had not been any necessity for such a concentrated strike force earlier in Alexander's reign or indeed for many years before. In later years the Roman military machine was to be totally reformed, split between garrison troops (to be called *limitanei*, based mostly on the frontiers) and a mobile force used for campaigning (the so-called *comitatenses*). In this later structure the field army *expected* to be on the move, and was suitably trained and equipped and had the greater pay and prestige.[23] It must have seemed the other way round for Alexander's exotic troops: they were the unlucky ones taken from their home bases, forced to cover huge distances on the march and accept most of the risk while being on the same pay as their comrades left behind. Their only hope was enrichment through plunder. And whereas individual legions maintained a strong *esprit de corps* with proud insignia and battle honours, this ad hoc force had been welded together at short notice with a bewildering array of languages, equipment and fighting styles.

So in this context, the offer of gold must understandably have seemed like a sell-out and an affront to the army's professionalism: an admission of defeat to add to the ignominious withdrawal from Persian lands. Many old soldiers would have known that to buy off barbarians would only foment trouble for the future. Men began to speak more openly of the cowardice and incompetence of the young Alexander and of the hold his mean-spirited mother had over him. Even if Alexander's reasoning was strategically sound for the empire as a whole, there is no doubt he had misjudged the mood of his men and a dangerous and potentially mutinous situation was developing.

The Purple

The only thing to dispel the boredom and keep warm through that long winter of discontent in the uninspiring land of Mogon was constant fitness training, weapons practice and tactical drill. One of the main auxiliary camps was some way to the south of the city, alongside the recently frozen Rhine for reasons of supply and security. It was here, it seems, that the imposing figure of Rome's greatest general took on the daily duty of training the men. Throughout history there are many examples of extreme, even fanatical devotion that troops have afforded their leaders: as hero, conquerer and perhaps most significant, father figure to young and frightened recruits. Herodian tells us that Maximinus did not merely oversee the instruction of his soldiers, he took the lead in all tasks. It took great strength and skill to pull an Osrhoenian bow or launch a Mauretanian javelin, but the old soldier (now in his early sixties but still in great physical shape)[24] had both. He also cultivated the men's allegiance by awarding them prizes and honours and even taking them on in the wrestling ring. As far as Maximinus was concerned, this was still a fighting force and by treating them as such and showing them respect he managed to hold them together.

Friction in the high command may have spilled over to brawling on one occasion. The *Augustan History* has a story that an insolent and haughty tribune, himself of great stature and courage, criticized Maximinus for sparring with the common soldiers and challenged him to a fight. Maximinus strode forward, smashed the palm of his hand into the man's breast, knocking him flat, and said "give me another, and this time a real tribune".[25]

One day in early March the auxiliaries mustered for training as usual in their arms and armour. But this was to be no normal roll-call, for as Maximinus stepped up to address them, a soldier placed a purple cloak about him and the men around him theatrically acclaimed him *imperator*. Since the days of Augustus himself, such a cloak was the mark of an emperor. Mere possession of it was treason. This was a formal act of public rebellion from which there could be no turning back. All the troops on that parade ground were now in mortal danger because everyone knew that the emperor Alexander and the main Roman army were just a short march away in the city.

It is perhaps worth mentioning in passing that by unifying the concept of *augustus* (supreme ruler) with *imperator* (supreme commander), the Romans may have made a structural error of enormous significance for the history of their empire. The troops on the Rhine wanted a commander on the ground; someone with unquestioned authority to run the war, but not necessarily a new ruler for the whole empire. But in the Roman state, they were one and the same thing.

Maximinus was a famous soldier, even the greatest of his time,[26] but he was not a natural born aristocrat. He threw off the purple cloak and refused the acclamation. The group of senior officers around him then drew their weapons, showing steel, and insisted that he wear it on pain of death. With no choice, he donned the cloak and stepped forward to address the assembled soldiers. It is unfortunate that Herodian's history does not contain Maximinus's (supposed) address in full, just an abbreviated summary (the suspected reason for this is that the work was incomplete at the time of Herodian's death: polished speeches abound in the earlier books but peter out in the later ones, as if they are missing the finishing touches):

> He addressed his soldiers and advised them that, although he accepted under protest in spite of himself, because he bowed to their desire, they must back up their decisions by action. They must get hold of their arms and quickly overpower Alexander before the news arrived, while he was still in the dark. The object was to overcome his attendant soldiers and his bodyguard, and either persuade them to acquiesce or compel them to do so without difficulty, catching them unprepared.
>
> Herodian, *History of the Empire* VI.8.7.

Either Maximinus was thinking very fast under pressure or the whole event had been orchestrated. It has so many parallels in history, both of Rome and many other states, that we must accept the latter as more likely. Nor was Herodian so gullible as to believe the occasion was unplanned: he also thought Maximinus must have been in on the plot from the very beginning, and later Roman sources agree that he orchestrated the coup.[27] The men who produced the imperial cloak and held a dagger to his throat are not named but their mere proximity to the commanding officer indicates they must have been senior officers who would be unlikely to act except by careful planning. The charade of the forced assumption of power may have been useful to convince weak-minded wavering soldiers that Maximinus had not betrayed his military oath until he had no choice, and so they too, in some sense, were absolved of theirs. But it was still an exceptionally dangerous situation and it is impossible that all the soldiers on the parade ground could have known what was going to happen in advance. So Maximinus announced that he would double the pay of the troops present (making them *duplicarii*; something that may have happened before, in the rebellion of Avitus/Elagabalus).[28] This was an enormous windfall for the men present. He also cancelled all punishments and especially marks of disgrace, which could last a lifetime. With the exits to the camp no doubt well screened, and confederates almost certainly placed strategically within the legions at Mogontiacum itself, a coup was under way. But unlike most previous occasions, the 'emperor' could claim no link whatsoever, real or imaginary, to any previous imperial dynasty.

The Legionary Fortress

Despite the requirement for urgent action it took a whole day and night before the rebel auxiliaries were ready to march out in the direction of the city. News of their treachery reached Alexander quickly. Herodian tells us that "he came rushing out of the imperial tent like a man possessed, weeping and trembling and raving against Maximinus for being unfaithful and ungrateful, recounting all the favours that had been showered upon him".[29] At short notice his only option was to gather his forces and crush the insurrection.

The situation was not lost, far from it. The bastion of Mogontiacum was impregnable, with its strong walls, defended gateways and overflowing garrison. Alexander had the rump of the regular army, which had been billeted in superior quarters, including the elite praetorian guard, and he held legitimate *imperium* bestowed by the senate and to which every man had sworn his sacred allegiance. He was popular in the empire, if no longer so much among the army. So the men declared they would stand by their emperor and promised to protect him in their stronghold. But the day ended in ominous silence, as communications from just up the road had been severed. And in reality the army was sorely split. Some, mindful of troubles ahead, no doubt cursed the rebellious auxiliaries for their lack of discipline. Many others may have sided with the rebels in spirit. Those not on guard duty would have retired to their barrack rooms as usual – eight comrades to a box-like room (the *contubinaria*) – and no doubt there were many whispered conversations that night, with peacemakers blaming the emperor's advisers and unpopular mother for the situation rather than Alexander himself. And it is quite possible that there was a division between the soldiers from Rome and those from the frontiers who had never even seen the world's greatest city but in whose name they were required to fight and die. Perhaps the native Romans urged support for the emperor who, although a Syrian, embodied Roman values more than the half-barbarian contender. As in most armies, the majority probably declined to be interested in high politics and waited for events to unfold.

The next day Alexander appeared before his troops and called them to a most critical task: their sworn duty was to destroy the rebellious contagion immediately before it could spread. This they must do by force. Again, we do not have a complete speech from Herodian, just a placeholder that he probably intended to elaborate upon at a later opportunity:

> Alexander begged them to fight for him and protect the emperor whom they had brought up and under whose rule they had lived for fourteen years without complaint. After appealing to everyone's sympathy and pity, he gave the order to arm and take up positions in the battle line.
>
> Herodian, *History of the Empire* VI.9.3.

Most of the soldiers continued to voice their allegiance, but it immediately became clear that support for action was far from solid. Some refused to take up weapons against their long-term brothers in arms, arguing, perhaps, for a diplomatic solution. Others responded by demanding that in return for their support Alexander should execute a certain hated senior prefect from his own household on the grounds that this man was responsible for the preceding military defeats. More worrying still, others began to heckle the emperor, criticizing his miserliness and his mother's greed. He might still bribe the men, but he could hardly turn over his own mother for execution.

As the dithering went on, a cloud of dust seen from the watchtowers marked the advent of the rebels. There was no way the approaching force could breach the walls, so their strategy from the first roadblock was to turn the soldiers' allegiance. Herodian recalls, or, more probably, imagines, the taunts: "desert your mean little sissy", give up the "timid little lad tied to his mother's apron strings" and instead join a man both brave and moderate and devoted to military action. Surely the army – and empire – deserved proper leadership by a man uncorrupted by riches who knew the ways of the army and was sure to look after their interests.

The strategy of the rebels began to work, and some men at various levels in the command chain began to see the inevitable outcome. Before long almost the whole army rebelled, including those manning the gates. Alexander, his personal staff, some loyal supporters and his most noble mother soon found themselves trapped in the command tent at the centre of a fortress that had turned against them. Boldly, Maximinus himself entered the gates to great acclaim and was noisily proclaimed *augustus* by the whole army on the parade ground, while the legitimate emperor cowered just metres away, clinging to his mother's robes, we are told, alternately hugging her and berating her for bringing about the calamity. They did not have long to wait. A party of tribunes and centurions arrived and killed everyone inside with cold steel.[30] Some of the inner circle managed to escape the tent, perhaps crawling under the flaps and guy ropes, but were cut down outside. Those killed seem to have included the commander of the praetorians who evidently did not desert Alexander at the last.[31] For Mamaea, this was the dreaded fate she had fought so long to avoid. Herodian summarized the reign of Alexander thus:

So Alexander met his end after a rule of fourteen years which, as far as his subjects were concerned, was without fault or bloodshed. Murder, cruelty and injustice were not part of his nature; his inclination was towards humane and benevolent behaviour. Indeed, his reign would have been notable for its complete success, but for the blame he incurred through his mother's faults of avarice and meanness.

Herodian, History of the Empire VI.9.8.

And on that 'but', the history of the civilized world lurched upon a new and very uncertain path. Over camp fires that evening there must have been many men wondering whether Rome, the empire and its many generals in far-flung places would endorse this most unexpected *coup d'état* with its unlikely figurehead.

Chapter VI

Soldier-Emperor

Consolidation

Maximinus was by no means the first general to be hailed *imperator* by his troops in defiance of the law, nor was he the first non-Roman to claim supreme office. Severus Alexander himself had been from the east, and his half-brother Avitus ('Elagabalus') and supposed grandfather Septimius Severus were also non-Romans who had ruled. By the third century, the Roman empire was, generally speaking, inclusive of its provinces and provincials. The really shocking difference was that Maximinus was low born and, so the rumours went, of barbarian extraction, and not even a Roman citizen at birth. Being Thracian cannot have helped, except in parts of the army. Whether he currently held equestrian or even senatorial rank was in a way irrelevant: he was a common soldier made good, and that was deeply shocking to the formally layered society of the Roman empire that held its rulers to be but one small step from divinity. Rome loved its square-jawed heroes in the military, but for the revered man at the top, deep-seated conservatism still preferred a lisping aristocrat like Claudius or depraved prince like Caracalla.

Ideally Maximinus would have rushed to the capital to consolidate his power among the ruling elite and the people, soothing raw nerves and making strategic alliances with the rich, ambitious and influential. But he also had his great army to contend with, poised as they were on the eve of a new campaigning season and with expectations raised to the highest pitch. The enemy had been made bold by Alexander's promised concessions and needed to be shown that a new man was in charge, so Maximinus had little option but to give the army what it wanted: a major campaign carefully designed to end in glory for Rome and booty for the soldiers. His personal survival would depend on delivering what Alexander had dared not attempt. As Herodian put it: "Since he had apparently been selected for his size, strength and military experience, he wanted to confirm his reputation and the soldiers' opinion of him by action".[1] A conspicuous victory over the barbarians would of course go some way to retrospectively justifying the assassination and silencing the critics in Rome and elsewhere.

Following the precedent set by Macrinus and Elagabalus, a delegation was dispatched to the senate in the name of the new emperor bearing letters demanding confirmation of his offices. It is not difficult to imagine the consternation these men brought with them as they stomped into the exalted marble halls of the capital. Yet again the military had demonstrated its power over the senate and people of Rome in an elemental way. Alexander and Mamaea had been loved and respected by many and embodied hope for the future, such a welcome contrast to the previous tyrannies; but now they were dead, and so were their praetorian prefects and others of the senior administration. Those once-powerful men, now eliminated, would have had many friends and allies in the city, especially among the senatorial class among whom proximity to Alexander had lately been a matter of extreme competition. Now even the mention of his name would be dangerous.

One option for the senate was to refuse to recognize Maximinus and declare him an enemy of the state. We can be sure that this was considered privately in the airy mansions clustered on the upwind slopes of the city's superior hills. But that would have entailed civil war in which the outcome was most uncertain. The senators were well aware of the usurper's hero status. No doubt Maximinus, in his dispatches, reassured the senate of his reluctance to rule and that his first priority was to deal with the German menace which would still have been a real worry in Rome. So the senate legitimized the coup and Maximinus was formally confirmed in his *imperium* and tribunician power and conferred with the great titles *augustus*, *pater patriae*, and *pontifex maximus*. The consulship would follow as normal at the start of the next consular year. This all happened by 25th March 235 at the latest, because a surviving inscription from Rome of that date records Maximinus's co-option into the sacred college of the guardians of the imperial cult (*sodales antoniniani*), 'by decree of the senate'.[2] And so it was that a man rumoured to have been a shepherd boy and one-time brigand of the Thracian hills became *princeps*, the legitimate emperor and master of the world and, incidentally, its most wealthy inhabitant because he was now the personal owner of a vast portfolio of imperial property and estates.

Before waiting for Rome's response Maximinus would surely have sent riders to all the army bases on the frontier, demanding allegiance from the commanders and provincial governors. Perhaps the only man who could have organized effective resistance was Timesitheus, overlord of the Rhine provinces, who had been given his extraordinary emergency powers by Alexander; but, presumably after a war council with his staff, he did not rise in opposition (and he was subsequently rewarded by Maximinus with some choice appointments).[3] There would be a nervous wait for several months to find out the reaction of other powerful armies in more distant parts like Britain, whose weather-beaten troops traditionally fancied themselves the equal of the Rhine armies, and the eastern provinces also. If either proclaimed their own commanders then a civil war would inevitably follow, like a repeat of the one fought by Septimius Severus over 40 years before. Perhaps it is testament to the new emperor's popularity and prestige in the army that no such rival emerged. Possibly it was also because Severus had wisely divided the more militarized provinces like Britannia and Syria so that no one man now had command over more than two legions, or maybe it was because all the provincial armies were under-strength and demoralized after the eastern war.

An immediate problem for Maximinus as emperor was the fawning imperial court: what to do with this retinue of highly-educated functionaries and officials who had served the previous emperor for many years? Maximinus took a soldierly approach and dismissed them all, executing those suspected of disloyalty in the takeover and sending the rest back to Rome. It must have been a challenge to set up a brand new imperial administration at Mogontiacum, so far from the real centre of communications. No doubt many middle-ranking civil servants kept their heads down as the axes fell, switching loyalties and retaining their jobs as always happens in such circumstances. But the real and most pressing problem for the administrative machine was money. It was customary (mandatory, in reality) for a new emperor to offer a large donative to the troops: not just those under his immediate command but right across the empire. This was an especially important priority for a soldier-emperor wanting to avert civil war, and so the cash was issued, further depleting the treasury. Maintaining the army and waging war against the barbarians was also going to be expensive. One way to raise money quickly was to confiscate the estates of any man suspected of treason, and the occasion of regime change always gave a new emperor a chance to root out real or potential opposition and at the same time generate revenue.

The great mint at Rome was evidently able to issue high-quality coins within just weeks, perhaps days, of the accession of an emperor. In normal times, it is likely that the themes were selected in person by the emperor. In this case, the responsibility probably devolved to magistrates on the spot. The first coins in Maximinus's name were probably delivered to the provincial strongboxes in late spring of 235: the issues were in gold, silver and bronze.[4] Most of the earliest types directly honour the army, showing the new emperor in armour addressing his troops between the sacred legionary standards (see Plate 6). Others proclaim *fides militum*, the faith of the soldiers, and *pax augusti*, the peace (through war) guaranteed by the emperor. These messages were for the whole empire, but would surely have been a major morale boost for the men who had risked all to put their favourite on the throne.

The soldiers knew there could be no more prevarication when the marching season opened. A detailed plan of campaign would have already been developed over the winter, and it is likely that Maximinus had been one of its architects. It surely involved, as a first step, re-crossing the Rhine from Mogontiacum and fully restoring control over the Taunus salient. This would be accompanied by one or more sweeping incursions into barbarian territory designed to spread terror, punish the Germans in their tribal homelands, and capture slaves and booty. As the eve of operations approached, Maximinus continued to train his troops hard, including getting into arms himself and leading by example despite now being emperor. Meanwhile the bridge across the Rhine was, presumably, reconstructed. This was a major task because the river was now in spate from the melted snows coming down from the Alps.

Magnus and Macedo

When the Rhine bridge was nearing completion, probably only about a month or two after the coup, the new emperor was informed of a plot against him that was already in an advanced stage of preparation. The plan was simple but clever. After Maximinus had led his army across the river into the forests beyond, a rebellion would erupt in his rear. The main base at Mogontiacum would be re-taken by the rebels and the newly restored bridge would be destroyed, cutting off the emperor and his troops from any obvious return route. A replacement emperor would be proclaimed on the west bank, who would be instantly ratified as *augustus* by the senate. Loyal troops would rush into the area to contest any re-crossing that the outlaw army might attempt. Without a supply route or any boats, and with the river still comparatively high, Maximinus would be stranded on the far bank for some time and quite probably harassed by barbarian raids. Whether his soldiers would stand by him in such circumstances, only time would tell.[5]

Herodian tells us that the plot involved "many centurions and people from the senate downwards"[6] and that it was centred on a patrician called Magnus. Historians have identified this man as Gaius Petronius Magnus, a former consul. The evidence for this is that his name was subsequently erased (although it is still just legible) from a surviving bronze tablet (see Plate 7). This plaque, which is known as the *Album of Canusium*, is a list of patrons of a city in southern Italy of that name. The removal of names was a standard part of the *damnatio memoriae* of a disgraced man. So Gaius Petronius Magnus had evidently done great wrong and his identity with the 'Magnus' of Herodian seems assured.[7]

Interestingly, Herodian suggests that the plot may have been fabricated by Maximinus himself as an excuse for a purge and a money-raising ploy. In essence, Herodian's reasoning is that the men who were implicated and executed could not be considered guilty because the charges were never tested in court. Nobody was brought to trial: all the suspects were ruthlessly killed without being allowed to exercise their right of defence.[8] This argument is legalistic and sounds a bit like a point of order, which makes one think that perhaps Herodian knew some of those who had been condemned in these trials, or their families, and their subsequent rehabilitation was a matter of politics at the time he was writing. Despite Herodian's reserve, the existence of a genuine senatorial plot at this time does seem highly plausible.

To get to this advanced stage of planning so quickly, it is fair to assume that the conspiracy must have been initiated among a group of disaffected senators at the time of Maximinus's accession, men keen to avenge the death of Alexander and make their own bid for power. Each senator commanded a great chain of patronage and could have identified individuals in the army who could be called on to do their part. Decisive and fast action was needed before Maximinus could consolidate his rule. The history of Rome abounds with brave men who were prepared to risk all in daring deeds, with the direst of consequences if they were discovered. The chief objection that could be raised to the plot – that an entire Roman army would be betrayed in the process – may have been softened somewhat by the fact that the troops were mostly foreign auxiliaries that had instigated the rebellion. Even so, the army did include many Romans, including senior commanders intent on their most patriotic of duties, and this may have been the plan's fatal weakness. If a friend of any one of these men got wind of the designs it was likely to be discovered. And that seems to have been what happened: for the perpetrators of the blown conspiracy the horror of the situation is hard to imagine. Retribution was merciless for them, their families and their dependants. The *Augustan History* says that over 4,000 men were executed in the purge and all their property confiscated.[9]

Another much more ham-fisted plot occurred around the same time from among the ranks of the Osrhoenian archers. Herodian tells us that Maximinus had dismissed from the army a man called Quartinus (possibly Titius Quartinus, a former provincial governor).[10] The reason for this is not given, but close association with Alexander can be presumed, and perhaps that he had been one of the latter's *amici*, or inner circle. A group of the archers, led by a man called Macedo who was presumably one of their senior officers, kidnapped this Quartinus and forced him to assume the imperial power at sword point. Their motive is unclear: Herodian says they "bitterly resented Alexander's death", which may hint at some sort of tension between the Germanic and eastern components of the army, or possibly even religious unrest, as Alexander's regime had reputedly been pro-Christian. It may even have been related to politics back in Osrhoene. Curiously, that city never minted coins in honour of Maximinus, although there is no evidence that it was captured by the Persians.[11] We can assume that the archers' encampment was some way from the main base at Mogontiacum because Quartinus, the unfortunate captive, survived for at least one day. But this time no great uprising occurred. Dismayed at the lack of support for his rash deed and rightly fearing the consequences, Macedo quickly changed his mind and murdered Quartinus then, with some panache, brought his head before Maximinus, demanding a reward. Unsurprisingly, Macedo was himself condemned for both treason against Maximinus and, with studied irony, disloyalty to the dead 'emperor' Quartinus that he himself had forced to wear the imperial purple.

Before moving on it is worth mentioning that the *Augustan History* gives a very garbled version of this same story, which it directly attributes to both Herodian and the lost work of Dexippus. This account[12] can be found in a very peculiar book known as the *tyranni triginta* (Thirty Tyrants), which is a low point even for the *Augustan History*, reading as it does like the output of a waffling student in an exam hall desperately resorting to fabrication to fill out some meagre remembered factoids (perhaps historians should examine this conjecture). Here the supposed author, Trebellius Pollio, names the reluctant pretender as 'Titus' (which nevertheless may fit with the scholarly identification of the man as Titius Quartinus). It then provides a fabulous account of the life of this 'Titus' who, it claims, had been tribune in Africa and, rather bizarrely, ruled the empire wisely for six months. Pollio then continues: "You will not, indeed, wonder that there is such diversity of statement about this man, for even his name is scarcely known." Rallying in his prose, however, he goes on to tell us that his wife Calpurnia was of a famous noble line, owner of Cleopatra's pearls, no less, and a giant silver platter weighing a hundred pounds, and that her golden statue could still be seen in the Temple of Venus in Rome at the time of writing should anyone wish to check the detail. After this apparent padding, the writer exclaimed: "I seem to have gone on further than the matter demanded" and moved on to an even more unlikely topic.

Battle of the Bog

Spring 235, and the kings and chiefs across the Rhine were monitoring events with a mounting sense of alarm. Failure of the plots against Maximinus meant that Germany had lost any hope of avoiding invasion. Herodian, it seems, was not present on the Rhine, but for what followed he would have eagerly gathered news from the front and he very probably spoke to veterans of the campaign when compiling his narrative. An independent account, probably by Dexippus, is transmitted to us via the *Augustan History*, a very uncertain filter. Both versions are quite condensed, but by combining them with archaeological evidence and making reasonable assumptions about the likely rate of progress, historians have pieced together an outline account of events.[13] With an experienced general, now emperor-on-the-spot and in full control of the decision-making, we can perhaps think of it as the type specimen of a Roman punitive campaign.

Maximinus and the main army crossed the pontoon bridge in the early summer, no doubt mindful of the Magnus plot and leaving behind a strong guard of unquestioned loyalty to protect the bridge. It was a late start to the campaign season because of the dramatic events of the spring. Herodian describes it as an enormous army, practically the entire Roman fighting strength, and it included the North African and Eastern missile troops whose job it was to take on any small group of raiders that might be encountered. The *Augustan History* also lists Persian cataphracts – those 'boiler boys' from the east – extraordinarily exotic troops in such an environment. In a satisfactory confirmation of this oft-maligned source from archaeology, the graves of such men have been discovered in two places in Germany, one of which commemorates brothers called Saluda and Regretho and the other a decurion called Biriba.[14] Such was the nature of the ancient world that these very same men could have fought with Ardashir beyond the Indus just a few years before.

Tacitus memorably described Germany as a land "bristling with forests and foul with swamps".[15] The logical first move was to reoccupy the Taunus salient while repairing roads and bridges along the frontier zone.[16] Then, according to the standard interpretation, the army swept south. The usual reading of the *Augustan History* suggests an incursion of thirty or forty Roman miles into barbarian territory.[17] This led to the view that the army devastated the frontier area to the south of the Taunus for perhaps hundreds of miles parallel to the border but without penetrating deep into *barbaricum*. This contention will be revisited in the following chapter, but whatever the direction of the thrust or thrusts, with the main forces of barbarians falling back in front of them, the troops fanned out to pillage and plunder everything in their path. As Herodian says, they devastated all the countryside, deliberately destroying the ripening corn and burning villages. He also mentions how easily the houses caught fire that hot summer and attributes it to the fact that they had wooden frames with little brick or stone in use. The farm animals were slaughtered for food, leaving no stock for reproduction. And while the army rampaged across the countryside, detachments were set to work restoring and reoccupying the entire Rhine defence line. Inscriptions dedicated to Maximinus have been discovered at several forts in the area documenting this work.[18]

Inevitably the ruthless policy provoked resistance. Herodian says that initially it was in the form of guerrilla raids and traps set in the woods and marshes, where local knowledge and experience gave the defenders an advantage and allowed escape. But as the devastation spread and large areas were cleared of their population the barbarians started to gather into concentrations, as much for their own mutual protection as their capacity to strike back. Their chiefs and kings would have been a focus of organized opposition, so it is most unfortunate for us that their names and tribes are nowhere reported. Late in the campaign season, perhaps in autumn or even early winter, the main barbarian army was located in an area of wooded swamp. We do not know where this was, although the issue is discussed further in the next chapter in the light of new discoveries on the ground. For Maximinus, after months of skirmishing, here was a chance for something more resembling a pitched battle. The Germans had fortified their position as best they could by preparing pits, traps and dead-ends in the marshes. We can imagine that the Roman forces were carefully distributed around the area to block obvious escape routes before the main attack was launched. But when it came, the soldiers were wary of making the assault because they feared being massacred on prepared ground. Herodian (who had no love for Maximinus and so can probably be believed on this point) tells us that the emperor himself took the lead, plunging into the bog on horseback, killing many barbarians and encouraging his men to do the same. Large numbers on both sides were killed in the ensuing slaughter and the swamp became so full of bodies and thick with blood that the scene resembled a naval battle. The end result was clear victory for the Romans. We are also told that there were many other lesser engagements during the campaign in which Maximinus again shared the dangers of battle with his men and was commended for bravery.

The campaign of 235 was an outstanding success from the Roman point of view and for Maximinus in particular. Here at last was a real victory against a foreign foe for the whole empire to celebrate: the first, indeed, for 40 years. The emperor was able to leave the German provinces with a robustly restored frontier and, beyond it, an area of devastation that would take years to mend and a chastised barbarian people who would think twice about entering Roman territory in future. Perhaps most importantly for the economy of the empire, many captives were taken: most would have been deported as slaves but inscriptional evidence suggests that at least some of the men of fighting age may have been enrolled as auxiliaries and posted to northern Britain shortly afterwards.[19] The soldiers had done comparatively well in plunder. The emperor himself had made a series of decisive strategic moves and distinguished himself by leading from the front on more than one occasion. Many of the men had displayed their own heroism, skill and discipline on successive occasions and would now think of each other as veterans and comrades-in-arms. Although the successes were surely exaggerated and local reverses ignored, the contrast with the feeble and dithering offers of gold by Alexander could not have been greater.

Pleased or not, the senate had no option but to award Maximinus, in his absence, a second imperial acclamation following that initially given to him on his elevation at Mogontiacum, hence *imperator II*,[20] and the title *germanicus maximus*. In lieu of his presence and a triumph in Rome, Maximinus ordered a series of giant paintings of the German campaign to be set up in front of the senate house, with himself in a starring role for all the people of Rome to see. It was a tradition stretching back at least 500 years.[21] The work was, perhaps, a placeholder for a future victory monument in stone, as had become *de rigeur*, but we can be sure the work on such an important imperial commission was very fine. These paintings were described by Herodian, who may very well have cast his own critical eye over them as he went about his daily business in the forum. A special issue of coins from Rome was commissioned, showing *Germania* as a tied captive at the foot of the goddess Victory who holds a palm frond and laurel wreath, symbolizing peace through victory (Plate 8).

One regional mint, Anazarbus in Cilicia (part of modern Turkey) went even further by issuing a medallion showing the emperor mounted on a fine stallion in the very act of spearing a fallen enemy, with Victory (or Nike as she was known in the east) fluttering before him, proffering a wreath over the horse's head (Plate 8). This coin is fascinating for several reasons. Most obviously, it is interesting in that it shows Maximinus doing what he was trained to do. More significantly, perhaps, it is one of the first Roman coins to show an emperor actually participating in the blood and gore of a battle scene, although the motif would become standard in later years (the horseman must be Maximinus because only the emperor could be awarded a victory). Moreover the image is strongly rooted in imagery used for centuries by Roman auxiliary cavalrymen on their tombstones, and by the Thracians in particular. There is a long-standing iconography depicting the so-called "Thracian rider" or "Thracian hero", sometimes identified with their top god Sabazios, in exactly this way, charging to the right over a fallen enemy (or animal, if the scene is a hunt) with his horse rearing on hind legs and his cape flowing out behind. It is said that the image was so strong that it persisted into the Christian era in the form of St. George slaying the dragon. And the highly strategic location of Anazarbus had been a provincial campaign base of the imperial horseguard from the time of Severus, the unit that Maximinus had been enrolled in, at least according to the *Augustan History*. So it may not be too much to imagine that the message on this coin was for the cavalry troopers themselves, a celebration that the emperor himself was one of their own corps, able to deliver a victory for the empire in a way the soldiers understood.[22]

As tradition demanded, the soldiers would have been allocated a share of the spoils and the proceeds of the slave auctions. But the army was given little time to celebrate. With winter closing in, the bulk of the troops were evidently made to force-march all the way back to the upper Danube (possibly the fortress at Radasbona [Regensburg]), where river transports took them on the long journey downstream to the big military base at Sirmium. The march was, under the circumstances, a herculean effort and illustrates the decisiveness and broad strategic vision of the new emperor: it also demonstrates that for Maximinus the campaign against the Germans was complete for now at least, and the guilty tribes across the Danube would be the target of the next campaigning season.

One man who seems to have made the journey but got no farther was Barsemis Abbei, an officer of the Osrhoenian archers, whose tombstone has been found at Intercisa fort south of Budapest in Hungary, and hence is one of the few names (along with the Persians, Saluda, Regretha and Biriba mentioned above) we can attach to these events.[23] Another is an ordinary soldier called Aurelius Vitalis of *legio IIII flavia felix* who died aged 25 after seven years of service as recorded on an inscription in the Rhine fort of Noviomagus (modern Speyer). One other man who may have fought alongside them is Tadius Exuperatus, aged 37, a native Briton whose memorial stone from Caerleon in South Wales records his death on an unspecified 'German expedition' (*expeditio germanica*) about this time. Caerleon was the fortress of *legio II augusta*, about as far across the empire as it is possible to be from the homeland of Barsemis.

Across the Danube (236–238)

It is noteworthy that while the mobile army was being transferred to winter quarters near the Danube frontier, Maximinus chose not to travel to Rome, where he was guaranteed a triumphal entry and would also have bolstered his position among the people. Herodian says "he wanted to be left on his own surrounded by the army, without anyone being near him who had the advantage of being aware of their own nobility". The *Augustan History* says he "feared that the nobility, because of his low birth, would scorn him".[24]

This may be fair comment, as Maximinus had been in the army for virtually his whole career. It is quite likely that he loathed the snobbish senatorial class just as they despised him in return. He may have feared the very real risk of assassination.

Despite staying with the army, Maximinus naturally kept a close eye on developments in the capital and the rest of the empire. The first day of January 236 was the allotted date for the emperor to be given tribunician power for the second time and be invested as *consul ordinarius* for the first time. A key choice, therefore, was who to take as his companion in the consulship? The mad emperor Caligula, we are told,[25] planned to nominate his favourite horse, Incitatus, as consul; whether to demean the office or because he really was mad we do not know. In marked contrast, Maximinus chose for his colleague a widely respected senator called Marcus Pupienus Africanus Maximus. This man was from a noble family; both his father and grandfather had been senators and his father (Marcus Clodius Pupienus Maximus) had served his second term as consul under Alexander just two years earlier. Perhaps the move was designed to reassure the senate and people that there was no intention of sweeping away the old ways. Even so, it seems unlikely that Maximinus would have entrusted the consulship to someone he did not know. The elder Pupienus had served a term as governor in a German province where he had distinguished himself in military service and had many influential supporters. It seems possible therefore that he, and possibly his son, had been involved with Maximinus in the planning of the German expedition under Alexander. Perhaps they were even party to the coup, which would be a most interesting possibility considering subsequent developments. Or perhaps by bestowing the consulship on the younger Pupienus, the aim was to win the support of the elder who was city prefect at that time and hence the most important official in Rome.[26]

The emperor had enormous powers of patronage for appointing individuals to all the other high offices of state. If, as seems likely, he devoted most of his energy to military affairs, he must have selected trusted men to advise him on practical matters including appointments. The most important of these was his personal representative in Rome, who would be given the office of praetorian prefect. The historical sources name this man as Vitalianus (most likely Publius Aelius Vitalianus, who had recently been governor of the province of Mauretania Caesariensis).[27] Possibly he had been commander of the Mauretanian auxiliaries in the Persian war and then in Germany, and had been a central figure in the coup. He might even have been an ex-officer of the horseguard, like Maximinus himself, if indeed it was traditional for governors of Mauretania to be chosen from among their ranks, as has been suggested. In any case, Vitalianus would have been chosen for his administrative talent and unquestioned loyalty to the new regime. Exactly who Maximinus's other closest advisers were is not known, but whoever had the emperor's ear was in an extremely influential and no doubt lucrative position as far as the civil administration went.

The army transferred that winter to Sirmium, then one of the major cities of the known world with up to a hundred thousand inhabitants, but now a small town in Serbia called Sremska Mitrovica. It was the capital of the province of Lower Pannonia, sited on the north bank of a large tributary to the Danube called the Savus (now the River Save). Its great commercial importance was that it commanded the overland supply route between Italy and the east. About 50 miles downstream of Sirmium, at the point where the Savus flowed into the Danube, was the great fortress of Singidunum (modern Belgrade). As Sirmium itself was a major trading city rather than a military camp, it suggests a more congenial over-wintering for the army than had been the case the previous year at Mogontiacum. Perhaps this indicates that Maximinus attended more closely to the comfort of his troops than had Alexander. Even so, if a large proportion of the army was billeted at Sirmium for the winter, it would soon have taken on the feel of a fortress.

For the men, winter life was all about regular training in which the imposing figure of Maximinus himself, more than ever a hero with the army, was once again seen regularly on the parade grounds. His presence, and the fact that the army was not dispersed, made it plain to everyone that as far as the emperor was concerned, there was still a war on. For the staff officers, winter was devoted to planning the forthcoming campaign. The previous incursions of barbarians across the Danube had yet to be avenged. Except for occasional aberrations such as under Alexander, Roman policy was forever constant: aggressive incursions could not go unpunished. The tragedy for the tribes across the Danube was that Maximinus was committed to this policy without mercy.

In contrast to his account of the war against the Germans, Herodian gives us very few details of the campaigning across the Danube; he simply credits Maximinus with further strategic successes and gives the impression that things progressed very well. In the event, Maximinus campaigned on the Danube frontier for two full seasons, using Sirmium as his winter base again in 236/7 and 237/8. Inscriptional evidence tells us that several military detachments in the area were awarded the honorific title *maximiniana*.[28] Perhaps, one day, archaeology will help fill in the details of the fighting.

Until then, all we have available to reconstruct events is the series of titles and imperial acclamations that the emperor was awarded. These do not all appear on his coins: the style of coin with very long legends that listed all the emperor's titles had long gone out of fashion, so we must rely on rarer inscriptions from across the empire and especially surviving papyri from the east. But this leaves some extra sources of doubt special to that kind of evidence, in that occasional writings by officials in far-flung parts of the empire do not necessarily get the titles right. Bearing in mind these caveats and the fact that Maximinus had already taken the tribunician power once (on his accession) and the imperial acclamation twice (on his accession and then after the victory in Germania) the facts seem to be as follows: 236 CE coincided with Maximinus's first consulship and second tribunician power, and inscriptions are known that combine *trib. pot. II* with the titles *imp III, dacicus maximus and sarmaticus maximus*. The fourth imperial acclamation, *imp IV* was probably also awarded in 236 in acknowledgement of another significant victory. In 237, along with his second consulship and *trib. pot III*, Maximinus was awarded two further salutations, *imp V* and *imp VI*.[29] So if the propaganda is to be believed, it was a period of outstanding military success and conquest with at least four major battles won, each of a similar significance to the Battle of the Bog.

Of course, the war did not go well for everyone. Of several inscriptions dedicated to the fallen, the most interesting is that of Publius Aelius Proculinus, a centurion of *legio II adiutrix*, who had transferred to the seventh cohort of praetorians and fell at an unknown place called Castellum Carporum (village of the Carpi). The others are troopers from *legio I adiutrix, legio II italica* and another man from *legio II adiutrix*. All these legions were stationed along the Danube at this time.

These clues give us a rough chronology on which to hang events. We can deduce that Maximinus and his great army crossed the Danube in 236, presumably in the spring, and campaigned in both Dacia and Sarmatia, claiming victories in both areas. A reprisal of the strategy used in Germany could have seen the Danubian legions crossing the river at the legionary base of Viminacium (home of *legio VII claudia*) then marching up through Dacia. The route would have taken it to the legionary base at Apulum (*legio XIII gemina*) and then on to the most distant outpost at Potaissa (*legio V macedonica*), while at the same time detachments would have been sent to secure the frontier to the west. These legions were probably in a better state than the Rhine armies had been in 235, as evidenced by the fact that Alexander had at that time chosen to deal with the Germans first. Also, it is possible that the Dacian units had been reinforced in 235 with detachments from the eastern army, or they had been able to restore order on their own. No doubt the new emperor's entry into these camps was accompanied by great shows of loyalty and devotion (and relief, for these far-flung garrisons had been surrounded by enemies). Old soldiers around the campfires might just have recalled that Maximinus himself had distinguished himself as a junior officer in Dacia many years before.

Combining his main army with detachments of local troops, Maximinus could have campaigned against the Carpi on the northern border of Dacia. Then he is likely to have swept west into enemy territory as his engineers reconnoitred the banks of the River Tissus (modern Tisza) for a future fortified frontier (*limes*). This area was controlled by a formidable Sarmatian tribe knows as the Jazyges. These were a nomadic people known to the Romans for many generations, and their horsemen were especially feared. Detachments of Sarmatian cavalry auxiliaries had been drafted into Roman service since the time of Hadrian; thousands of them showed up as far away as the great wall in Britain. But on this occasion the tribe was to feel the might of Roman vengeance. After penetrating far to the west, the army would have fanned out and used the same scorched earth policy as had been applied against the Germans, herding the fleeing enemy into sufficient concentrations that could then be systematically destroyed. In this way the pattern of attack would also have followed the general strategy of the philosopher-emperor Marcus Aurelius 50 years before in the same area.

A great arc would have brought the army back to Singidunum on the Danube by the end of the marching season, in time for river transport back to Sirmium for the winter. Such a campaign would have secured the western border of Dacia and subdued a large area of the Sarmatian salient, equating to what is now the lowlands of western Romania, and it would account for the titles *dacius maximus* and *sarmaticus maximus* awarded that year.

Despite the intrinsic aggression of such a strategy, it would still have left a broad zone untouched, equating to the north-south strip between the Tisza and the Danube (now eastern Hungary). This area may have received similar treatment in 237, possibly with Aquincum as the jumping-off point, while a second pincer repeated the route of 236. Such a move would have trapped any remaining people in the salient for capture and sale as slaves. Even so, being nomadic, many refugees would presumably have escaped north into the steppes of the Ukraine to avoid the Roman war machine the previous winter. The two imperial acclamations of 237 could refer to separate victories inflicted by the two wings postulated here. Another possibility is that Maximinus campaigned against the Goths east of Dacia and north of the lower Danube although he was never, so far as we know, given the title *gothicus maximus*.[30]

Although the overall strategy of these expeditions may have been similar to the German campaign, the main difference on the ground would have been tactical: the problem of moving the army safely across an open and flat terrain. Ambuscades were unlikely but, equally, good natural defensive positions were also scarce. The Romans would presumably have built many fortified marching camps to provide protection against surprise attacks and look-out towers to survey the plains. Further details of the progress of these campaigns will surely be forthcoming from archaeology if they can be disentangled from earlier and later warfare in the region.

Waging this kind of war was, put simply, genocide, but it was consistent with Roman mores. If an area posed a threat to the empire and could not be subdued efficiently, then its entire populace could legitimately be destroyed, either by the sword or through famine. The strategy has several precedents in Roman history, including the original Dacian campaign of Trajan. We can imagine that by the autumn of 237 the entire area formally occupied by the Jazyges had been turned into a wasteland. What the emperor himself thought of this – with his mother allegedly a Sarmatian peasant – we do not know, but it is difficult to think that he would have had any scruples. Whether Maximinus himself partook in the cut-and-thrust of battle we have no record, although the aforementioned death of Proculinus, one of his own praetorian guardsmen, may indicate that he was involved in battle as usual.

Back home, the people of the empire had by now become accustomed to the new imperial family and the imposing figure of the emperor Maximinus, the pious *augustus*, victor in Germany, Dacia and Sarmatia, on their statues and public inscriptions. Nobody could deny that renewed security on the river frontiers was a great relief and news of successive victories would have filtered back home through letters and communications. But there may also have been grumblings that the emperor still did not deign to show himself in Rome, let alone anywhere else in the empire, and nor did his son. There was no sign, so far, of any new architectural plans for the great cities, still less any support for the arts, sciences or philosophy. Even circus games had been severely curtailed, with the public money normally raised for such spectacles diverted to the army. And so it may have seemed in the more peaceful lands, where the problems of the frontier were of less immediate concern, that the entire Mediterranean economy and culture was being drained away toward wastelands on the edge of empire. Perhaps it was becoming evident that the new administration was, in fact, a military dictatorship. Paraphrasing Voltaire's comment on Prussia, it may have begun to seem that the Roman empire no longer possessed an army: the army possessed an empire.

Chapter VII

Echoes in Eternity

"Fratres! Three weeks from now I will be harvesting my crops. Imagine where you will be, and it will be so. Hold the line. Stay with me. If you find yourself alone, riding in green fields with the sun on your face, do not be troubled; for you are in Elysium, and you're already dead! Brothers, what we do in life echoes in eternity."
General Maximus Decimus Meridius to his cavalry wing, *Gladiator*, 2000.[1]

Detection

In the year of the millennium some metal detectorists set out to look for a long-lost medieval castle on a wooded limestone ridge called the Harzhorn, near a village called Kalefeld, south-west of Hannover. They did not find a castle but they did find some iron spearheads, a shovel and an enigmatic twisted iron object with hooks that they put aside as a curiosity. Years passed, until June 2008 when the collection was shown to district archaeologist Petra Lönne, who immediately recognized the unidentified object as a 'hipposandal' or Roman military horseshoe. It was an astonishing find: perhaps a Roman marching camp had been discovered far beyond the borders of the empire.

Later that year a campaign of archaeological metal detecting was organized and immediately started to turn up a spectacular array of finds: more spearheads, a broken sword, a fitting from a cart, bits of chain-mail, ballista bolts, arrowheads and hundreds of hobnails from the boots of Roman soldiers: over 700 finds in all, and that was just the start. Fortunately, the alkaline soil had preserved the objects beautifully. Even more exciting was the dawning realization that this was not a military camp but an actual battlefield, on one side of which was a fully-equipped Roman army and on the other, Germanic tribesmen. The presence of many ballista bolts strongly suggested that this was the action of at least one full legion.[2]

The media got hold of the story and inevitable parallels were drawn with the opening scene of the film *Gladiator* (2000), which features a spectacular recreation of a pitched battle between a disciplined Roman army and a horde of axe-wielding Germans. Strangely, the wooded hillside of the Harzhorn and the terrain of the film look identical (see Plate 7).[3] And then a coin turned up as dating evidence. As if written by a journalist, it portrayed the emperor Commodus (177–192), the bad guy in the film as memorably played by Joaquin Phoenix. True, in the film, Commodus arrived on the scene the misty morning after the battle too late to take part, and he was not yet emperor. And the coin was very, very worn. Nevertheless the find attracted a lot of attention and established the *terminus post quem* – the earliest possible date for the battle – which was 177 CE.

Modern Germans are famously proud of the fact that they, or at least most of them, maintained their independence from the Roman empire following a great victory in 9 CE, when Augustus's general Publius Quinctilius Varus was double-crossed by his auxiliary cavalry commander Arminius (sometimes known as 'Hermann the German') and all three of his legions were utterly destroyed on the march. Hence the late date surprised just about everyone because the Romans were not supposed to have penetrated this far into Germany after the first century. The first speculation that the battlefield could have been related to Maximinus's punitive campaign was soon aired, but other commentators disparaged such attempts to link the archaeology to any historical event (archaeologists are rightly concerned with extracting impartial evidence from the ground which can spill over into indignation at any attempt to link specific finds with history). Nevertheless, over the following year several more coins, including denarii of Severus Alexander and Julia Mamaea, were discovered, advancing the *terminus post quem* to 228. Radiocarbon dating of wooden artifacts tied the battle unequivocally to the first half of the third century. All this made the campaign of Maximinus look a much more likely explanation, especially in view of the fact that there was no other known major Roman incursion across the Rhine until 270 and that was most likely defensive rather than punitive.[4] If this theory is correct, future finds might include coins up to early 235 but no later: the dream find would be one from Maximinus's first issue, which might have reached the troops before they marched off that summer.

But the problem, indeed the big surprise to all involved, is the location. The battlefield is no less than 350 kilometres across barbarian territory from the base at Mogontiacum and would have taken a Roman legion the best part of a month to approach in hostile ground and just as long to retire, assuming this is the very limit they penetrated. And the layout of the battle suggests the Romans were engaged on their *return* journey. Moreover the place is much further north and east than anyone had predicted, because the previous evidence relating to the campaign of Maximinus, discussed above, comes from central and southern Germany.[5]

Although Herodian says that Maximinus "advanced a very long way"[6] before the decisive battle, he does not give a distance. The *Augustan History* does: the phrase, as has usually been reproduced in various editions of the work since the seventeenth century, is *ingressus igitur germaniam transrhenamam per triginta vel quadraginta milia barbirici*: "He marched, then, into Germany across the Rhine, and throughout 30 or 40 miles of the barbarians' country." A Roman mile (*mille passum*) was defined as 1,000 left–right pace cycles or 2,000 marching steps, and is regarded close to a modern mile. Curiously, however, the most important manuscript version of the text, the so-called Palatine codex from which all other manuscripts are ultimately derived, actually states *trecenta vel quadringenta milia barbirici*, or "300 or 400 miles of the barbarians' country". The script of the original, which is now viewable online at the website of the Vatican Library, is as perfectly clear now as the day it was copied down, from an earlier text, by a scribe in a monastery of the Holy Roman Empire, sometime in the ninth century. This is a rare example where most scholars – including the standard English translation by Magie in 1924 – preferred a later version of the text over the Palatine codex, presumably because the claim to have penetrated tens of miles sounded less far-fetched than several hundred. Now it seems that was wrong.[7]

The Romans, of course, might have divided their forces into two or more self-sufficient armies, each with the orders to march deep into Germania, seek out the troublemakers, and cause as much devastation as possible. But the available history suggests a single incursion by a very large force, hence the most likely interpretation of the Harzhorn battlefield is that this was the army commanded by Maximinus in person on its way back to the empire having laid waste to the North German (Saxon) plain. Herodian, it should be recalled, after discussing the Battle of the Bog, does say "There were other engagements too, in which Maximinus personally took a leading part in the battle and was always commended for bravery."[8] Perhaps this was one of them.

Engagement

Lessons can be learned from archaeological investigations into that other great Roman battlefield in Germany, that of Varus and Arminius in the Teutoborg forest from 9 CE in the reign of Augustus (as told, for example, in a most entertaining and insightful account by the British metal detectorist Tony Clunn who was instrumental in discovering it).[9] Investigations revealed several battle sites spread over a wide area as the Roman column fought running engagements with German tribes whose tactic was to constrict the route, throw up obstacles and prevent it from forming up for pitched battle. Eventually, the whole army was destroyed down to virtually the last man. The big difference though is that at the Harzhorn the German tactics seem to have been unsuccessful and Maximinus was on the winning side.

What can be said about the course of the battle from the evidence on the ground? The first thing to say is that the Harzhorn might sound like some lofty peak, but in point of fact it is a relatively low ridge, although no doubt strategically important. Archaeologists have concluded that the action there was very brief, perhaps lasting no more than half an hour. The Romans evidently attacked the hill from the north because the great majority (80 per cent) of projectiles were found embedded in the ground pointing south (presumably these were the ones that missed their targets). A marked concentration of Roman hobnails from the soles of their leather sandals along the bottom of the hill suggests the engagement began with a close-quarters infantry struggle involving considerable scrabbling and kicking (hobnails quite easily became detached and frequently had to be replaced). A beautiful high-status Germanic decorated spearhead is one of the finds from this area. The Germans probably scattered uphill to prepared positions in dips on the hillside, which were then subject to Roman artillery fire from wagon-mounted ballistae brought forward to assist the assault. These weapons are extremely powerful with a lethal range of about 300 metres and close accuracy within 100 metres. Several modern re-creations exist and they are most impressive: whereas arrows loop high into the air before descending on their target, ballista bolts are much heavier and fly with low trajectory at frightening speed, impossible for a man to dodge. The ballista bolts are highly concentrated in certain areas (no fewer than 70 are closely grouped at one particular point behind an undulation near the hilltop), showing that strong points were singled out and pounded with these machines before the infantry resumed the assault and cleared the heights. The arrowheads, significantly, are of a three-sided type consistent with the reflex bows used by the Osrhoenians.[10] These are much more widely distributed across the hillside than the bolts, presumably having targeted more dispersed opposition or been less accurate, or most likely both.

The broader strategic situation of the engagement can be guessed at. The Harzhorn overlooks from the west a major ancient thoroughfare (now the A6 autobahn), (see Plate 6). The Romans were presumably on their way back towards the empire, moving south-west along this road. The Germans would have known they were likely to come this way and set an ambush. Just opposite the Harzhorn there are more hills, the fingertips of the ancient crystalline massif of the Hartz mountains, hence the landscape causes a constriction at this point which would have forced the Romans to become strung out as they passed. The obvious tactic for the Germans would have been to conceal themselves on the heights and block the route at the far end while the army filtered into the valley. Having thus lured the Romans into a defile (perhaps not as steep as the ambushers would have liked), they would attack from both sides and inflict as much damage as possible before the invaders could get organized. Then they would fall back along the route to other prepared ambush points.

All the evidence suggests that in 9 CE, Varus was complacent on the march and walked into just such a trap, but not so Maximinus two hundred years later. Instead of marching along the valley, the Romans formed up in battle order and assaulted the western ridge, the Harzhorn. Whether a parallel battle also occurred on the eastern hill, as seems strategically likely, we do not positively know, and probably never will because that area has been subject to landslides, which would have buried much of the evidence.[11]

Aside from the historical texts, one odd fact and one eerie suggestion point to the conclusion that the Romans won the engagement. The odd fact is the lack of shoe buckles among the many small metal finds. Shed hobnails indicate substantial activity on the part of the legionaries, but dead soldiers also leave behind buckles as is the case all over the Varus battlefield. None has been found at the Harzhorn, and nor in fact have any bodies, German or Roman, although there is one dead horse in a pit. So it seems that the Romans had time to collect their wounded and recover the dead, which implies they controlled the battlefield in the immediate aftermath. Then, after they had left, the Germans would have scoured the area and cleared their own casualties, which may be why rather few German artifacts have been discovered.

Now the eerie fact: many of the bolts and arrows must have stood upright in the ground literally for years in order to preserve their orientation. Evidently the Romans were sufficiently in a hurry that no order to 'gather weapons and ammo' was given.[12] This is hardly surprising given how far they were from home and in an exposed position. But why were the arrows, bolts and spears not collected afterwards by the Germanic tribesmen when they removed the bodies? Could it be that the site remained taboo for the local people for years to come? Perhaps a German king, unknown to history, was killed on the Harzhorn, and the area was left unmolested in his memory. It is even possible that the buried horse, found at the epicentre of the fighting, was his mount.

Whether any of this speculation is along the right lines, one thing is clear: this is not the Battle of the Bog described by Herodian, which raises the intriguing possibility that the main battle site too may soon be discovered. It could lie almost anywhere in the North German plain, as far east as the Elbe or as far north as the coast. But there has to be a reasonable chance that it preceded the Harzhorn engagement by a matter of days, and hence probably occurred in the area beyond the Harzhorn, that is, the general direction from where the Roman column was marching. There are several candidate boggy areas and lakes within 40–50 kilometres, especially around and about the low-lying cities of Hannover and Brunswick. Even if such a discovery has been made by the time of writing, it would very properly be kept secret for further study so as not to attract the treasure hunters. But this should not deflect us entirely from speculation. For example (this author having toured likely spots), one area that fits the bill is the semi-enclosed drainage basin west of the medieval city of Goslar, not so far from the Harzhorn battlefield itself. This would have been a good strategic focus for the tribes to congregate and set traps in the manner described by Herodian, while maintaining escape routes to the mountains in their rear. A Roman army would not have been able to advance very far into the Saxon plain without the risk of being cut off at the Harzhorn gap by forces gathered in that area. This, then, might have been the strategic background to the great Battle of the Bog. Unfortunately the area in question is now entirely drained and managed, with two large dams and reservoirs (the Granestausee and Innertestausee) flooding what would have been the marshy areas, and little of the original landscape remains.

Grand Strategy?

These considerations finally allow us to plot the various campaigns of 235–237 on a map (Map 3). The details are, of course, necessarily tentative, but some conclusions can be drawn. The first is that each season the army probably marched well over 1,000 kilometres, perhaps as far as 1,000 Roman miles, which means it must have been on the move for much of the time, no doubt wreaking havoc as it went. It was, then, a "mobile field army", to use a phrase more often associated with later Roman marching forces.

The army has left little trace of its activities beyond the Rhine and Danube, which suggests that its purpose was punitive rather than the annexation of territory, although the goal may have been to soften up the invaded areas and gather intelligence for future wars of conquest. This much is consistent with the historical sources, such as they are. It does, however, reinforce the impression that the first consideration for planning each expedition was to define the start and end point and the distance to be covered. A major strategic limitation facing Maximinus and his commanders was that even with the budget stretched to the limit, the empire could only afford one such expedition per year.

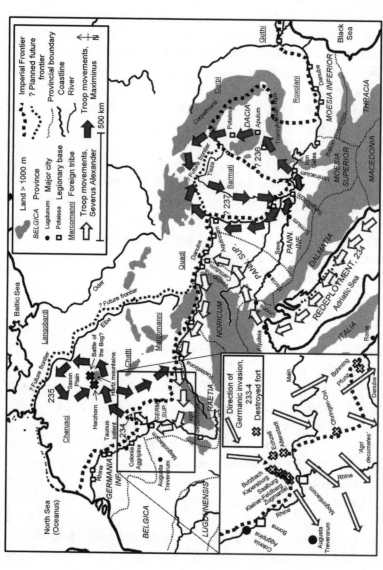

Map 3. Sketch map of campaigns on the Rhine and Danube in 234–237, with inset: the Germanic invasion of 233–234. Based mainly on Herodian, *History of the Empire* VII.2.1–9 and *Scriptores Historiae Augustae* (Julius Capitolinus), *Maximini Duo* XI.4–XIII.5, plus archaeological finds and other considerations discussed in the text. The campaigns were punitive but the ultimate strategic goal may have been to push back the imperial frontier to the Elbe–Danube–Tisza line.

What is more surprising, and is perhaps the main message of the discovery at the Harzhorn, is the degree of penetration into barbarian territory. What were the Romans doing so far from the Rhine? The area they were returning from was the heartland of tribes called (in earlier centuries) the Cherusci and (in later centuries) the Saxons. Perhaps these folk had been the main instigators of the pillage of the preceding year, thinking they were insulated from Roman reprisals by sheer distance. This interpretation puts a different complexion on the general challenge faced by the Roman empire regarding the barbarian incursions of the third and fourth centuries. It was not sufficient deterrent to cross the nominal frontier and chastise the first people encountered. The more Romanized tribes in those areas were not responsible for the destruction and had probably suffered themselves from the incursions. Such people were valuable trading partners.[13] To deliver effective retribution the Romans had to determine who was actually responsible for a given outrage and march hundreds of miles to their distant homelands, a potentially risky venture necessitating significant resources and extended supply lines.

There is a passage in Herodian hinting that Maximinus developed a more ambitious and creative strategy to protect the security of the empire. After discussing the Sarmatian campaigns, he says that Maximinus aspired to conquer "all the lands to the German Sea". The *Augustan History*, probably paraphrasing this, says "in his heart he desired to bring all the northern regions up to the Ocean under Roman sway".[14] What can this mean? The area of operations is nowhere near the German (North) Sea. But a look at a map of the empire shows that the trans-Danubian province of Dacia, conquered by Trajan for its mineral wealth over a century before, was like a large Roman salient projecting into barbarian territory, or looking at it the other way round, the flat lands between Dacia and Pannonia, roughly equivalent to eastern Hungary, western Romania and northern Serbia, constituted a large barbarian salient projecting into Roman territory. If this land could be swallowed and the border pushed back to a new east–west line that joined the great bend in the Danube at Aquincum (Budapest) to the northern border of Dacia along the heights of the Carpathians, the length of the imperial border overall would be greatly reduced, making it easier and more economical to protect. The line would have to be heavily fortified, of course, but the result would be that finally, from a Roman perspective, a fairly straight border would at last be drawn from the Black Sea to Oceanus, or the German (North) Sea.

Conquest of deep Germany, east of the Rhine and up to the Elbe, so recently reconnoitered in force during the campaign of the Battle of the Bog, may also have been on the planning board. Augustus had initially attempted just that (until cut short by the Varus catastrophe), and Marcus Aurelius had also planned something similar.[15] So perhaps Herodian's phrase, which no doubt made sense in terms of the rhetoric of the time, even points to a true grand strategy that transcended emperors and dynasties. If Maximinus could achieve these conquests, new provinces would be added to the empire for the first time in 100 years. They would add wealth, resources, and perhaps most importantly, manpower to the empire as a whole, increasing its overall strength in the same way that Ardashir had recently strengthened Persia. All prospect of a direct barbarian threat to Rome would be finally removed and of course a number of long-term tribal enemies (the Cherusci, Chatti, Marcomanni and Sarmati) would be pacified or eliminated in the process.

The excellent work done by teams of archaeologists at the Harzhorn means it is already the best-studied Roman-era battlefield in the world and the discoveries look set to go on for many years as further meticulous observations are made in surrounding areas.[16] News keeps seeping out either in the press or on blog posts of enthusiasts or, increasingly, in published reports. Unsurprisingly, by analogy with the extended reach of the Varus battlefield, new finds are cropping up away from the Harzhorn itself. The most spectacular of these is an axe-head (*dolabra*) with the inscription *leg IIII S A* on one side and *FAV* on the other, found several kilometres from the Harzhorn down the valley along with many other small finds, indicating another engagement (see Plate 8). This identifies *legio IIII flavia felix*[17] and the initials *S A* probably means *severinae alexandrinae*, or the fourth legion as reconstituted by Severus Alexander. Although that emperor had recently been killed, his initials might very well still be found on the legionary equipment. Other evidence of the involvement of the fourth legion is the tombstone of Aurelius Vitalis of that legion, mentioned previously. The fourth legion was from Singidunum (Belgrade) and may have been the one placed under Maximinus's command during the reign of Severus Alexander if the story in the *Augustan History* has any truth to it. By coincidence, the *felix* legion, symbol the lion, was the command of Russell Crowe as General Meridius in the film *Gladiator* (although there, for no apparent reason, it is '*legio III*').

Chapter VIII

Maximinus Augustus

Imperial Family

Following the victorious campaign of 235 the title *germanicus maximus* was also awarded to the emperor's son Maximus, who was probably raised to the rank of *caesar* at that time, making him a clear heir to the throne.[1] Maximus, who was about 18, had accompanied his father on campaign to learn the art of war. Coins were issued in the young *caesar's* name, some of which show him in military garb. Inscriptions dedicated to him give the traditional titles *nobilissimus* (most noble) *caesar* and *principii iuventutis* (Prince of the Youth, a title invented by the first emperor Augustus to identify a young heir to the throne). In the historical sources he is described as young and handsome and of tall stature… and quite a ladies' man if the *Augustan History* is to be believed. That work alludes to stories of his many and diverse sexual adventures but these, it says, were beneath it to report but could all be read in Cordus, which is an entertaining deception if Cordus was a fabrication as many scholars believe.

On his coins Maximus looks intelligent and commanding, if somewhat haughty. Despite being tall, Herodian tell us that he did not have his father's large frame and heavy features and this much at least is borne out by the coins.[2] If there is a resemblance, it is the penetrating gaze (Plate 9). We are told that unlike his father, Maximus was very well educated in Latin, Greek and oratory, but also that he was excessively vain, and even wont to appear in golden armour with a bejewelled shield and a gold-inlaid spear.[3] It seems difficult to imagine the gruff old man's approval of such paraphernalia.

There is a story in the *Augustan History* that Maximus was briefly betrothed to a patrician lady called Junia Fadilla, a direct descendant of Antoninus Pius. Historians treat this with suspicion like everything else that is uncorroborated in that work, but there is no reason intrinsically to dismiss it. A good marriage into an old imperial family would have been a sensible policy. A son and heir born from such a match would be the great-great-grandson of a famous old emperor as well as grandson of Maximinus. The *Augustan History* does not tell us why the wedding was called off, but it may have been at the prince's instigation because the lady was allowed to keep her betrothal gifts. These, it reports, according to the testimony of the dubious Cordus, were a necklace with nine pearls, a network cap with 11 emeralds, a bracelet with four sapphires, some gowns of gold and other items.

Maximinus's wife Paulina is known from a special posthumous issue of commemorative coins and a single inscription[4] which gives her family name Caecilia Paulina and the title *augusta*. The coins refer to her as *diva* (the divine) Paulina and show her *apotheosis*, or ascension to the heavens, aboard a flying peacock. This was the culmination of an elaborate funeral ceremony in which the body was burned on a tiered pyre from which a bird was theatrically released, symbolizing the empress's soul being carried to her place among the gods. Only emperors and empresses could be thus deified, so if the coins refer to an actual event, the implication is that Paulina was empress for a short time before she died in 235.[5] Almost nothing else is known about her except that centuries later it was claimed that she had been a positive influence on her husband.[6]

The elevation of Maximus to the rank of *caesar* and the issuing of coins in Paulina's name were normal in their own way and a very useful means of conveying propaganda to the peoples of the empire. They signalled that there was not just a new emperor in charge but a new imperial dynasty to be venerated in the many shrines that fostered the imperial cult. Perhaps most importantly the highly orthodox symbolism of the coinage showed that the ancient religion of the Romans was not being challenged by this new emperor despite his ethnicity and lowly origins. The coins all refer to the piety of the emperor and traditional religious motifs are common. Maximinus may well have been a religious man – many soldiers were – or he may simply have been using the state religion to bolster his authority. Either way the people would have been relieved that he was no new Elagabalus set to force foreign gods and peculiar customs upon them.

Times Most Flourishing?

The tiny village of Zraia in modern Algeria was once, anagrammatically, the small town of Zarai in the Roman province of Numidia. Here a dedication stone was once unearthed from 237 CE that refers to the rule of Maximinus as *florentissimum saeculum*: a most flourishing age.[7] The historical sources for this period are not as kind, and Africa it seems, in particular, was suffering. Herodian, who was now in his early sixties and probably living in Rome,[8] is still our primary witness. His description of the years 235–238 is condensed but heartfelt, and in its bitter and personal tone it is unlike anything else in his history. After a generally factual (and indeed praiseworthy) account of Maximinus's campaigning, he continues:

> So much for Maximinus's military exploits. His achievements would have won him a reputation, if he had not proved so oppressive and fearsome to his own people and his subjects. There is little point in destroying barbarians, if even more people are being murdered in Rome and the subject nations; nor in carrying off prisoners and plunder from the enemy, when the people at home are stripped bare of their possessions.
>
> Herodian, *History of the Empire* VII.3.1.

The phrase "his own people" as contrasted with "his subjects" seems to be a reference to Maximinus's barbarian ancestry, and so could be interpreted as a case of moral condemnation of the emperor's genocidal policy against his kin. It also underlines Herodian's claim, dismissed by most modern historians, that he was part-barbarian. Then:

> Informers were given complete licence, even encouragement, to damage people and stir up old troubles, if there was a chance, without the cases being heard or any real evidence. A person simply had to receive a court summons from an informer, and straight away he lost his case and his property was confiscated.
>
> Herodian, *History of the Empire* VII.3.2.

This complaint sounds so personal that it is difficult to resist the idea that someone close to Herodian was condemned at this time. He goes on:

> Men who were rich one day and beggars the next were a daily sight, so tremendous was the tyrant's greed for wealth, though he pretended he needed a continuous supply of money to pay his troops. His ears were quick to pick up charges, sparing neither a person's age or position. Many men in posts of trust in the provinces and the army, who had held the honorable office of consul or earned the distinction of a triumph, he caused to be whisked away on some trifling, petty charge. Orders were issued that they should be put in a carriage on their own, without any attendants, and brought to him, travelling night and day from East or West, as the case might be, or from the South to Pannonia where he was staying. Then, after tormenting and insulting them, he punished them with death or exile.
>
> Herodian, *History of the Empire* VII.3.3–5.[9]

The detail that men were summoned on the long journey without attendants (household slaves) is suggestive of some direct testimony. Although Herodian's account is condensed, he does not seem to be describing here the initial purge of those men most loyal to Alexander, because Maximinus is located in Pannonia. It reads rather more like an indictment of the whole period up to 238. But we have already seen, with the plot of Magnus, that Maximinus had good reason to fear conspiracy and treason. He may have felt that the only way to retain power, and hence his life, from his base afar was to rule by terror.[10] From the point of view of the tyrant, repression can produce security through fear, but it can also foment unrest. It is a dangerous strategy, but history shows it can be sustained more or less indefinitely, if vigorously pursued. One thing is certain: Rome had seen these kinds of purges many times before. It is a recurring theme from the days of the Republic onwards and, incidentally, the main reason why it is very difficult to trace the senatorial families through the centuries. But in Herodian's time the most recent senatorial purges had been decades ago in the reigns of Caracalla and Elagabalus, allowing the ruling class to develop a certain feeling of security and continuity.

Despite the treason trials, Maximinus was not engaged in a revolution of government or destruction of the entire senatorial class. He probably dissolved the cabinet of advisers set up by Mamaea, but the offices of state continued to function normally, and wealthy senators who remained in the clear continued to be elected to the highest office, including that of *consul*. A detailed analysis of Maximinus's appointments to consular honours and provincial governorships reveals nothing unusual.[11] Many men who had been given high office under Alexander remained in their posts. Wealthy and ambitious senators were encouraged to adapt to the new realities and some of them no doubt found this very easy. Maximinus might have found genuine support from far and wide among those men who agreed that running the empire required a firm hand. Although Herodian, in the account relayed above, is sceptical that he needed the money for his wars, this may just reflect personal disgruntlement. The emperor still had a large mobile army to support as well as regular troops stationed across the empire and he needed to reward them for their loyalty. Plunder from the campaigns in *barbaricum* would not have produced great riches. If, as seems likely, Alexander's decision to pay off the Germans had been partly a financial calculation to avoid the expense of keeping such a large army together, the situation can only have become more critical in the succeeding years, as Maximinus refused to scale down the military operation.

One thing that Maximinus did not do was reduce the silver content of the currency, nor did he reintroduce the despised double-denarius of Caracalla. He may have been advised that in the long term the effects of such a move would be counter-productive to the economy by driving inflation (as had occurred under Caracalla and also proved to be the case later on). Perhaps a more immediate reason for maintaining the quality of the coinage was that in the hands of the ordinary people his image on the silver epitomized his personal prestige, and his position was still insecure despite repeated military victories.

Nevertheless the financial situation deteriorated and we are told that Maximinus resorted to other ways of raising money, including stripping public buildings of their gold and silver adornments and turning it into coin. Such an activity was expected in times of desperation – Athens had famously done this to finance its war against Sparta – but not in the ordinary course of events. On the frontier, where the emperor surveyed his frightful opponents across rivers and marshes, the sense of danger may have seemed imminent and the need for cash overwhelming but in more settled, distant places, with the border seemingly now secure, this move was sure to provoke outrage. Even more so was the decision to extend the order to encompass the temples across the empire. Religious buildings were a particularly rich source of money for the treasury because they contained many precious statues and dedications that had been left for the glory of the gods by private citizens, supposedly for all time.

The regime tried to spin its policy with an appeal to the common good. Men were dying on the frontier and the whole empire needed to resist the combined pressure of the uncivilized tribes and the Persians. But commandeering religious donatives must have caused deep dismay and indignation across a much wider population than was felt by just purging the rich. Herodian tells us that such moves were sometimes violently opposed; ordinary people refused to allow some provincial temples to be looted, leading to rioting. They improvised guards at the shrines and sometimes paid with their lives in the name of their gods. Soldiers found themselves being criticized by their own families for their part in despoiling the temples.[12] Naturally enough, people began praying to the injured gods for revenge, whether Jupiter, Isis, Mithras or Jesus Christ.

Turbulent Priests

Christianity had grown steadily through the first and second centuries and by the time of Maximinus there may have been about a million adherents (or about 1 per cent of the empire's population).[13] Most concentrations were in the east, but there were also well-developed communities in many of the western cities including Rome. By this time the religion was well organized into dioceses with bishops at their head, between whom there was much intercommunication on doctrinal matters which were not, however, very settled. The bishops of Rome were trying to assert some sort of primacy in church affairs based on their claim that the disciple Peter had founded the Roman church on Jesus's specific instruction. But the Roman Christians were themselves in a state of doctrinal schism, very much a foretaste of things to come. The current issue at dispute was whether the 'Word of God' (*logos*), as central to John's Gospel, and 'God the Father' were one and the same. The official bishop of Rome, Pontianus (or Pontian), held that they were, but another influential bishop called Hippolytus comprehensively rejected this view and set himself up as a rival pope, gathering a significant following in the process.

It is worth digressing for a moment on Hippolytus. His chief legacy today is that he was the first person to propose the date of 25th December for the birth of Jesus based on his interpretation of prophecies in the Book of Daniel. But despite, then, having a claim to be the original Father Christmas, he was not a cuddly character. As befits someone whose name means 'a horse turned loose', he was a true firebrand, constantly and graphically predicting the imminent end of the world, and warning all heretics (by which he seems to have meant anyone who disagreed with him) to expect the boiling flood of hell's eternal lake of fire to engulf them, and so on. But he did have another side: his writings show he thought a lot about the contentions of others, including ancient and foreign thinkers. His principal surviving work is the magnificently hubristic *Refutation of All Heresies*, in which he violently condemned not only Pontianus's Roman church but almost everyone else. His principal target was gnostic Christianity, at that time thriving in the east of the empire; he called the gnostics mere 'plagiarists' (a term he himself seemingly invented) of the Greek philosophers and so not true Christians at all.[14] Others who attracted his ire included astrologers and magicians, jugglers, the scribes of Egypt, the Brahmins of India and the Druids of Britain, all of whom would suffer an eternity of torment. Paradoxically, in refuting all their beliefs, he did us the invaluable service of preserving some of them by actually writing them down in a context that later Christian censors would pass fit for further copy.[15]

The doctrinal wrangling between the Christian intellectuals regarding their acceptance, or not, of ancient Greek philosophy had been going on for years and Maximinus evidently decided to put a stop to it. Perhaps, as it was later claimed, Maximinus was biased against all Christians because they had been associated with Alexander's regime and had been supported by Mamaea.[16] Possibly the schism was affecting morale among the Osrhoenian archers and other Christians in his army. So in one of his first acts as emperor he ordered pope and antipope alike to be banished to the silver mines of Sardinia so that they might continue their dispute underground. A poignant church record shows that Pontianus formally resigned his pontificate on 28 September 235 so that another could take his place in Rome. (He was the first pope to resign, setting a precedent cited in 2013 by the infirm Benedict XVI on his own resignation.) The mines were hard places, worked manually by slaves and prisoners, and would have been especially merciless for old men of letters. Both Pontianus and Hippolytus were dead within weeks "as a result of inhuman treatment and privations". The Christian annal, the *liber pontificalis* (book of popes),[17] tells us that Pontianus died on 30 October after having been beaten with clubs, but church tradition maintains that there was, after all, a subterranean theological reconciliation wherein Hippolytus returned to the true church and instructed his followers to do the same. This was of course very convenient for the Church of Rome. The following year the bones of both men were quietly brought back to the city for burial and both were henceforth regarded as saints and martyrs by the Catholic church. From the point of view of Maximinus, the supposed reconciliation of the Christians was a policy success.

From the earliest times the two martyrs shared a feast day on the Ides (13th) of August, one of relatively few original saints' days as recorded in the oldest list of holy days, the *Chronography of 354*. By medieval times Pontianus's feast had been moved to 19th November but fittingly, at the Second Vatican Council in 1969, it was decided to move it back to August so that once again he would share it with Hippolytus.[18] The *Chronography of 354* also records that the two men were buried in different catacombs, Pontianus on the *via appia* and Hippolytus on the *via tiburtina*. Satisfyingly, an ancient statue of Hippolytus was found in a tomb on the Tiburtina in 1551 and is now on display at the Vatican, and Pontianus's tomb was rediscovered in the Catacomb of Callixtus on the Appian Way in 1909.

The book of popes records that Pontianus's successor, Anteros, was pope for just one month and 12 days and was martyred "at the time when Maximin[us] and Africanus were consuls" (i.e. in 236). The timing doesn't quite add up unless Anteros had also been forced to resign and was later killed. But the man who followed him (Fabianus) was unmolested thereafter, holding office for 14 years. Interestingly, it is Fabianus who is recorded in the book of popes as having brought back Pontianus's body to Rome (and presumably that of Hippolytus at the same time, although it doesn't specifically say so). Therefore it seems likely that it was Fabianus who brokered the reconciliation of the two factions in Rome, and in so doing brought the church back into harmony.[19] Anteros may have copped it for unwisely continuing the bickering.

There is evidence that other prominent church figures also suffered death or banishment in 235. For example, a work by Origen (a man we have already met when he was summoned to explain Christianity to the empress Julia Mamaea and who, incidentally, had just been excommunicated by Pontianus), entitled *Exhortation to Martyrdom*, was written in Caesarea in Palestine during the purges of that year. It is dedicated to two of Origen's colleagues who had just been executed: Ambrose, a very wealthy and learned gentleman and deacon of the church at Alexandria, and Protoctetus, a priest of Caesarea. Why Origen himself was spared by the authorities is not explained. Possibly the turmoil was related to the edict of the stripping of the temples, as related by Herodian, in which case we must deduce that the early Christian churches would have had precious objects worth protecting (gold chalices, perhaps?). The *Exhortation* is frustratingly short on factual details and long on the supposed joys of martyrdom, that pernicious doctrine, but a few historical tidbits can be discerned. For instance:

> I pray that... in the presence of the tribunals and of the naked swords drawn against our necks they may be guarded by the peace of God... What greater joy there can be than the act of martyrdom? A great multitude is assembled to watch the last hours of the martyr. And let each of us remember how many times we have been in danger of an ordinary death, and then let us ask ourselves whether we have not been preserved for something better, for the baptism in blood which washes away our sins and allows us to take our place at the heavenly altar.
>
> Origen, *Exhortation to Martyrdom*, 39.

So the executions were public. An interesting feature of this work that foreshadows the medieval cults of the saints is that martyrs were attributed special powers of interceding with God through prayers directed to them, and they also protected against evil: "The voluntary death of one righteous man for the community will avert by expiation evil demons who cause plagues or famines or tempests at sea." The bones of the martyrs were surreptitiously exhumed and brought into the churches. Origen himself repeatedly stressed his own intense desire for the martyr's fate[20] and that the reward in heaven would be proportionally greater for all the possessions left behind (which, if we are charitable, may just help explain contemporaneous reports that he was angry to have been cut out of the rich man Ambrose's will!).

More evidence of persecution comes from a surviving letter from Firmilian, the bishop of Caesarea in Cappadocia (now Kayseri in Turkey) to Cyprian, the bishop of Carthage.[21] The letter was written in 256 but refers back to events following the time of the emperor Alexander, when one Serenianus, a "bitter and terrible persecutor", was provincial governor there. Inscriptions identify this man as Licinius Serenianus, appointed by Maximinus as governor of Cappadocia in 235–236, so perhaps he was one after the emperor's own heart.[22] There had been a series of earthquakes in the province including the destruction of unnamed cities, and the Christians were blamed for this, sparking the persecution. Interestingly, Firmilian's letter goes on to describe the exorcism of a demon from a 'prophetess' who had the temerity to baptize people and celebrate the Eucharist: an early example of a woman priest.

Despite these events, historians have concluded that Maximinus did not order a general crackdown against Christians in the empire in 235–236. Indeed Firmilian states that the persecution in Cappadocia was "not over the whole world, but local", so that many in the Christian community were able to escape it by fleeing the province. The fourth-century history of Sulpicius Severus simply states that Maximinus persecuted the clerics of some churches.[23] Christians were convenient scapegoats for natural disasters, but so long as they kept the peace and conformed to imperial policy, the leading churchmen of the day seemed to have been permitted to continue as normal across much of the empire, and the cult continued to flourish.

Imperial Businesss

Neither Herodian nor the author or authors of the *Augustan History* was interested in reporting the day-to-day workings of government, so evidence for it under Maximinus is hard to come by. The fact that even three years into his rule he had not set foot in Rome does not necessarily imply a neglect of civic duties because other rulers before had spent long periods at war or on tour. Rome had a city prefect appointed by the emperor who could make decisions in his absence, and it seems Maximinus had also stationed a praetorian prefect, Vitalianus, there as his personal representative and the highest civilian authority.[24] From across the empire there are scattered inscriptions, papyri, and the like that record local events and building works but they do not add up to much of a general picture except that there seems to have been a large amount of road building. Evidence for this comes from an abundance of milestones bearing the name and titles of the emperor. In particular there are many such milestones from the provinces of Hispania and Africa, which were far from the front line, possibly hinting at some crisis in olive oil production in those areas. It seems this effort was more about maintenance and renovation than laying down new routes. Improving the arteries of commerce would also have improved the economy, of course, but only in the long run.[25]

The only other source of information on the government that survives are copies of so-called imperial rescripts (formal replies to legal issues from petitioners from across the empire) issued on behalf of the emperor, and signed off by him, and then kept on the public record. Many of these were collated in the sixth century during the reign of the early Byzantine emperor Justinian I (in the *codex iustinianus*, Code of Justinian). This work is a fundamental building block of so-called 'Roman Law' that profoundly influenced medieval law across Christendom and, by descent, modern law in many parts of the world. Unfortunately just three rescripts from the period survive, one from 235 and the others from 236. For later years there is nothing, which is not in itself surprising, as much of the third century legal record is missing. The paucity of rescripts (especially compared to Severus Alexander) might be evidence of neglect, but even three in the first two years is more than some other emperors managed. Perhaps one reason for the small number of rescripts is that emperors of the period may not have processed legal requests while on campaign.[26]

But since we have them, we might as well look at what they say, if only to get a glimpse of jurisprudence at the time. The first is dated to 13 August 235 is the most enlightening in that it seems to confirm sweeping legal powers for the praetorian prefect:[27]

> The same emperor to Restitutianus: If a rule made by the praetorian prefect is general, and not contrary to the law or constitutions, and no innovation has been subsequently made therein by my authority, it should be treated as valid.
>
> *Codex Iustinianus* 1.26.2.

This may have been part of Maximinus's attempt to delegate much of his civil authority to his prefect in Rome[28] after some controversy over the legal extent of his powers, possibly related to the fallout from the Magnus plot. The date indicates that it was possibly made just before the army began its campaign in Germany in 235. It might be the day that Maximinus signed off the law, or more likely it was the date that it was entered into the books in Rome. Anyway, the ruling seems to have remained in force until Byzantine times. The other two rescripts relate to specific points of law that evidently needed clarification, for reasons that are lost in the mists of time, one with respect to the relationship between a collateral agreement relating to a separate, binding, contract (lawyers everywhere love this kind of thing), and the other with respect to property ownership in a case about a dowry. Here they are:

> Emperor Maximinus to Marinus: In the case of equitable (bonae fidei) contracts an action arises on a pact made[29] in connection therewith only if

the pact is made as part of the same transaction; for whatever is agreed on thereafter, gives rise not to a claim but to a defence only.

Codex Iustinianus 2.13.3.

Emperor Maximus (sic) to Sulpicius. Your grandmother, who gave a dowry for your daughter, could, although no stipulation was entered into, transmit to you, if you became her heir, a right of action on the simple agreement made concerning the dowry. For the cause of action on the agreement of the mother and of the father is not the same, since the agreement with the mother gives rise to an action on the special facts; but, it is believed that the father's right of action which he has by reason of a dowry, given to him out of his own property, cannot be changed by a simple contract.

Codex Iustinianus 5.12.6.

These last two cases were probably passed up the legal chain to the highest court of appeal, but it is difficult to imagine Maximinus himself taking an interest in such issues: almost certainly the rescripts are the work of top legal officials in the imperial service.[30]

Maximinus may not have been much concerned with legal minutiae and the daily tasks of administering his empire but he did know one thing: the military job on the Danube was still not complete. As the new consular year of 238 began, the emperor and his advisers were no doubt considering their campaigning options. At the same time reports probably began to arrive telling of a new threat on the Persian front. Ardashir, it seems, had licked his wounds and was now re-mobilizing and ready to take on the Roman Empire once more. Confronted by these developments the very last thing the military council would have wanted was news of serious insurrection *within* the empire, and from a totally unexpected quarter.

Chapter IX

Provok'd Rebellion

African Spring

Of the several cities that vied with each other for the claim to be the second of the empire, Carthage (now located in a suburb of Tunis) was one. Arguably no war in all of human history quite compares for tenacity with that fought between the two cities in the third and second centuries BCE (if a series of wars and dubious peace treaties spanning over a hundred years can be styled as one conflict). It was a case of two emerging superpowers, arranged along very different lines and with irreconcilable cultures, both intent on controlling the lucrative trade of the Mediterranean and its hinterlands by force of arms: Rome on the Italian peninsula, and Carthage, not so far away on the adjacent coast of North Africa. Like evenly matched prize-fighters who would not give up, both sides suffered almost intolerable losses by sea and land only to keep hitting back. For the Romans a series of catastrophic defeats culminated in the virtual obliteration of their army at the hands of Hannibal, with the deaths of about 50,000 men on a single day at the Battle of Cannae in 216 BCE. But after unbelievable privation and endurance the Romans finally achieved total victory, venting their fury by utterly destroying the city of Carthage, enslaving all survivors, and symbolically sowing its surrounding fields with salt so that it could never be re-established.[1]

But even the Romans could not destroy the wonderful strategic location of Carthage or its excellent natural harbours and so the city grew once again, this time as a Roman vassal. Inevitably, and despite the proscriptions, traces of its old Phoenician (or Punic, to use the Roman adjective) culture and language re-emerged. By the third century, Carthage and the other great Roman cities of North Africa were fully integrated into the empire and, far from the barbarian frontiers, they were among its most secure and peaceful quarters. The only military threat was from Numidian tribesmen and bandits to the south and west, but the great desert wasteland that intervened ensured there would never be anything like the external pressure that was being felt along the Rhine and Danube or in the eastern provinces. Testament to this pacific situation was that there was no permanent legion stationed in the entire province of Africa (which, it should be emphasized, corresponds to just a small fragment of the modern continent of the same name, corresponding to modern Tunisia, plus eastern Algeria and western Libya). There were just a few local units to protect the desolate border and police the big cities. For this reason, governance remained in the hands of the senate rather than the emperor.

The province of Africa was in its ascendancy in the early third century. Vast fortunes were being accrued by the nobility while the arts, law and scholarship flourished. Africa had prospered in particular under Septimius Severus who came from Lepcis Magna along the coast and rewarded his home province with many great buildings and public works. The African nobility had enjoyed new levels of prominence around the empire under his dynasty. Men of the senatorial class were required to journey to Rome to further their public careers and also to invest part of their fortune in Italy, stipulations that helped bind the interests of Rome and Africa. Business was good: Africa supplied grain, olive oil and slaves to Rome as well as figs and pomegranates and luxury items such as ivory, gold, ornamental stone, sponges, and exotic wild animals for the circus. Irrigation was widespread and better organized than at any other time in history. Money, and the many other fruits of the empire, flowed the other way, in large quantities. With a consistent trade surplus, Africa was a province on the make, and the top men became so rich they hardly knew what to do with their wealth.

Not everyone prospered under this system of course: the slaves and serfs suffered under the yoke as they did everywhere else, perhaps more so because there was a large concentration of industrial-scale farms (*latifundia*) growing cash crops for the overseas market. These great estates can be thought of as historical forerunners of the cotton plantations of the American south. They existed to supply an insatiable demand and were run for profit by a dandy elite on the backs of the hard labour and short lives of the many people they owned.

The accession of Maximinus must have been wholly unwelcome news to the nobility of Africa. All pretence that the incumbent emperor was descended from Severus the African was now at an end. Rumour had it that Maximinus was a semi-barbarian peasant who had mostly avoided the *cursus honorum*, the very system that cemented such provincial elites into the hierarchy of the empire. The first wave of purges could have affected some of the African families. Then, by staying with his armies and shunning Rome, Maximinus also effectively snubbed the whole empire. Unfavourable tales of the behaviour of the haughty young prince Maximus would hardly have generated much optimism for the future. On the other hand, in these early years of the reign, the potential for a counter-coup remained high, and perhaps there were many who hoped that the emperor might very well be killed leading one of his reckless charges against the northern barbarians. If Maximinus was able to protect the distant frontier while business remained good at home, perhaps the situation was tolerable.

But the constant need for money to fund the ongoing campaigning meant that Africa began to be directly affected. Support of the imperial army must, by necessity, be borne by higher taxation of the peaceful districts as had happened many times before, but Maximinus seems to have gone further than his predecessors in his rapacity. The decision to confiscate public funds earmarked for games and festivals could hardly have been calculated to gain broad support.[2] Then the edict to strip the precious metals and dedications of the public buildings and temples of the whole empire may have been especially resented in the rich and peaceful provinces. Of more direct impact on the local economy was a sharp increase in the oil and corn levy, the tax in kind that Rome exacted to maintain the supply to the capital (*annonna*) and its armies (the *annonna militaris*). It has been suggested that extensive upgrading of the African road infrastructure at this time was conducted to allow more efficient passage of the grain wagons.[3] What had started under Alexander as a military emergency was turning into a permanent state of affairs in which the wealth of the empire was being sucked into the military machine on the Danube, with rich Africa being milked for all it was worth.

Bad as this might have seemed, the situation in the province deteriorated further with the appointment of an especially harsh procurator of a kind that crops up repeatedly in Roman history. Procurators were senior imperial agents effectively independent of the senate and with a range of sweeping powers to facilitate their work, including taking military command when necessary. This man's role in Africa would have been to directly oversee the emperor's personal estates and liaise with the senatorial governor to ensure prompt execution of imperial dictat. We do not know his name, but Herodian tells us that he was wont to exact 'absolutely savage' sentences and confiscations from the people in the hope of being noticed by the emperor and promoted to higher positions.[4] The *Augustan History* suggests he went further in his depredations than even Maximinus would have allowed, by repeatedly issuing death sentences and banishments on the flimsiest evidence.[5]

Because it was a senatorial province, the actions of the procurator produced a confused chain of command. The governor at the time was an old man named Marcus Antonius Gordianus Sempronianus, or Gordian as he is known. He had been appointed several years previously and was, supposedly, beloved by the populace. Gordian was no ordinary man: he was reputedly the richest private citizen of the entire empire, owning more extensive estates than anyone but the emperor himself. Of noble birth, he did what Roman patricians had done for centuries to gain the approbation of the people: he funded major public works and lavish spectacles. His great gift to the people was just then approaching completion: a huge amphitheatre to rival any except Rome's Colosseum, with seating for over 30,000 spectators. Carthage had had an amphitheatre for about a hundred years but this new construction would eclipse even that. The building survives more or less intact in the twenty-first century despite an Ottoman-era cannonade and is one of the most spectacular of all Roman remains (Plate 10).[6] No doubt the populace were eagerly looking forward to the inaugural games, which would be famous throughout the empire, if they would be allowed in this time of enforced austerity.

The stadium was in the city of Thysdrus about 175 kilometres from Carthage. Just as Carthage styled itself the second city of the empire, so Thysdrus claimed to be the second city of Africa. Situated conveniently at a great road intersection, the city had enjoyed a prolonged boom time through the early third century.[7] Surrounded by huge *latifundia* estates, it was a major centre of olive production and therefore an integral part of the imperial economy. Olive oil was one of the empire's most important tradable commodities: apart from its use in cooking, medicine and cosmetics, it was the only major source of domestic and public lighting, fuelling the ubiquitous clay lamps that flickered in cities, towns and hamlets all across the empire after dark.

In early 238 tensions were running high because it was time to arrange collection of the annual oil levy. An increase in the demand for shipments to the army, possibly coming from Maximinus himself, would have been much resented because this was a tax-in-kind and so it was not paid for. Both the hated procurator and the popular provincial governor, Gordian, were present in the city to ensure compliance. There was no love lost between these two men, and the atmosphere of discord was quite probably exacerbated by additional friction between these agents of government and the city merchants, landed aristocracy, and ordinary people. The rumour was that Gordian had been trying to restrain the procurator's measures and the latter had retaliated by threatening the governor himself.[8] It is perhaps understandable that such a wealthy man as Gordian would have come into conflict with a rapacious procurator at a time of general belt-tightening. Tension in the chain of command between governor and procurator was not unknown: the jurist Ulpian himself had recently ruled that although the governor was the prime representative of the emperor in a province, he also had to respect the independent authority of the procurator.[9]

The imperial agent had ambitions beyond taxing olive oil to the limit. While in Thysdrus he managed to bring about a major prosecution that involved several young men from some of Africa's richest and most noble families. The fact that the prosecution was directed specifically at young men from several different families suggests that whatever they were accused of, it was in some way in association. That the death penalty was not demanded indicates that it was not an accusation of treason. Lesser charges of black magic, impiety or debauchery could easily be manufactured using paid informers.[10] In the prevailing climate of the day, a guilty verdict was certain whatever the truth of the matter. Even so, the men would have had the right to defend themselves in the courts and the progress of the trial would have made big news in the province and possibly further afield. Despite the publicity, gossip and intrigue, the trial wound eventually to its inevitable verdict and sentence was pronounced: all the young men were fined huge sums of money and ordered to surrender their estates to the emperor (which meant of course that the estates would pass to the direct control of the procurator himself). To the convicted, this sentence entailed not only financial catastrophe but social ruin. Membership of the senatorial or equestrian classes had financial stipulations. Stripped of their wealth and estates, the aristocrats could no longer hope for advancement in Rome, or perhaps even to hold up their heads in public again.

Gordian's Knot

The 'opulent youths' as Gibbon described them – we do not know how many there were but the story implies no more than about a dozen – were granted three days to find the money. But instead of acquiescing to the court's demands they privately vowed revenge, summoning to their cause their many dependants and all those who had already suffered under the procurator, plus other sympathizers who feared they might be next in line. There was substantial support. Assembling agricultural workers from the estates around the city, they stole into town at night with axes and clubs concealed. The condemned men themselves went to the procurator ostensibly to discuss payment of their fines only to spring upon him and stab him to death. The mob from the countryside easily disarmed those few soldiers stationed in Thysdrus that might have resisted. As the residents awoke it became clear that one of the empire's significant cities was in a state of dangerous rebellion.

If any of the plotters held the idealistic view that they might be able to appeal for justice and clemency to the imperial administration they must soon have realized that a line had been crossed: the only way now to save their lives and property was to turn the situation into a full-scale insurrection against

Maximinus, with the hope that military support would be forthcoming from other equally disgruntled parts of the empire. The *Augustan History* gives us a name for the leader of the enterprise – a man called Mauritius – who summoned the town council, of which he was a decurion (senior councillor), to a meeting at his estate. The first step was to try to bring Carthage into the rebellion, including the provincial administration appointed by the senate.

Mauritius will remain forever in the shadows of history, but the man now thrust by fortune to the centre of events was the distinguished old provincial governor himself. According to the *Augustan History*, Gordian had held the consulship twice during his earlier career, although this assertion has not been confirmed by any known inscription. Indeed historians have struggled to trace the details of his life. Herodian tells us that he had held many provincial commands and proved his ability by "important achievements", but no more. Inscriptional evidence suggests that he served as governor of Britannia Inferior in Eboracum (York) in 216, a few years after the dubious peace with the north Britons had been concluded on the death of Severus. After that stint, there is evidence that places him as governor, and then suffect consul, of one of the Greek provinces, Achaia (a suffect consul was replacement for a man who had died in office).[11]

The account in the *Augustan History*, which may have been derived from the lost work of Dexippus or could be bogus, has him descended on his mother's (Ulpia Gordiana's) side from the emperor Trajan, and via his father's (Maecius Marullus's) from the ancient line of the Gracchi.[12] This was nobility indeed, because there were many previous consuls on both sides of the family. As a young man he is supposed to have written poetry, including a versified account of the reigns of Marcus Aurelius and Antoninus Pius: some of his early poetry could supposedly still be found in the libraries at the time of writing. The *Augustan History* also says, perhaps more reliably, that he owned the 'House of Pompey', a famous palace on the Esquiline Hill in Rome that was originally built by Pompey the Great;[13] and moreover that in that house, mosaics depicting Gordian's wild beast shows could still be seen a century or more later.

Whether or not any of that is true, Gordian's family background was certainly wealthy and it seems likely he rose to high military office and possibly the consulship with Caracalla in 213. There is some suggestion he was a friend of Caracalla's mother, and Severus's wife, the matriarch Julia Domna. A philosopher, Philostratus of Athens, had dedicated his *Lives of the Sophists* to him,[14] which may tally with his intellectual credentials as described in the *Augustan History*. Exactly which other offices he may have held is, in some ways, immaterial: the fact is, he was a senior senator of consular status at the end of a long and distinguished career. This means he must have had significant property holdings in Rome and Italy and, just as importantly, a network of contacts in the highest circles and patronage across the empire. The ancient texts agree he was a true-blood Roman and we have no reason to doubt that evaluation.

According to Herodian the plotters deliberated all morning before marching with the mob on the governor's residence in Thysdrus at mid-day, with the object of proclaiming him emperor. Perhaps the intervening hours were taken up with patching together an imperial cloak from purple cloth taken from military standards. Gordian was about 80,[15] which is an excessively advanced age for the period. Evidently he had not been alerted to the events of the night before, for he was resting on a couch when the young men, led by Mauritius and backed by the mob, burst in brandishing their weapons and threw the purple cloak about his shoulders. Gordian dropped at their feet and begged for mercy, not knowing the reason for the uprising.

Herodian informs us that one of the young nobles was famed for his rhetorical skills. This was very convenient of course, because he was to step forward and deliver one of the historian's set pieces (these speeches, by the way, are best imagined being declaimed aloud as they were intended):

> There are two risks you face, one here, the other in the future; one clearly predictable, the other open to the vagaries of chance. You must choose today whether you are to be safe with us and put your trust in the brighter prospects we all believe in, or whether you are going to die now at our hands. If you choose safety now, we have plenty of advantages to make us optimistic – the universal unpopularity of Maximinus, the desire to be rid of a cruel tyranny, the reputation of your past record, your celebrated name among the senate and people of Rome and your long distinguished position of honour. But, if you refuse to join us, then this day will be your last, even though we have to die ourselves. For we have undertaken a deed of daring that needs a still greater act of desperation. The servant of the tyrant has been struck down, paying the penalty for his cruelty by his murder at our hands. If you join us as a partner in our risks, your own reward will be the office of emperor, and we shall be praised, not punished for the deed we propose to do.
>
> Herodian, *History of the Empire* VII.5.5–6.

With the guards overpowered there was little the old man could do but bow to these demands. Besides, Herodian adds the believable psychological detail that "being now an extremely old man, he did not find the prospect of a possible death while holding imperial honours such a terrible thing".[16] Having prospered under Severus Alexander, Gordian probably shared his class's antipathy to the upstart soldier-emperor Maximinus. Perhaps he saw himself as destined by fate to dispose of a hated and feared tyrant for the glory of Rome, like some latter-day Brutus. The date, according to the most likely chronology, was around 22 March, three years to the day since Maximinus had been proclaimed emperor in the fortress of Mogontiacum on the German frontier.[17] But it would of course take some time before the news penetrated back across the empire: a precious breathing space that Gordian must use to his advantage.

Res Publica Replica

So Gordian illegally, albeit necessarily for his own skin, claimed the usual honours associated with *imperium*: the tribunician power, the high priesthood, the consulship and the title *pater patriae*. This was, by now, following a well-trodden path for provincial usurpers, although what the senate in Rome would make of it was another matter. Gordian's son, also called Marcus Antonius Gordianus, was with his father serving as legate. He was also proclaimed *augustus* by the rebels and consequently is known to history as Gordian II.

The elevation of the younger man to the highest office was a sensible move because his father was so excessively old he could not lead the troops in battle and, people must have realized, might die at any time leaving a power vacuum. Both men were given the title *africanus* in patriotic celebration of the nearly bloodless takeover of the province and in conscious emulation of the famous general Scipio Africanus who had achieved fine victories for the Romans in the Punic Wars. The elder Gordian seems also to have taken the name *romanus* – the Roman – that at least is evident from some of his inscriptions, and it has been suggested that this was to contrast his patriotism and nobility with the semi-barbarian Maximinus.

Striding on to the world stage at this moment, the younger Gordian was about 45 years old. Not much is known about him to this point but coins reveal one detail: unlike his father he had a receding hairline, which is quite possible as the gene for male pattern baldness can be inherited through the maternal line. According to the potted biography in the *Augustan History* he was a genial and intelligent man and, like his father, a diligent servant of the state. He was something of a scholar, with an envied library of 65,000 books. And he was also a great lover of women. He did not marry, but instead chose to keep a house of concubines with whom he fathered many illegitimate children, which led him to be called the Priam of his age after the legendary king of Troy who fathered

50 sons, although the vulgar jested it would be better to call him the Priapus of his age after the ever-erect god of male fertility.[18]

The two Gordians spent the first few days in Thysdrus drawing up a plan of action and monitoring the local response. Early indications were good: the urban cohorts (armed police force) of Carthage pledged their support as the entire area rose in revolt and all the dedications to Maximinus were torn down and his inscriptions were erased by the excited populace. Archaeological evidence confirms that the insurrection spread quickly throughout the province and included the great cities of Tripolitanea (including Lepcis Magna, birthplace of Septimius Severus, in modern Libya).[19] Then, confident of a joyous welcome in Carthage, the Gordians entered that great city with all the pomp of an imperial procession, led by the senior man surrounded by a bodyguard "chosen from the tallest young men" and supported by the urban cohorts. Marks of imperial distinction included Gordian's purple robe and laurel wreath. A ceremonial fire was carried before him, and attendants called lictors carried the *fasces* garlanded with laurel (this object was a bundle of sticks and an axe used on ceremonial occasions symbolizing the power to punish, and is root of the modern word 'fascist'; when garlanded with laurel it was indicative of the emperor himself). The crowds ecstatically acclaimed the Gordians as emperors and their saviours from tyranny (and taxes, some might have coughed). Herodian tells us that for a time Carthage became a "replica of Rome", although one obvious thing was missing: anything resembling a regular army.[20]

Apart from the urban cohorts, the nearest concentration of imperial troops was a single legion (*legio III augusta*), together with auxiliaries, stationed in Numidia to the west under the control of the governor of that province, a man called Capelianus. Gordian knew that the Numidian soldiers would be useful in any future struggles, especially should an army have to be taken overseas to contest Italy with Maximinus. So as one of his first decisive acts, he dispatched a delegation to relieve Capelianus of his command, led by a loyal replacement. Depending on the wind, the journey by sea could take several days.

After the ceremonials, still more urgent action was needed. The Gordians might be figureheads for an empire-wide rebellion but it was obvious that somebody else was going to have to provide most of the muscle. So the *de novo* emperors used their only other weapon: the pen. Letters, highly treasonable of course, went out to their contacts all over the empire and presumably anyone else that they thought might be persuaded to provide support. The content of these letters can be guessed at: the reluctance of the elder Gordian's accession would be mentioned; his illustrious and loyal career in the service of Rome, the senate and its people over more years than virtually anyone else could recall;

the depredations of the impious barbarian Maximinus and his desecration of holy sites; and perhaps the glory and deserved divinity of the great emperor Severus Alexander, so cruelly murdered by his own treacherous general on the point of victory. Herodian gives us some rather more prosaic details: the Gordians promised great restraint and clemency, exile for informers and retrials for all those unjustly condemned – and, the clincher – a larger cash handout to the troops than had ever before been granted by any emperor on his accession.

Some historians, spurning the simple story given by Herodian, have speculated that the rebellion in Thysdrus must have been premeditated in Rome and carefully planned, with Gordian in on the plot from the beginning.[21] But apart from the inherent plausibility of Herodian's narrative, there is one significant fact that argues strongly against any planning, namely, the timing. With the rebellion occurring in March, the news would be bound to reach Maximinus on the frontier about a month later, perhaps a little less. At this time the army of the Danube, composed of war-hardened veterans renowned for their merciless campaigning, would still be in winter quarters, thoroughly rested, retrained and re-equipped. Surely a planned African coup would have been conducted in high summer, with the main army remote and engaged in barbarian country, depleted, tired and under fire. In fact, the timing could not have been any worse.

Chapter X

The Noble and the Brave

Assassins

The Gordians knew that the key to their rebellion would be Rome and, in particular, its senate, who would be forced to choose between the widely despised but legitimate emperor and the dubious claimant from Africa. The elder Gordian was well known of course, and of impeccable aristocratic descent. If the senate could be persuaded to back him, then it had the power to summon military assistance from all over the empire to engage in civil war. If, on the other hand, it declared Gordian a public enemy, then there was no option but suicide for the plotters. The Gordians knew that the senators, presented with this dilemma, would have no time to dither. Half-measures would surely be interpreted as treason by Maximinus, and another excuse for a ruthless purge. All would depend, therefore, on the audacity of the deputation sent to Rome and whether or not the senate, so long a plaything of aberrant emperors, still had a spine. If at all possible, Gordian's messengers would arrive before news of the revolt had reached the city, which meant that the fastest ships in Carthage would have been requisitioned for their use. The leaders of the coup would have had very little time to instruct the messengers. It seems that the young men from Thysdrus who had instigated the rebellion were sidelined at this moment. Another set of young men picked from the higher nobility of Carthage, stepped into a transport on the city's great dockside to take the fight to Rome herself.

As we have seen, the senior representative of Maximinus's government in Rome was the praetorian prefect Vitalianus. With the emperor absent, he had an enormous workload to deal with, including judicial matters as the highest court of appeal. Given the recent purges he was a hated figure, and he is supposed to have exhibited great cruelty: a true representative of the regime, then. It was obvious to Gordian and his co-conspirators that Vitalianus had to be disposed of immediately if the rebellion had any chance of success. So beside the diplomats on their way to the senate, on the boat from Carthage, there was a team of assassins. Command of this critical aspect of the mission was entrusted to a young man of senatorial rank, described as "inherently brave, physically tough and in the prime of his youth". The early Byzantine author Zosimus identifies him as Publius Licinius Valerianus, a later emperor no less.[1] He was accompanied by a band of centurions and soldiers carrying secret messages for the senate, sealed in folding tablets. It seems possible amid the confusion of the historical sources that another key personage in the embassy was Gordian's young nephew, a third person of the same name, Marcus Antonius Gordianus, who was only about 13 years old. Perhaps it was thought that it would be helpful if there was a representative of the dynasty in Rome, however young.

With Vitalianus busy at official business all day, and no doubt well protected by bodyguards, it was going to be difficult to find an opportunity for an attempt on his life. The assassins were instructed to arrive in Rome before dawn, presumably after entering the great harbour at Ostia the evening before, and surprise the prefect while he was alone at the start of his day examining secret papers behind closed doors in a small courthouse. This court was probably attached to the imperial palace on the Palatine Hill, which Vitalianus had made his residence in the emperor's absence. Clearly the plotters in Africa had detailed information about his daily routine.

The account of the events of that day given by Herodian is so detailed and exact that historians have concluded that he must have been in Rome to witness the drama.[2] Initially the timing went according to plan: as the sun began to rise the hit squad arrived at the palace. Pretending to be messengers from Maximinus himself on urgent business, they requested a private audience. Vitalianus had finished with his pre-dawn duties but was not yet at the main legal business of the morning. The assassins were shown in to deliver their message, and while the hated prefect examined the seals – perhaps suddenly suspicious that not everything was in order – he was assailed and stabbed to death. All his attendants ran away in fright, assuming, quite understandably, that the murder had been ordered by Maximinus, and so the assassins were able to make their getaway from the heart of government and into the city.

So far, so good. Some of the plotters then ran down the main thoroughfare from the palace to the forum and Colosseum, the *via sacra*. Nailing up copies of Gordian's letter to the people as they went, they fanned out to deliver their carefully prepared messages to key senators and other influential individuals. The revolutionaries also spread the rumour that Maximinus himself had been assassinated, realizing that fear of vengeance was going to be the main obstacle to the senate's acceptance. Rumours, false and true alike, spread quickly, and no doubt people rushed to crowd around the posted copies of Gordian's decree. Gordian was a well-known figure in the city, renowned for his long-term generosity in staging gladiatorial extravaganzas. Indeed he had been scrupulously even-handed in his generosity, distributing the finest

Sicilian and Cappadocian horses among the circus factions without favour, which contrasts strongly with Maximinus's neglect of the city and the games.[3] To the delight of the plotters, hatred of the emperor quickly won out over fear. Sensing safety in numbers, the common people began to riot, tearing down statues and dedications to the Thracian upstart. Soon enough, Herodian tells us, people were rushing around as if possessed. It began to look like the coup was going to succeed.

Viri Clarissimi

Amid these scenes, those senators who dared converged on the senate house for the most important meeting of that august body in living memory. With the mob rioting outside and no firm news on whether Maximinus was alive or dead, the parliament of Rome was forced to address its dilemma. They had been manipulated into a position to choose between two rival emperors, each a very different proposition. Among their number was a high proportion of African provincials and associates of Gordian and men who perhaps had been given private and secret assurances of advancement or riches. On the other hand there were those who had been promoted by Maximinus and had ties of loyalty to what was, after all, the legitimate regime.

Who in fact were these men that held the fate of the western world in their hands? Unfortunately, no list of senators survives from antiquity, so the only way to reconstruct the membership is to collate and assemble passing mentions in the historical sources and those that survive in inscriptions, papyri and dedications from across the empire. This is the domain of an arcane historical art called prosopography, a discipline to charm anyone who delights in the making of lists. The German scholar Karlheinz Dietz has applied such methods to the senate of 238, producing a roll call of 87 individuals who are firmly known to have been senators at this moment. He has also collected all the available information on where each man was born, where he held estates, to what rank he had ascended by that time, and his known major appointments. Some of the senators are very well known from multiple sources, but all we know of others is a single incomplete inscription and just a few letters of their names.[4]

According to one account, the consul Julius Silanus read out Gordian's letter to the senate, taking a neutral stance, saying that he would respect their decision. By another version, the leading consul actively encouraged the senators in praise of the Gordians. Either way, the temper of the house soon mirrored that of the mob outside. This was surely the moment to rid the empire of a hated emperor who had been forced on them by the army and at the same time avenge the death of the beloved emperor Alexander. So the senate passed a historic decree declaring Maximinus and his son Maximus *hostes publici* (public enemies), stripping them of their titles, powers and imperial estates, and placing a price on their heads. In effect the senate was asserting sovereign power over the emperor. It was unknown for a legitimate emperor to be deposed in this way, the only partial precedent being Nero in 68 CE. Unbeknown to Gordian himself (as communications were so slow), the old man in Carthage was now officially ruler of the empire and all his titles were confirmed, as were his son's. Although there is some debate as to whether this senatorial decree was intended to be kept secret for the time being, the crowd outside immediately found out the gist of it and rejoiced.[5]

But the Romans were very superstitious and it cannot have been seen as good news when around that time, possibly the very morning of this decree, that there was a partial eclipse of the sun "so black that men thought it was night and business could not be transacted without the aid of lanterns". Not surprisingly, the omen was interpreted as indicating a short and truncated reign for the Gordians. We know from the physics of the solar system that there was indeed a partial eclipse occluding up to 95 per cent of the sun's surface on 2 April 238, peaking at 10.20 a.m. Spookily, we can now see (as the Romans, of course, could not) that the eclipse track spanned almost precisely the entire Roman empire, from Mauretania in the west to Mesopotamia in the east. Rome itself was somewhat off centre and would have experienced lesser occlusion of the sun, although enough to cause significant dimming, a strange atmosphere and riffling breezes (but not to turn day into night, it must be said).[6]

Omens aside, a council of 20 of the most influential senators of good military repute was elected to look after the affairs of the city and empire in the name of the distant Gordians. A dedicatory inscription exists to one of them, which gives the name of this elite body: the *XX viri ex senatus consulto rei publici curandae* (20 men appointed by the senate to take control of state affairs).[7] But of this so-called vigintivirate we have just seven names, one of which was added as recently as 1997 after discovery of an inscription listing his career. For the record these are: Decimus Caelius Calvinus Balbinus, Lucius Caesonius Lucillus Macer Rufianus, Marcus Clodius Pupienus Maximus, Rutilius Pudens Crispinus, Tullius Menophilus, Lucius Valerius Claudius Acilius Priscilianus and Marcus Cnaeus Licinius Rufinus.

These men immediately imposed martial law. What then followed was a bloody convulsion seen all too many times in history when a brutal regime is overturned. Informers (that is, private investigators), imperial tax collectors, jurymen – all those who had had a part in the recent purges – were ruthlessly hunted down and slaughtered, their bodies desecrated and dumped in the sewers. Much of this was on the orders of the senate. Homes and property were raided without warning and looted, in Rome itself and then across the surrounding countryside, especially in the imperial estates. Families hid in terror and some fought back in desperation. Innocent people were caught up in the mayhem and many were murdered just to settle old scores that had nothing to do with regime change. Districts of the city and perhaps the countryside became barricaded by their inhabitants. The situation was fast running out of control: Herodian himself described it as a state of virtual civil war.[8]

Soon enough, and despite the chaos, new inscriptions and statues were raised for the Gordians, and the indefatigable engravers at the great mint went to work on a new coinage in their images (Plate 10). If one examines these coins, the elder Gordian does not look his age: perhaps the die-cutters only had an old statue to work from, or more likely they were under orders not to bring attention to the fact that he was an octagenarian. The new issue of coins celebrated Eternal Rome, Victory and the Virtue and Security of the new emperors: standard motifs. Analysis of coin hoards has shown that these issues must have been minted within days of the emperors' confirmation by the senate. But the suggestion that this proves that the Gordians' coup was preplanned in Rome seems far-fetched. What plotters would have been so reckless as to include mere die-cutters in on their plans? And in any case, as previously mentioned, the revolution occurred at the very worst time of year from a campaigning perspective. A more sensible conclusion is that the die-cutters (*celators*, as they were known) were so professional they could turn their hand to a new portrait in no time at all.[9]

A convulsion that had started as an unjust sentence against a group of dandies had developed into a revolt in a provincial town, followed by a rebellion in a province. Now, having gained the approval of the senate, the disturbance swept the entire empire in the form of impending civil war. The great capital city may not have been the focus of military power any more, but it was the centre of communications: all roads lead to Rome, as the saying goes. Messengers radiated out by sea and land declaring Maximinus a public enemy and demanding allegiance to the new and rightful *augusti* Gordians I and II, who now exercised lawful power on behalf of the senate and people of Rome.[10]

Swift Justice

The official news was no doubt accompanied by whirling and contradictory rumours regarding the actual facts. Provincial governors and military commanders everywhere faced the same awful dilemma that had been forced on the senate: with whom to side? This calculation meant deciding first whether the messages they received were real and had not simply been sent to test their loyalty (a cunning ploy that had been used by some of the more paranoid emperors in living memory) and then assessing the local mood in cities and army camps and the likely course of the inevitable war for their area, and more importantly picking a winner overall and how they might profit from the aftermath. Some may even have been so scrupulous as to wonder who was constitutionally in the right in this unprecedented situation: the deposed emperor or rebellious senate? And while many men in power may have been tempted to delay, the situation forced a more or less instantaneous decision on most. An unprecedented example of studied neutrality occurred in the city of Pergamum in Mysia (part of modern Turkey) where the dithering magistrate Aurelius Nilus ordered the coinage to be struck with the heads side left blank. It is difficult to see how such vacillation would have endeared him to either side.[11]

One by one the provinces began to declare for either the Gordians or Maximinus, with their decisions influencing their neighbours. The result was dire division. Some of the senatorial emissaries were well received, but in other cases the unfortunate heralds were put to death, imprisoned or sent to Maximinus for summary punishment. Scholars have made various attempts to determine who sided with whom at this time based on the outputs of the provincial mints, the destruction of statues and the erasure of inscriptions, and also the pathways of subsequent careers. In general, it seems, the eastern provinces sided with Rome whereas Numidia, Spain and the provinces of the Danube frontier remained with Maximinus.[12] There seems to have been a local fight for control in Maximinus's home provinces of Thrace and Moesia. The situation along the Rhine is less easy to determine.

But with the mint still banging out the new issue declaring the security of the Gordians, the supreme irony of the situation was that by this time both of them were dead. Their joint reign as official *augusti* had lasted just 21 days by the most likely count, and it is possible that neither man actually lived long enough to hear news of his ratification by the senate.

This is what had happened: as mentioned before, the Gordians had dispatched an 'imperial' delegation to Capelianus, governor of Numidia, relieving him of his command of the local legion and expelling him from the province while another man was appointed in his place. Numidia was a minor province on Africa's more threatened flank, having been split off some years before by Septimius Severus on his tour of North Africa. On a personal level, Capelianus was a sworn enemy of the Gordians following some earlier legal dispute, and whereas Gordian had been appointed to his post by the senate, Capelianus was a direct appointment of the emperor himself. Hence the formal chain of command was ambiguous. Gordian and his entourage had miscalculated. To have relinquished command and fly abroad at this juncture would have been, for Capelianus, to put his life on the line under charges of cowardice or complicity from Maximinus. With news from Rome not due for weeks, a local decision was necessary, and his duty, it seemed to him, was clear. Outraged by the order, he either imprisoned or more likely executed his supposed replacement.

Capelianus is described by one source as being a *veteranus* (an old soldier).[13] His one regular legion, *legio III augusta*, on paper about 5,000 men but no doubt depleted from detachments having been sent to the frontier wars, was supplemented by a draft of local Numidian auxiliaries. The Gordians had few regular troops but could muster a large number of militia from the populations of Carthage and Tripolitanea. With the situation on a knife-edge, Capelianus assembled his force in the big African legionary base at Cirta and reinforced their sacred oath of loyalty to the emperor Maximinus. He probably reminded them that they had previously taken the loyal epithet *maximiniana*, which is attested by a surviving inscription.[14] No doubt he promised the looting and great rewards that would be theirs for crushing Gordian's feeble revolt, not to mention the gratitude of Maximinus who had always been so generous with the army.

Fast and decisive action was necessary. As soon as it could be arranged, Capelianus led his men on to the Carthage road. If his dispositions went by the book, the Numidian horsemen would have fanned out along the flanks and set up advanced pickets along the route. All the logistics necessary to maintain and supply a significant army had to be organized in an instant. At first, the situation would undoubtedly have been chaotic, but with a professional army staff at the core of the force, order quickly emerged. The occasion is in fact one of the few times in Roman imperial history which proves that a single legion with its auxiliaries really did have the wherewithal to fight a war all on its own, and win.

The march was a little over 400 kilometres along a relatively well-made road and could be completed in good order in less than ten days, forced. News would have been travelling back and forth somewhat faster by boat, depending on the wind. Good though the road may have been, the terrain was not. Eventually the route climbs and is flanked by hills with difficult ranges on both sides. Small bridges and awkward undefended villages among the orange groves were scattered along the way. Capelianus would have aimed to break out of these hills and on to the plain of Carthage before his enemy was able to organize ambushes. This was exactly the same strategy of the Americo-Anglo First Army that marched the same route advancing on Tunis after landing at

Algiers in 1942. Fortunately for Capelianus, spring was coming to the hills and survival in the open was less of a daily challenge than it would have been just weeks earlier.

As the forces converged on Africa's great city some of the Carthaginians, guessing the outcome, apparently deserted to join the invading force, giving the author of the *Augustan History* an opportunity for a traditional jibe at 'Punic faith'.[15] The armies eventually clashed on the city outskirts around late April 238. The battle was preceded by a violent storm that, it has been suggested, prevented the defenders from mustering in good order.[16] The defenders were led out by the playboy prince, Gordian II, while the old man stayed in the city. His was by far the more numerous force but it was composed of only a few trained troops and included many ordinary people of all ages armed with hunting weapons or whatever they could manufacture. Their shields had been made on the spot from wood and leather in a hastily arranged production line. Capelianus, on the other hand, had a well-trained and equipped army of tough young men. Particularly menacing were the fearsome Numidian cavalry, whose special skill (Herodian tells us) was to control their horses at a gallop with no reins and just a riding crop. Wearily, and expectantly, in the cold and wet, the two sides assembled against one another on the muddy plain outside the great city.

Most ancient battles started with the two sides closing on one another and attempting to raise a deafening war cry to intimidate those opposite. Then missiles were exchanged and finally the ranks clashed shield against shield and steel against steel, each man relying on the discipline and training of his comrades for support and encouragement. Predictably enough,[17] the set-piece engagement quickly became a rout, with the Carthaginians falling back on their city in disarray while the wounded, brave or slow were cut to pieces by the well-drilled cohorts in the centre of Capelianus's line. It was said that more were killed in the stampede than on the battlefield, which was in fact normal in ancient warfare. The women and children of this huge, previously peaceful city, looked on in horror as rout turned to massacre, just as their ancestors had done centuries before when Scipio Africanus took Carthage. The troops of the third legion then flooded in and thoroughly looted the city, while all the prominent people involved in the rebellion were rounded up for execution. No doubt many leading citizens now pleaded their eternal loyalty to Capelianus and the emperor Maximinus.

In the following days the army was allowed to roam the countryside in search of food and riches on the grounds that the rebellion had started in the great estates. Presumably the decurion Mauritius and his comrades were top of the most wanted list, but history has no more to say about them. Further detachments were sent onward to chastise the other undefended cities of Africa that had supported the rebels and, no doubt, bring in loot and booty. According to the *Augustan History*, Capelianus "over-threw cities, ravaged shrines, divided gifts among his soldiers, and slaughtered common folk and nobles in the cities".[18] Some inscriptions are known in which the name of Maximinus had been chiselled off and then restored, which presumably happened at this time. Another tangible relic from this time is a poignant inscription on a tombstone from the nearby city of Theveste in modern Algeria that records a man, Lucius Aemilius Severinus, who died *pro amore romano quievit ab hoc capeliano captus* ("for the love of Rome while fighting against Capelianus").[19]

The younger Gordian also fell in battle with his makeshift bodyguard, and his corpse was never recovered. There are conflicting accounts regarding the fate of the older man. Herodian gives us two versions: one that he hanged himself in despair before battle was joined and another, perhaps more plausible, that he killed himself as Capelianus and his troops entered the city. The *Augustan History* agrees with the latter account. Either way, hanging was considered a shameful method of suicide in comparison to self-administration of the blade, so it is probably true. A much less likely version is found in the late source of Zosimus, who said that both Gordians took ship for Rome but died "in a tempest in the midst of their navigation". Gibbon described this as indicating "a strange ignorance of history, or a strange abuse of metaphors!".[20]

Capelianus must have accrued substantial riches from the looting of the virtually defenceless province with its great cities and industries. For now, he was master of the empire's second city and the surrounding provinces, with jubilant troops and an impeccable claim to have acted out of duty and loyalty to Rome. He had also thoroughly settled an old score against Gordian, so he must have been dismayed to say the least when news from Rome of the old man's legitimacy arrived. The sack of Carthage had been conducted in the name of Maximinus, who was now an outlaw. Capelianus convened a war council with his closest officers, at which time he considered all eventualities, including planning a bid for the empire should fortune turn against Maximinus and present him with a suitable opportunity.[21]

Trouble in the East

Africa was not the only place experiencing violence, because with impeccable timing, Ardashir went on the attack. Having disbanded most of his great army after the war of 232, the great king of kings must have viewed the ensuing uprisings along the Rhine and Danube with relish, as crack Roman and allied units were drained away from the border zone to fight distant barbarians.

There had been no hurry on his part to renew the Roman war: in fact he had had a similar pressing need to subdue turbulent tribes around the far fringes of his own mighty empire. But in 237, with Maximinus and the main Roman army still engaged in Sarmatia, Ardashir evidently decided the time was ripe for a new campaign against the big enemy and started mobilizing en masse. No doubt his men were spoiling for a fight: that the foe could be beaten had been proven, and that they were weaker in the east than in 232, with their most experienced generals absent, was obvious.

The parallels between the two great leaders, Ardashir and Maximinus, are striking, beyond the simple fact that both had overturned previous dynasties and were hungry for conquests beyond their traditional borders. Both relied on their martial reputations to establish them in the eyes of the people, in contrast to the weakness of previous regimes. Both were skilled and calculating generals, consummate in the art of war and ruthless against all opposition. Ardashir was accompanied on campaign by his princely son called Shapur, just as Maximinus shared his command with Maximus, each young man embodying the promise of a long dynasty.

Ardashir seems to have set limited but firm strategic objectives for his campaign of 238. This was not going to be another raid, instead he aimed to take and hold territory that was currently part of Roman Mesopotamia, pushing the Romans back up the Euphrates and developing a new line of fortifications that could subsequently provide a launch pad for an invasion of Syria. For two centuries the Romans had advanced, bit by bit, down the Euphrates and their progress had seemed inexorable. Now Ardashir aimed to turn this tide. And by once again making war on the Romans, he would reinforce his supposed ancestral claim to all of Asia, including the eastern third of the Roman Empire.

The main target of his attack was the area of the Chaboras (Khabur) River, the principal tributary of the upper Euphrates. This river was flanked by extensive tracts of irrigated lands, including idyllic vineyards and orchards, and was dotted with many prosperous towns and villages. Stacks of military papyri discovered in the sand of Dura Europos in the early twentieth century tell us that many of the smaller settlements in the area were fortified with little detachments of soldiers to keep order. Retired army officers were wont to buy up parcels of land here and live out their remaining days farming and trading around the riverbank in the cradle of civilization. The area was dominated by the formidable garrison cities of Singara, Nisibus, and Carrhae, and, below the confluence of the Chaboras and Euphrates, the great fortress of Dura Europos itself. For hundreds of years these strongholds were key to the balance of power in the area. But as Ardashir knew, they had all once been in the Persian sphere of influence. If some or all could be retaken, the geopolitics would take a decisive shift along the whole frontier region. The near-impregnable desert fortress of Hatra, which had withstood various Roman attacks and then his own siege in 230, becoming a Roman ally before the war of 232, would be completely surrounded by these advances and must necessarily sue for peace. Then Armenia would start to look isolated and vulnerable. Ardashir, it will be recalled, was a sworn enemy of the Armenians, not only for harbouring dissident Parthian nobility but also for supporting Alexander's great invasion a few years before. Another factor in Ardashir's calculation was that the Christian city of Edessa may have been in a state of revolt from Maximinus, and had certainly been stripped of many of its elite archers for the German war.

We know very little about the events of 237–238 on the eastern front because the historical sources are very sketchy. Even the year in which certain moves took place is a matter of debate, relying mostly as it does on much later Byzantine sources. Direct evidence comes from the coinage, in that all the Roman Mesopotamian mints ceased to operate in 238. So it seems that early that year, Nisibus and Carrhae were subjected to siege and both fell, as was also recorded by Zonoras. Presumably this was after a fight, as both were well defended. The loss of either city would have been a major defeat for the Romans: to lose both was a first-order disaster. The loss of Carrhae was a particular blow to the Roman empire as it was so close to Edessa, capital of Osrhoene (a mere 30 miles away). It is also probable that Singara and the Roman frontier outpost of Ain Sinu to the east of that major centre also fell in 238. Any survivors from the garrison at Singara would have been enlisted by the Persians or sold into slavery. [22] It is hard to believe that the transfer of the enormous contingent of Osrhoenian archers to the west had nothing to do with this weakening of defences in the east. For the archers, when they inevitably heard the news, it was a mirror image of the situation faced by the Rhine troops in 232, who had similarly been taken to a distant war only to hear of foreign incursions in their weakened homeland.

It is reasonable to assume from these conspicuous successes that Ardashir's force was large and well organized. After stabilizing the administration in his newly-conquered cities on the Chaboras and with no major Roman force threatening retaliation, Ardashir turned his sights once again on the toughest nut of all, the fortress of Hatra, and began another siege. This traditionally independent city under its king Daizan[23] was newly allied to Rome, but whether it still contained its contingent of Moroccan archers from the far end of the Roman Empire is uncertain. Once again Hatra was going to have to rely on its walls and wells. Meanwhile the garrison at Dura Europos, base of the new *dux ripae* (possibly by now, Domitius Pompeianus) must have looked on in alarm as the Persian incursions swept up-river beyond them.

The Roman response to the loss of the Chaboras was radical, perhaps cynical; the province of Mesopotamia was dissolved and the client kingdom of Osrhoene was restored as an independent (buffer) state. Perhaps this was in response to the King of Osrhoene (Abgar X) demanding to be allowed to manage the crisis without further interference. It is difficult to believe that the Romans would have allowed Edessa to fall into enemy hands if they could help it. These diplomatic moves may well have been orchestrated by Maximinus from afar as a delaying tactic while he developed a strategy for counter-attack. It has been suggested that in 238 Maximinus planned to return to the eastern theatre himself, although the grounds for that seem to be a misreading of the historical evidence.[24] Even so, the basic idea is not implausible if intelligence of Ardashir's mobilization reached Maximinus early in 238. It would have made sense for him to return to the east with part of the mobile army, including the eastern auxiliaries who had been away from their homeland for so long, perhaps leaving a trusted general to continue the pacification of Sarmatia. Maximinus might easily come back to Sarmatia a year or two later to found a new province when the eastern war was concluded. But all such plans were overtaken by the news from Africa.

Gothic Horror

If this conspiracy of events was not enough, the military fragility of the empire was underscored that year by a totally new threat and a harbinger of things to come: bloody incursions by the Goths. As previously related, these were a west Eurasian people who had lived for centuries beyond the fringes of the Roman empire, seemingly migrating *en masse* from the area of the Baltic to the northern fringes of the Black Sea. Trading contact with the empire would have impressed them greatly. Many of their young men had served in the Roman army and knew it from the inside. To aggressive war leaders in the tribal homelands, the opulent cities of Asia Minor were appealing targets for raiding and plunder. The disincentive was the fearsome reputation of the Danubian legions (the empire's best) and Rome's habit of extracting brutal and efficient reprisals against the heartlands of the perpetrators, as recently demonstrated in Germania and Sarmatia.

Details are very sparse, but it seems that the Goths in 238 took advantage of the chaos in the empire by launching at least two major raids that spring and summer aimed at Roman lands to the west of the Black Sea. The Greek colony and port of Istros on the Black Sea was sacked. However these were not naval raids; the Goths had yet to learn the benefits of massed fleet actions, which later proved so effective for them.[25] They were probably mounted war bands descending on the peaceful agricultural districts of the Thracian plains, incidentally the likely homeland of Maximinus himself. In doing so they would have cut off Byzantium from landward communications via the Danube, although the city itself was not under direct threat on account of its walls, garrison and harbour. The incursions imply defeat of the upper Moesian legions *legio XI claudia* and *legio I italica*, or at least some of their outposts. Quite likely these units had just been depleted by Maximinus for his frontier wars, triggering the Gothic raids.

To some Romans, the Goths may have seemed fairly insignificant in the grander scheme: just another barbarian tribe to contend with. But others, mindful of their independent culture and tradition, and perhaps also aware of the burgeoning population behind the frontier, may have perceived a general problem that was emerging: a rich, well-organized but underpopulated empire was beginning to be surrounded by a press of humanity looking for a better life, so that when the empire was also threatened by a warlike Sasanian Persia, there were simply too few troops to secure all the borders at any one time. This was the start of the great geopolitical problem of the centuries to come and, incidentally, endless miseries for the people of Thrace and the Balkans. The historian Dexippus, who, 30 years later, himself played a starring role in later wars against the Goths (or Scyths as he called them) noted that it was in 238 that "the Scythian war began" with the destruction of Istros.[26]

Sirmium

News of the Gordians' rebellion and the senate's treachery reached Maximinus at about the same time that, unbeknown to him, at the other end of the empire, the Battle of Carthage was being fought in his name, possibly even on the same day in late April.[27] We are told that Maximinus was enraged, and with good reason, for he would have seen himself as the empire's protector, doing its dirty work on the frontier only to be forced to give up a position of strength against the barbarians because of the weakness of others. He may also have been secretly concerned about the Gothic threat to his own homeland and Ardashir's attacks in Mesopotamia, although we do not know how far events had proceeded by that time. Most important for Maximinus was of course the direct challenge to his own position. Not only did the extraordinary news immediately change his military priorities, it also cut off his army's supply of money, grain and oil. Clearly the senate had to be brought back into line, and fast. It was very fortunate for him that his army had not yet left winter quarters.

The *Augustan History* makes the interesting claim that Maximinus was particularly angry with his son, whom he had previously ordered to take personal control in Rome but who had refused to go. If Maximus had indeed been in Rome, perhaps the senate would not have dared oppose him. More likely though is that he would have been first to die. That source also tells us that the emperor drank so much wine that night that the next morning he could not remember what had happened and the bad news had to be broken to him afresh. For two full days he remained locked up with his military and imperial council, planning his response and, presumably, nursing his hangover. Herodian tells us that although the entire army and all the locals immediately learned the news from Rome, everyone feigned ignorance of it, and during these days Maximinus himself kept a close watch on what people were saying and "on the flicker of their eyes".[28]

On the third day the emperor emerged to address his veteran army, with a speech conveniently prepared for him by one of his staff because he was illiterate, according to Herodian:[29]

I am sure what I am going to say to you will be incredible and unsuspected [given the rumours, it was an amusing start] – it is not in my opinion so much a matter for astonishment as for laughter and ridicule. Someone is pitting his arms against you and your courage. But not the Germans, who we have defeated on many occasions, nor the Sarmatians, who regularly come to beg for peace. The Persians, after their invasion of Mesopotamia some time ago, are now quiet and content with their own possessions. Keeping them in check is your reputation for bravery in fighting and their knowledge and experience of my activities when I was commander of legions on the frontier banks of the river.[30] It is not they (and this surely is ludicrous news) but the Carthaginians who have gone mad. They have persuaded or forced a feeble, old man, who has taken leave of his senses in the extremity of old age, to be Emperor, as though it were a game in a procession. But what sort of army are they relying on, when lictors are enough for them as attendants on their governor? What sort of weapons will they use, when they have nothing but the lances used by gladiators in single combat against wild animals? Their only combat training is in choruses or witty speeches and rhythmic dances. No one should be disturbed by the news from Rome. Vitalianus was caught and murdered by a deceitful trick, and you know perfectly well about the fickle infidelity of the Roman populace. But their bravery only extends to shouting. They have only to see two or three armed soldiers to be pushing and trampling on each other, each man runs away from the threat to his own person, without a thought for the common danger. If some of you have heard about the Senate's reactions, you should not be surprised that our disciplined moderation is aggravating for them, and that they prefer

Gordian who shares their dissolute habits. They say that courageous, sober deeds are intimidation, whereas they favour undisciplined incontinence as though it is toleration. So, they are hostile to my rule because it is strict and well-regulated, but welcome the sound of Gordian's name – and you know the scandals of his past life. These are the kinds of people against whom we are at war, if war is the right name for it. I am convinced that we only have to set foot in Italy for almost everyone to hold out olive branches and bring their children to us, begging for mercy and falling at our feet. The rest will run away because they are poor cowards. Then I shall be able to distribute all their property to you, and you can take it and enjoy it without restraint.

Herodian, *History of the Empire* VII.4–8.

Hurrah! Maximinus may have stalked off dreaming of dissolving the senate and other institutions of state that had treated him so treacherously, but he was also aware that not all his troops relished the prospect of war with Rome. Tellingly, he increased his own security and urgently sent for Maximus (who was further up the border) to join him.[31]

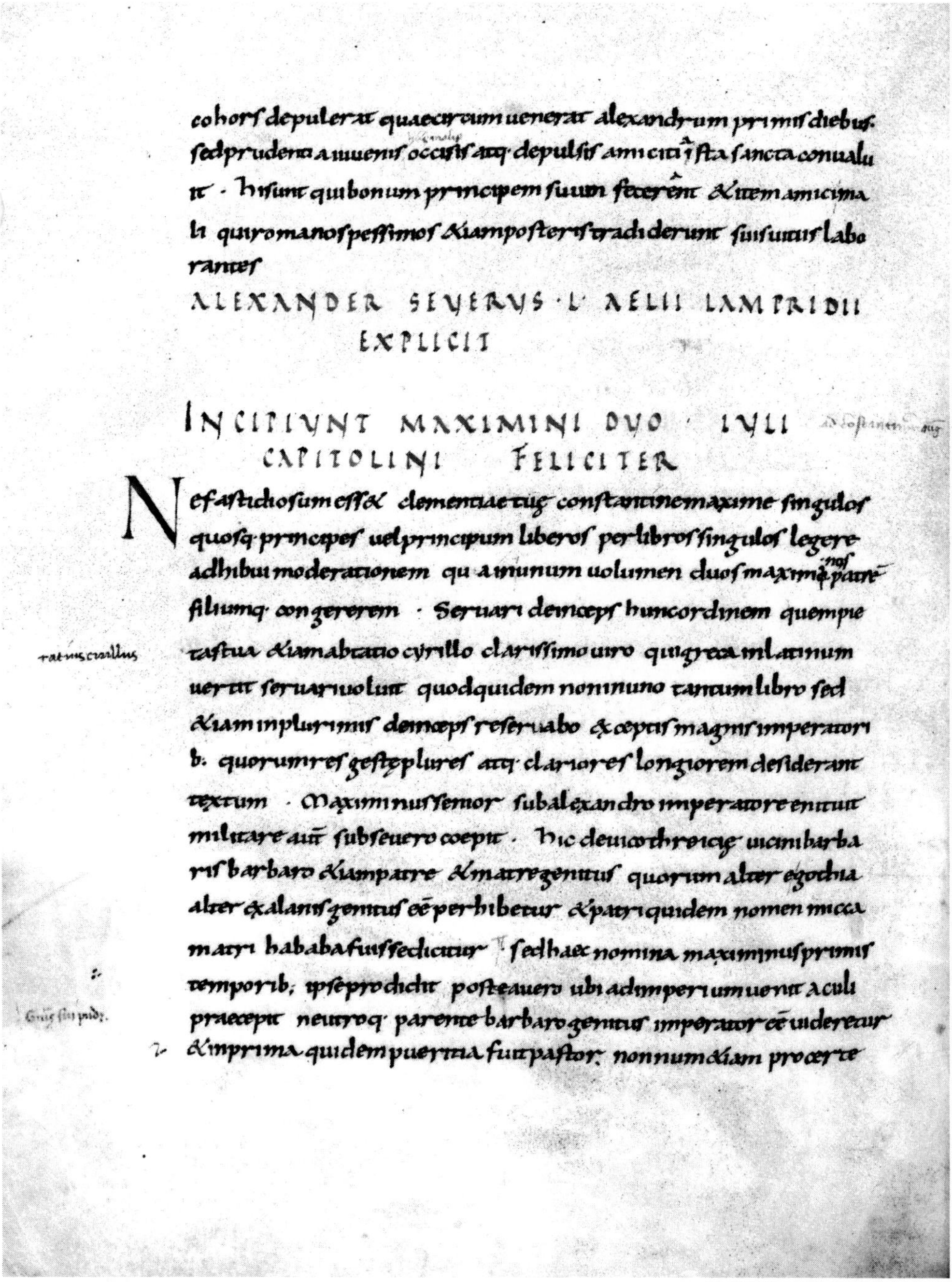

PLATE 1

cohors depulerat quaecumque uenerat alexandrum primis diebus
sed prudenter amiuens occisis atq depulsis amicitia ista sancta conualu
it · his sunt qui bonum principem suum fecerent &item amicissi
li qui romanos pessimos &iam posteris tradiderunt sussuuris labo
rantes

ALEXANDER SEVERVS · L · AELII LAMPRIDII
EXPLICIT

INCIPIVNT MAXIMINI DVO · IVLI
CAPITOLINI FELICITER

Nefas ratus sum &clementiae tuae constantine maxime singulos
quosq principes uel principum liberos per libros singulos legere
adhibui moderationem qu a uiuum uolumen duos maxima patre
filiumq congererem · Seruari deinceps hunc ordinem quempie
castua &iam ab tatio cyrillo clarissimo uiro qui graeca in latinum
uertit seruaui uolui quod quidem nomi nuno tantum libro sed
&iam in plurimis deinceps reseruabo &ceptis magnis imperatori
b· quorum res gestae plures atq clariores longiorem desiderant
textum · Maximinus senior sub alexandro imperatore enitui
militare au subseuero coepit · hic deum cthroicie uicum barba
ris barbaro &iam patre &matre genitus quorum alter egothia
alter ex alanis genitus ee perhibetur &patri quidem nomen micca
matri hababa fuisse dicitur · sed haec nomina maximinus primis
temporib; ipse prodicht postea uero ubi adimperiium uenit a culi
praecepit neutroq parente barbaro genitus imperator ee uideretur
&imprima quidem puertia fuit pastor: nonnum &iam procer te

A page from the oldest surviving manuscript of the *Augustan History* in which the life of Maximinus begins *(reproduced with permission of the Biblioteca Apostolica Vaticana in Rome).*

PLATE 2

P. SEPTIMIVS GETA
(African noble)

JVLIVS BASSIANVS
High priest of El Gabal
(Syrian noble) d. 217

THE HOUSE OF SEVERUS

m. JULIUS
AVITUS
(Syrian noble)

L. SEPTIMIVS SEVERVS
145-211
(Augustus 193-211)

JVLIA DOMNA
170-217
(Augusta 193-217)

JVLIA MAESA
165-224
(Augusta 218-224)

M. AVRELIVS
ANTONINVS
'CARACALLA'
188-217
(Augustus 198-217)

L. SEPTIMIVS GETA
189-212
(Augustus 209-212)

JVLIA MAMAEA
180-235
(Augusta 222-235)
m. GESSIUS
MARCIANUS
(Roman noble)

JVLIA SOAEMIAS
180-222
(Augusta 218-222)
m. SEXTUS
VARIUS MARCELLUS
(Roman noble)

ORBIANA
208-235
(Augusta 225-227)

M. AVR. SEVERVS
ALEXANDER
208-235
(Augustus 222-235)

m. JVLIA PAULA (Augusta 219-220)
(2) AQVILIA SEVERA (Augusta 220 and 221-222)
(3) ANNIA FAVSTINA (Augusta 221)

V. AVITVS BASSIANVS
'ELAGABALUS'
203-222
(Augustus 218-222)

The dynasty of Septimius Severus. Note that both Elagabalus and Severus Alexander claimed Caracalla as their natural father (*coins with the permission of CNG coins*).

PLATE 3

Geta, the boy prince,
c. 200 CE (*CNG coins*).

Septimius Severus, 196 CE, with an imposing bodyguard
(*CNG coins*).

Tombstone naming the troop of Julius Maximinus
of the *equites singulares*, c. 200 CE.

Mosaic floor and part of a surviving wall of the *palaestra* (exercise space) attached to the bathhouse
of the imperial horseguard in Rome (*photograph by the author with permission, Vatican museums*).

PLATE 4

Julia Mamaea, 230 CE.

Severus Alexander goes to war (*profectio*), 231 CE.

Severus Alexander, 232 CE.

Ardashir, Persian king of kings, c. 230 CE (*all coins with permission of CNG coins*).

Boiler boy: Persian armoured horseman, third century graffito from Dura Europos.

PLATE 5

The walls of Dura Europos and the palace of the *dux ripae* overlooking the Euphrates (*www.colorado.edu*).

Restored Roman-style temple at the Armenian Royal Fortress at Garni, Armenia (*author photograph*).

The harsh Armenian terrain traversed by the Roman army invading Persian Medea (*author photograph*).

PLATE 6

The Album of Canusium with
the name of Petronius Magnus
erased from the first column.
Modified from Salway (2000).

Maximinus addresses the troops
(*adlocutio*): from his first issue of coins,
235 CE (*CNG coins*).

The Harzhorn in Germany (arrows show
line of ancient trackway and Roman assault)
(*author photograph*).

HARZHORN
RIDGE

PLATE 7

Distribution of finds on the Harzhorn ridge (*arch.rwth-aachen.de*).

Roman horseshoe (*Thorsten Schwarz, Wikimedia Commons*).

Roman ballista bolts (*Braunschweigisches Landesmuseum, Wikimedia Commons*).

The Harzhorn battlefield: the Romans attacked up this slope (*author photograph*).

PLATE 8

Germanic spearpoint from the Harzhorn (*Thorsten Schwarz, Wikimedia Commons*).

Roman *dolabra* (axe head) inscribed
LEG IIII S A, Harzhorn region (*Martin
Oppermann, Wikimedia Commons*).

Victory coinage
(VICTORIA
GERMANICA),
235-6 CE
(*CNG coins*).

PLATE 9

The imperial family: Maximinus Augustus, the divine Paulina (reverse: ascending to the heavens on a peacock) and Maximus Caesar, Prince of Youth (PRINCIPII IVVENTVTIS)
(*coins with the permission of CNG coins*).

PLATE 10

The amphitheatre at Thysdrus (El Djem) attributed to the elder Gordian (*Jerzystrzelecki, Wikimedia Commons*).

Coin of Gordian I advertising the Security of the Two Emperors, and Gordian II (*CNG coins*).

The forum of Aquileia, Italy (*author photograph*).

PLATE 11

Foundations of hastily built defences, Aquileia, 238 CE. This was originally the river dock front. Semicircular towers, probably mounting artillery, were added either side of the steps down to the river (*author photograph*).

Roman crossing point of the river Sontius (Isonzo), Italy, at low water before the spate (*author photograph*).

PLATE 12

Pupienus: *fathers of the senate*.

Balbinus: *mutual faith of the emperors*.

The victory altar in Aquileia.

Gordian III and Tranquillina from the mint at recaptured Singara, c. 242 CE.

Fortuna with rudder, cornucopiae and wheel. From a coin of Gordian III c. 243 CE (*all coins with the permission of CNG coins*).

PLATE 13

Type 1 portrait:
first emission,
235 CE.

Type 2 portrait:
early 236 CE.

Type 3 portrait:
236 -238 CE.

A curse on
Maximinus:
'health of
the emperor'
filed flat
(*all coins with
the permission of
CNG coins*)

PLATE   14

Variations of the Type 3 portrait, 236-238 CE (*with the permission of CNG coins*).

PLATE 15

Busts of Maximinus.

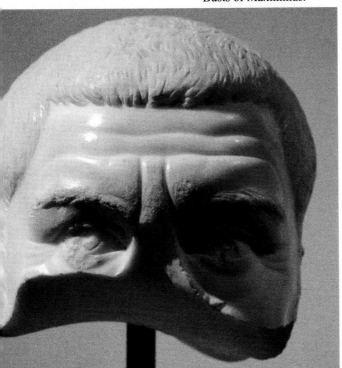

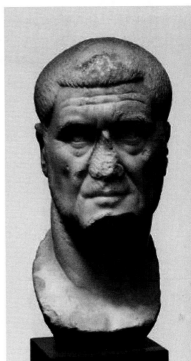

The Palatine fragment.

The Copenhagen bust.

The Capitoline bust.

The Louvre bust.

PLATE 16

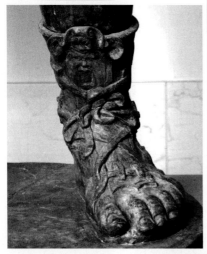

The eight foot statue
in the Metropolitan
Museum of Art, with
detail of the sandal.
Modified from Hemingway
and others (2013).

Trebonianus Gallus in
the Vatican Museum
(*author photograph*).

The Met statue
(*photograph as above*).

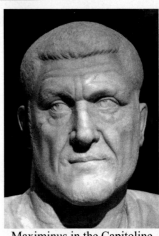

Maximinus in the Capitoline
Museum (*author photograph*).

Chapter XI

Bellum Civile

Power Play

News of the mobilization of Maximinus's army and the death of the Gordians at the Battle of Carthage reached Rome almost simultaneously. The first piece of news, terrifying as it was, could have been no surprise, but the second was a true body blow. Rome, at war with the professional core of its own army, now even lacked a figurehead, and Africa was lost, threatening the grain and oil supply. There was little prospect of appealing for clemency from Maximinus: diplomatic manoeuvres were already in play all across the empire that surely guaranteed civil war.

A second crisis meeting of the senators was quickly arranged, and to underline the extraordinary nature of the occasion they met not at the senate house but in the inner sanctum of the temple of Jupiter Optimus Maximus on the Capitoline Hill.[1] Jupiter's temple was the city's most sacred site, already over 700 years old, although it had been rebuilt several times. The location was deeply symbolic: a similar convocation had been held there once before on the assassination of Caligula almost 200 years before when the empire had, similarly, found itself suddenly leaderless. At that time the idea of restoring the republican system of government had been openly discussed, but without effect because while the senators debated, the praetorians took action and installed as emperor the aristocrat Claudius, Caligula's uncle (against his will we are told). Now a similar but even more extreme crisis was under way. Herodian tells us that the meeting was held behind closed doors, which probably means that the usual scribes, slaves and civil servants were not admitted. The reason: the very constitution and nature of the state was on the agenda.

The meeting began as always with offerings seeking divine guidance for the proceedings, presumably led by the *flamen dialis*, Rome's supreme priest (apart from the emperor) and guardian of Jupiter's temple. As the first speeches were made it became clear that the mood was decisive and radical. After years of being humiliated and marginalized by tyrannical emperors the venerable institution began to find something of its old spirit and dignity. The senators were all motivated by the usual ties of patronage and the need to protect their lives and fortunes in an uncertain future, but something more seemed to be stirring.

The obvious question, of course, was who would be emperor? Surprisingly, the first weighty decision made was that they would appoint *two* new emperors of *equal* status, and that the elected men would come from their own ranks. This sharing of the supreme power echoed the consular system of the old republic but unlike the republican model, in which power was granted for just a year at a time, both men would be given the title of *augustus* and their appointment would be for life. The decision to appoint two men may have been driven partly by expediency: an imperial presence was required both to maintain order at Rome, and at the head of the army that was being formed to face Maximinus. But, as Herodian suggested, it may also have been a deliberate attempt to insert a constitutional check on the unlimited power of the emperors that had plagued the empire under a succession of cruel rulers since Commodus. It is telling that the sons of the elected men, even though of high rank and merit themselves, were not given the rank of *caesar*. This may suggest that the senate was seeking to move away from the hereditary tradition and instead sought to allocate itself the role of electing future successors to the imperial title, thereby cementing its role as the supreme power in the empire. This new constitution was no democracy, of course – the common people were excluded, as always – but the senate evidently thought it would provide a more stable basis for power and law than the effective monarchy, so abused of late.[2] And, of course, men elected from their own wealthy ranks could be expected to wield power in the interests of the rich.

This motion seems to have been passed with overwhelming support. The next decision was equally critical: who, in fact, would be appointed? A shortlist was produced consisting of "men of distinction and consular rank", which may have been identical to the list of the 20 senior senators who had been administering affairs in Rome since Gordian was recognized as emperor: the *vigintivirate*.[3] Herodian (who, if he was a senator himself, may have been there) tells us that the voting was not straightforward. Many men on the list received some votes from the house, but eventually, by a process of elimination, the number was reduced to two. We do not know who was third, fourth or fifth: we do not even know who was first. That, at least, is testament to the secrecy of the proceedings and to the tact of Herodian and his sources.

The two winners of this extraordinary ballot were Marcus Clodius Pupienus Maximus (generally referred to in history as Pupienus) and Decimus Caelius Calvinus Balbinus (generally referred to as Balbinus). Both had excelled in the *cursus honorum* and in doing so had gained enormous experience, patronage and power. Each had served as consul on two previous occasions and both were well respected for their integrity and proven industry under previous regimes. These men were invested with full imperial honours on the spot. In another constitutional innovation, the title of *pontifex maximus* (chief priest) was shared between them (when previous emperors had shared the title of *augustus* with a son or other named successor, they had not both held this title). If this offended the traditionalists, at least it signalled that this was no ordinary change of government. This was a dyarchy: absolute power to be wielded equally by two individuals.

The two men were of very different character and background. Pupienus may have been of humbler origin than his colleague, although a late Roman story that he started life as a blacksmith is almost certainly a muddle with a later emperor, or just false. It is interesting that the fact that his son had been chosen to share the consulship with the tyrant Maximinus a couple of years before did not count against him in the eyes of his colleagues. Then aged about 60, he was a military man and known as a strict disciplinarian. According to Herodian, public opinion (by which he presumably means the upper classes) held him as intelligent and of sober habits. Unsurprisingly he was appointed commander-in-chief of the army. The coins minted in his name show him with an appropriately severe, glaring expression. Balbinus was the elder, already in his mid-70s according to the sources, and was from one of Rome's noblest families, related to the former emperors Trajan and Hadrian, and possibly, like them, ultimately from Spain where he still held estates. He had served a long career with many offices of state, including a stint as a respected provincial governor. His coins and statues reveal rather portly features and a double chin, and he usually wears a more genial expression than his colleague. The *Augustan History* describes him as "somewhat fonder of pleasure" than Pupienus.[4] He was given control of the civil administration of the empire and the law. Presumably the imperial treasury was made available to both men for the public good.

With these two meritorious individuals no doubt reeling from their unexpected elevation to semi-divinity, the senate then went on to debate the crisis and the immediate course of action. The agenda would no doubt have included such important items as the defence of the city, law and order, the defence of Italy, the raising of new troop levies, the prospects of summoning soldiery from loyal parts of the empire, and the continued suppression of Maximinus's interests in Rome and elsewhere. Senior figures were allocated special commands and responsibilities for the duration of the mobilization.

Arguably the senate had just enacted more serious business in an hour than it had done in the preceding 100 years, but inevitably the election of two new emperors must have affected the finely balanced and intricate mesh of patronage and obligation that characterized the highest stratum of Roman society. Unsurprisingly, given the size of the senate, not everyone was happy with these developments. A particular complaint was that the legitimate heirs of the Gordians had been overlooked. Apart from the inherent justice of that claim, the men who had stood to gain most from the Gordians' revolution, possibly with secret promises and agreements entered into, now found themselves wrenched from the centre of power just as suddenly as they had been thrown into it. The delegation from Carthage that had instigated the coup were obviously among those most disconcerted at the turn of events as Roman interests solidified around a new reality.[5]

As the day wore on, and despite the supposed secrecy of proceedings, word leaked out to the throng outside regarding the appointments of the joint rulers. Perhaps stirred up by pro-Gordian agitators, the reaction in the city was far from positive. Many free citizens may well have felt suddenly marginalized at the very time that they too might have had a say on the direction of governance. Presently, an angry mob began to assemble at the temple gates brandishing sticks and stones. Pupienus in particular was very unpopular among those whom Herodian describes as "the unstable rabble of the lower classes" because of his reputation of severity arising from his time as urban prefect: we do not know exactly what he had done to earn the hatred of the masses, but it is interesting that this strict reputation was the very virtue that had contributed to his elevation by the senate. And as the meeting wore on it became apparent that an extraordinary situation was developing wherein the Capitol in the sacred centre of the city and the Temple of Jupiter itself were surrounded by a baying mob. The senators found themselves virtually imprisoned by the very people they aspired to rule. Death threats to the new 'emperors' began to ring out. The main demand resolved itself on the idea that a legitimate heir of the popular Gordians should be elevated in place of these self-elected nobodies.

As closure of the meeting approached, the situation descended into utter chaos in the streets outside. The senators realized they would actually have to force their way out of the temple precinct. To facilitate this operation, a bodyguard of young men from noble families loyal to the senatorial interest was summoned (mainly their own sons and grandsons). Swords in hand, the youths tried to force a path through the crowd from the outside but were met with a shower of sticks and stones in response. According to one story Balbinus himself "almost suffered a blow with a stone and, according to some, was actually hit with a club". As the hours wore on, the senatorial party retreated back to the sacred precinct for an ignominious rethink.[6]

The impasse was resolved by quick thinking on somebody's part, possibly one of the Carthaginians. The Gordians' legitimate heir was a boy, aged 12 or 13. He was grandson of Gordian I by his daughter Maecia Faustina and the senator and ex-consul Caius Junius Balbus. Conveniently he was present in the city, possibly, as we have seen, having travelled to Rome with the initial delegation. A decision was made to compromise with the crowd and acknowledge this boy as *caesar* and hence heir to the imperial throne. As both emperors were fairly old he might not have to wait that long. One can imagine that some of the senators, seeing their dreams of a quasi-republican future evaporate, turned away in disgust, but the decision was enacted immediately and a party was dispatched to locate the boy: Herodian gives us the colourful detail that he was found alone at home, quietly playing with his toys. The boy was then carried aloft through the streets "on the neck of a very tall man" to great acclaim and showered with flowers by the people who hailed him as Gordian *caesar*.[7] Eventually the mob dispersed and the senators were able to slink back to their expensive residences, while the new emperors made their way to the imperial palace.

The atmosphere in Rome that evening must have been electric. Some celebrated the new senatorial control. Others may have concluded that Balbinus and Pupienus were acceptable as emperors *pro tem* but the real future of Rome was the boy's. Just about everyone would have feared the celebrated armies of the Danube and their revered commander Maximinus. The new regime had survived a tumultuous day but danger was everywhere: Herodian tells us that from this moment all the men of the city began to go about armed with daggers, concealed or, increasingly, openly on display (which was illegal in the city). This, presumably, included himself.

One of the first public acts of any new emperor was to distribute largesse to the crowds and provide a donative to the troops, in return for which the soldiers would swear their allegiance. These solemn vows were to be repeated every ten years in the future, and hence were known as decannial vows. For Balbinus and Pupienus this was an especially significant occasion because of the extraordinary circumstances of their rise to power. It was also a possible flashpoint for renewed agitation and it must have been with some trepidation that the emperors emerged from hiding to show themselves to their public. Fortunately the event seems to have gone off peacefully, lubricated as it was with a new issue of coinage. The first coins bearing the heads of the new emperors commemorate the occasion. There were three reverse designs, each of which was issued for both men as befitted the power-sharing arrangement. The simpler of these types just bears the legend *votis decannalibus*, recording the decannial vows given by the troops. The second depicts the personification of the goddess Liberality with the legend *liberalitas augustorum* – the liberality of the emperors – and hence represents their side of the bargain, the doling out of cash. The third and most interesting has the same legend but actually purports to show the public occasion when alms were distributed to the people. Balbinus and Pupienus, together with the boy Gordian *caesar*, are seated on elegant thrones atop a raised platform accompanied by a soldier and the personification of Liberality, while a citizen mounts the steps to receive largesse. A similar design had occasionally been used for these occasions since the accession of the emperor Marcus Aurelius almost a century earlier, although with a much less crowded imperial stage.

The distribution of money and the taking of vows may have done something to stabilize the situation on the streets of Rome, but inevitably there were still deep divisions among the people and military. The rioting suggests that there was a continuing split between the pro-senatorial and pro-Gordian factions, possibly dividing along class or even ethnic lines. Perhaps some people wanted more from their revolution than simply to restore a few super-rich special interests to power. Others may have predicted a swift defeat for the new regime and began carefully aligning themselves for survival when Maximinus and his troops finally entered the city.

Praetorians versus Gladiators

There must have been many who supported the cause of Maximinus by honest conviction, especially among the soldiery, and they would have been keeping a low profile while awaiting news from the front. The military forces in Rome can be divided into three main categories: in ascending order of precedence, the *vigiles* or watchmen, the urban cohorts or military police, and the imperial guard comprising the praetorians and horseguards (the *equites singulares augusti*). The watchmen performed day-to-day policing and, in particular, firefighting duties and acted as night guards: they may have numbered about 7,000 men and were distributed in station houses across the various city districts. The urban cohorts provided the main armed reserve force that guaranteed order, especially if there were signs of unrest. At full strength they numbered at least 4,000 well-armed men, split into cohorts of 500, although in practice the numbers could have been fewer. The praetorians, as we have seen, were an elite soldiery who were supposed to be the emperor's bodyguard but who also performed other policing and ceremonial duties when called upon. Most of the praetorians and horseguard were absent on campaign with the emperor, but their numbers had no doubt been replenished somewhat. The praetorians and most of the urban cohorts, who were under the orders of the city prefect, were billeted in the praetorian camp, a huge barracks complex at the north-eastern edge of the city. The horseguards occupied their two barracks complexes on the Caelian Hill. There was also a separate barracks for secret police and the intelligence services.

These formal troops were not the only forces in the city. There were also various armed groups associated with particular senior families, districts, local gangsters or chariot-racing teams, such that wealthy Romans always seem to have found it easy to hire an armed mob whenever necessary. There was also at least one paramilitary youth organization and, as we have seen, the leading families were able to call on their sons at short notice to provide an armed guard. No account of the forces in Rome would be complete without mention of the famous gladiators in their schools around the Colosseum: slaves whose job it was to fight and often die in the arena as sacred public entertainment. The gladiators themselves may have numbered more than 1,000. All were highly trained in various styles of ritual fighting, whether it was against one another or dangerous wild beasts. Their number included magnificent athletes who were famous across the entire empire just as top sportsmen are today.

It was a good thing for the senate that most of the guard, who might have intervened at some stage on Maximinus's behalf, were abroad with the main army. There was, nevertheless, a reduced garrison of praetorians in the camp, composed mainly of old soldiers who would ordinarily have been discharged but because of the emergency had been retained to help keep the peace in Rome. Some of these men may have been kept hanging on ever since Alexander set off for the east in 231. These soldiers were in an especially difficult position because their absent units and commanding officers were of course still loyal to Maximinus despite the senate having declared him a public enemy. But even if they had wanted to intervene on Maximinus's behalf, they knew they were too small in number to directly challenge the will of the senate and people of Rome.

Although the historical sources are a little confused on this point, it seems that one of the first actions of Balbinus and Pupienus as emperors was to appoint a new man called Sabinus to the important post of urban prefect and hence take command of all the various official forces in Rome. This was an especially difficult brief, with the city tense and highly factionalized and with everyone worried about the consequences if the war was lost. Unfortunately for Sabinus the chaotic situation soon took a drastic turn for the worse.

Herodian tells us that one day a group of praetorian veterans were hanging around the senate house among a sizeable crowd of citizens, all of whom were trying to find out the latest news from inside the chamber. The men were in uniform but apparently off duty. Two or three of them actually entered the chamber, passing beyond the sacred altar of Victory where senators habitually offered incense before taking their places. Innocently, if Herodian is to be believed, these men had strayed beyond the permitted line. In reality they may or may not have been trying to spy on or intimidate the senators in session: we will never know, because two of the senators, who are named by Herodian as Gallicanus and Maecenas, suddenly attacked them with knives. Poignantly, the encroaching praetorians died at the very foot of the altar of Victory, and on searching the bodies they were found to be unarmed.[8]

Their comrades in the street outside ran off in terror, or perhaps in anger to fetch reinforcements. Gallicanus emerged from the senate house, and either fearing legal redress for cold-blooded murder or seeing their flight as evidence of guilt, he theatrically denounced the praetorians as treacherous agents of Maximinus. Brandishing a bloodstained dagger, he exhorted the masses to chase and slay the fleeing men. The praetorian camp was located at the edge of the city, over a mile from the senate house. In their flight the soldiers sustained some casualties from bricks and stones, but they were fitter than the chasing mob and managed to barricade themselves into the relative safety of the camp. The alarm was raised and the soldiers within – presumably a mixture of old praetorians and the urban cohorts – immediately manned the walls. It seems probable that the newly-appointed urban prefect Sabinus was in the camp at the time. An uneasy stand-off ensued.

Of the two named senators, Gallicanus has been identified by historians as Lucius Domitius Gallicanus Papinianus and 'Maecenas' may be Publius Messius Augustinus Maecianus (whose full names are known individually from surviving inscriptions).[9] It is intriguing that both these men were probably Africans and so may well have been part of the faction that had initially supported the Gordians and then, when their death became known, promoted the popular cause of the young *caesar* Gordian III. They may have been more or less openly hostile to the senatorial emperors as well as the supporters of Maximinus. Evidently they decided to continue stirring up trouble. With the crowd still apparently very much in support, Gallicanus encouraged the mob to break into the public armouries and seize weapons. These swords and spears were supposed to be used for ceremonial occasions, not battles, but they were nevertheless serviceable. Gallicanus also took the extraordinary step of summoning gladiators from their barracks, presumably with a substantial payment and the offer of a lavish reward for their help against the praetorians. Other men gathered axes and clubs from houses and workshops or fashioned their own weapons from whatever was available. Soon this ad hoc force started to besiege the turreted walls of the praetorian camp, and in response were met with arrows and spears from the disciplined men within.

It turned into a long hot afternoon of assault and defence, but the attackers failed to break in until eventually, exhausted and with evening approaching, they started to retire. This was precisely the moment for the professional troops inside to mount a sortie. Bursting from the gates, they hacked at the crowd, singling out and cutting down as many of the grimly resisting gladiators as they could find, while the mob fled in terror. Many were killed on both sides including, it seems, the garrison commander and urban prefect Sabinus himself. The historical sources are confused and contradictory on this point, but it seems than in attempting to quell the disturbance he was clubbed to death[10] although we do not know by whom or when. Frankly, the event is suspicious, and it seems most likely that the praetorians themselves could have disposed of their commanding officer, a senatorial representative, just as soon as the situation became clear. With nightfall approaching and the city in a state of anarchy, the troops had no option but to return to the safety of their camp. Now with a broken chain of command and unable to establish their own authority in the city, they seem to have decided to sit it out and wait for events to unfold. By not collaborating with the new regime, those soldiers loyal to Maximinus appreciated they could maintain a clear conscience and would escape retribution should he be victorious, as many probably thought inevitable. Meanwhile the greatest city in the world had just lost most of its police force and mob rule had arrived.

From the Frontier

There is an intriguing suggestion in the *Augustan History* that one of Maximinus's first acts was to dispatch emissaries to Rome to open peace negotiations with the senate "promising to redress the past". Presumably he would have argued that the empire could not afford a civil war at a time when external threats were still so very real. There has been very little speculation in the academic literature about precisely what Maximinus might have proposed to the senate, and whether it might have been sincere, but one person who evidently did think about this was a cunning twentieth-century numismatic forger who doctored a coin of Maximinus to show the legend *LIBERA AVGGGG*.[11] The four Gs imply recognition of four emperors simultaneously, who presumably would have been Maximinus, Maximus (now raised to the rank of *augustus*), Balbinus and Pupienus. Whether Maximinus in fact offered a deal like this we do not know, but any peace proposals were turned down flat and no such coin was ever issued: *caveat emptor*.

The war aim of Maximinus with his battle-hardened troops was simple: invade Italy and crush all opposition before Rome could rebuild its strength and especially before any experienced armies from other areas arrived. He lacked a navy and so had little option but to take the direct approach from the east, crossing Illyria and then the Julian Alps (a range named after Julius Caesar) and descending upon Italy from the north-east. There could be no element of surprise in this strategy except what might be achieved through speed. If all went well, the eternal city would be forced to welcome him as emperor in person for the first time, although not in circumstances either party would have chosen. A ruthless purge of all antagonistic forces and individuals would be automatic. It might even prove necessary to rearrange the politics of the empire once and for all by dissolving the senate so as to prevent it from scheming against the *princeps*. With Rome sorted out, the rebellious regions and provinces would be brought into line through fear.

Maximinus offered his troops an enormous donative as pre-payment for the campaign ahead, draining his treasury in the process. From now on riches would have to be gained by looting. The logistical problems of a large army turned inside out and cut off from its main supply lines were immense. The main routes between Italy and the Danube all became clogged. Front-line units consisting of the trusted Pannonian legions were sent westward, only to meet the last wagon supply trains rumbling up towards them. Absolute priority would have been food and weapons to the spearhead, which was ordered to move against Italy as fast as possible.[12] The organized chaos could not hide the fact that one of the great armies of antiquity was on the move again, and this time Rome itself was the target. If Gordian had indeed styled himself *romanus* (the Roman), perhaps there was a corresponding sense of Danubian national pride in the marching army: after all, these were sons of the men who had installed Septimius Severus in 193 in a similar march on Rome and then subsequently defeated all his enemies one by one.

It was obvious to both sides that the towns of northern Italy were in an exposed position. Maximinus would not want to leave substantial enemy forces in his rear, so he would have to confront and defeat any major troop concentrations there and reduce hostile cities in his path before moving on Rome. The topography and road network, not to mention lessons learned from previous centuries of turbulent history, indicated that Maximinus's advance would first require the acquiescence or subjugation of the great trading city of Aquileia in the north-east (recall that the Adriatic port of Aquileia had previously been used by Maximinus to land Severus Alexander's eastern forces before he marched them to Germany). From there the army would likely skirt inland of the Po delta, and then track back to the Adriatic coast at Ariminum (Rimini). Then the direct route was by the Roman superhighway, the Via Flaminia across the Apennine mountains, although there were in fact other options once Italy was invaded. As the army advanced, many wealthy towns, cities and senatorial estates would be at its mercy, and since much of the land was owned by the rich, little clemency could be expected. To some extent the army could hope to live off the land, but an organized supply line from the east would also be necessary, especially if the war dragged on. The ideal outcome, however, would be that fear would drive the great cities to open their gates, and eventually Rome would do the same, betraying their unpopular newly-elected emperors to the mob and the city police just as Didius Julianus had been abandoned by everyone on the approach of Septimius Severus.

In Rome, as the awkward stand-off at the praetorian barracks continued, the first priority of the tottering regime was to mobilize as many men as possible and devise a way of defeating the advancing veteran army. This was the duty of Pupienus, who went about his task with alacrity as if his own life and many others depended on a successful outcome. Senior military commanders were rapidly appointed from among the senate and a general enlistment was enacted all over Italy, especially from the paramilitary youth groups.[13] Echoes of the tumult come to us from archaeology: for example, we know from inscriptional evidence that a senator called Clodius Celsinus was dispatched to the province of Moesia Inferior on the lower Danube with the especially dangerous job of trying to persuade the remaining legions in that area to turn against Maximinus and attack his army from behind.[14] Many other provinces must have received similar delegations and urgent demands for military assistance.

The loyalty of the Rhine legions would have been a particular concern to the generals on both sides. One might have expected them to side with Maximinus, as they had been party to his coup in 235. But if they could be turned to neutrality or even recruited to the senatorial cause they might prove critical in the ensuing conflict. Pupienus was well respected on the Rhine with strong bonds of loyalty following his own successful governorship there. History is silent, but he surely must have dispatched an important emissary, and the logical choice would have been his son, Marcus Pupienus Africanus Maximus, who had served as consul with Maximinus and therefore personified regime change more than any other individual. If the younger Pupienus was sent on such a mission, a mad dash across the Alps would have been followed by urgent negotiation with the senior commanders in the region, while at the same time he would have to frustrate any emissaries of Maximinus.

The best option for the elder Pupienus and his staff officers was to play for time while forces hopefully flooded into Italy from the rest of the empire. As the late Roman military manual of Vegetius put it, if a commander "knows himself inferior, he must avoid general actions and endeavour to succeed by surprises, strategems and ambuscades ...To distress the enemy more by famine than the sword is the mark of consummate skill."[15] One possibility would be to ambush and delay Maximinus in the difficult mountain passes of the Julian Alps, if it could be organized in time. Failing that, the cities of the north would have to be encouraged to resist behind their walls (those that had them) as best they could until the senatorial army was sufficiently strong and concentrated to seek a decisive encounter. Evidence of this activity survives in the form of an inscription recording a senator called Annianus, who had the extraordinary task of organizing recruitment and weaponry in Mediolanum (Milan).[16] This would be a key strongpoint on Maximinus's flank as he marched on Rome. No doubt similar preparations were under way in the other northern cities. Meanwhile Pupienus set up his command in Ravenna, blocking the approach to Rome. The senatorial forces would also do what they could to sap the morale of the approaching army and encourage desertion, but that might prove an uphill struggle when the stuttering regime was finding that it could not even command the enthusiastic support of its own people of Rome.

All eyes turned to Aquileia at the head of the Adriatic Sea (Map 4). Today it is a sleepy town of just 3,500 inhabitants near the Italy–Slovenia border. It lies on the Italian plain but the snow-capped peaks of the Julian Alps make a spectacular distant backdrop. In the third century it had a population of over 100,000 and was one of the biggest cities in the world. Just like Rome, the city was a few kilometres inland of the coast and supplies reached its heart via a bustling river port just a few hundred metres from the great central forum. Among other amenities it had many temples, several theatres, a sizeable amphitheatre and, on the western edge of town, a circus or chariot-racing circuit with a lap length of about a kilometre and seating for over 25,000 people. Most of this now lies under flat fields, the view interrupted only by the occasional bus stop or tennis net. The site has deservedly been designated a world heritage site (Plate 10).[17]

Aquileia was a key part of the imperial communication network that linked Italy to the Danube frontier, and a major industrial centre in its own right. Various goods and raw materials that came towards Italy from the Illyrian provinces and beyond had to pass through the gates, while luxury goods from across the empire went the other way. The town was famous for its artisans, especially those working amber imported from the Baltic for distribution throughout Italy, as well as glass and gemstones. The surrounding area was crowded with vineyards for cash export, as is still the case today. Aquileia also supplied the frontier provinces with grain and other goods from Africa and the east via its Adriatic port.

In the centuries BCE it had originally been a fortified frontier town but conquering armies soon extended the borders of the empire well to the east

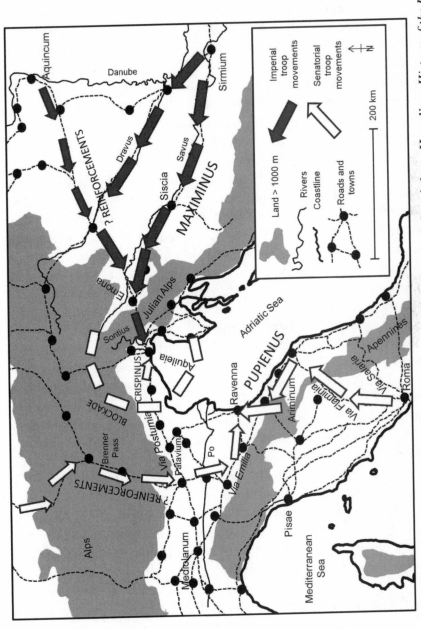

Map 4. Sketch map of the advance on Aquileia in 238. Reconstruction based mainly on Herodian, *History of the Empire* VII.8.9–11 and VIII.1.1–VIII.5.7 and other considerations discussed in the text.

and north and the war zone receded beyond distant mountains. But when Italy was threatened again during the Marcomannic wars of Marcus Aurelius in the second century CE, that emperor rediscovered its strategic situation, and so it was turned once again into a fortress with strong defensive walls, an unusual measure at that time. That was in 163: Herodian tells us that by 238, after a long period of uninterrupted peace and prosperity, the walls had once again fallen into disrepair.

Pupienus selected two senior men from among the council of 20 to prepare the city's defence. These were Rutilius Pudens Crispinus and Tullius Menophilus. Nothing is known of the career of Menophilus to that date. However we have met Crispinus before, as the probable commander of invasion forces that Alexander assembled in Palmyra in 232 and possible leader of the ill-fated southern column that had been annihilated by the Persian archers and armoured knights. Before that, however, he had enjoyed a stellar career including both military and government postings; he had been at one time commanding officer of *legio XV appolinaris* and then governor of Lusitania, Thrace and Syria Phoenice. Things had taken a downturn after the Persian war when he was made governor of Achaia which, it has been suggested, was like a demotion in the *cursus honorum*. Perhaps the defence of Aquileia was regarded as almost a suicide mission and Crispinus volunteered for the job to redeem his reputation or die in the process.[18] No doubt the senators brought with them a garrison of handpicked men. Large quantities of supplies were also rushed in but the task of preparing the defences was complicated by waves of refugees that kept coming in from the countryside to shelter within the walls, bringing more hungry mouths to feed.

Once in the city, the two senior senators supervised a programme of hasty repair work, including strengthening sections of the perimeter and adding towers and parapets. Direct evidence of this was uncovered during archaeological excavation of the river port area in the 1930s.[19] The dock front was clearly a vulnerable point so the road entrances were blocked off and crude towers added, the foundations of which can still be seen today (Plate 11), and their hasty construction is obvious: a jumble of old broken slabs, some inscribed, and bits of broken columns were mortared together on a very approximate ground plan. Another motley set of assorted towers seem to have been added all along the external wall of the circus race-track and a new wall was built in the south and west of the city, providing an additional line of defence. Elsewhere the city benefited from being partly encircled by rivers, providing the defenders with a moat. Eventually, as scouts detected the enemy approaching, the gates were closed and those within awaited a fight to the death. With all this rebuilding and reinforcement, there had been no time to set ambushes in the hills.

The two obvious directions for Maximinus's advance were via the Save and Drave valleys and, given the logistical challenge, it seems likely that he would have sent detachments along both routes to expedite progress. Eventually the routes converge in the plain of the upper Save, where the forces from Sirmium could have linked up with loyal Pannonian detachments coming south from the great bases at Vindobona (Vienna), Carnutum and Aquincum (Budapest) on the Danube. This would be a sensible rendezvous point and location for a rearguard logistical supply and communications base, where the army command could monitor the progress of the Italian campaign while at the same time keeping an eye out for trouble on the Rhine frontier which the senatorial forces were possibly trying to foment.

It is a peculiarity of ancient geopolitics that the border of *Italia*, the Roman province, lay just beyond the natural boundary created by the Julian Alps.[20] When Maximinus and the army approached this formal line, the political situation would have started to clarify a little as they learned of the death of the Gordians at the hands of Capelianus at Carthage, providing a huge morale boost. Herodian tells us that Maximinus was hopeful that Italy would now surrender before a show of force. So, perhaps consciously imitating Caesar and his ceremonial crossing of the Rubicon, he formed his army into fighting array as he entered *Italia*. The order of battle is described in some detail by Herodian. The infantry, he tells us, were spread out in line across the plain of the upper Save, with the equipment and baggage train following in the centre. On the wings were the missile troops, including the exotic African and Eastern slingers and archers, and beyond them the heavy cavalry. These would have included elements of Persian cataphracts alongside the more regular Roman cavalry wings. Barbarian light German horse (presumably including men captured and conscripted in the Rhine campaign) took up forward positions for scouting and initial skirmishing and, if an enemy was encountered, they could be quickly reinforced by the missile troops in the preliminary exchanges. (Herodian, by the way, acknowledged the bravery of the German cavalry but says they would have been of little value in a pitched battle; the Roman mantra, as always, was that mass discipline won battles.) The infantry held the centre of the line. A strong rearguard was provided by the elite praetorians whose job was to protect the emperor, who himself would come forward into a central command position should a general engagement develop. In a pitched battle the elite troops would be held in reserve unless and until absolutely needed. The arrangement described by Herodian was classically orthodox and, aside from the absence of gunpowder, it would have been recognized by Napoleon or Wellington.[21]

Why did Maximinus form up in battle order? Of course a decisive pitched battle would have suited him perfectly, and an army from Rome might just about have had time to reach the upper Save had it been dispatched in good order at the time the Gordians were elected. Much more likely is that he wanted to make a show of strength to boost his troops' morale and intimidate the cities in his path, and we should not forget the fact, recommended by Vegetius, that it was useful to rehearse the challenging task of forming up. Maximinus, it seems, was flexing his considerable muscles.

The first substantial city ahead was Emona (modern Ljubljana, Slovenia), which was nominally part of *Italia* despite being on the eastern foothills of the mountains. So the great army, morale high, with trumpets sounding and messengers galloping about, descended on the city which was to be their campaign base. Unsurprisingly, the remaining inhabitants had fled to the hills, taking all their valuables. The *Augustan History* tells us that in their place a howling pack of 500 wolves had occupied the abandoned streets, which was taken by the more superstitious of the troops as a fearful omen, the wolf being Rome's ancient symbol.[22]

With Italy formally entered, aside from killing wolves, the next obstacle was to take the army over the passes of the Julian Alps. These form an imposing and often snow-capped range with few good routes: Herodian describes them picturesquely as part of Italy's natural fortifications. The passes range in elevation from about 800 to 1,600 metres, and although there were at least two ancient roads capable of transmitting a substantial volume of trade, each would certainly be a pinch-point for an invading army. The main route rises rapidly west of Emona and, after a considerable distance of hard climbing, it drops once again through several steep defiles into a series of sharp switchbacks, only to climb again to a high and desolate saddle. Beyond this, as the vanguard turned into a long column flanked by dense forests and high rocky walls there would be many opportunities for ambush.

Scouts went on ahead in search of enemy units, working stealthily by night if standard procedure was adopted.[23] To their great relief, the passes were undefended. So Maximinus sent his spearhead units across the mountains with orders to press forward to the other side as fast as possible, securing the route towards Aquileia, while the main army reorganized itself at Emona after the long and hasty march. Maximinus chose to remain at Emona for the time being, directing the logistical operation. Nobody would have thought to interpret that as a lack of courage.

Fire!

Back in Rome, the situation at the praetorian camp was worsening. Despite renewed attacks on the walls by the citizen militia and gladiators, with many casualties on both sides, the defences stood firm. The emperor-on-the-spot, Balbinus, attempted to end matters by negotiation, promising a general amnesty to the soldiers within, but this was contemptuously ignored. According to one account "he issued a thousand edicts, to which no-one listened".[24] The praetorians, horseguard and urban cohorts were evidently waiting for Maximinus's expected victory, whereupon they could emerge to receive his thanks and mete out revenge on the city's rebellious inhabitants, the portly Balbinus no doubt foremost among them.

The besiegers, however, were not content to await this outcome, so they decided to cut the camp's water supply by diverting the pipes into new culverts. When the wells ran dry the soldiers had no option but to mount another major sortie, hacking once again at their fleeing opponents, while a squad of engineers fixed the plumbing. The district near the camp (on the Viminal and Quirinal hills) was crowded with multi-storey apartment blocks, many of which had overhanging wooden balconies on the upper floors. As the street fighting surged back and forth some of the citizen mob climbed up the apartments to throw missiles and tiles down on the cohorts. The soldiers responded by setting fire to the houses (just as they had threatened to do years before in the Ulpian riots during the early years of Alexander). Inevitably the fires spread rapidly through the crowded neighbourhood and soon raged out of control. It then became a horrendous conflagration, all the worse because the men who would normally try to put it out were the ones doing the arson. Herodian says that a significant fraction of the city burned down and many innocent people died in the flames, and that the area destroyed was as large as any single city of the empire other than Rome herself. This suggests at least 100,000 people were made homeless, the worst such conflagration since Nero had famously fiddled.

Into Italy

As Rome burned, the first of Maximinus's Pannonians descended on to the plains of Italy, singing in triumph and relief at the lack of opposition in the mountains. Many had never seen Italy, let alone Rome, and waging war on the capital must have seemed an awesome prospect. But now their feet were on true Italian soil, the weather was good – it was mid to late May by now – and the enemy had fled. But as the soldiers advanced through the rich agricultural land they began to come across the first hints of opposition. The country had been stripped bare of its livestock and provisions and the famous and beautiful bridge over the River Sontius (called the *pons aesonti*) had been destroyed to impede their advance.[25] But the river was low, so it was no problem for them to simply wade across the rocky riverbed, hardly getting their feet wet and no doubt chuckling at the folly of their opponents (Plate 11). Reports indicated that a day's march beyond, Aquilea had closed its doors and the walls were manned. So, acting by the book, the forward commanders gathered the available troops and launched an immediate attack on the walls. It proved unsuccessful and the experienced Pannonians were driven back, suffering heavy losses from stones, spears and arrows.

The news that Aquileia was resisting was passed back down the column to the furious Maximinus at his headquarters in Emona. This had not happened to Septimius Severus.[26] Maximinus knew the city well, of course, having been in command there as Alexander's great army of the east was landed in 234. Its position on the main highway and strategic significance was such that if he wanted to maintain communications with his troops on the frontier it simply had to be taken before the march on Rome could resume. He therefore decided to try negotiation. Among the forward army – no doubt there for just this eventuality – was a senior tribune (general) who was a native of the city and whose wife and family were within the walls. Maximinus ordered this man to approach the walls under a flag of truce to deliver terms. The choice was stark and impeccably traditional: an amnesty for all, or annihilation for all.

To many of the peaceful citizens it might have made sense to open up the gates and let the army occupy it rather than suffer the brunt of an attack by an enormous force which, to the dismay of the inhabitants, could be seen hourly increasing in size. It seems likely that the town would have accepted this offer were it not for the senatorial forces that had been rushed in during the preceding days and weeks. Their aristocratic commander Crispinus ran about the ramparts rallying the defenders and persuading them to stand firm. Herodian gives him a speech that contains a surprisingly un-heroic and utilitarian analysis of the two sides' asymmetric motivations for war. Like some of the other set pieces in Herodian's great work, it reads like notes for a speech that he intended to craft but never completed:

Earn yourselves the title of saviours and defenders of all Italy. Do not believe the promises of a tyrant who breaks his word and deceives people. Do not be enticed by fine words into surrendering yourselves to certain destruction when you can rely upon even chances in war. Numerically smaller sides often defeat bigger armies; supposedly weaker sides frequently overthrow those with a reputation for bravery. So do not be disconcerted by the size of the army. Those who are fighting for the benefit of another person, and have to depend on him for any future happiness that might occur, are only moderately enthusiastic for a fight, because they know that, though they will have their share of danger, someone else will reap the greatest benefits from the victory. Those who are fighting for their own land can expect more from the gods, because they are asking not to appropriate others' property but to save their own. Their motivation to fight is not someone else's order, but their own essential interest, since the entire fruits of victory will be for them.

Herodian, *History of the Empire* VIII.3.4–6.

With this argument Crispinus was successful in persuading the citizens to continue in their resistance. It might have been because of his famed rhetorical skills, or it could also have been down to occult forces because at the same time sacrifices were being made to the local god Belenus by Tullius Menophilus, the other senatorial representative. Belenus is a fierce Celtic sun god whom the Romans had identified with Apollo (and, in more modern times, was frequently invoked by Asterix the Gaul in the classic comic books of Goscinny and Uderzo). Belenus's cult was popular across the empire but was apparently strongest in Aquileia where many dedications survive. So sacrifices were made, the entrails were read and, to the relief of the populace, the omens were good: Belenus would protect the walls and Aquileia would emerge victorious from the siege.

A few days later Maximinus himself descended from the foothills with the rump of the army, where at a point located precisely by Herodian as 16 miles from the city he came upon the ruined bridge. But the Sontius was by now in spate: melting snows in the mountains had raised the level so that it was now difficult to cross safely. This detail, incidentally, confirms that it was by now May when the peak flood still occurs.[27] Some German cavalry tried to swim their horses across (it was a task they were specifically trained for) but were swept away by fast-flowing currents which, Herodian pointed out, they were unused to in the rivers of their own country. With the vanguard still besieging Aquileia, the main army was forced to pitch camp and figure out a way of getting across this chilly torrent.

This was a job for the famous army engineers. There was very little mature timber in the area, so normal bridge-building was ruled out. The solution, we are told, was ingenious. The marauding troops discovered that there were many empty wooden wine barrels in the district, awaiting production of the new vintage later in the season. They were very large containers used for export in bulk. The country was scoured for such barrels, which were lashed together and piled with brushwood and soil. After just two or three days the structure was strong enough to support the passing army that was then able to resume its march.

But even this short delay was potentially important. As each day passed, all the men and animals of the huge invading force required feeding, and rations were dwindling fast. Foraging parties were sent far afield but the countryside was found to be devoid of villagers, animals and crops. The land was fertile but it had not been used to grow food: viticulture dominated almost exclusively. Unripened vines covered the landscape that, Herodian tells us, the soldiers destroyed out of vengeance as they began to go hungry (and in so doing they destroyed "the natural beauty that once belonged to the countryside").[28]

Defenders of all Italy

The Romans had learned the art of siege warfare from the Greeks and by the third century it had become a highly developed part of the war machine.[29] Indeed the essence of siegecraft hardly changed from ancient times until the advent of gunpowder: accordingly, the defending force had to rely on its walls and towers to keep the enemy out while at the same time maintaining access to fresh water and rationing the available food. Every effort would be made to inflict losses on the enemy by attrition, firing from the heights or else preparing devilish traps and surprises for the attackers. An occasional sortie could be mounted to destroy men or equipment if the besiegers became complacent.

For the attackers, the first option was to try to seize a city by *coup de main*, that is, an instant frontal assault in the hope that the shock would be enough to open the city before the inhabitants settled into the routine of defence. That had already failed. The next strategy was to negotiate surrender with threats; that too had failed. Then it was advisable to try to take the city by treachery, which was always a good bet in a civil war: there may have been many within whose true loyalties lay with the besieging force and who might be tempted to save their lives and property at the expense of the rest. Such individuals might open a gate at night or usher a commando force into the city by some other unexpected route. If the population stood firm, however, then the attackers could try to starve them into submission, but Maximinus knew he did not have the time to accomplish this, with his own army going hungry and other forces in Italy rapidly organizing against him. So a costly direct assault would have to be made, either in one place or several spots simultaneously to stretch the defenders. An attack could be made using ladders on an intact part of the perimeter – a so-called 'escalade' – or a breach could be made using battering rams and artillery. Other options for the attackers were trickery (as in the Trojan horse), tunnelling in, undermining the ramparts, running large siege towers up to the walls or building a huge ramp. In any of these scenarios the first wave of attackers would be in an extremely exposed position and unlikely to survive, hence the highest award for bravery was traditionally given to the first man over the walls.

As the main army arrived after their long forced march (in a state of exhaustion, according to Herodian) they continued the encirclement of the city, keeping carefully out of bowshot, with each unit allocated a particular sector. It must have been most disconcerting for the defenders to see the huge army spread out facing them from all directions for many miles in circumference. The remaining supply lines were cut off and the city was henceforth subjected to a formal siege. Once again it is to Herodian that we are indebted for a detailed account of what happened.

Maximinus deployed the "complete range of siege engines". Some had been manhandled by the legions over the mountain passes,[30] although the larger pieces were probably locally constructed from materials collected from demolished buildings outside the walls. These would certainly have included the ballista, a kind of heavy crossbow that fired rocks or large iron darts. Every century of a regular legion was supposed to have such a machine, making a total of 55 per legion, so there may have been hundreds on the field, possibly including some that had fired bolts on the Harzhorn. The power was provided by putting coiled sinew under extreme tension using cranks and winches to pull back a bowspring. If flinging rocks, it would be aimed at weak parts of the walls. It could also send burning projectiles over the parapets to try to start fires within the city. A smaller fixed crossbow on similar principles was the scorpion, which was more of an anti-personnel device.

But the really heavy machine was the onager (or kicking ass) which had a massive spring-loaded bar and more of a slingshot action to fire rocks or other projectiles at or over the walls; of these there was one per cohort, or ten per legion, according to the manual.[31] These machines were on wheels and the operators were normally protected from incoming fire by screens and earthworks because the defenders had their own ballistae and scorpions mounted on the towers.

Under cover of the first artillery exchanges, the battering rams were trundled up to the walls, each with a squad of men under a protecting roof made of supposedly inflammable materials. Despite this precaution the defenders fired incendiary arrows of pitch and resin down upon them, and with some success. When a ram reached the wall's base the wheels were removed and the structure was affixed permanently to the ground to prevent recoil, which would have taken time and considerable nerve under fire to accomplish. The battering ram itself was a great timber beam with a tempered iron cap, often actually cast in the shape of a ram's head, which would be repeatedly swung against the base of the wall to weaken it and hopefully open a breach. The first knock of the ram was, across the ancient world, a symbolic moment because everyone knew it meant that those within had at that point relinquished any claim to mercy, such was the ancient version of the rules of war.

Despite this ghastly threat, one by one the siege machines were destroyed and the walls held. Maximinus then ordered a general assault. Men charged forward with ladders and started to climb, only to be met by the Aquileians' secret weapon: incendiary tar. This evil substance was concocted from a recipe of pitch, oil (presumably olive oil), sulphur and bitumen. It had been ladled into jars and dispersed around the walls so that each group of defenders could quickly react to an attack in their sector. It is not clear whether the jars were thrown like petrol bombs or simply tipped over the walls in flaming cascades, or both. Either way, the burning tar proved devastating against troop concentrations at the foot of the walls and easily destroyed their ladders. Herodian emphasizes not the men killed, which may have been comparatively few, but the many injuries and disfigurements that this nasty weapon caused. Many men lost their eyesight as they looked up into the flaming rain while scaling the walls; exposed parts of the body were badly burnt as the cloying substance charred away the skin; others lost hands and fingers. Perhaps most terrifying was the effect the blazing goo had on plate armour where it stuck, heating the metal to a red incandescence while at the same time the leather straps and buckles around the torso hissed and shrunk in desiccation. Soldiers were in danger of cooking to death, so many stripped off and fled, leaving their cuirasses piled up and looking like so many captured trophies at the foot of the wall.

Stalemate developed as the siege settled down into a rhythm and the attackers probed day and night for weaknesses. Within the city, everyone helped in the 24 hour defensive effort, including the many refugees from the surrounding country. One source gives us the colourful if dubious detail that the women of the city donated their long hair for the manufacture of bowstrings.[32] The watch needed to be incessant: a single slip-up could lead to an enemy encroachment that might easily turn into a rout and then a general massacre. By daylight the outlaw emperor was himself a most conspicuous figure on the plain, regularly greeted by the foulest of insults from the walls whenever he appeared. At first both sides achieved some successes but as the days passed the situation became progressively more worrying for the besieging force. The city had plenty of food and drinking water, whereas the huge attacking army with its enormous supply footprint was finding it increasingly difficult to feed itself. As morale declined outside so, in proportion, it rose within.

Infamy!

As the siege stuck so the wider strategic situation was deteriorating for Maximinus. Pupienus was rapidly building and training his strike force at Ravenna, steadfastly refusing to march prematurely to the city's aid and thereby risk defeat in battle: instead he ordered checkpoints and roadblocks all over Italy and a naval blockade of the Adriatic to prevent any unscrupulous merchants from delivering much-needed provisions to the invaders. Herodian tells us that even the local footpaths around Aquileia were blocked off so that news of the outside world could not reach his army.[33] This detail might indicate that senatorial forces managed to break the supply and communication line back over the Julian Alps; if so that would have been a major strategic achievement on their part. Despite this precaution (or perhaps because of it) Herodian talks of stories spreading among the besieging troops; that all of Italy was mobilizing against them, armies were approaching from the east and south and that a huge force was being mustered in Moesia to attack their home bases from the rear. All of these rumours may have had some truth in them.

And so the besiegers became, in a wider sense, the besieged. It was an old cliché but real enough for those confronted with the situation. Most of the men slept in the open, exposed to the elements as hunger gave way to starvation. A famous maxim of ancient warfare was that "famine is more terrible than the sword".[34] Presumably men gazed hungrily at the pack animal corral, but these could not be slaughtered because they would be needed for the advance on Rome. As the first men actually began to die of hunger, the elite assault troops, presumably better fed than most, made increasingly reckless assaults on the walls, fighting their way past the decayed bodies of the fallen and the charred remains of siege engines. No doubt every weakness in the city was probed and attacks were made at dead of night as well as during the day, but each attack was repulsed with heavy losses and the returning troops were berated by their increasingly desperate commander. To make matters worse, some of the attackers reported seeing terrifying apparitions of the god Belenus himself in the sky above the city: "I am not sure whether the god really appeared to some of the men or whether it was their imagination", Herodian remarked, in his typical sceptical spirit.[35]

According to the *Augustan History*, Maximinus had two of his generals executed for cowardice, presumably after a failed assault. Making an example of them was no doubt calculated to inspire the men to even greater feats of daring and sacrifice, but it could also backfire by creating resentment, including among the senior army staff. It seems to have been a desperate move, especially as none of the sources suggest that Maximinus risked his own life in any of the attacks. Some may have wondered what would happen if Maximinus was killed: would the war simply end?

About a month into the siege during a midday lull in the fighting, a group of soldiers from *legio II parthica* approached the praetorians on guard outside the imperial command tent. Some sort of parley took place, followed by a commotion. The soldiers, bodyguard included, started to tear down the sacred imperial images from the standards about the tent. This was a treasonous act. Zosimus tells us that in those feverish moments Maximinus sent his son out to reason with the troops, hoping that his youth and beauty would incline them to compassion. It did not work, because they murdered him "in a most barbarous manner". His most senior general, a military prefect, was also killed when he appeared. Whether Maximinus, the old soldier, put up a fight is not certain. According to one account, on seeing his son killed, he was permitted to take his own life. Another late source tells us that a daughter, otherwise unknown to history, was also killed on this occasion "to the accompanying military jest that a whelp from inferior stock must not be kept". The conspirators then rushed into the command centre and massacred all the senior advisers. It was just three years and three months since Alexander and his entourage had been similarly slaughtered in their tent at Mogontiacum. If we accept the most likely chronology, Maximinus was in his 65th year when he met his death, while his son was about 21.[36]

The motive for the assassinations appears straightforward. The military situation had reached a costly stand off and parts of the army, especially its Roman core, would have been profoundly affected by the news that the once legitimate emperor had been declared an enemy of the state. The conspirators of Aquileia may have calculated that the deaths of a few men, who themselves owed their position to violence, could bring a costly war to an end. Herodian specifically alludes to the fact that the men of the Second Parthian Legion who instigated the plot were based at Mount Alba on the Appian Way near Rome and that their wives and children lived in the capital. Many of these men were actually Romans by birth. It has been suggested[37] that the praetorians and second legion were very closely connected, on account of them both being recruited from Rome; historians have been able to demonstrate from inscriptional evidence that pairs of brothers served in both units. So there were no doubt personal as well as patriotic interests at stake. And there was, of course, a substantial bounty on the head of Maximinus.

The death of Maximinus could not suppress the people's fascination at the old emperor's extraordinary physique. There is a story that one half of the royal footwear ended up on display in a grove between Aquileia and another town, which is otherwise unknown but possibly its seaport, called Arcia. Whether this was some religious site or more in the line of a circus exhibit is not clear, but it became famous. The *Augustan History* tells us men agreed that the boot was twice the normal size, "whence also is derived the vulgar expression, used for lanky and awkward fellows, of 'Maximinus's boot'".[38]

Chapter XII

A New Start

Heads on Sticks

At this point, with the subject of the book dead, it is worth remarking that we shall be examining his image and legacy in a future chapter. But the situation was still developing, so for now we will return to the narrative.

With the blood still flowing, the conspirators must have been in great danger from potentially loyal soldiers nearby. Evidently they were sufficiently organized to prevent an immediate riot around the command tent, which suggests a degree of forward planning. It was imperative for the assassins to present the rest of army with a *fait accompli* and gamble on the fact that morale was sufficiently low that the situation would simply be accepted. The news spread through the encircling army in an instant. Herodian tells us that the soldiers in general "were nonplussed and by no means all pleased at the event".[1] Most displeased of all were the Pannonian and Thracian legions who had been responsible for Maximinus's elevation and had been his most trusted troops. To them he was a hero, raised from their own ranks. Many of their officers were, no doubt, chosen men. But with the bulk of the starving army willing to accept the situation, they had to pretend, however reluctantly, to be pleased by the development. More genuine quiet celebrations no doubt began in various quarters. The praetorians hacked off the oversized head of Maximinus and severed his son's more elegant neck, throwing their bodies to the assembling crowd for ritual desecration, as was the Roman way. The heads were retained as proof positive of the death of the erstwhile *augustus* and his *caesar*.

The leaderless army stood in a state of indecision until some of the soldiers approached the city walls under flag of truce to inform the defenders that the war was over, and to beg admittance to the city. The Aquileians, of course, were much too canny to let anyone in. Initially they may have suspected that the whole thing was an elaborate ruse. Even when they had been shown the heads of the tyrants they would have feared the consequences of admitting large numbers of armed, ravenous and, to them, barbaric, soldiers into a city packed with refugees, women and children. Perhaps their hatred was such that many of the inhabitants were happy to watch the army continue to starve outside. Wiser counsel prevailed, however, presumably from the two senior senators Crispinus and Menophilus. A ceremony was arranged in which the images of Pupienus, Balbinus and the young Gordian Caesar were brought to the walls, garlanded in laurel, and the troops outside were required to formally acknowledge them as legitimate emperors and shout up their new oaths of allegiance. The defenders also demanded retrospective recognition of the legitimacy of the two elder Gordians who had died at Carthage; that is, that they were rightly gods who had ascended to heaven. With varying degrees of reluctance or enthusiasm the encircling army acquiesced to these demands in the face of a celebrating and perhaps jeering populace on the walls.

After that, and presumably as part of the bargain, an extraordinary market spontaneously developed. Herodian tells us that "every commodity – all the things a prosperous, flourishing city might offer to satisfy people's wants" was sold or bartered down from the ramparts, including "all kinds of food and drink, clothes and shoes". Shoes in particular must have been in short supply in a great army that had marched over mountains with no prior preparation. The encircling troops were astonished, realizing that they could never have starved this city into submission. Herodian tells us that for a time the situation still *looked* like a siege, with the army set in its encampments encircling the city, but it was not. Best Aquileian wine was being shared around the camp fires. Dead heroes were buried and mourned, within and without the walls, and a condition of "peace and friendship" evolved. But the gates remained firmly shut.

Meanwhile a group of trusted officers were selected for the job of crossing the lines in search of the emperor Pupienus, with a precious cargo: the heads of Maximinus and his son. Presumably this delegation included the assassins themselves, or men very close to them, including senior officers from key units of the invading army. Local towns opened their gates to the horsemen, rejoicing in the news of the surrender. The squad learned that Pupienus was in Ravenna. It was not so far away – just 100 miles or so down the Adriatic coast, but very difficult to approach directly because of the marshes and lagoons of the Po delta. And so, presumably with consideration of the prevailing winds, the emissaries decided to take a boat. Soon they pulled into Ravenna harbour and hurried up the narrow streets to the imperial headquarters conveying the priceless news that the whole army now recognized the senatorial regime as legitimate.

The co-emperor was at that time still busy assembling his elite battle troops, including a significant force of cavalry from the German legions who were personally loyal to him from his time as provincial governor. If these units had indeed travelled from the German frontier they must have endured the high Alpine passes at a less-than-optimal time of year. Their presence signifies that the Rhine legions, which the histories are otherwise silent about during these momentous events, had not declared for Maximinus, and it emphasizes just how isolated the forces at Aquileia had become.

Naturally there was much rejoicing at the unexpected end of hostilities. But while it is not difficult to imagine the relief felt among the men at Ravenna, the future was still very uncertain. The immediate problem for Pupienus was to reassert control over the half-starving troops massed around Aquileia. And the wider strategic situation across the empire was a thorough mess.

Thanksgiving

The morning after the delegation arrived, sacrifices were made to the gods and omens sought in the bloody entrails in the traditional manner. The signs were favourable, so Pupienus ordered the men to make haste towards Rome carrying the heads of the tyrants to lay before Balbinus and the senate. A separate messenger was dispatched to go on ahead, with orders not to stop for any reason whatsoever. All these envoys would have used the imperial posting system, requisitioning fresh horses at regular stations on the way. The best interpretation of the garbled accounts in the history books is that the single messenger's journey took just three days, while the main delegation arrived on the fourth day. According to one story, games were being held in Rome, with Balbinus and Gordian in attendance, when the first man arrived. As he made his way to the imperial box the crowd guessed the meaning and cried out "Maximinus is dead!" The emperor and *caesar*, after some urgent consultation, theatrically nodded their assent to the crowd. The performance was immediately curtailed and the people rushed to the temples to give thanks.[2] The senators assembled spontaneously in the Senate House. One of them, Cuspidius Celerinus was first up, proposing a motion that equestrian statues should be made of the emperors and the boy *caesar* in celebration (this was quick thinking, it seems his son was soon made governor of the rich province of Cappadocia by the joint emperors).[3] Heroic sentiments abounded. It was without doubt the senate's highest point since the end of the Republic.

The following day the main delegation arrived. Herodian's account seems to be that of an eyewitness:

It is impossible to describe the scenes of celebration that day after the arrival of the messengers, and their sudden entry into the city with the head of the enemy stuck on a pole for all to see. People of all ages ran to the altars and temples; no one stayed indoors. They were swept along as though a spirit was in control of them, congratulating each other and all rushing together to the circus, as though there were a public assembly there... while all the magistrates, the senate and every ordinary man was bursting with joy, as if he had shaken off a sword that was hanging over his head.

Herodian, *History of the Empire* VIII.6.7–8.

Balbinus, in his capacity as joint highest priest of the empire, led the official thanksgiving, presumably at the Temple of Jupiter Optimus Maximus, where he "actually in person sacrificed hecatombs"[4] as thanks to the gods for the safe deliverance of the city, followed by a general feast and party. A hecatomb was a hundred cattle, so it sounds like hard work for the portly old gentleman. Official messengers wearing laurel wreaths were dispatched to the provinces bearing the news, while the already rotting heads of the tyrants were burned on the Field of Mars "as the mob capered".[5]

As this was going on in Rome, the other emperor and chief priest, Pupienus, had made his way north and entered Aquileia where he was greeted by the heroic leaders of the defence, Crispinus and Menophilus, and the rest of the garrison, and was showered with flowers by the joyous populace. Yet another hecatomb of unfortunate beasts was sacrificed, and no doubt the old god Belenus was specially honoured by the faithful for his role in delivering the city from its mortal foes. Delegations from other northern cities converged on Aquileia bringing their own priestly rituals and sacred statues, emphasizing that they too had been ready to fight the tyrant just like the heroic Aquileians.

Archaeological excavations have produced a poignant relic from precisely this time,[6] which currently stands exposed to the elements in the archaeological park near the ancient port area of Aquileia (see Plate 12). It is a marble altar showing the personification of Aquileia kneeling before Roma herself and is dedicated, for joy and victory ("*pro salute et victoria*"), to Juno, Minerva and Mars. It is an appropriate trio of deities for a siege: Juno, consort of Jupiter himself, had a special role as a protector of those who honoured her, as did Mars, the god of war, who in this inscription is specifically given the epithets "Protector" and "Victor". Minerva is another warlike deity who was invoked especially for military victories that were earned by cunning, courage and perseverance. The altar recorded the emperors Pupienus and Balbinus and Gordian *caesar* and was set up in the names of the commanding officers of a specific unit, the *cohors I ulpia galatarum*, who refer to themselves as "agents in the survival of Aquileia" ("*agentum in protensione aquileia*"). The officers' names are Flavius Servilianus and Flavius Adiutor. The latter has the extraordinary title of *praepositus militum*, which seems to have been an ad hoc temporary command: at least in later times *praepositus* came to mean something like 'commanding officer'.[7] These men are otherwise unknown unless, by a long shot, Adiutor is one and the same as a man who 20 years earlier was recorded as a beneficiary of an irrigation scheme at Lamasba in Roman Numidia (now Tunisia), where he is specifically recorded as being an army veteran.[8]

As the sacrificial blood flowed over this and other altars, the encircling army assembled once again in peaceful posture, carrying laurel branches and acknowledging Pupienus the man (and not just his image) as their rightful emperor, who then formally addressed them. Herodian's account is worth reproducing in full as it contains interesting insights from the period, albeit through his imagining, into the political stance of the new regime and the senate's attitude to itself, the empire and its subjects:

> You now know from experience the value of changing your minds and falling into line with Roman policy. In place of war you are at peace with the gods in whose name you took your oaths, and you are now being true to your military vow, which is the sacred secret of the Roman Empire. For the future you must always enjoy these benefits by keeping your pledges to the Romans and to us your emperors. The senate and the Roman people decided to choose us because of our noble birth and many achievements in a long series of offices, which we held like graded promotions before reaching this final position. The empire is not the private property of a single man but by tradition the common possession of the Roman people. It is in the hands of the city of Rome that the fate of the principate is placed. We have been given the task to govern and administer the empire with your assistance. If this is done in a disciplined and properly ordered way, with respect and honour shown to the rulers, you will find a pleasant life which lacks nothing. And in the provinces and cities everyone will live in peace and obedience to their governors. You will live as you want in your own homes, not in foreign lands undergoing privations. It will be our care to see that the barbarian nations keep the peace. There are two of us emperors, so there will be more efficient rule at Rome and abroad if any emergency arises. One of us will always be quickly on the spot for service as it is demanded. None of you should imagine that there is any recrimination for the past on our part (since you were under military orders), nor on the part of the Romans or the rest of the nations that rebelled when they were unjustly treated. There must be a complete amnesty, a firm treaty of friendship, and a pledge of loyalty and discipline forever.

Herodian, *History of the Empire* VIII.7.4–6.

Pupienus sensibly cemented the amnesty with a large distribution of money to the troops outside the city so that they might once again pay their way as individuals and be formally re-integrated with the Roman army. Then, with the high politics played out, the army retired to its encampments and everyone fit to do so no doubt reflected on the fact of their personal survival, waiting anxiously for new orders and postings.

Soon enough, Maximinus's legions were sent back to their bases on the upper Danube as Pupienus had promised, where the imperial propaganda was quick to celebrate them as protectors against the barbarians.[9] Tullius Menophilus was apparently given the command because he later appears in charge of these legions on the Danube front. In contrast, the elite core of the army, the praetorian guard, was to return to Rome in the service of the new emperors. The praetorian barracks on the edge of the city was their rightful base, and no doubt their arrival was intended to help ease the stand off with the defiant veterans back in Rome. Pupienus also took with him the force of German cavalry who, it seems, had recently and dramatically crossed the Alps and mustered at Ravenna in his personal service (it being a long-established tradition for a commander to have a personal bodyguard of German cavalry).[10] Our sources do not mention in this context the men of *legio II parthica*, the unit from Rome that had instigated the assassination, but it seems consistent with the general policy that they too would have accompanied Pupienus back to their home station as reward for their action.

Despite these pragmatic and seemingly wise arrangements there were still serious tensions. According to Herodian the show of loyalty from Maximinus's core troops had effectively been forced upon them by the situation, and the majority was quietly resentful and angry. Although they had not been publicly disgraced, the prestige of the elite Pannonian legions whose star had ridden high since the days of Septimius Severus had been greatly diminished. Many individuals must have thought back wistfully to those heroic days of rebellion that had brought their beloved champion Maximinus to supreme power, and how they had subsequently delivered victory after victory in the name of Rome against assorted tribes deep in barbarian territory. They might justifiably have felt betrayed by the city they had fought for.

Pupienus marched south at the head of his ad hoc force and some time probably around late June he finally approached Rome, where there was another staged ceremony, the *adventus* (arrival) of the emperor. His co-emperor Balbinus and the young *caesar* Gordian III came out to meet him, leading the senators and people of the city. As was traditional on such an occasion, sacrifices were made to the goddess Fortuna for the safe return of the emperor. There were further scenes of wild celebration and rejoicing at the happy turn of events and Pupienus received the thunderous applause of the senate.[11] The task for the co-emperors, as they looked out over a partly smouldering capital, was now to secure this very uneasy peace.

Diffidentia Mutua Augg

Those raucous days of celebration must have helped remove the stain of odium associated with the two emperors' unorthodox means of elevation to supreme power. A brand new and highly distinctive coinage was issued, emphasizing harmony and partnership at the top (Plate 12). The six issuing departments (*officinae*) at the great mint were divided equally between Balbinus and Pupienus. All the new reverse types show their hands clasped in a universal sign of partnership. The types for Balbinus are *concordia augg* (concord of the two emperors), *fides mutua augg* (mutual trust of the two emperors) and *pietas mutua augg* (mutual piety of the two emperors). The three reverses of Pupienus advertise *amor mutua augg* (mutual love of the two emperors), *caritas mutua augg* (mutual charity of the two emperors) and *patres senatus* (fathers of the senate). This latter type is especially interesting: the title *pater senatus* in the singular crops up occasionally in Roman history, but the plural usage very aptly represents the unique constitutional role of the joint emperors as leaders of the senate. All these coins, incidentally, were double-denarii, the denomination that had successfully been avoided by Alexander and Maximinus but was now reintroduced in response to the dire financial situation. The average weight of these pieces was 4.75 grams compared with 3.0 grams for the single denarius, but the silver quality was good, and it has been suggested (optimistically, perhaps) that this was a pragmatic new re-launch for the currency after the debasement of the single denarius which had occurred in the preceding decades of turmoil.[12]

The spirit of the times demanded that the two emperors receive honours equally, but there might have been worry in some quarters that sharing glory was not the way of Roman patricians, at least not for hundreds of years. Each man had his own nexus of patronage to support and their lines of influence must, in many places, have been in competition with one another. Pupienus had gained by far the most personal credit from the war by leading the army. According to strategists such as Vegetius, the most praiseworthy kind of victory a Roman general could win was one achieved by guile, by outmanoeuvring and starving the enemy and avoiding the risk of pitched battle. By this strategy, Pupienus had even preserved Maximinus's fearsome Illyrian legions more or less intact and suitable for immediate redeployment on the Danube against the barbarians. In contrast, the administration of Balbinus in Rome had been farcical. The corpulent old man had been unable even to control the senate, and his attempts to impose order had been flatly ignored by most of the factions. It cannot have reflected well on his personal standing that a large part of the city had been burnt to the ground on his watch. Later tradition has it that he was "a timid soul by nature, who trembled when he heard Maximinus's name".[13]

Herodian tells us that with the immediate danger over, the emperors "began a tug-of-war for personal power",[14] both secretly aiming for sole rule. Balbinus considered himself the senior man by age and because he had served his second consulship first. Pupienus had the greater reputation as a soldier and administrator and had served as urban prefect, which Balbinus had not (although in that capacity he had made himself conspicuously unpopular with the lower orders). And then there was young Gordian *caesar*, who was an inconvenience to both emperors and especially to their potential hereditary heirs, should either achieve sole rule. We know that Pupienus had two sons in the senate, both of consular status. The elder, Titus Clodius Pupienus Pulcher, had been made suffect consul in 238 even before his father's proclamation; the younger, Marcus Pupienus Africanus had shared the ordinary consulship with Maximinus in his first year (236).[15] There was also a young grandson in the line. If Balbinus had male descendants it is not known, but it remains perfectly possible, given the scanty evidence. In contrast, the boy Gordian was champion of the African faction in the senate and favourite of the people, many of whom believed him to be the rightful emperor by dynastic succession. Everyone knew that the rebellion had been started by the elder Gordian and his son who had died heroically on the field of battle, that their legitimacy had been formally ratified by the senate, and also that the senatorial emperors would have willingly and quietly passed over this legacy had they not been forced into an embarrassing U-turn on the very day of their elevation by acknowledging the young nephew as *caesar*.

On the plus side, Herodian tells us that the new regime began to rule the city efficiently and sensibly and the emperors enjoyed a deluge of popularity stemming from the defeat of the common enemy. Even the great fire would have had its advantages in that it had cleared a less-than-genteel district of the city, providing an opportunity for improved town planning. Meanwhile there was a major reshuffling of senior appointments across the empire, both of provincial and military commands, as men who had been too closely identified with Maximinus were removed and supporters of the senatorial emperors rewarded. A particular problem was the province of *hispania citerior* (nearer Spain, roughly equivalent to modern Catalonia), which had been resolutely pro-Maximinus in the war: Rutilius Pudens Crispinus, hero of Aquileia, was apparently sent there to settle matters tactfully.[16]

And so it was that in 238 the common people of Rome were once again ruled by true patricians, which is seemingly how they liked it: Herodian asserts this[17] and he was there. The cluster of grand and historic buildings in the centre of Rome was, once again, a seat of real power and influence. Rome's relief and joy morphed into a summer of sport as everyone's attention turned to a month of games, the so-called Capitoline games which were held every four years, and had become so important that they replaced the ancient olympiad in the imperial calendar. They were a mixture of athletic tournaments, recitals and shows: poetry, history, oratory, comedy and magic were included. According to Herodian, everyone was busy attending the performances and one can't help wondering if he himself contributed in the historical line (although the book that survives was written after this date). The contrast with the reign of Maximinus, who had confiscated the games budget, was obvious to all.

But not everyone was happy. The residential north-east of the city had to cope with a displaced population, and looming beyond its ruins, there was the massive praetorian camp. Across this smouldering wasteland, enmity between the people of Rome and their well-paid military police force was deeper than ever.[18] And within the camp there were basically two sets of comrades united by hatred of the city and its popular rulers. There were the older men who had stayed behind when Alexander had departed for the east in 231 and who had subsequently been assaulted by the populace on account of being supporters of Maximinus. Some of their friends had been killed in the street fighting and they had ended up being holed up in the barracks, besieged by the mob, hoping for a favourable outcome on a distant battlefield that never came. Then there was the praetorian core of the army that had departed in such pomp with the Alexander's *profectio* but had just returned in ignominy, if not actual defeat. Some assuaged their wounded pride by grumbling that their failure to capture Aquileia could not in fact be considered a victory for the senatorial troops, as it had been an act of the god Belenus, who had somehow been offended.[19] Others, it is true, had colluded and even participated in the assassination of Maximinus, so there must have been a diversity of opinion, but all of them would have felt the very real shift of power away from the army towards the upper-class regime. To add insult to injury, Pupienus had brought with him a loyal guard of his own, the cavalry units from the German legions, who now acted as a *de facto* horseguard. The potential for bar-room brawling between opposing units must have been running high.

As they watched the people enjoying the games, Rome's senior generals must have appreciated that the external strategic situation remained dire. The civil war had drained resources from the troubled frontiers. Unsurprisingly, a new insurrection was once again brewing in the difficult province of Dacia beyond the Danube. Reports of large-scale raiding in Thrace by the Goths were coming in, and Africa was still in the hands of Capelianus who, although he had technically never opposed the senate (his defeat of the elder Gordians was probably achieved before either he or they knew of their legitimization), must have realized he would be unlikely to expect favour from the new regime. His third legion, victorious at Carthage and fat on pillage, was in the same exposed position. Far more worryingly, Ardashir had made stunning conquests in the east and was now in possession of a large tract of once-Roman Mesopotamia, including several fortified cities that everyone had confidently assumed would be Roman forever. Dura Europos was severely exposed, possibly even surrounded. Such a situation was unprecedented in hundreds of years of imperial expansion. A firm hand was needed to restore the imperial borderlands and protect the tax-paying regions whence many of the troops themselves originated.

Suddenly, probably sometime in early August – the chronology is not fully determined – there was another momentous development. A band of disillusioned praetorians set out for the imperial palace with the intention of leveling the score and assassinating the emperors. The old men received advanced warning of what was happening and fortunately still had time to respond. Pupienus sent for his loyal German bodyguard, but Balbinus countermanded this order because he was suspicious that it was actually an involved plot against himself ordered by his colleague. Critical minutes passed, making the coins that advertise the 'mutual faith' of the emperors deeply ironic. The prevarication proved calamitous. When the praetorians arrived, the palace guards, uncertain of the chain of command, deserted their posts rather than be slaughtered. The patrician emperors were hunted down and captured among the sumptuous galleries and porticoes (surprisingly, perhaps, there were no panic rooms or escape tunnels), then stripped naked and subject to "absolutely degrading insults" by the soldiers. Their beards and eyebrows were yanked out and their naked flesh was mutilated as they were dragged out towards the praetorian camp. The reason for not killing them on the spot, according to Herodian, was that the prateorians wanted to extend their agony, such was the degree of hatred.

Yet even now it was not too late for them, as news of the palace assault finally reached the German guard. Weapons were seized, horses mounted and a hastily assembled squad set off to rescue the emperors. But when they approached, the praetorians simply slit the two men's throats in the street. By the best estimate it had been just over three months since their dramatic elevation in the senate and only two months since the death of Maximinus. Presumably there was a dangerous stand off in the streets before the opposing forces realized that the need for fighting was over. In some ways the contending interests of the empire had reached a consensus. The constitutional coup of the senate had failed. And given the fact that Herodian clearly disapproved of boy emperors, his great history has a stark ending:

This was the end of Maximus [i.e. Pupienus] and Balbinus, a death that was undeserved and desecrated for two respected and distinguished old men, who had come to power through their high birth and by their own merits. Gordian, aged about thirteen, was saluted as emperor and took over the Roman empire.

Herodian, *History of the Empire* VIII.7.8.

Chapter XIII

Empire of Fortune

Turn of the Wheel

Aand so it came to pass that Marcus Antonius Gordianus, an aristocratic boy with a strangely pointy nose, became the most powerful person on the planet. Just a few months earlier the eventuality would have seemed laughable, but the Romans had a way of rationalizing such twists of fate: they called it fortune, as made flesh in the shape of the goddess Fortuna, daughter of mighty Jupiter. Whereas we might associate 'fortune' with a piece of extraordinary good luck or a large sum of money, to the ancients – pious, superstitious and ambitious in equal measure – Fortuna was mistress of worldly events. It was the duty of mortals to venerate her, and in doing so she might be appeased or actively enlisted in a personal cause. Confidence, ambition, cunning and avarice were clear virtues in her eyes. Those saved from death on the battlefield honoured her just as those whose children were taken by plague or accident wailed lamentations to her. The origin of her cult in Rome is accredited to one rich and worldly Roman who, in a supreme combination of piety and arrogance, worshipped the fickle goddess as his personal intimate. In the modern world she would be venerated from Shanghai to Gao Bang and from Wall Street to the Bronx, the muse of banker and beggar alike.

In statues and coins (see Plate 12) Fortuna is usually shown holding a ship's rudder resting upon a globe or orb. In her other hand she holds the cornucopiae, the fabled 'horn of plenty' (a sacred object superabundant with fruit and flowers, symbol of wealth, fertility and, to the Romans, the all-important concept of dynasty). The meaning is clear: to embark on a journey, whether literal or metaphorical, is to entrust your destination to her. The orb and rudder could represent navigating the physical world, but the orb was also seen as a symbol of worldly sovereignty, a symbolism that lived on into the days of medieval kings, who would generally be depicted orb in hand. But the most ominous and enduring of Fortuna's symbols, rarely absent from her side and still resonant today, is her turning wheel. The wheel of fortune implies that situations change and eventually repeat.

To those who contemplated fortune's wheel in 238 it must have been clear that the Roman state was in danger of entering yet another cycle of violent destruction. Gordian was the same age as Severus Alexander had been when he had become supreme ruler of the empire just 16 years before. Would the new emperor survive even to manhood? It was now six months into the consular year and so far no fewer than six individuals had legitimately held the title of *augustus* (fully a fifth of the grand total since the original Augustus over 260 years before) and another (Maximus) had been *caesar*.

But against the odds, the waves of factional suspicion and hatred that had washed over the empire now began to dissipate as, variously, the supporters of the old Severan regime, of Maximinus, the Gordians, and of the senatorial emperors, all began to sense that enough was enough. The boy emperor was of impeccable aristocratic ancestry and an innocent compromise candidate that few could object to. Even so he was placed under close protection as the senate ratified his advancement as sole *augustus*, handing him all the levers of power (theoretically at least). Tellingly, his titles included the traditional *pater patriae*, father of the fatherland, and he was never advertised as *pater senatus*.

Loose Ends

Herodian's cliffhanger ending to his history of the times is all very well but there is something rather fishy about it. Neither he, nor anyone else, reported public outrage at the deaths of the senatorial emperors as might have been expected, especially at the slaying of Pupienus, the hero of Aquileia. Balbinus and Pupienus, men of very different character but intertwined fates, were never deified by the senate despite their previous heroic actions and undeserved (according to Herodian) end. There is no notice that the soldiers who tortured and killed them were ever held to account. So perhaps also there is something in a claim made much later, in the early sixth century by Zosimus, that Balbinus and Pupienus had been secretly conspiring together against the boy Gordian. They had ordered some soldiers to dispose of him, and when the plot came to light they themselves were murdered by the praetorians in retaliation.[1] Perhaps it is relevant that there are instances of their names having been chiselled out of inscriptions, including the very one in Aquileia raised by the first cohort of Galatians that celebrates their victory over the forces of Maximinus. Their statues in the harbour at Piraeus may well have been tipped into the sea deliberately at this time.[2]

Be that as it may, it seems the two were not subject to formal *damnatio memoriae* by the senate although there may have been confusion at the time that persists to this day.[3] Balbinus, we know, was buried at his opulent villa beside the Appian Way because that is where in modern times his fine and unmolested sarcophagus was discovered. Perhaps with the emperors dead and unable to defend themselves against the charges, with complex family interests at stake, and with an extremely tense and factional situation in the capital, a collective decision was to leave the affair uninvestigated and move on.

It is surely a regret that Herodian tells us nothing about the reign of Gordian III, despite the fact that the old historian is thought to have lived for up to a decade more. But it was dangerous to write about current affairs so perhaps that is not surprising. The unreliable and intriguing *Augustan History* has a brief account of Gordian's reign, seemingly derived from the chronicle of Dexippus;[4] and of course epigraphy, numismatics and archaeology also continue to be invaluable. From these clues, a broad outline of what happened can be assembled.

At the time of their murder the senatorial emperors had been in the early stages of planning two military campaigns, with Pupienus to lead an army against Persia and Balbinus against the Carpi, who were once again troubling Dacia. These wars would restore order to the empire and also, hopefully, bolster the martial reputations of the new *augusti*. Most of that planning was now quietly shelved, except that Tullius Menophilus, one of the heroes of the defence of Aquileia, was awarded the prime military posting to lead a campaign against the Goths and Carpi.[5] Although it was imperative for the Roman state to provide security for its eastern provinces and respond to Ardashir's continuing aggression, the new regime seems to have instead adopted a policy of defensive recuperation there. Accordingly there was no new call to arms and it was even claimed that peace had descended on the empire.[6] The great cities of Nisibus and Carrhae (and possibly also Singara) were left in Persian hands, which suited Ardashir who was able to consolidate his historic gains. As far as can be determined the rest of the year 238 passed peacefully enough in the east.

The power behind Gordian's throne seems to have been an alliance of senior men including, probably, the consuls, praetorian prefects and urban prefect. According to lists and inscriptions, the ordinary consuls for 238 were Fulvius Pius and Pontius Proculus Pontianus, but these men had been appointed by Maximinus and we do not know how successfully they had negotiated the power struggles of that difficult year. Praetorian prefects around this time were men called Pinarius Valens and one 'Domitius', but unfortunately the historical sources are equally silent about their actions. The consuls for 239 were the boy Gordian III (as was normal for an emperor in the first full year of his reign) and a man called Manius Acilius Aviola, a member of an ancient and noble line and a close relative of one of the vigintivirate who had been appointed to oppose

Maximinus in the civil war,[7] but he too is otherwise unknown to history. From these very meagre clues, it seems likely that Aviola could have been effectively in charge of the imperial administration as regent.

One man who did eventually emerge as a major political force in the new regime was Gaius Furius Sabinius Aquila Timesitheus. We first met him when he was transferred by Severus Alexander from the east to be emergency military governor of the Rhine provinces at the time of the Germanic invasion in 233/4. We have noted that he was probably the one person powerful enough to have attempted opposition of Maximinus's coup in 235 but chose not to act at that time and was rewarded with lucrative eastern postings. His later prominence throws up an intriguing possibility that Timesitheus had taken a prominent role in the civil war of 238 in opposition to Maximinus.

In 239 (the first full year of Gordian's reign), the main Persian force evidently felt itself sufficiently strong to launch an assault on Dura Europos, the exposed forward Roman stronghold on the Euphrates. This was the base of the *dux ripae* (riverbank commander), as we have seen in the account of Alexander's Persian war. For the inhabitants of Dura, knowing that several great cities in their rear had fallen the year before, it cannot have been much of a surprise. Direct evidence for the attack comes from a poignant graffito scribbled on the wall in the 'House of Nebuchelus' uncovered by archaeologists in the 1930s: "On the thirtieth day of the month of Xandikus of the year 550, the Persians descended upon us."[8] Xandikus was a month in the old Macedonian calendar and the counting system is that of the Seleucid empire which formally began in October 312 BCE. (It is interesting that this system, so much more convenient than the Roman method of naming the years after the consuls, was still in use in Dura.) The date translates as 20 April 239, near the beginning of the campaigning season. Also dating from around this time, from a private house in Dura, is an epitaph to a senior Roman commander: "Julius Terentius, tribune of the Twentieth Cohort of Palmyrenes, the brave in campaigns, mighty in wars, dead – a man worthy of memory, Aurelia Arria buried her beloved husband, whom may the divine spirits receive and the light earth conceal."[9] It seems that besieged Dura held out *in extremis* despite losing this senior officer (who, incidentally, is also depicted in a colourful surviving wall painting from the city).

Later that year the boy emperor and his entourage made a state visit to the east, beginning in Antioch and then moving on to the city of Osrhoene. The evidence comes partly from a Byzantine legal document referring to a case heard in Antioch, which implies the emperor's presence, and the coinage of the eastern cities.[10] For example, a piece from Alexandria shows Gordian on horseback trampling an eastern barbarian, suggesting a military campaign. But the most interesting coin is from Osrhoene, featuring a scene in which Gordian is being presented with a figure of victory by King Abgar X; Gordian adopts the pose of a Roman consul, which contrasts with Abgar's flowing eastern garb. The message on this coin is most easily explained if the Roman military, and in particular the Osrhoenian units, had had some success against the Persians in 239, possibly repelling the enemy from the walls of Dura. These forces might even have included some of the men who had fought with Maximinus in the German forests and at Aquileia, now returned to the east. The coin also implies that the constitutional status of Osrhoene was re-normalized, having either rebelled or been told to fend for itself the previous year, or possibly before.

In 240 Gordian returned to Rome as is evidenced by the coinage commemorating his safe arrival, with the standard type for a returning emperor: *fortuna redux*. But with the situation in the east temporarily stabilized, if not fully redressed, trouble now broke out in Africa. The *Augustan History* gives us a very brief and confusing account,[11] presumably summarized from Dexippus:

> In the consulship of Venustus and Sabinus [i.e. 240], a revolt broke out in Africa against Gordian III under the leadership of Sabinianus. But the governor of Mauretania, who was first beset by the conspirators, crushed it for Gordian so severely that all of them came up to Carthage to surrender Sabinianus and confessed their wrong and sought pardon for it.
> *Scriptores Historiae Augustae* (Julius Capitolinus), *Gordiani Tres* XXIII.4.

It has been suggested that this Sabinianus was the governor of Africa,[12] presumably having been sent there by the senate on the death of the elder Gordian. The account has strong echoes of the African rebellion of two years before. At that time, as we have seen, the elder Gordian's Carthaginian militia was defeated by Capelianus with his force from Numidia comprising *legio III augusta* and auxiliary Numidian horsemen. We do not know the fate of Capelianus or his supporters who had ransacked Carthage and the other great African cities in 238, but it seems that one of the first acts of Gordian III as emperor was to disband the third legion and disperse its troops to other units across the empire.[13] The fact that Capelianus never raised a serious rebellion and was never heard of again may be testament to some unseen stroke of diplomacy. The reason for Sabinianus's revolt is unknown but it might have been related to the power vacuum left after the disbandment of the third legion. Perhaps he was forced to claim imperial power by a faction from Thysdrus in a copycat emulation of the successful elevation of the elder Gordian two years earlier – so much is possible, at least. The text quoted above implies that the rebellion was initially successful before being defeated. Whatever the truth of it, it does show that the chaos continued in the once peaceful and prosperous province of Africa.[14]

In 241, Gordian III was proclaimed consul for the second time. His colleague this time was Clodius Pompeianus about whom nothing is known. Gordian officially came of age and took for his wife the daughter of Timesitheus, a girl called Tranquillina. Like Alexander and Orbiana in 226, the royal couple were both aged about 15 or 16. At the same time, Timesitheus was appointed praetorian prefect and head of the prateorian guard. The *Augustan History* tells us that Gordian appointed Timesitheus because of his erudition and eloquence, but this is hardly convincing: muscle and influence seem more likely.

Meanwhile, something strange seems to have happened on the Danube front. Tullius Menophilus, hero of Aquileia, was removed from power and presumably executed then damned to the memory and his name erased from inscriptions. According to the *Augustan History*, Gordian himself took command of the legions in Moesia.[15] The dramatic fall from grace of Menophilus suggests some treasonable act on his part, although nothing more is known about it. It also seems likely that Gordian's government secured the uneasy peace by paying tribute to the Goths for the first time.[16]

Decline and Fall

It can hardly have been a surprise when major hostilities flared up once again with the Persians in 241. A large force under Ardashir's son Shapur finally captured the desert stronghold of Hatra (by treachery on the part of a Hatran princess, according to legend), presumably putting to the sword any remnants of the Roman garrison that had been installed a few years before. It seems likely that, as a reward for this victory, Shapur was promoted co-ruler of the Persian empire as Shapur I, and was given overall military command. In response, Gordian and Timesitheus decided on a major new campaign against the Persians in order to recapture Mesopotamia and then invade their empire, very much in the manner of Alexander a decade before.

Gordian ceremonially opened the great gates to the ancient Temple of Janus in Rome in 242. This symbolic act, which was obviously recorded in state annals and was consequently one of the few facts of his reign known to some later historians, signalled a declaration of war, although there had hardly been peace across the empire before that. The young emperor left for the east in the company of his powerful father-in-law. The event was, presumably, just as magnificent as the *profectio* of Severus Alexander in 231, although there was no historian to describe it. A detailed study of the coinage from the eastern provincial mints has allowed a reconstruction of the main events that followed.[17] Just like Alexander, Gordian made Antioch his base and took some time to assemble and train his forces. The army finally left the city in the spring of 243, crossed the Euphrates at Zeugma and, under the command of Timesitheus, inflicted a major and crushing defeat on the Persians. The site of this battle was recorded much later in the history of Ammianus Marcellinus as Rhesaina in Mesopotamia (now Ra's al-'Ayn, Syria);[18] Ammianus simply records that Gordian vanquished the Persian king (presumably Shapur) and put him to flight. The victory was so overwhelming that the Persians were forced to vacate Nisibis and Singara in the aftermath. For this we have the incontrovertible evidence that the cities once again began to issue coins in Gordian's name (and also Tranquillina's), (see Plate 12).[19] In this way Rome recovered its province of (upper) Mesopotamia and control over the Khabur River which had been lost about five years before, as well as a great deal of lost prestige.

And so, with Mesopotamia restored, and a popular young emperor preparing for a new assault on the Persian heartlands, it is time to abandon the narrative of events lest the story starts to become too repetitive. Suffice to say that Fortune was about to take another drastic turn for the worst as far as the Romans were concerned, with strong echoes of the coup of Maximinus. Gordian was either killed in battle or murdered by his generals. The bloody convulsions associated with Fortune's accelerating wheel then continued for decades. By 270 there was such widespread rebellion and disorder that it seemed the empire was in its death throes. By that time, a Roman emperor (Decius) and his heir had been killed fighting the Goths, the first time an emperor had fallen in battle against a foreign enemy, and another emperor Valerian, a man reputed to have been part of the Gordians' delegation to Rome in 238 and the assassin of Maximinus's prefect Vitalianus, had been captured by the Persians along with his entire staff and was being kept in miserable captivity. The empire fragmented as rival confederations of provinces emerged in both the east (centred on Palmyra, but including Egypt and most of the east) and west (with a rival imperial dynasty in control of Gaul, Britain and Spain for a decade). A horde of Goths had overrun Greece and sacked Athens, no less, while other armies threatened the Rhine–Danube frontier as never before. One Persian incursion led by a resurgent Shapur had managed to invade as far as Syria's Mediterranean seaboard, capturing many cities and culminating with the sack of Antioch itself. Inflation, economic stagnation, plague, and weak leadership assailed what remained of the 'legitimate' Roman empire, which became hunkered down in Italy and a few surrounding provinces. One military coup after another failed to reverse the process and only added to the anarchy. Meanwhile the Persian empire went from strength to strength under the long reign of Shapur, who became known as Shapur the Great, and Roman prisoners were put to work building cities and bridges and improving the irrigation system of Mesopotamia. The contrasting fortune of the two great empires is best seen, perhaps, in their respective coinage. On the Roman side, the silver double-denarius as reintroduced by Balbinus and Pupienus quickly became so debased as to become a small bronze coin, hastily manufactured in huge quantities and worth very little, driving all the old denominations out of circulation. In Persia, on the other hand, the silver coinage continued with no debasement or reduction in quality, the coins of Ardashir mixing indiscriminately with those of his successors for many years to come.

This was not, however, the end for the Roman empire. Against all the odds the emperor Aurelian (ruled 270–275) managed to reunite the provinces east and west in a series of brilliant campaigns before he too was assassinated by his staff officers. Later, another strong soldier emperor, Diocletian (ruled 284–305), steadied the body politic, effected a series of deep structural reforms to the empire (economic, military and, especially, constitutional; he set up a tetrarchy of four co-emperors) and, after actually retiring from office twice (something unheard of), managed to die peacefully in his bed: the first emperor to achieve this since Septimius Severus at York almost a century before. Soon after that a strong ruling dynasty along more traditional monarchical lines was established by Constantine I (ruled 307–337) and the empire was re-founded in comparative strength.

But by this time it was not really a Roman empire any more. The most important city in the late empire was Byzantium in the east, renamed Constantinople. Even in Italy, Rome became second choice as residence of the emperors after the more conveniently situated and comfortable Ravenna. Many rulers of the 'Roman' empire never set foot in the supposed capital, or perhaps only made short visits for sightseeing purposes. The senate of Rome became marginalized as far as the imperial administration was concerned. A second senate was set up in Constantinople while a court and civil service sprung up around the person of the emperor, wherever he happened to be. Culturally and artistically the late Roman empire was a far different entity from its classical forebear. The imperial persona became modelled on Persian customs. Strange religions flourished, including Sun worship and Mithraism; and another eastern cult, Christianity, actually became state policy under Constantine and most of his successors.

Using the long lens of history, the tumult of the third century is seen by many historians as the end of the classical era and the beginning of a new period known as Late Antiquity, which in turn blends with the early medieval period (depending, critically, on which country one happens to be from). The snobbish fourth-century historian Aurelius Victor was probably the first to identify the death of Alexander and his replacement by the 'practically illiterate' common soldier Maximinus as a decisive turning point:

> Henceforth, as long as the emperors were more intent upon dominating their subjects than upon subjugating foreign peoples and preferred to fight among themselves, they threw the Roman state into steep decline, as it were, and men were put into power indiscriminately, good and bad, noble and base-born, even many of barbarian extraction ...So the violent power of fortune, once it had acquired unfettered freedom, drives on mortals with destructive desire ...After almost all were overcome by depravity it entrusted the government even to the lowest in birth and training."
>
> Aurelius Victor, *De Caesaribus* XXIV.[20]

Or, as Gibbon put it more succinctly: "After the murder of Alexander Severus, and the elevation of Maximin[us], no emperor could think himself safe upon the throne, and every barbarian peasant of the frontier might aspire to that august, but dangerous station."[21]

Chapter XIV

The Giant's Legacy

Damnation

Maximinus, emperor of Rome, was formally subject to *damnatio memoriae* by the senate on the day he was deposed in the spring of 238, the precise date being uncertain. This meant there would be no solemn ceremony of deification when he died and his birthday and date of accession would not be marked with sacrifices in the temples of the empire ever after, as he had no doubt hoped would be the case. The memory of his wife Paulina and son Maximus *caesar* were also damned. All their public images were destroyed or defaced by order. Their names and titles were carefully chiselled out of inscriptions but, as was usual in such circumstances, the inscriptions were generally left standing as mute testament to their disgrace. They would forever be omitted from the list of "good emperors", fondly recalled.[1]

There were of course limits to what such a campaign of rewriting history could achieve: some inscriptions escaped destruction, especially in the farther reaches of the empire or, it seems, in military establishments where enduring sympathy with the man may have resided. One such relic was dug up in 1838 among the ruins of an army blockhouse at Roman Brocolitia (now Carrawburgh) on Hadrian's Wall in Britain, recording some repair work undertaken there. It is worth reproducing as a rare survivor (albeit fragmentary) of countless similar inscriptions that would have been seen across the empire formally advertising the victories of the emperor and his son. The stone says:

IMP CAES G IVLIV VERO MAXIMINO P F AVG GERM MAX DAC
MAX SARM MAX PONT MAX TR P III IMP VI COS PROCOS P P
ET G IVLIO VERO MAXIMO GER MAX DAC MAX SARM MAX
NOB CAES NOS SVB ...VCCIANO V C LEG AVG PR PR COH I
BATAVORVM FECIT CVRANTE BVRRIO ...STO PRAEF PERPETVO
ET CORNELIANO COS

(For the Emperor Caesar Gaius Julius Verus Maximinus most Holy and
Fortunate Augustus, greatest in Germany, greatest in Dacia, greatest

in Sarmatia, High Priest, holding tribunician power three times, hailed imperator six times, consul, proconsul, Father of the Fatherland; and for Gaius Julius Verus Maximus, greatest in Germany, greatest in Dacia, greatest in Sarmatia, most-noble Caesar. We, the First Cohort of Batavians, have made this, during [the administration of governor ...T]uccianus, the most illustrious of men, legate of the emperor with propraetorian power, under the supervision of the prefect Burrius[...]stus, in the consulship of Perpetuus and Cornelianus.)[2]

The imperial titles and acclamations date this inscription very accurately to the end of the year 237. The Batavians were long-term stalwarts of the wall garrison, originally from what is now the Netherlands.

Once before, on the death of Caligula, the senate had attempted to recall the coinage, melt it down and re-mint it under the name of a new emperor but it had proved an impossible task, and after that episode there is no evidence that coins were systematically withdrawn from circulation on the death of a damned emperor (except, perhaps we may speculate, the gold aurei, which seem to be very rare for the disgraced emperors including Maximinus). So his regular coins continued to circulate, indiscriminately mixing in pots and purses with those of Balbinus, Pupienus and Gordian III. There are a number of instances of provincial coins where the images of Maximinus or his son were defaced by disgruntled owners in antiquity.[3] In one case the portrait has been doctored to show his head on a stake. Presumably this coin was passed on tails upward. Another coin was defaced in a different way (see Plate 13): the reverse design which probably featured *salus augusti* – the health of the emperor – has been filed flat as if in a curse, and although the name of Maximinus and his title Germanicus remain on the obverse, the titles *pius* (associated with the priesthood) and *augustus* have apparently been defaced, presumably after the senatorial proscription.

The very large number of surviving and unmolested coins gives us the most important evidence of the man's appearance in life, but they also provide us with a puzzle because there are three distinct styles of portrait, which look almost like different people (Plate 13). (This does not count the provincial issues, which sometimes look like one of the official portraits of the Rome mint, but sometimes seem to be largely imaginary, charming as they are.) To try to unravel this we must first consider whether the official image was actually intended to be lifelike.[4]

The portraiture of Maximinus on the coins has been discussed by several authors,[5] although not with much agreement. Ignoring the provincial issues, the first style of portrait (which for convenience we will call type 1) is found exclusively on coins of the first emission from the mint in 235, which are associated with the first tribunician power. The more gracile of these resembles quite closely the image of his predecessor Severus Alexander, although the nose is hooked, the chin is more angular, and – perhaps a significant clue this – the hairline usually has a right angle bend similar to all later versions of the portrait and distinctly different from that of Alexander. The portrait on the second emission (type 2) associated with the second tribunician power awarded on 1st January 236 is quite different in profile. Above the eyes it is similar to type 1, but it has a straighter nose and distinctly jutting chin. These features give the emperor a lifelike but smugly prognathous expression that can hardly be called handsome. The third portrait style (type 3) first appears in a special issue of 236 celebrating victory in Germany, in which the title *germ(anicus)* appears on the obverse legend for the first time. Here both the forehead and chin jut forward, sometimes to an extraordinary degree. This style of portrait is found on all subsequent emissions from Rome up to 238, and so was presumably the one endorsed by the emperor himself. It is one of the lines of evidence that has led to the diagnosis of acromegaly (giantism).[6] Despite this, most regional mints in the east of the empire seem to have stuck with an image resembling the type 2 portrait.

Despite Maximinus's damnation, several fragmentary and defaced statues survive and they are all apparently on the same model.[7] The most poignant relic is a fragment found on the Palatine Hill itself, in the very centre of Rome, the city's sacred birthplace where Romulus himself supposedly ploughed out the original city limits, and, in imperial times, site of the emperor's palace complex (the word 'palace' itself derives from 'Palatine'). Now on display in the Palatine Museum, it is the upper half of a head, showing a close-cropped military haircut and furrowed brow. This piece is of exquisite quality made of the best Luna marble (Plate 15) and is probably a remnant of an official statue that had been sited outside the opulent residence that Maximinus never visited as emperor, possibly the type from which others were copied. As such it was very likely destroyed on the very day the senate outlawed him. It appears to have been attacked with a mallet or sledgehammer after the eyes and ears were roughed up with a pick.

Three much more complete versions of the same statue survive (Plate 15). One, now in the Louvre, was discovered during nineteenth-century excavations of a wealthy villa on the Appian Way. It too had been deliberately smashed and the fragments discarded as rubble, but it has been restored. Another similarly reconstructed statue is on display in the Capitoline Museum in Rome. A fourth bust, now at a museum in Copenhagen, has had its nose, ears and chin lopped off in an act of deliberate mutilation. It is displayed alongside a bust of Maximus that received similar treatment. All in all, the restored works show that the sculptor managed to give the big man an intelligent if careworn expression. He looks a statesman, hard and commanding but certainly not an ogre. Although one commentator has suggested that "the heavy, protruding jaw and bulging, ape-like brow ridge seem to be emphasized to the point of caricature",[8] the features are certainly not as extreme as on the coins.

Curiously, perhaps, when viewed in profile, the surviving statues most resemble the type 2 portrait. There are several ways of reconciling these observations and the following explanation is just one possible scenario. When the senate ratified Maximinus's advancement to *augustus* in the spring of 235, the emperor was of course absent, and the mint workers were under pressure to put out a first issue of coinage as quickly as possible. An equally pressing need was to replace the statues of Severus Alexander with ones of the new emperor. A statue may have been available in the city, perhaps from a previous sitting of the illustrious general, or possibly a master sculptor was put to work to produce a likeness from memory, advised by people who knew the emperor well. This formed the basis of the official statue on the Palatine Hill carved from finest marble, and the type 2 portrait on the coins. Multiple copies would be made for private houses, public spaces and temples to the imperial cult all over the empire. But perhaps the mint could not wait for the final version of this statue and so, as has been suggested quite reasonably, the engravers may have based their initial portrait on Maximinus's murdered predecessor Severus Alexander,[9] beefing up the features. They usually got the hairline right from the beginning, however, which seems more than a coincidence, so the resemblance to Alexander may be more due to the fact that the dies were made with the same hub as had been used before, giving a similar curve to the head and jaw line, but with the external features such as the nose and hairline altered. Thus the type 1 portrait is very unlikely to be a good likeness of the man.

Meanwhile it seems perfectly plausible that a master sculptor was dispatched to the frontier on the orders of the senate to bring back a true likeness of the new first citizen. Hence it was probably on the Rhine or Danube that the emperor's features were captured after the victorious army had returned from Germany during the winter of 235/6. This sculpture could account for the type 3 portrait, and by this reckoning it is probably most lifelike, even if it is the oddest-looking of the three. The appearance of this portrait on the coins coincides with the news, in early 236, of the German victory. The new design was not, so far as we know, used for replacements of the official statues. Maximinus never came to Rome as emperor and the budget was tight, so a new set of statues based on the type 3 portrait was probably never ordered.

This may be the best we can do from the standpoint of over 1,500 years. But we can be sure the engravers were delighted to have a new emperor to depict, and especially one with such strong features. The best medium for their art was the large-flanned bronze sestertius. When well executed, these exuberant pieces capture a bold and powerful portrait with a penetrating and intelligent eye, which was no doubt the intention, although others, it has to be admitted, verge on the grotesque and have something of Mr. Punch about them (Plate 14). It is unusual to find two coins struck from the same die, so each specimen that survives can be thought of as a more or less individual work of art produced by an unknown engraver in antiquity. These extraordinary relics are not very expensive to acquire, especially in a worn condition, but any prospective collector should beware of Internet fakes.

The peculiar features of Maximinus on these coins was, of course, one line of evidence that led to the suggestion that he had a pituitary disorder. According to the neurologist who suggested this,

> Acromegaly... has characteristic effects on the skull and face. The skull becomes enlarged and thickened, and all its bony ridges are exaggerated; the margins of the orbits, including the supraorbital ridge, the cheekbones, the external occipital protuberance, and most striking of all, the lower jaw, become enlarged. The mandible juts out significantly, resulting in prognathism.
>
> Klawans, 1982, p. 323–4.

This explanation is certainly worth considering given that cartoon-like exaggeration is not known from anywhere else in the repertoire of Roman imperial portraiture.

Roman Villain

Herodian's is the only contemporaneous account of the reign of Maximinus to survive. He was not a polemicist and was capable of forming a balanced judgement.[10] He wrote approvingly of the military victories but castigated Maximinus for his cruelty and rapacity, setting the tone for later authors:

> Once Maximinus had taken over the empire, he caused a great change, exercising his power cruelly and causing widespread fear. He tried to make a complete transformation from a mild tolerant autocracy to a savage tyranny, conscious of the hatred against him for being the first man to rise from the most humble origins to such a fortunate position. But by his birth

and normal behaviours he was a barbarian. Possessing the bloodthirsty temperament derived from his ancestors and his country, he devoted himself to strengthening his rule by cruel actions.

Herodian, *History of the Empire* VII.1–2.

Subsequent writers repeatedly emphasized Maximinus's barbarian origins and lack of a good education (a point stressed, for example, by Aurelius Victor).[11] He became identified as the man on the spot when the rot set in for imperial Rome, and was blamed by implication for half a century of misfortune that followed his death. In the fourth century the *Augustan History*, whether simply concocted out of thin air or based on earlier writings or tradition, added further to Maximinus's reputation for cruelty. That work portrays him as a veritable monster, and has the people of Rome offering prayers to the gods that he would never come to the city. His lowly birth was never forgotten; rather it was accentuated as he was associated with the feared Goths who threatened Rome throughout the third, fourth and fifth centuries.[12]

His reputation as a persecutor of the Christians also contributed to his deteriorating image when the empire formally adopted that religion. Following Eusebius of Caesarea he was to be placed sixth in the most heinous list of persecutors, although as previously discussed the direct evidence for a systematic crackdown against the sect in his reign is thin.[13] The early Byzantine pagan historian Zosimus, writing around the beginning of the sixth century, elaborated on his monstrous cruelty and injustice, accusing him of murdering out of avarice and plundering whole towns (which might just be a reference to the quartering of his army in Emona) and becoming "intolerable to all men".[14] By the tenth century he was described as "by nature a barbarian in character as well as in race, for his murderous behaviour was hereditary".[15] Such themes echoed for Edward Gibbon and his contemporaries in 'Enlightenment' Britain, and it is perhaps too easy to perpetuate this snobbish, even at times racist caricature into modern times. Thus from twentieth and twenty-first century writings: "He was a low-born barbarian and he behaved as such"; "Every anecdote and, indeed, all evidence suggest a man utterly unwilling to confront – and perhaps unable to comprehend – those aspects of the world that were not susceptible to intimidation and resolution by the force of his own two hands."[16]

Gothic Hero

In 410 the unthinkable happened: Rome was sacked by an army of Goths (quite respectfully sacked, in that religious buildings were left inviolate by order of their commander, Alaric). It was not actually the end for Rome or its institutions, and the rump of the Roman state fought back against the Goths and various other barbarian groups with some success over the coming decades.[17] Barbarian units served alternately as allies and enemies of Rome in a military and political barn dance that stomped across the western empire for many years. A decisive moment occurred in 452 when Atilla the Hun achieved what Maximinus and, after him, the Goths had failed to do, by successfully besieging and sacking heroic Aquileia, although it took Atilla so long that his starving forces were never the same again. In the end, the most prominent result of these struggles was twofold: the final defeat of the Huns and the collapse of central authority and provincial government in the western Roman empire. Local kingdoms sprung up across Europe and North Africa, ruled by descendants of the old barbarian elites who had hailed from outside the empire (Vandals, Franks, Goths, Burgundians, Saxons). Eventually, and astonishing as it must have seemed, a Gothic kingdom was established in Italy, with overlordship of Rome herself. All in all this was the inevitable result of the collapse of the Rhine–Danube frontier, as had long been feared by Rome's master strategists: Augustus, Hadrian and Marcus Aurelius, to whom we might, of course, add Maximinus. The eastern half of the empire continued to call itself 'Roman' and inherited its institutions, but it became a distinctly eastern Mediterranean power centred on Constantinople.

Inevitably, perhaps, the upper-class Goths who found themselves in Italy began to value education, art and the finer points of civilization that they discovered in the conquered territories (no doubt starting with good food and wine). They had long ago been converted to Christianity of the Arian variety (those who thought that Jesus, though divine, was subordinate to the all-powerful creator god: an idea that was no longer approved of in the remaining Roman empire) and their language was transcribed and their oral history investigated. This Gothic renaissance reached a new and fascinating peak in the reign of Theodoric the Great (ruled Italy 493–526). He employed noble Romans at court, including a most distinguished man and one time praetorian prefect of Italy called Flavius Magnus Aurelius Cassiodorus Senator (Senator being part of his name, not an office he held). Cassiodorus wrote a history of the Goths from the earliest days to his own times, which unfortunately survives only in an abridgement that was written quickly (in just three days according to its author) by a scholar of the next generation called Jordanes. This epitome was made sometime around 551, probably in Constantinople. Unsurprisingly, the history of Cassiodorus/Jordanes is more sympathetic to Maximinus than was the tradition of the Roman historians. Although it includes no new material, it reworks the version of Maximinus provided by the *Augustan History* (via the lost work of Symmachus, such are the tenuous threads of history at this time) in a more favourable light, focusing on Maximinus's Gothic ancestry, bravery and strength. The section on Maximinus concludes: "These matters we have borrowed from the history of Symmachus for this our little book, in order to show that the race of which we speak attained to the very highest station in the Roman Empire."[18] No doubt King Theoderic appreciated these sentiments fully as it gave him a legitimate historical precedent in the rule of Rome. Despite being generally positive about Maximinus, Cassiodorus was necessarily critical of his persecution of the Christians, which he attributed to "an evil vow".

The Prince

In 1513 the famous Florentine political adviser Niccolò Machiavelli wrote his great and controversial work *The Prince*, a handbook of advice to his patrons, the Medici, on how to retain power and rule effectively. As part of his analysis he took a thoughtful look at the Roman emperors and their fates "from Marcus the philosopher down to Maximinus". He identified the chief dilemma facing any new ruler in that period, namely that it was very difficult to please both the people and the army, and he divided the emperors neatly into those that favoured one or the other "because, as princes cannot help being hated by someone, they ought, in the first place, to avoid being hated by everyone".[19] Maximinus, of course, was an example of an emperor who was loved by the army and hated by the people, in stark contrast to his predecessor Severus Alexander. Machiavelli identified two reasons why Maximinus eventually failed to hold on to power: that he was low born, which was "considered a great indignity by everyone", and that he "deferred going to Rome and taking possession of the imperial seat". In his case, anger with him increased to the point that his own army at Aquileia, "disgusted with his cruelties, and fearing him less when they found so many against him, murdered him".

This is an interesting verdict in several ways. Maximinus, of course, could do nothing about rumours of his low birth except to adopt the trappings of nobility and, as he may have attempted, to marry his son into a legitimate imperial dynasty and thereby assure Rome of a blue-blood emperor in the long run. The second criticism is very pertinent; had Maximinus celebrated a triumph in Rome after the German war in late 235 he may very well have increased his popularity with the masses and his connections with the elite. He could have delegated the Sarmatian wars to one of his generals. Perhaps both Herodian and the *Augustan History* were right that he just did not have the appetite to rule in pomp surrounded by patricians in an atmosphere of mutual contempt. Hence that issue too comes down to the fact that he was not of the right social class to be emperor.

The interplay of fear of the prince, on the one hand, and anger (along with hatred, disgust and contempt) on the other, were central themes for Machiavelli, and of course very relevant to his own times. Both, he noted, are created by similar actions, although fear works in a prince's favour and anger against: "A prince, so long as he keeps his subjects united and loyal, ought not to mind the reproach of cruelty."[20] But the end for Maximinus came when, among his own troops, a critical point was reached as anger increased and fear diminished. What is so striking in Machiavelli's account of Maximinus, in contrast to other writers both before and after him, is its dispassionate and utilitarian outlook and the absence of moral comment. That is true of *The Prince* in general and why it has proved so controversial down the ages.

Gibbon

The story of Maximinus and his times first came to mass circulation in the English-speaking world through Edward Gibbon's magnificent *Decline and Fall of the Roman Empire*. This classic of English literature was published in instalments between 1776 and 1788 and has remained in print ever since. Gibbon's account of Maximinus and the events of 238 is from the first volume, and relies heavily on the dubious *Augustan History*, but it is succinct and beautifully written. The drama of the story is heightened by the contrast between the savage but effective Maximinus (with his "dark and sanguinary soul") and his noble but weak predecessor. After repeating the story of the games in which Maximinus first came to prominence, Gibbon describes his advancement under the regime of Alexander, continuing:

> Instead of securing his fidelity, these favours served only to inflame the ambition of the Thracian peasant, who deemed his fortune inadequate to his merit as long as he was constrained to acknowledge a superior. Though a stranger to real wisdom, he was not devoid of a selfish cunning, which showed him that the emperor had lost the affection of the army, and taught him to improve their discontent to his own advantage.
>
> Gibbon, 1776, p. 189.

The coup of Maximinus, and the repressive government that followed, gave Gibbon an opportunity to enlarge on the deficiencies of military dictatorship in general: "The army is the only order of men sufficiently united to concur in the same sentiments, and powerful enough to impose them on the rest of their fellow-citizens; but the temper of soldiers, habituated at once to violence and to slavery, renders them very unfit guardians of a legal or even a civil constitution." He also criticized democracy ("in a large society the election of a monarch can never devolve to the wisest or to the most numerous part of the people") and concluded that a benign hereditary monarchy is the most felicitous form of government: just like the Georgian England in which he was writing, in fact!

Maximinus and the Nazis

The attempted rehabilitation of Maximinus as a Gothic hero by Cassiodorus has a disturbing parallel in more modern times. In the Nazi era the German scholar Franz Altheim celebrated Maximinus as "the first German on the imperial throne" on account of his supposed 'Aryan' ancestry.[21] The sinister influence behind Altheim's work was Heinrich Himmler, head of the SS and himself a keen devotee of ancient history, archaeology and folklore and collector of Roman coins and other antiquities.[22]

But Himmler was a fantasist, apparently believing that a tall, blond Aryan race had descended from heaven and once lived on the continent of Atlantis before a great cataclysm had all but destroyed their civilization a million years ago (caused by an interplanetary catastrophe, no less). According to this 'theory', small remnants of the ancient master race originally survived in the high mountains of the Andes and Himalaya, and pre-war Nazi expeditions were actually sent in search of them. Other Aryans had survived in the frozen north, hunting mammoths and sharpening their spears while retaining some remnants of their original ancient written language and culture, long before civilizations emerged in Egypt and Mesopotamia. These were the so-called Nordic people, founders of the ancient Germanic tribes. Eastward migrations of such people (including the Goths) in ancient times had made them overlords of all the supposedly lesser races in the middle East and India, but of course ideology necessitated they were responsible for all the finer points of those civilizations if only evidence could be found to support the claim. Not only were the more prominent leaders of the ancient Greeks and Romans suspect Aryans, but Buddha himself[23] and even the Japanese samurai class. Himmler believed that the Aryans must have possessed superior weaponry and thought that the lightning-emitting hammer of the Norse god Thor was some sort of electrical super-weapon that just might be redeveloped to help the Nazis attain world domination in his own time.[24]

To develop these themes Himmler set up, in the pre-war period, a research institute called the *Deutsches Ahnenerbe*, or 'German Ancestral Heritage'.

Franz Altheim, who was a respected historian and not himself a Nazi originally, eventually decided to apply for funds from the *Ahnenerbe* to conduct an archaeological tour of the ancient near east with his lover Erika Trautmann. The trip was co-funded by one of Trautmann's friends: another prominent Nazi and then commander-in-chief of the Luftwaffe, Hermann Göring. The ostensible purpose was to find ancient evidence and artefacts of the Nordic master race that Nazi fantasists were trying to prove as the real power behind both the Roman and Persian empires. For Altheim and Trautmann it was probably more of a romantic archaeological expedition to places they had longed to see. But at the same time the pair spied for the SS, making contacts with far-right and anti-Jewish groups in Romania and Iraq and reporting back directly to Himmler.[25] It has been suggested that Altheim was the inspiration for the evil Gestapo agent Arnold Ernst Toht in the 1981 blockbuster *Raiders of the Lost Ark*.[26]

In a book *Die Soldatenkaiser* (The Soldier Emperors) published in 1939, in which he published the results of this expedition, Altheim argued that Germanic individuals had contributed much-needed fibre to the Roman empire at its time of crisis in the third century. Maximinus in particular was painted as a heroic figure, the embodiment of "the masculine principle in its raw and most natural way" and that his strength and vision had been misinterpreted as cruelty by the more effete and treacherous Romans.[27] According to Altheim, Maximinus was part Goth and part Persian (not Alan) in ancestry, which was acceptable to Nazi ideology because the Persians, or at least their nobility, were also claimed to have belonged to the mythical Aryan race. But the issue was hotly debated as other German scholars, notably Ernst Hohl (himself a Nazi affiliate since 1934) and Wilhelm Ensslin flatly rejected Altheim's characterization in their own counter-publications even as war was raging across Europe. This prompted a bad tempered response from Altheim in a 1942 paper entitled "'For the Last Time: Maximinus Thrax'".[28] Meanwhile scholars from the rest of the world were ignoring the racist nonsense emanating from Nazi Germany: "Everywhere outside of Germany, German science is seen as chauvinistic, without foundation", one of the *Ahnenerbe* prehistorians complained.[29]

All this would now be regarded as little more than pitiful nonsense if it were not for the extraordinary power wielded by Himmler as head of the SS and, increasingly in the war years, the second most powerful man in Germany. As the panzers smashed into southern Ukraine and the Crimea in 1942, Himmler received the führer's support for his grand plan of establishing a pure Germanic colony in the ancient heartland of the Goths (it was to be called Gotengau, land of the Goths). This would be repopulated from the west by an SS farmer-soldier peasantry who, through selective breeding (eugenics), would re-establish the Aryan master race in their primal strength and would forever insulate Europe from Asiatics from the east. *Ahnenerbe* archaeologists and racial specialists literally worked alongside an SS death squad as war raged around them. Himmler took time out from his despicable war crimes to enjoy a guided tour of the Gothic archaeology of the Crimea, while the Jews of the area were rounded up and massacred on his orders as a first phase of his Gotengau plan. At this time, 40,000 Jewish civilians of all ages died.[30] It is an almost unimaginable number, and the doing of it presented serious logistical problems at the time, but it was a comparatively small early phase of the eventual genocide as the 'scientific' Nazi regime proved itself more colossally brutal and morally deranged than any Roman emperor.

It is a matter of shame that genuine scholars like Altheim, who was rehabilitated into academia after the war,[31] had been responsible for playing along with Himmler's ridiculous fantasies. In retrospect it seems trivial to point out that painting Maximinus as a German hero is deeply ironic, as his main achievement as emperor was a punitive campaign *against* the German tribes, for which the senate voted him the title *germanicus maximus* (greatest victor over the Germans).

Drury Lane

The tale of Maximinus and the drama of 238 has largely been forgotten, but an exception is a play *The Siege of Aquileia: a Tragedy* by the Scots dramatist John Home (1722–1808), performed at the Theatre Royal in 1760. The starring roles were played by the famous Shakespearean actor David Garrick and his regular leading lady, Mrs. Cibber (herself a colourful character and subject of racy society scandals, which can all be read about in Cordus).

The plot centres on a Roman consul, Aemelius[32] and his wife Cornelia, each the last representative of a great Roman family, and their two sons; the elder Paulus (the embodiment of virtue) and Titus (a rash youth, yearning for honour and glory), all of whom are trapped in the besieged city. The brothers lead a valiant sortie from the north gate and destroy a siege tower that would necessarily have taken the city, but they are captured in the struggle. The brutal Maximinus orders them to be placed on a scaffold in view of the walls and sends a herald to demand the city's capitulation in exchange for their lives. Cornelia, full of maternal woe, pleads with her husband to agree to this ultimatum, and even the sympathetic townsfolk urge them to surrender, but the steadfast Aemelius will not accept such shameful terms. Then Titus comes to the city on parole, ostensibly to plead basely for his life, but after some misinterpretation of his motives he privately stiffens his father's resolve not to do a deal and nobly returns to his place of execution.

These heroics are observed by the tyrant's herald, a man named Varus, himself of good Roman stock and, it so happens, commander of a detachment of Britons in the army of Maximinus. Moved by what he has seen, Varus changes allegiance and attempts to stir rebellion in the besieging army but is captured and executed. At this point Cornelia thinks that it is her own sons who are being slain, and, in a heart-rending scene, berates her noble husband for his unyielding rectitude in condemning their offspring to death. But offstage the killing of Varus has moved the British legions to action. First they free the brothers, and then together they attack the giant Maximinus who, after an epic fight as befits his stature and martial reputation (also off stage), is slain. The fatal blow is delivered by Titus himself, who is then observed from the walls returning to the city in pomp. But joy turns to grief as it turns out he has been mortally wounded in the struggle and he dies nobly in his mother's arms, finally achieving his dream of winning glory to match the exploits of his forefathers. And so ends the play; Maximinus gets no lines at all.

Actually the play is based on the true story of a siege by an English army of a Scottish border town in 1333 and was originally written as *The Siege of Berwick*. Garrick, however, pointed out to the Scottish playwright that this plot line might not appeal strongly in Georgian London, so the drama was shifted to ancient times.[33] Home was a classical enthusiast and presumably obtained his material from Herodian and the *Augustan History*. Intriguingly, the playwright was himself no stranger to sieges. He had been among the defenders of Edinburgh against the 1745 Jacobite rebellion, and the following year was captured by 'Bonnie' Prince Charlie's highland clansmen at the battle of Falkirk and imprisoned in a lofty granite castle. Like a character from one of his own yarns, Home escaped this incarceration by descending the precipitous walls using a rope made from his own ripped and knotted bed sheets.

The elevated themes of Home's tragedy may seem rather hackneyed to modern tastes, but it is still possible to appreciate the elegance of his verse, which still reads fresh and lively today. Although now largely forgotten, he was considered one of the greatest playwrights of his age and even compared seriously with Shakespeare. *The Siege of Aquileia* was well received at the time and seems to have fared quite well in the minds of subsequent academic critics of eighteenth-century British drama, although it is doubtful if it was ever staged again. In the twenty-first century, we may appreciate it anew.

The play relies on the contrast between the noble and heroic sentiments of the Romans on the one hand and the tyrant's brutal nature on the other. The scene is set in the opening speech:

...o'er yon mighty host, that girds our walls,
Fierce Maximin commands: whether of Thrace,
Or wild Dalmatia, so obscure his birth,
Himself scarce knows; but sure Barbarian born.
This savage soldier, nurs'd in blood and war,
Whom military frenzy hath set up
To trample on mankind, abhors a Roman;
And marks for death the noble and the brave.
His yoke, at last, th' indignant senate scorns,
The slumb'ring Genius of our country wakes,
And rouses slothful Italy to arms.

Home, 1760, p. 6.

Home also notes the tyrant's "gigantick stature", "Whom nature for a gladiator form'd, To be the sport, and not the lord, of Rome".[34] Aemilius's refusal to open the city gates in exchange for his sons' lives provokes Maximinus to fits of primal rage. As the herald explains,

Incens'd at the refusal which I bore,
His fury rages like a fire confin'd.[35]

Of the minor characters in the drama, two stand out: first a heroic Numidian called Gartha, played by a certain Mr Scrase, who might be considered a distant precursor of many similar 'noble savage' roles up to the present day.[36] Second was Dumnorix, a perfidious Gaul, played by a Mr. Bransby, one of the regulars at Drury Lane. It was a wartime production, staged in the middle of the Seven Years War against France (1756–1763), hence it is no surprise to find a Gaulish villain among the minor characters. Dumnorix sides with the brutal Maximinus to the end, of course.

More recently Maximinus crops up occasionally in the increasingly popular genre of historical fiction. Most notably the prologue of Harry Sidebottom's swashbuckling *Warrior of Rome* series has the young hero, Ballista, leading an attack on the walls of Aquileia and narrowly escaping incineration from burning tar bombs. He then ends up stabbing the giant emperor in his command tent with a stylus, and the ghost of Maximinus haunts him ever after. At the time of writing, Sidebottom is publishing a new series of adventures set in the civil war of 238.[37] The series is highly recommended.

On the Internet, Maximinus's extraordinary reported size (over eight feet tall, according to the *Augustan History*) has been used as evidence that there were once giants walking the Earth, just as it says in the book of Genesis, hence he is cited in support of Biblical literalism. It has also been suggested that he was a denizen of Atlantis.

The Verdict

Despite the efforts of Cassiodorus and Altheim, it has to be admitted that history has provided a clear negative verdict on Maximinus the Thracian. But is it, in fact, possible to question this and see his contribution in a more positive light? Let us examine the case. Before assuming the purple, he was an able and diligent officer famed for bravery and apparently not associated with the failings of the eastern campaign of Severus Alexander. We should remember that there is a chance, albeit a small one, that this loyal general of Rome and lifelong supporter of the Severan dynasty did not in fact orchestrate the rebellion that brought him to power but was forced to accept the office of emperor on pain of death, just as he claimed. Herodian remarked that he had been chosen for his size and reputation by the army, implying at least that he may not have been the only one involved in the plot. Equally plausible is that Maximinus saw it as his duty to intervene and prevent the folly of Alexander's attempted buy-off of the German tribes and the inevitable disastrous consequences. In any case, no such coup could possibly have succeeded without widespread support among the top brass on the Rhine. Maximinus and the army staff around him may have concluded that regime change was necessary for the common good, and as such he was a figurehead for change.

No doubt there is much truth in the tales of Maximinus's cruelty and rapacity, and Herodian's testimony is especially valuable as coming from an eyewitness. But this reputation became exaggerated in the telling thereafter as it became bound up with his base reputation. There is a tendency among ancient historians, going back to at least the fifth century BCE, to separate the 'good' and the 'bad' in the storytelling.[38] In reality, Rome had endured many cruel emperors: it was a notoriously violent society throughout most of its history. Maximinus had enemies in high places and a string of plots to contend with, so perhaps he needed to be ruthless to avoid a violent end for as long as he did, which is not to excuse his actions; and if one examines the acts of many of the men who have gone down as 'good emperors' it is not difficult to find similar evidence of personal ruthlessness combined with genocidal tendencies in war. Julius Caesar openly boasted of the necessity to slaughter women and children in open view to cow an enemy[39] and may even have been responsible for the violent deaths of millions. The first emperor Augustus ordered countless executions among the upper classes[40] and, among other horrors, inflicted on his troops the ancient practice of decimation; that is, among a unit routed in battle, the disgraced survivors had to draw lots and every tenth man was killed on the spot by his comrades. This generalization is also true of other 'good emperors' such as Trajan, Aurelian, Diocletian, and Constantine the Great (supposedly the first Christian emperor). Even Marcus Aurelius, the stoic 'philosopher emperor', celebrated what would now be indictable war crimes on his public monuments.[41]

As far as taxation goes, one should remember that Herodian's criticism emanated from the upper class, and the rich have never quite seen the need for taxes. In 235, Maximinus was facing a genuine military crisis that threatened the empire, including Rome herself. If he confiscated the estates of the condemned and stripped the temples of gold, at least he did not use the proceeds to enrich himself. He built no pleasure dome, nor did he indulge in vanity projects such as covering his home town (wherever that was) in grandiose buildings. His measures might therefore be styled harsh but fair: recall that the procurator in Africa who started the rebellion was described by Herodian as going *further* than Maximinus himself, showing that there were limits.

Perhaps the most remarkable aspect of Maximinus's reputation, even among his enemies, is that he was never criticized for moral degeneracy, depravity or insanity. It was fair game for ancient historians to accuse the damned emperors of all manner of vices and deviances, especially of a sexual nature, so as to spice up their stories.[42] Unlike other acknowledged tyrants like Tiberius, Caligula, Nero, Domitian, Commodus, Caracalla and Elagabalus (to name some prominent examples), such accusations were not leveled at Maximinus; all we know of his private life is that he married once and honoured his wife Paulina after she died.[43]

In contrast to all the emperors from the time of his (supposed) mentor Septimius Severus to his own time, and many before, Maximinus proved to be a competent and imaginative leader, seemingly tireless in Rome's interest (as he saw it) and personally valiant in battle. Leading from the front had long been esteemed in ancient warfare, Alexander the Great being the type specimen. The *Augustan History*, which was written at a later time when emperors tended to decline the ancient honour of personally taking the field of battle, attributed his habit of engaging the enemy hand to hand not to bravery but to "barbaric rashness".[44] But he clearly inspired his men and provided Rome with genuine military victories, succeeding where Severus Alexander had conspicuously failed.

Moreover it is possible that he was working to a broad strategic plan. Had he lived to complete this work he may have greatly shortened the barbarian frontier, shoring up the defences by conquest and bringing the benefits of civilization to various foreign peoples by incorporating them into great new provinces. Such had been the legacy of Julius Caesar, for example, in annexing Gaul. Extending the empire far beyond the Rhine and Danube had also been the unrealized dream of Augustus and Marcus Aurelius.[45] Such an act may even have prevented the final collapse of the western empire. We should not forget that Herodian, who was no friend of Maximinus, judged that he might have actually accomplished this project if the privileged underbelly of the empire had not turned against him at a critical moment. But history is written by the winners, and one day beneath the walls of Aquileia, it transpired that the strongman emperor of Rome was not destined to be among them.

Chapter XV

Postscript: The Ogre in the Met

Nasty, Brutish, and Tall

The known images of Maximinus were discussed in the last chapter; however there is one other possible representation of the man, an 'oversize' bronze statue, which, if it is indeed him, is by far the most impressive to survive (Plate 16). The trouble is, up until now, nobody has suggested that it is.

The figure was allegedly dug up around the 1820s during excavations in a vineyard near the basilica of San Giovanni in Laterano (Saint John Lateran) on the Caelian Hill in Rome.[1] It was found in pieces, but that seems to be because of corrosion in the ground rather than deliberate destruction in an act of *damnatio memoriae*: the head, for example, is well preserved and not mutilated in any way (a point that may be significant, as we shall see). Now thoroughly restored, it is on permanent display in the Metropolitan Museum of Art in New York where it is identified as the Roman emperor Trebonianus Gallus (ruled 251–253). But while the statue is very likely to be an emperor on account of his heroic nudity and commanding pose, and is clearly mid-third century in style, the identification as Trebonianus is conjectural, based on supposed resemblance to features seen on coins. But even the Met's own notes highlight a problem with that interpretation: "The massive nude body itself resembles that of an athlete or gladiator... rather than what was typical for a representation of an emperor."[2]

The most striking thing about the statue is indeed its size (it stands nearly eight feet tall), its barrel chest and very long, muscular legs. The subject's right hand seems to be held up in a gesture of oration, as if he was in the act of addressing his troops (*adlocutio*), as is seen on some coins of the period.[3] The body is strong and powerful but hardly conforms to classical ideals, especially in the matter of belly fat. A recent author refers to "the figure's markedly un-classical features – its small head, contorted expression, enormous torso, and stilted pose"; another to its "brutish" visage.[4] The following account is a good summary of the way the statue tends to be interpreted by art historians:

...its disproportionately large muscular body intimidates through its sheer physical presence, and is reminiscent of over-muscled Herculean bodies of wrestlers, boxers and gladiators ...The massive nude body, then, marked out this emperor as an extraordinary physical figure in the midst of the third-century crisis, while preserving in the commander's paludamentum [cloak] (which is far too small for him) and the stern stubbled face, stout neck and cropped hair the auctoritas [authority] of a Roman military leader, and in the contours of the skin, wrinkled brow, fleshy torso and gently sagging pectorals the seniority and experience expected of an effective Roman emperor... Trebonianus was drawing upon multiple traditions and associations in this imperial image: its corpulence both contrasted with the waifness of recent emperors and tapped into the strength and vigour of the camp and the exceptional physical presence of professional fighters and athletes. And far from harmonizing these traditions, the artist went to great lengths to underline the composite character of the piece: the head is some two-thirds the scale of the body and the inflated torso is almost a caricature of the Polykleitian ideal from which it is derived [Polykleitos was an ancient Greek sculptor famed for his elegant standing figures]. The very disproportion of this extraordinary statue, represented most strikingly by its gutsy display of flesh, marked a bold (and typically late antique) rejection of the orthodoxies of classical portraiture.

Bradley, 2011, p. 31.

There was a profound artistic shift around the end of the third century when naturalistic representations in statuary gave way to much more stylized images. In art-history terms, that was the end of the classical age. Our statue clearly predates that revolution but it has often been argued, as above, that some of its 'un-classical' peculiarities may herald the beginning of the end.[5]

Thomas Hoving, a previous director of the institution in which it is now housed, went so far as to label the statue:

...the ugliest work of art in the Met. It's so unattractive that when I was director I wanted to relegate it to storage for fear that young visitors would have bad dreams. His patina is the color of offal. His anatomy is bulbous, syrupy, soft, waxy, and unconvincing. His pinhead is set incongruously into this ungainly body with too-long legs and the stomach muscles of an octogenarian. I'm convinced this is a phony concocted by that master of masters, Wolfgang Helbig, and made by a team of fakers in Orvieto.

Hoving, 1997, p. 328–329.[6]

That was in 1997. But subsequent meticulous scientific investigation has exonerated the Helbig gang, at least in this case, and proved that the statue is undoubtedly genuine although heavily restored in places. Moreover it has been confirmed that its current appearance is close to what it would have looked like in antiquity.[7] Perhaps Hoving's aesthetic expectation was that a Roman emperor ought to sport the six-pack and perfect bodily proportions of a young athlete or warrior, as is seen so often in ancient art.[8] But what if, as a point of fact, his physique was something entirely different?

A Case of Identity

When the statue was first described in the mid-nineteenth century it was identified as Julius Caesar, that most famous of all Romans. It does not remotely resemble Caesar, so that was either a ploy to maximize its value among the art collectors of the age or, more charitably, a combination of enthusiasm and ignorance (it was also kitted out with a laurel wreath and fig leaf, since removed). It is now identified as third-century, mainly on account of the imperial haircut and beard and the particular way the hair is stippled. Around 1905 the Dutch art connoisseur Alphonse Van Branteghem suggested, much more reasonably, that it might be Trebonianus Gallus, a mid-third century emperor.[9] Then, when the Metropolitan Museum of Art purchased it later that year, the acquisitions committee accepted that identification. In the notice of accession by purchase, it was claimed that the identity is obvious by comparisons with coins, and another article that year claimed "comparison with the authentic coins bearing his image establishes the identity of the subject conclusively".[10]

An intriguing possibility is that the identification was supported by one William M. Laffan, then editor of the New York broadsheet *The Sun* and amateur antiquarian. Laffan was on the acquisitions committee of the museum and donated a coin of Trebonianus from his own collection at the time of purchase that was used to put a seal on the identification.[11]

That the statue is Trebonianus has been repeated many times since. For instance, when it was exhibited in 1977 it was compared once again with Laffan's coin:

The head can be securely identified as a portrait of the emperor Caius Vibius Trebonianus Gallus through comparison with his coin portraits... Characteristic is the short, squarish face with pointed chin and hook nose. The short hair is cut squarely across the forehead, and the full, clipped beard begins over the cheekbones. The high, furrowed brow, which gives the portrait its intense expression, can also be found in some of the coin portraits.

Weitzmann, 1979, p. 8.

But by that time doubts were being raised by other experts because the features are not very like other statues that are more securely identified as Trebonianus. Most notable of these is a bronze bust in the Vatican collection. Two detailed treatises on third-century imperial portraiture were published in the 1970s, both of which compared and discussed the images of the various emperors of that period as depicted on the available statues and a wide range of coins, and both studies were sceptical of the identification (although neither went so far as to suggest an alternative). Interestingly, they both focused exclusively on the facial features and did not mention the peculiar body. More recently, the identification has usually been accompanied with an admission that it is, ultimately, uncertain: the most up-to-date study calls it "not absolutely certain but probable".[12]

The physiognomy described in the quotation above applies equally, if not more so, to the coins of Maximinus, although we have already noted there are three very distinct styles of his portrait to compare it with. Several other points might indicate that the statue is more likely to be Maximinus than Trebonianus or, indeed, any other third century emperor. Let us start with his ornate sandals, which are very curious and have been compared to those worn for wrestling, or in military exercises. This fits the historical accounts that Maximinus had long excelled in the training of soldiers, wrestling, and weapons practice. They are decorated with an outlandish stern face, presumably a god, with a wide open mouth surrounded by scrollwork (Plate 16). It is certainly not one of the traditional Roman pantheon (Jupiter or Mars, for example) so if the image could be identified, it might help with determining who the man is. Trebonianus was an Italian aristocrat and senator so is unlikely to have identified with regional gods. An idea worth floating is that it might be a depiction of the adult Dionysus, the Thracian god of wine (and we know Maximinus liked his wine!).[13]

More obviously, of course, the oversize physique fits the ancient descriptions of the man, both from Herodian and the *Augustan History*, and the image projected by his propaganda. One art historian went so far as to juxtapose a picture of the statue (claimed to be of Trebonianus) with the description of Maximinus's giant size from the *Augustan History*, suggesting that together they somehow represent a new kind of bodily ideal promoted by emperors of the third century in general.[14] Surely a less convolute notion is that the statue *is* Maximinus. Unfortunately, there are no surviving physical descriptions of

Trebonianus from his contemporaries[15] but on the Vatican bust and his coins he does not look like an especially big and powerful man. The stern expression of the statue is similar to the others of Maximinus, especially from the front (see Plate 16), and the body, with its slightly sagging musculature, arguably fits better with a man in his sixties than one in his forties (as was Trebonianus, in his short reign).

Perhaps one reason why nobody has suggested Maximinus before is that he is most often associated with the square-headed prognathous Type 3 portrait, which is very unlike the New York statue in profile. But as we have seen, that portrait only appeared on coins after the announcement of the German victory in early 236, and thereafter was the official *imagine* of the emperor for the rest of his reign. The demand for statuary in Rome would have peaked immediate following the senate's ratification of the coup in March 235 when there was no live subject to base the sculptures on. Hence our statue is probably better compared with the (possibly) more speculative Type 1 portrait on the coins, although it must be admitted it is by no means a precise match for that either.

Statues and Pedestals

There is another line of evidence that might support the identification of the Metropolitan Museum statue as Maximinus: the very interesting context of its discovery and subsequent history, which has recently become controversial. It is a fascinating story that involves some of the super-rich of Europe, acts of skullduggery and gambling, and the murky fine art market of the nineteenth century. Unravelling it could not only help confirm the identity of the big bronze in the Met, it could even lead to a better understanding of other major works of art from ancient Rome.

The first thing to note is that bronze statues are very rare, in fact this is the *only* surviving large bronze statue from the entire third century[16] although there must have been many thousands manufactured. The reason is simple: when broken, worn out, or out of fashion, they were worth more recycled or melted down for coin. This fate was no doubt virtually inevitable for statues of emperors damned to the memory, as were both Maximinus and Trebonianus, so the survival of this example indicates some unusual circumstance of preservation.

The original story of its discovery was written in 1849, about a quarter of a century after the supposed event, by its then proud new owner Auguste de Montferrand (1786–1858), a very distinguished St. Petersburg architect and himself a sculptor in the neoclassical style.[17] Montferrand writes of a certain 'mason' who claimed to have been there when it was first unearthed:

In my youth, when I was studying in Rome, a distinguished person from the Russian court obtained from his Holiness Pope Pius VII the permission to carry out, at his own expense, excavations in a vineyard, located not far from St. John Lateran. Many statues, including the one in question, bas-reliefs and other fragments of sculpture were the result of these excavations, which lasted almost two years, and whose cost reached 100,000 piastres [a piastre was a large silver coin descended from the old Spanish 'piece of eight', used in international commerce]. After so great an expense, Mr. N. N. de D. believed he had to suspend his research ...Our statue was found in these excavations; it was knocked off its pedestal, lying in pieces and buried beneath the ruins of a hall of which it had occupied the centre. Because it was feared that the statue would attract the attention of the directors of the pontifical museums, and that its importance would give rise to the desire to acquire it, the pieces were immediately packed up and sent to Florence, where, in the absence of their legal owner, they were neglected for many years. Eventually, they were restored and displayed to the impatient curiosity of scholars and connoisseurs.

Montferrand, 1849, p. 12–13[18]

It seems from the context that this 'mason' is a thin disguise for none other than Montferrand himself.[19] The "Mr. N. N. de D" is Count Nicolas Nikitich Demidoff (1773–1828), a Russian aristocrat and art collector whose family had accumulated a fabulous fortune in the mining industry. Demidoff had been an admirer of Bonaparte, but when France invaded Russia in 1812 he raised a regiment at his own expense, fighting at the Battle of Borodino and elsewhere, for which he was knighted. After the war, in 1817 or possibly 1819 (the sources differ), he was appointed Russian ambassador to the court of Tuscany in Florence. In any case, from 1817 to his death in 1828 he seems to have been dividing his time between Florence and Rome. (Italy at that time was not, of course, united, so they were in different jurisdictions.) When in Rome he apparently busied himself importing copper from his Russian mines with his own ships, funding philanthropic schemes and throwing lavish receptions.[20]

Demidoff was clearly fascinated by ancient sculpture and seems to have gone to great lengths to amass a personal collection while in Italy, both by purchasing works on the general market and funding excavations himself. He seems to have sourced some of his sculptures from digs in Campania and Tivoli, as well as Rome. A measure of his ambition is that he was planning to excavate the entire Roman forum to a depth of ten or 12 feet using a gang of 500 convicts, but had to shelve the scheme on being forced to leave the city by the secret police: the reason for this, we are told, is that a French comedy that he staged fell foul of the cardinal censor because one of the actors exclaimed "Pardieu!", a blasphemy.[21] Later, it seems, he was rehabilitated, whereupon he dug up a site in the Via dei Quattro Cantoni about a kilometre from the Lateran cathedral, recovering some important art works in the process. There is no contemporaneous published account of the excavation referred to by Montferrand, but if it lasted two years and at such great expense, something must have kept him engaged, so it seems possible that an outstanding cache of ancient art had been discovered.[22]

But in an article published online in October 2014 (shortly before the completion of this book), the scholar Elizabeth Marlowe expressed strong doubts about the veracity of Montferrand's story.[23] Her argument, in short, is that it could be a fake provenance, and a self-serving one, because a statue from central Rome would be worth much more than any old statue (just as a Julius Caesar would be worth more than any old emperor). There is not space here to run through all the circumstances outlined in support of that claim, but if it is true, it means the Met's statue could have come from almost anywhere in the Roman empire; Marlowe suggested the Balkans, for example. And yet it does seem a strange story for Montferrand to concoct. The pope's permission is an odd detail to invent because it might have been checked in the Vatican archives, and also that the digging took two years, and that the bronze statue (and presumably the many other statues from the same location) was whisked away from under the noses of the authorities: why admit to that? Moreover if a false provenance was needed, why not just claim that the statue came from one of Demidoff's genuine digs?

Evidence that Montferrand's story may be true is that the area of San Giovanni in Laterano is exactly the kind of location that a collection of statues might have been unearthed. It boasts extremely well preserved archaeology, and has produced many other sculptures, friezes and inscriptions dating from the second and third centuries. For example, excavations in 1934 and surveys ongoing at the time of writing under the basilica itself uncovered extensive and very well preserved third-century remains, including lofty rooms in two stories with steps. The buildings have been identified as the supplementary barracks complex (*castra nova*) built by Septimius Severus when he expanded the numbers of his elite imperial horse guard, the *equites singulares augusti*.[24] But because Demidoff's dig is supposed to have been conducted in a vineyard near the church, and not beside it or underneath it, a more likely location for it is the area of the original fort (*castra priora*) of the *equites*, which was 200–300 metres to the north-east of the new fort, in the area of what is now the Via Tasso.[25] A detailed map of Rome from 1748 shows that this area belonged to a grand house called the Villa Giustiniana and was cultivated in rows, which may indicate a vineyard. One eighteenth century print might actually show the very plot in the distance, with its vines.[26] So while it may not be possible to prove Montferrand's account, it is at least plausible and fits the pattern of Demidoff's activities.

It so happens that this area was later uncovered in 1885, in another dig financed by a Monsieur Maraini, and although there was no excavation report, several notices were published in learned journals and art magazines at the time.[27] The distinguished archaeologist Rodolfo Lanciani provided some evocative details about these later discoveries in his book of 1901:

> I shall never forget the wonderful site we beheld on entering the vestibule of the old barracks of the Equites Singulares in the Via Tasso. The noble hall was found to contain forty-four marble pedestals, some still standing in their proper places against the wall facing the entrance, some upset on the marble floor, and each inscribed with the dedicatory inscription on the front and with a list of subscribers on the sides. Some bear dedications to the Emperor commander-in-chief, as, for instance: "To the Genius of our Emperor Antoninus Pius. The Thracians honorably dismissed from the regiment of the Equites Singulares after twenty-five years of service... have raised by subscription this marble statue.
>
> Lanciani, 1901, p. 180–182.[28]

Also recovered in the dig were two statues: another account written by Lanciani in 1886, tells us more about these, and gives some significant additional details:

> I cannot speak of these finds without a certain degree of enthusiasm, because I have never seen forty-three marble pedestals or marble slabs inscribed with nearly one hundred pages of minute records discovered in one and the same hall, and in less than a week's time. The portion of the barracks brought to light in the Via Tasso runs parallel with an antique street 13 ft. wide, and contains a hall more than 90 ft. long, and small apartments on each side of it, the whole built in the reticulated work of Hadrian's time ...Of the statues which stood on the pedestals above described two only have been brought to light, besides many fragments of others. The first, head-less and of rather common workmanship, is considered by some to have represented the genius of the barracks; the second is a noble work of art indeed, one of the most perfect marble statues discovered in Rome within my recollection. It represents a young Bacchus, whose curly, silky, womanly hair, tied on the forehead with a vitta and crowned with ivy, falls in graceful ringlets on the shoulders.
>
> Lanciani, 1886, quoted in Frothingham, 1886.[29]

The current whereabouts of the Bacchus is unknown. The headless statue was identified more recently as Mercury.[30] Sadly, the ancient hall seems to have been destroyed shortly after Maraini's excavation to make way for new building, although there is a chance that parts of it may yet survive, because another wall of the old barracks just a hundred metres or so away was recently uncovered in works on the Rome Metro system.[31] The Via Tasso is now a typical crowded Lazio street lined with modern town-houses with the ubiquitous graffitied shutters and parked-up vestas, and no indication of the treasures that might lie beneath. Incidentally, the locality of Maraini's excavation is either below, or very close to, a building that was subsequently used as a headquarters by the Gestapo in Rome during the Second World War, the site of many tortures and executions. It is now the National Museum of the Liberation, and the cells can still be visited, with the poignant graffiti of the condemned still preserved behind glass.

Fortunately some of the 'marble pedestals' were saved and seven of them can be seen in a courtyard in the National Museum in Rome at the magnificent Baths of Diocletian. A detailed catalogue of the collection was published in 1994, when they were described as being of very fine quality.[32] The various dedications run from the oldest, from the time of the emperor Trajan in the early second century, to the youngest, in 241 in the reign of Gordian III.[33] They seem to be a mixture of pieces. Most are second-century dedications set up by groups of up to about 50 men of the *equites singulares augusti* on the occasion of their honourable discharge from the army after 25 years service. This was a great occasion for the men, who were given a large lump sum, a pension, and the full benefits of Roman citizenship. Evidently, on at least some of those occasions, the old comrades had a whip-round to purchase a marble plinth which was engraved with all their names, and in some if not all such cases, they also purchased a fine statue to go on top of it (occasionally the names of one or other subscribers have been erased, presumably after they defaulted on the payment!). One imagines there was a solemn dedication ceremony led by their commander-in-chief, followed by a big party.[34]

It seems likely from these details that the 'noble' marble hall dug in 1885 was the cross-hall or *basilica* of the unit's headquarters, the place where regimental ceremonies were carried out. Halls of statues are not ten a penny in archaeology, even in Rome, so, as Lanciani intimated, it must have been frustrating for the diggers to find so many empty pedestals. So can we put two and two together and suggest that Lanciani's hall is one and the same as that described by Montferrand as having been partially excavated by Demidoff around the early 1820s, who then carted away the many statues he found, along with fragments of statues and bas-reliefs, leaving just debris behind? The detail that the 1885 excavation took less than a week as opposed to nearly two years for the earlier one suggests that it may have been mostly removing the backfill of a prior clearance, or at least uncovering less valuable contents. That there were pedestals on the floor of the hall is common to both accounts, and it may also be significant that, in Montferrand's original story, the pedestal belonging to the big bronze in the Met was left where it was. There is nothing strange about that: Demidoff was more interested in art than archaeology (which was very much a nascent field in the 1820s), and the pedestals are very heavy and would have been tiresome and expensive to move.[35] As for the statue of Bacchus found in 1885, it is indeed very fine, and Demidoff would surely have removed it had he found it, but Demidoff's excavation is recorded as having stopped when the money ran out.

Demidoff amassed a large collection of artworks in his home in Florence, some of which were shipped to St. Petersburg by his sons Paul (or Pavel) and Anatole[36] on his death in 1828 and subsequently formed the nucleus of what became regarded as one of the great art collections of the world. The bronze in the Met was very likely part of this shipment because the customs licenses from 1828 refer to a "*statua colossale di bronzo*" among a total of over 600 pieces that were exported.[37] This significant detail helps corroborate that the statue did indeed come from Demidoff's collection in Italy in the early nineteenth century (if not certainly from Rome).[38] In St. Petersburg the pieces were split between the brothers. The big bronze was later separated from the rest of the collection when Anatole supposedly gifted it to Montferrand, who was quick to claim it as a masterpiece. Montferrand had befriended the Demidoff family, who were neighbours in St. Petersburg, and indeed Montferrand had re-designed the Demidoff mansion inhabited by Powel on his marriage in 1835. In Montferrand's account he asked for the statue "in jest", and claimed to have been confused and delighted when it actually turned up at his door, posted by the generous Anatole, who may have been happy to get rid of it. An alternative story that emerged at the beginning of the twentieth century is that Anatole may have given it to Montferrand to settle a gambling loss.[39] Whatever is the case, it seems Montferrand greatly loved his 'Julius Caesar' that had pride of place among his sculpture collection in his St. Petersburg mansion. One report gives us the charming detail that "any Sunday he indulged in rearranging the statues, using 25 labourers from 9 a.m. to lunch time".[40]

When Montferrand died, the statue was sold by his heirs and passed through the hands of several dealers and collectors, making its way to Paris, where it was acquired by Evangelos Triantaphyllos, who then sold it to the New York Museum. The rest of the Demidoff collections were later dispersed on the general art market in sales in the 1860s and 1870s.[41] Before that, however, seventeen pieces of statuary were acquired by the Hermitage Museum in St. Petersburg.[42] These are now on display, where most are simply described as being from ancient Rome. Some of them can be matched with the descriptions of the six statues reportedly recovered by Demidoff's diggers from the site on the Via dei Quattro Cantoni. According to the Hermitage records, others come from Tivoli, Naples, and via purchases made by the Demidoff from pre-existing collections.

Sadly, none of the published inscriptions from the 1885 excavations[43] appears to correspond to a pedestal of a missing statue of Maximinus (or, for that matter, Trebonianus). Although several of the plinths had statues, we only know for sure what one of them was, namely the emperor Antoninus Pius (as described above, it was dedicated by a group of Thracian *equites* who, on their retirement, "inscribed and joyfully dedicated a statue with its marble base to the emperor Antoninus" [on 1 March 139 CE]).[44] The Antoninus Pius in the Hermitage is a most excellent piece and would be a fitting memorial to the Thracian horseguard, if indeed it proves to be the statue that once stood on that very pedestal. Intriguingly, this statue is the odd one out in the Demidoff collection, recorded as "found in 1825 near the Lateran Gate". This description would fit the Via Tasso site, which is about 350m from that gate (one of the major fortified gateways in the ancient Aurelian Walls) and would have been in clear view at the time across cultivated fields.[45]

Changing of the Guard

So what happened to the *equites singulares*, and in particular, to their barracks complexes? For this we have to fast-forward by about 70 years from the time of Maximinus to the early third century, passing over an interval of almost unremitting chaos and disaster for the empire, followed by something of a resurgence. Out of the tumult a new and very powerful figure emerged, Flavius Valerius Aurelius Constantinus, or Constantine I (the Great), subsequently revered as the first Christian emperor of Rome, and even Saint Constantine. This man was proclaimed *augustus* by his troops in Eboracum (York) in 306. In 312 he invaded Italy with an army of Gauls and Britons to fight the incumbent emperor in Rome, Maxentius, for control the western empire. Maxentius drew his army from Italy and was supported by the horseguard and praetorians (although they were much depleted from their glory days because of continuous warfare and the loss of their traditional recruiting grounds to the regime in Rome). On the eve of battle, Constantine is supposed to have seen a cross of light in the sky with the message *in hoc signo vinces* (with this sign you will be victorious). The reality of that story is endlessly debated and need not detain us here, except to remark that it is likely that Constantine's mother was a Christian and he was generally sympathetic to that religion, unlike other senior figures who had been trying to stamp it out using dire persecution.[46] The point is relevant to our story.

The troops of the emphatically non-Christian Maxentius (he had restored the ancient temples of Rome) bravely came out of the city, crossing the Tiber by the Milvian Bridge, where they began to array themselves in battle order with the river at their rear. Constantine was significantly outnumbered but was in a better tactical situation. Seeing the enemy unprepared, he quickly attacked and won the battle. As the army of Maxentius routed, many men drowned or were killed in the stampede along the riverbank. The praetorians and horseguard stood firm with their emperor until near the end, but eventually they too were defeated and put to flight, and Maxentius himself ended up being swept away by the river.[47] Constantine then marched triumphantly into Rome, styling himself the great liberator.

Constantine could not risk a hostile power in the capital, especially one made up of Danubian soldiers devoted to regional gods and the old religion, so the defeated and abject remnant of the praetorian guard of Rome was immediately cashiered, and with them the horseguard. The circumstance has echoes of Septimius Severus over a hundred years earlier, but Constantine was even more ruthless. Entirely new units of horse were to be levied under a different regimental structure. The barracks complexes were hastily levelled in order that their prime locations could be re-used and all memory of the defeated guards obliterated. Perhaps to emphasize this regime change, Constantine ordered construction of the world's first Christian basilica atop the demolished barracks. The altar of this basilica was termed the *sancta sanctorum*, or holy of holies, in emulation of the Jewish Temple in Jerusalem, and it is reputed to have housed holy relics later brought back from Jerusalem by Constantine's mother, Helena, including pieces of the "True Cross". It has been suggested that this altar was consciously sited above the destroyed shrine of the imperial horseguard, where their sacred standards had once been housed.[48] This church became the official seat of the Christian bishops of Rome, the popes, and it remains so down to the present day. Meanwhile, perhaps with similar symbolism, a great mausoleum was built atop the graveyard of the *equites* to the east of the city. Constantine initially planned to be interred there himself although in the event he ended up being buried in his great new city Constantinople (a rebuild of Byzantium; there were riots in Rome when the populace found out they had been snubbed in this way).

In the rush to clear the ground, both the new and old forts of the horseguard were evidently very quickly pulled down,[49] filled in, and levelled. Little or no attempt seems to have been made to rescue the overwhelmingly pagan artworks and dedications that simply became part of the backfill. The bottom stories of these buildings survived reasonably intact, preserved below ground (see Plate 3). The leading historian of the *equites* has remarked:

> In one of history's fair ironies... Constantine raised a striking monument to the horse guard. When he razed its fort and graveyard, he hoped thereby to blot out its memory – instead he saved it. The rubble of the fort and the graveyard safeguarded vast treasure troves of inscriptions and graven images. In the shrine of the old fort alone, 45 dedications were unearthed, more than in any other sanctuary of the Roman army; and in the basilica of St. Peter and Marcellinus, built over the horse guard's graveyard, has yielded 609 headstones, more than all other known cavalry gravestones taken together.[50]

One of those gravestones, by the way, is that of the aforementioned soldier who had identified himself as belonging to the troop of one Julius Maximinus back in the time of the emperor Septimius Severus.

All this allows us to speculate that the great bronze statue may have been on display right down to the time of Maxentius, and not in some peripheral position, but in the very centre of the regimental headquarters (Principia) of the *equites singulares augusti*, the elite unit in which Maximinus had supposedly served as a young man. Such a location would be entirely fitting, of course, but it leaves us with a final puzzle: how could the statue have been on display if he had been damned to the memory, expunged from history, and never to be spoken of again?

The first thing to say about this is that the problem is not resolved by speculating that the statue is instead Trebonianus or almost any other of the crew-cut emperors of the mid third century. Almost all such men were violently killed by the next man to take charge, and so it went on, with virtually all of them being subject to *damnatio memoriae* when their time came. The one exception to this pattern is Claudius II who reigned from 268–270, in which short time he won a major battle against the Goths and then managed to die of the plague (probably smallpox) rather than from a knife in the back and was subsequently honoured, and he achieved deification, not damnation. But the image of Claudius on the coins is that of a *small* hard man, rather than a *big* hard man, although we are told that he too could smash a horse's teeth with his fist![51]

A solution to the conundrum might be found in the politics of late 238. By that time Maximinus was dead and the Aquileian war was over. Recall, however, that the praetorians had never accepted the legitimacy of Balbinus and Pupienus and according to Herodian they "hated having emperors chosen by the senate".[52] In the end they had hauled the senatorial emperors from the palace and butchered them in the streets, and there were at least some attempts underway to damn *their* memory. There is no record of the praetorians having been held to account for that act. The new regime of the boy Gordian III needed to bring together the warring factions and certainly required the backing of the guard. It therefore seems inevitable that a peace conference was held. And it seems reasonable to suppose that high on the agenda would have been repeal of the constitutional innovations of the rogue senate of early 238, especially to emphasize that there should be just one emperor and the senate did *not* have the power to appoint and depose emperors, not least because a very dangerous precedent would have been set for the boy Gordian. So perhaps the various parties were able to shake hands by agreeing that the damning of Maximinus had been an unconstitutional act by an illegal regime, and in return that the senatorial emperors should not themselves be damned to the memory either; nor would any of them be raised to the gods. Balbinus was laid to rest in his fine unmolested sarcophagus on the Appian Way and, just possibly, the statue of Maximinus may have been returned triumphantly to its rightful place in the horseguard barracks.

Of course that is all so much speculation so as to fill a historical lacuna. But it does provide an explanation of how our statue could have been permitted to remain centre stage in the hall of the imperial horseguard right down to the time of the Milvian Bridge. Almost all of the intervening 'soldier-emperors' hailed from the Danubian legions, or depended heavily on men who did, and hence would have approved of Maximinus's legacy, or at least pretended to.

The statue is certainly an oddity, and its peculiarities have taxed art historians. Perhaps it can be interpreted as a depiction of emperor-as-drillmaster, a special image for the troops he commanded, commissioned on his accession to power. And perhaps the statue is not 'oversize' with a 'pin head', but *life size*[53] (or nearly so) and realistic: a genuine attempt by a sculptor to depict of a man who everyone at the time admired as being freakishly tall. This peculiar object might even corroborate the accounts of Maximinus's appearance given by the ancient authors, all too easily dismissed as mere propaganda, fantasy or invention. His impressive physique, possibly the result of a pituitary disorder, had made Maximinus bodyguard to the emperor as a young man. That breakthrough then allowed him a dramatically accelerated career. Bravery, hard work, and excellence in the arts of war then took him to the very top, a true hero for the Roman army and especially the provincial soldiers that increasingly made up its fighting strength.

Appendix I

Sources

T he principal ancient sources for the events described in this book are
as follows (in the order they may have been written):

- **Cassius Dio, *Roman History* (mostly written after 229 CE but
covering events to 232).** It is unfortunate for our purposes that one of the
most important, thoroughly researched and well respected of all Roman
histories, that of Lucius (or perhaps Claudius) Cassius Dio Cocceianus,
ends in the early 230s, probably around the time of his death, just before
the main events of this book. It is nevertheless invaluable for setting the
scene and for providing many details of Roman life in the early third
century. Cassius Dio, Greek by birth, was a senior senator and served
as consul twice, the second time under Severus Alexander in 229, and
hence was directly acquainted with goings-on in the empire in its highest
political stratum. His was a history of extraordinary breadth, ranging
from the earliest days of Rome right up to the period of his life. One of his
chief limitations, from a modern perspective, is his credulous fondness for
supernatural signs and portents.

- *Marius Maximus* **(written after 222).** If correctly identified, this author
was twice consul and moreover military hero in the wars that brought
Septimius Severus to power. He wrote a series of lives of the emperors
from Nerva (reigned 96–98 CE) to Elagabalus (reigned 218–222). His work
is lost, but it is universally regarded as genuine, and was cited by various
later authors, notably including the *Augustan History*. Like Cassius Dio,
the lost work of Marius Maximus does not extend to the main period of
interest but, via later works, it does convey some useful information. It also
contained copies of important texts from official senatorial and diplomatic
sources that were summarized by later writers.

- *Herodian* **(written c. 244–249).** Easily the most important of our sources
is Herodian's *History of the Empire from the Death of Marcus Aurelius* (there
are various alternative titles), which covers the years 180–238. Because of
the work's political stance, scholars think it was written in the 240s during
the reign of Philip I (244–249) when the author was a very old man by

Roman standards, or even later.[1] Little is known about Herodian except that he appears to have come from the eastern part of the empire (possibly Antioch) and held public office, perhaps in a relatively minor capacity, and dwelt for some time in Rome itself. Some nineteenth-century historians thought that he might have been a senator, a theory that has gone out of fashion, but perhaps should be examined afresh. That he himself was not a Roman is obvious from the fact that he wrote in Greek and felt it necessary to explain Roman habits and customs from the perspective of an outsider. Herodian's history has various failings and contradictions, and has sometimes been compared unfavourably with that of Cassius Dio on account of minor errors of content and style, but for our period it is by far the most reliable source. The oldest surviving manuscript is eleventh century but other, later versions are derived from a different source, the common root (archtype) of which is seventh century.

- *Aelius Junius Cordus* (**written after 238? Or bogus?**). This is a lost work referred to over twenty times in the *Augustan History* (see below) as a source, sometimes as Aelius Cordus and occasionally as Junius Cordus. Most modern writers consider that Cordus is a fictional invention.[2] There are (according to current thinking) many fictional authorities in the *Augustan History*. However only Cordus is referred to more than a few times and it may be suggestive of his possible authenticity that, chronologically, the references to Cordus start abruptly at the reign of Septimius Severus and end with the three Gordians. Cordus, if he existed, was certainly sensationalist and superficial in outlook. His may be a genuine lost *fictional* history of the salacious lives of the emperors, almost totally unreliable, which was used by the authors (or author) of the *Augustan History*.

- *Dexippus* (**written after 270**). An important early source is the Chronicle of the Athenian statesman and historian Publius Herennius Dexippus. Originally in 12 books, the *Chronicle* covered a thousand years up to the death of the emperor Claudius II (270). Unfortunately only fragments survive through later authors who quote him; worse still, historians regard what remains of his work as poor and unreliable. However, Dexippus is a major historical character in his own right, having led the Athenians against the invading hordes in 269 when Athens was overrun. Dexippus may have used a combination of oral and written sources for his history and was undeniably well connected. His is the last known work when there is any possibility of information from our period being recorded first hand. Dexippus was used by the authors (or author) of the *Augustan History* and Zozimus (see below) among others.

- *Augustan History* (ostensibly early fourth century but perhaps late fourth or fifth century). This controversial source was discussed in the beginning of this book, so those arguments will not be repeated here. But now the narrative has been told, it is worth pointing out that the life of Maximinus hangs together surprisingly well for what is commonly thought of as pure invention, and there is at least some element of independent corroboration. Details associated with the games of Severus are plausible, as is Maximinus's career as a bodyguard. An inscription names one Julius Maximinus as a squad commander in the elite imperial horseguard in Rome at about the right time. His retirement from the service to his native province under Macrinus seems psychologically appropriate and fits the wider historical pattern, as is the idea that the dubious regime of Elagabalus in its early days, so concerned to secure the loyalty of the army, would have tried to persuade a famous old soldier associated with the old dynasty back into service by offering him equestrian status and senior command. The governorship for Mauretania Tingitana, a post revealed in an inscription as having been occupied by him, was a known progression for an ex-officer of the horseguard (as only the *Augustan History* places him). And that work also has him march 300–400 miles into barbarian Germany, which was a seemingly fanciful idea until 2009, since when it has received strong support from archaeology.

    Two other curiosities are worth mentioning. First, the degree of consistent detail (verisimilitude) in the story of Maximinus contrasts strongly with that of Maximus and the Gordians, which are essentially superficial, despite being supposedly by the same author, Julius Capitolinus. Second, that although Herodian's convincing account of the coup of 235 was available to the author or authors of the *Augustan History*, a rather different account was preferred, insofar as Severus Alexander was murdered by discontented soldiers in Gaul, or even Britain. All this suggests that it is possible, at least, that Julius Capitolinus (if indeed it was him) had access to a life of Maximinus independent of Herodian, possibly one that was sympathetic and in the military tradition. This may have been transmitted via Dexippus or some other source. Cordus, if he existed, may have had access to it too. Mixing of pro- and anti-Maximinus propaganda could account for various curiosities in the narratives of Aelius Lampridius (for Severus Alexander) and Julius Capitolinus (for Maximinus, Maximus, and the Gordians).

    Historians since Dessau have emphasized the obvious similarity of certain sections of the *Augustan History* and mid- to late-third century sources such as Aurelius Victor and Eutropius. Some passages are almost word-for-word the same. The inference is that the author of the *Augustan History* simply copied such passages. However determining if A copied B or vice versa, or if both copied some unknown source, or if the suspect passages are later insertions, is not as simple as it may seem. And one has to ask, if the supposed fraudster went to such elaborate and heroically sustained lengths to pose as six different, earlier authors, deriving (but disguising) information from Ammianus Marcellinus among others, then why then risk all by lifting certain short passages from these works word for word?

One further point can be made; even if the Dessau/Syme view is correct, the *Augustan History* is not necessarily worthless. Syme (1968) developed an interesting thesis that it uses material from Ammianus Marcellinus, even though he is not named (that would have been an obvious *faux pas* on the part of the supposed fraudster who was pretending to be writing before Ammianus was even born). An implication of this viewpoint, although apparently not spelled out by Syme, is that the *Augustan History* could therefore contain unattributed information pertaining to the third century from Ammianus's lost books. We know that those books contained information on the reign of Maximinus and the Gordians (e.g. Frakes, 1995, p. 243).

- **Multiple other lost first-hand sources.** Herodian is clear that he was by no means the only historian of his times, nor was he necessarily the most authoritative; his is simply the work that has survived intact. In Roman times the telling of history was a recognized genre and a respectable pursuit for retired noblemen, even a competition sport in events like the Capitoline games. So we must accept that there may have been any number of other first-hand sources of various degrees of reliability and inherent merit, some written and archived in the great libraries of antiquity, others transmitted verbally, that may have been used by later writers. The *Augustan History* refers frequently to various individuals, otherwise unknown, who supposedly wrote accounts of their times. The question of how information was transmitted seems irresolvable, except through the distant hope of archaeological disinterment of some ancient library.

- *Kaisergeschicte* (c. 340–360). This is the name given by Enmann (1884) to a hypothetical series of lives of the Caesars written in Greek, now lost, that was used as a common source for several later works including Aurelius Victor, Eutropius and, more controversially, the *Augustan History*. Its existence is betrayed by a series of errors common to all these later sources. The work may have synthesized any number of lost histories, notably including Marius Maximus (see above). Other authors speculate on an additional lost source similar to the *Kaisergeschicte* but in Latin.

- *Aurelius Victor* (c. 361). Sextus Aurelius Victor is the supposed author of a history of Rome from Augustus (27 BCE) to Julian (360 CE) called *De Caesaribus*, plus other minor works which together are referred to as the *Historia Romana*. The third-century information is possibly derived mainly from the hypothetical *Kaisergeschicte* (see above). As such it represents a different tradition from our other main sources and is full of interesting snippets; unfortunately it is also replete with known errors. Perhaps its main value is in reminding us just how little educated Romans of the late fourth century knew of their own history.

- *Epitome De Caesaribus* (late fourth century). Sometimes attributed to Aurelius Victor, this anonymous work is a much abridged list of the emperors mostly derived from Aurelius Victor. It contains a few comments or character details relating to third century matters that are found nowhere else.

- *Ammianus Marcellinus* (after 378). Ammianus Marcellinus wrote one of the greatest of all Roman histories, which is an invaluable source for the late fourth century. Ammianus's history originally extended from the accession of Nerva (96) to the death of Valens (378). Unfortunately, only the later, extended, period of his history (from 353) survives, although in it there are occasional references to earlier events, including from our period of interest.

- *Eutropius* (around 380). Flavius Eutropius wrote a highly abbreviated Roman history, running from the foundation of the city to the accession of the emperor Valens in 364. As in Aurelius Victor, the third-century information is thought to have been derived mostly from the Kaisergeschicte.

- **Church sources.** Early Christian churches kept records, including a book of popes (*liber pontificus*), which contains brief biographies with incidental details. Other early Christian writers recorded martyrdoms and persecutions. When the Christian church became established as the state religion of the empire, this information was synthesized by the so-called 'Fathers of the Church'. The most important works for our period are various writings by the ascetic Origen (c. 185–254 CE) who witnessed the religious purge of 235; the anti-pope Hippolytus who died at that time; the letters of St. Cyprian, bishop of Carthage; the *Ecclesiastical History* of Eusebius of Caesarea (early fourth century) which derives much from Origen; the so-called *Chronography of 354*; and the church *Chronicle* of Sulpicius Severus (403 AD).

- *Vegetius* (around 380, possibly early fifth century). Publius Flavius Vegetius Renatus wrote a manual of military affairs in the declining days of the Roman empire that consciously looked back at the long history of Roman and ancient Greek military successes and failures and the reasons for them. It reads like a white paper on what had gone wrong in the military of the late fourth century and how to restore discipline and organization in the traditional manner. Although there is no direct reference to our period of interest, it remains an invaluable guide to Roman military science. We may use it, with caution, as a guide for how third century armies operated in matters such as conscription, training and tactics.

- **Agathangelos (probably fifth century).** This is the name of an Armenian Christian writer of a *History of St. Gregory and the Conversion of Armenia*, of which various versions and embellishments exist.[3] The history has some colourful details from the third century that must have been transmitted via Parthian/Persian scribes independent of the Roman tradition.

- **Zosimus (circa 498–518).** This pagan historian lived in Constantinople in the early Byzantine period. He wrote a work called the *Historia Nova* (new history), apparently making primary use of a possibly complete copy of Dexippus for the period of our investigation, and he also transmitted fragments from Cassius Dio that would otherwise be lost.

- **Jordanes (c. 551).** This man wrote his work *Getica*, on the Goths, in a few days as a summary of a lost work on the same subject by Cassiodorus, a Roman who worked in the service of the Ostrogothic king Theodoric the Great. It contains no new material (except some slightly variant details that are nevertheless clearly derived from the *Augustan History* via Symmachus), but provides a somewhat more positive view of Maximinus than is found in the other ancient sources.

- **Agathias (c. 560).** This Greek poet and historian is one of the chief sources for the reign of Justinian I. His *Histories* contain some interesting information on the early years of the Sasanian empire which he copied from Persian Royal archives, now lost to us.

- **Peter Patricius (c. 560).** This Byzantine official and diplomat wrote a history of the Roman Empire from 44 BCE to 361 CE of which only fragments survive but which could contain independent information from Dexippus and possibly other unknown channels.

- **George Syncellus (c. 800).** This Byzantine churchman wrote a Chronicle that transmits some earlier works including fragments of Dexippus.

- **John Zonoras (after 1118).** This man was a scholar and theologian at Constantinople. He wrote a work called *Epitome Historiam* (Extracts of

History) summarizing many earlier writers. For our purposes, the most important part of his work is the interval of the third and fourth centuries because Zonoras certainly used sources that are otherwise unknown to us. It is interesting that Gibbon regarded Zonoras as one of the 'moderns' rather than the 'ancients'. No subsequent historian seems to have had any independent source of information about our period of interest apart from archaeological data.

The oldest surviving manuscripts of the most important texts – that is, physical objects that can be opened and read today – mostly date from the ninth century or later. The unknown scribes who copied and recopied these works in the intervening centuries transmitted everything we know of the period, aside from the archaeological remains, and we are all in their debt. The thread of history was thin and delicate until the fifteenth century when the invention of printing changed everything, as, more recently, did the Internet. We can fantasize that a complete text of Marius Maximus or Dexippus – or even Cordus! – might one day come to light, or even the work of an unknown historian, perhaps buried in some anoxic sludge or desiccated cave. Until that day, we must fill in the gaps as best we can.

Appendix II

Chronology of 238

Various authors have attempted to draw up a chronology for 238 based on the historical sources combined with analysis of inscription, papyri, and the coinage. The issue has been discussed at length by Haegemans (2010, p. 21–27) who emphasizes the uncertainty. The following summary is from Dietz (1980) and Haegemans (2010):

Event	Carson (1959)	Whittaker (1969)	Loriot (1975)	Schwartz (1977)	Haegemans (2010) based on Peachin (1990)
Proclamation of Gordian I and II	22 March	ca. 1 March	15–20 January		Second half of March
Recognition of the Gordians in Rome: Maximinus made public enemy	1 April (eclipse, 2 April)		End of January/ beginning of February	March	Beginning of April
Battle of Carthage	12 April	ca. 22 March	ca. 20 February	March or April	Late April
Departure of Maximinus from Sirmium		24 March	ca. Middle February		
Elevation of Balbinus and Pupienus (and Gordian III, as *caesar*)	22 April	1 April	28 February or 1 March		First half of May?
Maximus in Emona		10 April			
Vanguard arrives at Aquileia			15–20 March		End of May
Arrival of Maximinus at Aquileia		20 April	ca. 10 April		
Death of Maximinus	24 June	End of May	ca. 10 May	Before 27 July	First half of June

Event	Carson (1959)	Whittaker (1969)	Loriot (1975)	Schwartz (1977)	Haegemans (2010) based on Peachin (1990)
Pupienus arrives in Aquileia			ca. 15–20 May		
Pupienus arrives at Rome			End of May		
Death of Balbinus and Pupienus	29 July	8 July	6 or 7 June	Before 29 August	First half of August
Decannial vows of Gordian			8 June		Unknown

Endnotes

Introduction

1. CE, the Common Era, a term that is increasingly being used in place of AD, *Anno Domini*, which begins with the supposed year of Jesus's birth. We will meet, in passing, one of the early scholars who first tried to determine this date. It is usually said that the empire reached its greatest extent under Trajan in about 117 CE following the conquest of Dacia (roughly modern Romania) and lower Mesopotamia, but the latter province could not be held. The borders were more or less constant for the following century and a half. That the empire was already declining in the first decades of the early third century, especially in the wake of the Antonine plague, is a widely held view, and owes much to Cassius Dio's memorable statement that in his time an age of gold had given way to one of 'iron and rust' (*Cassius Dio, Roman History* LXXII=LXXIII.35.1). But it was traditional for educated nobility of the empire to lament a previous golden age. The idea that the early third century was Rome's peak was the view of Aurelius Victor in the fourth century (*Aurelius Victor, De Caesaribus*, Chapter 24). The phrase 'golden age' of Latin was introduced by Teuffel (1870).
2. Haegemans (2010). See also Bersanetti (1940), Bellezza (1964), Balil (1965) and Burian (1988) for earlier works focused on Maximinus.
3. The quotation is from Le Bohec (1994, p. 8). It may be pause for thought that the revered Thucydides wrote virtually nothing other than battle-history and events!
4. Regarding Herodian's non-senatorial status, see, for example, Whittaker (1969, Volume 1, p. xix–xx), who argued that Herodian's knowledge of a secret senatorial decree (which we will come to in due course) is hardly evidence of him having been a senator, as had been argued long before by Volkmann (1859) and others. That may be true, but there are several other instances where Herodian recounts what is arguably 'inside information' from the senate, and events in and around the senate house. Of course he could have obtained those details from a senator but I see no positive evidence that he was not a senator, and as Whittaker does point out, writing history was a respectable occupation for a man of senatorial rank. Whittaker's argument that he was not a senator comes down largely to the fact that his writing is less concerned with senatorial matters than is Cassius Dio's. But Dio was twice consul, and nobody is suggesting Herodian was *that* eminent or as privy to state matters. On Herodian's value as a historian see, for example, Syme (1971, p. 255) who dismissed him as "a Greek rhetorician passing himself off as a writer of history" and Potter (2004, p. 232) who describes Herodian's history as a "mixed blessing". Speidel (1994b, p. 56) went so far as to claim that Herodian "set the truth at naught", and Birley (1988, p. 204–205) also gives a very critical assessment, but arguably all these authors are trying to hold him to the standards of a modern academic historian. More balanced and

positive views have been expressed by a range of authors including Sidebottom (1998). An excellent recent discussion on critical views on Herodian and his 'partial rehabilitation' by academics in recent years is given by Haegemans (2010, p. 14–16). We await his full rehabilitation. One very positive thing we can say about Herodian is that he rarely engaged in discussing supernatural signs, dreams and portents, unlike Dio and many other ancient historians. Just one example of his scepticism is his comment on the dreams of Septimius Severus that supposedly predicted high office: "These prognostications are all believed to be absolutely true later when in actual fact they turn out well" (*Herodian, History of the Empire* II.9.3).

5. That this kind of claim for objectivity was standard fare among historians from Thucydides onward does not mean we should necessarily discredit it. For his imperial service see *Herodian, History of the Empire* I.2.5.

Prologue

1. As they progressed, Severus had ordered an advance guard under the command of his loyal general Claudius Candidus to cross the Sea of Marmara and this force was now manoeuvering against Niger's forces in Asia Minor. Severus may have been held up on the European side of the straits because the pro-Niger city of Byzantium refused to surrender and so had been put to siege. With Byzantium holding out behind its formidable defences and a substantial garrison within, the situation needed to be stabilized before the main force could safely cross into Asia (Birley, 1988, p. 108–112). Incidentally, the commander of the force besieging Byzantium was none other than Marius Maximus who later wrote an important historical work that is now lost to us, but information from which was reworked by later authors (see Appendix 1).

2. *Scriptores Historiae Augustae* (Julius Capitolinus), *Maximini Duo* II:4–III.7. The story is also repeated in the ancient history of the Goths by Jordanes (*Jordanes, Getica* XV:83–87), where it is there copied via the lost work of Symmachus as summarized by Cassiodorus (see Appendix 1 on these sources). For the sake of the prologue I have developed the context, working with the assumption that such an event actually happened. The *Augustan History* does not give a year or a location for the games, the only clue of the timing being the birthday of Geta, of which we know the date from other sources. The gist of the story is that Maximinus was initially a civilian, hence if indeed such an event actually happened, his home province of Thrace is the most likely setting for it (as Gibbon also concluded long ago; Gibbon [1776, Chapter 7]). Geta's birthday was in early March. Severus was probably camped out in Thrace in the spring of 194 (Birley, 1998, p. 109, 112) so this seems the most plausible time that such games might have been held. With the army of Candidus already in the Asian theatre of war and distinguishing themselves by winning victories, and others besieging Byzantium, it would have been important to maintain morale among the strategic reserve. The date also fits well with Maximinus' age as reported by Zonoras: he would have been about 21–22 years old and hence not yet too old to be recruited, especially in an army that was preparing for war. Of course none of these incidental details guarantees the authenticity of the story.

3. Thracian was an important Indo-European language that died out in the Middle Ages (Hummer, 1998).

4. Information on the *torquatus* is from *Vegetius, Military Institutions* 2.5. Milo of Croton is one of history's more extraordinary characters, a famous wrestler and strongman, military commander, and associate of Pythagoras (see Boardman and Hammond, 1982, p. 194). The claims about Maximinus's eating and drinking and similar passages are dismissed by Syme (1968, p. 67) as fantasy, although he himself exaggerated the *Augustan History* by writing that Maximinus drank that much "each day". Regarding sweating, Haynes (2013, p. 173) has pointed out that it was seen as a macho characteristic in the army. As for the horse's teeth, a similar claim was made of the emperor Claudius II Gothicus, who "often by a blow of his fist he would dash out the teeth of a horse or mule": *Scriptores Historiae Augustae* (Trebellius Pollio), *Divus Claudius* XIII.5.

5. He first gained the epithet 'Thrax' in the *Epitome de Caesaribus* and it has subsequently been used to distinguish him from a later emperor of the same name, Maximinus Daia (the Dacian). Alternatively he is known as Maximinus I. For a critical discussion of the contention that his accession was a turning point in Roman history, see Haegemans (2010, p. 3).

6. *Herodian, History of the Empire* VII.1.12.

7. King (1990, p. 130) discusses imperial portraiture on the coinage. The issue of Maximinus' depiction is returned to in the final two chapters.

8. Klawans (1982). See also Sheaves (1999). The claim is debated by Pearce (2003).

9. http://en.wikipedia.org/wiki/Acromegaly#Notable_cases.

10. The Roman foot or *pes* was estimated at 295.9 mm, or 0.9708 English feet, by Smith and Anthon (1851, p. 1024–1030). But this figure seems to be spuriously accurate! A German horseman at the time of Augustus named Pusio ('the little one') was reportedly over *ten* feet tall (Speidel, 1994b, p. 18).

11. See, for example, Rhodes (1977): "It now seems certain that Richard did not have a hunchback" and many statements by other scholars and the King Richard III Society (although, to be fair, Rhodes did consider other conditions that might raise a shoulder). For the discovery of Richard's skeleton see Buckley *et al.* (2013). Klawans's idea of acromegaly has been cited just three times in over three decades since it was published (source: Google Scholar) but, intriguingly, it is mentioned on the Wikipedia page: http://en.wikipedia.org/wiki/Maximinus_Thrax#Appearance.

12. This is the usual title in English; there are other varieties, and Herodian himself gave no title.

13. In our story, the account of Severus Alexander's construction programme in Rome is one example where only the *Augustan History* records details that can be confirmed in the surviving bricks and mortar. The building of a great wall in Britain by Hadrian is another striking instance: almost all other ancient sources attribute Britain's most impressive surviving Roman monument to Septimius Severus (Birley, 1976, footnote to p. 69; the exception to this is the Dark Age work of the monk Gildas, *De Ecxidio et Conquesto Britanniae*). The existence of the short-lived emperor Domitian II, rejected by some scholars as a typical invention of the *Augustan History* (where a senior general named Domitian appears), was recently proved beyond doubt by the discovery of a second coin bearing his image, the first from the same dies having been found a century before and dismissed as a forgery (see Abdy, 2009).

14. The impression one gets from reading the *Augustan History* is that the *scriptores* are happy to repeat a certain number of dubious claims from Cordus but only up to a point.

For example, on elaborating a number of scarcely believable signs and portents from Cordus, the supposed author, Julius Capitolinus wraps the topic up with "It is a lengthy business to enumerate all these things; and if anyone desires to know them, let him, as I have often said, read Cordus, who has related them all, to the point of telling idle tales" (*Scriptores Historiae Augustae* (Julius Capitolinus), *Maximini Duo* XXXI.5.

15. For a discussion of a range of historical views on Cordus, with references, see Syme (1971, p. 76) and Haegemans (2010, p. 19).

16. The radical view of the *Augustan History* as a single late work was made by Dessau (1889). The first reference to it was by Quintus Aurelius Memmius Symmachus, author of a Roman History that is also now lost, but which was quoted in detail by a later writer, Jordanes (see Birley, 1976, p. 20). The key story that links Jordanes to the *Augustan History* is none other than that of Maximinus at the games.

17. See the masterful introduction to the *Augustan History* by Magie (1924, Volume I) which, in the opinion of this author, is rather spoiled by a short "Editorial Note" of 1991 by 'G.P.G.' (Magie, 1924, Volume I, p. xxxviii) that contradicts Magie's position, citing the later works of Ronald Syme (1968, 1971) and his pupil T.D. Barnes (1978). See also White (1967). The most authoritative opponent of Dessau was Klebs (1892).

18. Birley (1988, p. 206).

19. For an account of the history, problems and pitfalls of stylometrics see Holmes (1998). For application to the *Augustan History* see Marriott (1979), Syme (1980), Gurney and Gurney (1998a, b, c): especially Gurney and Gurney (1998b, figs. 1 and 3), and Tse *et al.* (1998) and the critique by Rudman (1998); there are also several other significant contributions cited in those articles. Rudman's critique contains many good points and some not so good ones (why must a stylometrician also be expert in Greek and Latin and have a knowledge of ancient rhetoric as a *sine qua non* [whatever that means!]?), these important results have been cited just a handful of times and have been ignored by most subsequent commentators on the *Augustan History* except for Den Hengst (2002) who concludes the controversy cannot be resolved by sweeping statements. So from a small selection of recent writings, Haegemans (2010) did not question the single authorship and late date of the work and makes no mention of stylometrics; nor does Wiegels (2012), who reports that the *communis opinio* is in favour of a single author around the time of Theodosius. Rohrbacher (2013) briefly reviewed the debate but considered it settled, while at the same time raised interesting questions that are engendered by assuming a single author: what sort of person might have done it, and what was their purpose?

The main technique used by Gurney and Gurney (1998b) is a method called canonical discriminant analysis in which the authorship of the vitae is 'given' and the analysis seeks the best way of differentiating them along multivariate axes. The method successfully achieves this if given frequency data on a sufficient number of words. However because the six categories are given in advance, the method does not provide an absolute demonstration of the authorship, as Gurney and Gurney accept. Comparing the degree of cluster separation against a large number of randomized controls might achieve that. However techniques for multivariate clustering now exist in which the authorship is not 'known' and the number and membership of clusters is determined automatically from the data alone using thresholding criteria and principal components (Ezard *et al.* 2010). Demonstration by this method would be the utopia for stylometric studies of the

Historia Augusta. Pending that, however, the Gurney and Gurney (1998b) discriminant analysis stands as a provocative study in favour of multiple authorship that should be taken seriously.

The full implications of the stylometric result of Gurney and Gurney (a, b, c) have hardly been explored. It seems to this author that if one half of Dessau's thesis (single authorship) is rejected, the other half (the late date) must also be highly questionable. It is possible, of course, that the dedications to Diocletian and Constantine are later additions by an editor, to make the collection appear older than it is, especially as they do come at the start of their respective *vitae*. But with wholesale fraud ruled out, that conjecture surely becomes less likely, as indeed does the non-existence of Cordus. In essence, the 'believability threshold' of everything in the *Augustan History* increases by a significant notch if the texts can be shown to be consistent with the six authors as stated.

Chapter I: Nurs'd in Blood and War

1. For Zonoras see *Zonoras, Extracts of History* 12.16: for the other works see Haegemans (2010, p. 50). Syme (1971, p. 181–182) urges caution on the date, partly on the grounds that Maximinus does not look like a sexagenarian on his coins, and suggests he may have been a decade younger. However it must be admitted that many of the older emperors, from Augustus onward, are flattered by their portraits, and it seems pointless to contradict what little evidence we have on such thin grounds. For Herodian see *Herodian, History of the Empire* VI.8. Most other sources agree on his Thracian origin although one late source, Syncellus, described him as 'Maximinus the Moesian'. Whether this is an inference from the *Augustan History* or because of other information, now lost, we do not know (see Dodgeon and Lieu, p. 43). The extended quotation is from *Scriptores Historiae Augustae* (Julius Capitolinus), *Maximini Duo* I:6–7, although the text of the original codex reads 'hababa', not 'ababa'.

2. That Thrace and Moesia would have been a fine distinction for an easterner like Herodian to make was discussed by Syme (1971, p.186) and Syme (1973, p. 313). To this we can add that Upper Moesia was later incorporated into the later diocese of 'broader Thrace' at the time of Diocletian. For wealth see *Herodian, History of the Empire* III.5.

3. For anti-Thracian prejudice in Greece and the Roman empire, and especially their bloodthirsty reputation, see Webber (2011) who also gives a fascinating account of the many Thracian tribes.

4. For religion see *Ammianus Marcellinus, Roman History* XXXI.2.18. For Thracians see Matthews (2007, p. 334–335). For Chinese sources see Alemany (2000). The modern-day Ossetians of the Caucasus may be direct descendants of the Alans (Alemany, 2000, p. 5).

5. For the Goths' history see *Jordanes, Getica*. For archaeology see Heather (1996, p. 11–50). It should be noted that the more cautious archaeologists reject this generalization but support it in detail.

6. The wide range of opinions on Maximinus's likely origins, including widespread distrust of the *Augustan History*, is summarized by Weigels (2012, p. 451–452). Syme (1971) thought it likely that he would have been the son of an army officer, and Syme (1973), by "making allowance for prejudice and defamation", was confident he must have been a Roman citizen from Moesia, but without evidence. Syme (1971, p.186) suggested the most likely place of birth is the vicinity of the fort at Oescus in Treballian Moesia, but this

precision seems to be unwarranted by the available evidence. Petraccia Lucernoni (1997) suggested Nova Italica in Moesia as the birthplace (see also Speidel, 1994b) but this may be a misunderstanding of an inscription. More recently, Potter (2004, p.168) dismissed the accounts in Herodian and the *Historia Augusta* as "wild slanders" although also without citing evidence. Haegemens (2010, p. 51) pointed out there is no real reason to discount his lowly origins but also states (p. 52) "a birth as a son of a local dignitary or officer, perhaps even of equestrian rank, is definitely a possibility". Regarding enriching one's home town, Philip the Arab (reigned 244–249) adorned Philippopolis with magnificent buildings (Potter, 2004, p. 238). On the possibly Gothic etymology see Bellezza (1964); for the alternative see Syme (1968, p. 37, p. 173: "an allurement to the learned or the credulous") and Haegemans (2010, p. 50). Heather (1996, p. 38–39) suggests contact between Goths and Romans from after the second century Marcomannic wars.

7. *Inscriptiones Graecae in Bulgaria Repertae* 3, 1. n. 1126; see discussion in Haynes (2013, p. 109). For the sanctuary see Tsonchev (1941).

8. See Goldsworthy (2000) for an engrossing narrative account.

9. The etymology of *augustus* is discussed by Suetonius; see Haverfield (1915). For the advice see *Tacitus, Annals* I.11. Its interpretation is discussed by Whittaker (1994, p. 25–26).

10. I state this in full knowledge that equating Hadrian's British and African walls has been described, by the French, as the *pons asinorum* of Anglo-Saxon historians (Trousset, 1981; see discussion in Whittaker, 1994, p. 91).

11. For Roman attitudes to their frontiers see Whittaker (1994).

12. It is standard to regard Augustus as the first emperor, but he did not claim this himself. A better case can be made for regarding Julius Caesar as the first, from the moment he had the Senate proclaim him *dictator perpetuo*: dictator for life and put his portrait on the coinage. It was this move that precipitated his assassination. Suetonius placed Julius Caesar as the first of his *Twelve Caesars*.

13. These were termed *consul ordinarius*. Other men were usually appointed consul in their place later in the year to spread the honours around.

14. There may have been sound reasons for this because such men could be lifelong professional soldiers. The trend was to continue until the emperor Gallienus actually banned senators from taking senior commands, or so it was said; see Haegemans (2010, p. 40) and Mennen (2011, chapter 4). For a discussion of the formal and practical relationship between the senators and *equites*, see Haegemans (2010, p. 29–32).

15. Nothing in third century history is debated more than Caracalla's decree: both the reasons for it, and its consequences (see, for example, discussions in Hekster, 2008, p. 47–55, and Ando, 2012, p. 52–54). The latter will forever be difficult to judge, although it undoubtedly affected the relative status of army units (Haynes, 2013, p. 89) but the fundamental reason for the move may just be obvious: Caracalla was by descent part African and part Syrian. Extending the citizenship was his affirmation that the Roman empire was no longer just about the big city, but an international collective of the rich and powerful with its historic centre in Rome. And as Dio pointed out, that meant he could tax everyone as a citizen too!

16. For a general discussion of the intrinsic versus face value worth of money up to the modern era see Coggan (2011). The distinction was first articulated by the jurist Paul (Julius Paulus Prudentissimus) in the reign of Severus Alexander, for which see Ando (2012, p. 216, footnote).

17. See Birley (1988) for a detailed biography and account of his reign. A family tree is provided by Birley (1988, p. 216–217).
18. The orthodox view that debasement caused inflation in the third century (e.g. Sutherland, 1974, p. 225) has been questioned in recent years, especially because the evidence for price rises does not tally well with data on the metallurgical content of the coins (see, for example, Rathbone, 1996, and the discussions in Prodromídis, 2006, and Ando, 2012, p. 214–216). The issue is too complex to enter here, except to remark that archaeological evidence shows unequivocally that the people clearly understood that heavier coins of better precious metal quality were worth more than others of the same face value, hence, in accordance with 'Gresham's law' that bad money drives out good, the finer pieces (e.g. republican denarii) were hoarded for their metal content rather than their face value, often for centuries. Moreover bullion also passed as a means of exchange. All this means it would be premature to dismiss the old paradigm, which, as pointed out by Prodromídis (2006) is based on sound economic principles. For Commodus's illness see McLynn (2009, p. 446). For the re-naming of the months see *Cassius Dio, Roman History* LXXII.15 and *Scriptores Historiae Augustae* (Aelius Lampridius) *Commodus Antoninus* XI: 6–10. See also Birley (1988, p. 85). Of these, the only month we would now recognize is August.
19. For example, *Scriptores Historiae Augustae* (Aelius Spartianus), *Severus* I.6–10.
20. See *Cassius Dio, Roman History* LXXIV.11, 1–6. One modern historian prefers to regard Cassius Dio's detailed account of this auction as false propaganda, although evidence for that thesis is not presented (Potter, 2004, p. 97). Soldiers' pay was traditionally a *denarius* (4 *sestertii*) per day, but pay rises in the time of Severus and Caracalla had increased this (Frank, 1936, p. 86).
21. Conveniently, one of Severus's first acts as emperor was to issue a series of coins in honour of these legions and to fund his campaign, which confirms their support: see http://dougsmith.ancients.info/legion1.html.
22. *Cassius Dio, Roman History* LXXIV.17.2.
23. For the disgrace of the praetorians see *Cassius Dio, Roman History* LXXV.1.2. Banditry in Italy was a problem subsequently.
24. *Cassius Dio, Roman History* LXXV.7.5.
25. *Cassius Dio, Roman History* LXXVI.4.1–6.

Chapter II: Cursus Maximini

1. *Scriptores Historiae Augustae* (Julius Capitolinus), *Maximini Duo* III.1.
2. Quotations from Vegetius in this chapter are from *Vegetius, Military Institutions* 1.1, 1.4, 1.5, 1.7, 2.7, 2.9 and 3.15.
3. An example of this comes from a second century papyrus which refers to an Egyptian called Isidorus who was known as Julius Martialis in the army (Haynes (2013, p. 72).
4. Bellezza (1964) noted that Micca might mean 'big' but did not draw a parallel with the name Maximinus; for an alternative view on the name Micca see Syme (1968, p. 37 and p. 173) and Haegemans (2010, p. 50). There was a provincial governor called Caius Julius Maximinus in the third century (Whittaker, 1969–1970, Volume II, p. 131) who might have given Maximinus his name but that idea has been called far-fetched by Haegemans (2010, p. 53).

5. Haynes (2013, p. 98).
6. For the *ala* see Dixon and Southern (1992, p. 23, 80). That thirty-two troopers formed a *turma* is from the ancient historian Arrian, but some historians prefer thirty (see Haynes 2013, p. 53, note 8). See also Goldsworthy (2000, p. 127).
7. Livius, *Ab Urbe Condita Libri* XXII.38. See also Van Slyke (2005, p. 170).
8. *Stipatores corporis* is the term used in the *Augustan History* (*Scriptores Historiae Augustae* (Julius Capitolinus), *Maximini Duo* III.5. A *stipator* is a bodyguard. Haegemans (2010, p. 52-53) provides a discussion of whether this was one and the same as the *equites singulares augusti*: Because a man cannot have thousands of bodyguards, it is likely the *stipatores* were selected from the latter. On bodyguards and their physical size see Speidel (1994b, p. 14, 22, 64, 79 and 120).
9. This is according to Diocletian's price edict of the late third century, see Speidel (1994b, p. 104).
10. The main contender is the Chinese capital, Lu-Yougong on the Yellow River (Keay, 2008).
11. *Scriptores Historiae Augustae* (Julius Capitolinus), *Maximini Duo* VIII.7. *Cassius Dio, Roman History* LXXV.2. 6, although, it is fair to say, the quote is from before the date of Maximinus's likely enlistment.
12. *Scriptores Historiae Augustae* (Julius Capitolinus), *Maximini Duo* III.6.
13. On the career, see Speidel (1994b, p. 148–149). On establishments near the Caelian barracks see Speidel (1994b, p. 126–138). The remains of the new barracks (*castra nova*) of the *equites* has been uncovered in excavations beneath the basilica of San Giovanni in Laterano (see Haynes *et al.*, 2012, and Chapter 15).
14. For the inscription, see Speidel (1994a, p. 132). For Maximinus see Speidel (1994b, p. 68). Most other historians dismiss the story that Maximinus was an imperial bodyguard as an invention of the *Augustan History*, and it is often claimed that he was the first emperor never to have visited the city.
15. *Herodian, History of the Empire* III.11.9.
16. Haegemans (2010, p. 53).
17. *Corpus Inscriptionum Latinarum* VII, 513.
18. On the troubles in Caledonia see *Herodian, History of the Empire* III.13.14. On the possible refugee camp see http://explore-hadrians-wall.com/roman-sites/vindolanda.php. On preparations for war see *Cassius Dio, Roman History* LXXVII.13.1. Of course the strategy to secure Britain did not happen, and the ongoing instability spawned a series of insurrections through the later third and fourth centuries.
19. *Herodian, History of the Empire* III.14.2. Other ancient sources referred to in this section are *Herodian, History of the Empire* III.14.6; and *Cassius Dio, Roman History* LXXVII.13.2., LXXVII.15.3, LXXVIII.15.4.
20. Birley (1988, p. 175); Speidel (1994, p. 39).
21. Bowman (1994, p. 103).
22. It seems strange that serial defeats of the Romans plays little part in modern Scottish national myth-making, as it does, for example, in Germany. Perhaps this is because we know almost nothing of the experience from the Caledonian side.
23. On the deeds of Caracalla see *Cassius Dio, Roman History* LXXVIII.16.1–6 and LXXVIII.20.1; see also *Herodian, History of the Empire* IV.6.4, IV.7.3 and IV.9.8.
24. There have been various unconvincing (to this author) suggestion that the denomination may have been tariffed at 1.25 or 1.5 denarii (see discussion in Haegemans, 2010, p. 218;

also Reece, 2007, p. 131). The crown had long been the symbol of the bronze double *as*, the *dupondius*, a simple system for indicating face value, understood by the illiterate majority of the empire.

25. On centurion see *Scriptores Historiae Augustae* (Julius Capitolinus), *Maximini Duo* IV.4. On transfers see LeBohec (1994, p. 44). On the Dacian war see *Scriptores Historiae Augustae* (Aelius Spartianus), *Antoninus Caracalla* V.6-7. On Porolissum see http:// en.wikipedia.org/wiki/Roman_Dacia#cite_note-Grumeza-1. On *primus pilus*, the particular phrase used by the *Augustan History* is that he "commanded in the ranks of the centuries", which is interpreted as meaning this rank – see Magie (1924, Volume II, p. 233, footnote 3).

26. *Herodian, History of the Empire* IV.11.3. Also used in this section are *Herodian, History of the Empire* IV.11.9, and V.3.10.

27. Regarding Paulina's ring, enlargement of the hands is a characteristic feature of acromegaly, and this tale was used as possible support of his thesis by Klawans (1982, p. 323). Regarding the equestrian rank, most modern historians assume he must have been an equestrian from birth but this conflicts with the written sources. It was perfectly possible for a *primus pilus* to be raised to equestrian status as a further promotion (Mennen, 2011, p. 136). A step up from *primus pilus* to senior command had been possible since at least the reign of Claudius in the first century (Haegemans, 2010, p. 53, footnote). Advancement from the ranks may well have been more common under the cosmopolitan and militaristic rule of Severus and Caracalla than other emperors. For Caecilius, *Caecilius est pater. Metella est mater* (Cambridge Latin course)! For Zosimus see *Zosimus, New History* 1.13.1. For the daughter see *Epitome de Caesaribus*, Chapter 25.

28. Or possibly by beating her breast and rupturing a tumour; see Langford (2013) for discussion of this and other reflections on Julia Domna.

29. Although not necessarily true, it is characteristically dismissed as "pure fable" by Syme (1971, p. 186) without evidence that it is so. For Thracians returning home, see Roxan (1997, p. 487) discussed in Haynes (2013, p. 374)

30. See Hedeager (1987) and Whittaker (1994).

31. For 'bravest man', see *Scriptores Historiae Augustae* (Julius Capitolinus), *Maximini Duo* IV.9. For feigning illness see *Scriptores Historiae Augustae* (Julius Capitolinus), *Maximini Duo* IV.6. For tribune see *Scriptores Historiae Augustae* (Julius Capitolinus), *Maximini Duo* V.1.

32. Godbout (2004).

33. As imagined by the Victorian artist Lawrence Alma-Tadema in his famous painting *The Roses of Heliogabalus*.

Chapter III: Regime Change

1. *Herodian, History of the Empire* VI.1.5. Other ancient sources used in this section are *Herodian, History of the Empire* VI.1.3., VI.1.4, VI.1.6., VI.I.9, VI.1.10, VI.2.1, VI.8.1, VI.9.7; *Cassius Dio, Roman History* LXXIX.21.2, LXXX.1.3., LXXX.2.4.; *Scriptores Historiae Augustae* (Aelius Lampridius), *Alexander Severus* V.4, VIII.1, XIV.6, XV.2, XVI.2, XX.2, XXII.1, XXIII.I., XXIV.3, XXVIII.6; and *Aurelius Victor, De Caesaribus* 25.1.

2. Honoré (2002).

3. Mennen (2011, p. 164).

4. Honoré (2002); Herrin (2007, Chapter 7).

5. Carson (1962, p. 54).

6. *Scriptores Historiae Augustae* (Aelius Lampridius), *Alexander Severus* XXV.7; Magie (1924, Volume II, p. 224–225). The new water supply was also depicted on a special issue of coins; see Carson (1962, p. 63–64).

7. The inscription from Mauretania is PIR2 I 420. It is discussed by Spraul (1994, p. 250), Speidel (1994, p. 69. 178, and Haegemans (2010, p. 54).

8. This is from *Scriptores Historiae Augustae* (Julius Capitolinus), *Maximini Duo.* V.4 and VIII.1. Later sources prefer the version that Maximinus was not of senatorial rank, which fits his image as a semi-barbarian outsider portrayed in later histories (*Eutropius, Breviarum* VIII.1). A typically cautious view from a modern historian is that "there is no need... to assume Maximinus ever reached the rank of senator, as all the major positions he held were open to equestrian officers" (Haegemans, 2011, p. 56). See also Magie (1924, p. 322–323, note 1).

9. The fourth legion was always rendered *IIII* in inscriptions, rather than *IV*, an old-fashioned style that lived on in the conservative army. There has been a great deal of discussion about the likely identity of this legion and, in particular, whether it can be identified instead as *legio IIII italicae*, although the only evidence for that legion is from much later, the *notitia dignitatum* of the early fifth century (see Mann, 1999). That conclusion has been rejected by recent scholarship (Weigels, 2012) and the traditional view, dating back at least to Bang (1906) seems least problematic.

10. *Aurelius Victor, De Caesaribus* 25.1. See also Whittaker (1969–1970, Volume II, p.133, footnote 2). The title *praefectus* was normally associated with equestrian offices (Mennen, 2011), which is one reason why some historians assume Maximinus never made senatorial rank. Weigels (2012, p. 447) questions this view. Like most aspects of Maximinus's early career, it is difficult to achieve certainty.

11. *Aurelius Victor, De Caesaribus* 24.

12. The supposition is based on some fragmentary inscriptions and a garbled statement attributed to Dexippus in *Scriptores Historiae Augustae* (Aelius Lampridius), *Alexander Severus* XLIX.4–5 where the father in law is called Macrinus; see discussion in Whittaker (1969–1970, Vol. II, p. 86–87, footnote 2).

13. Carson (1962, p. 65).

14. Herodian does not name Orbiana but she is well known from the coinage.

15. For a succinct account of Zoroastrianism in Sasanian Persia see Holland (2012, p. 83–87).

16. Evans (2011, p. 109–112).

17. Edwell (2008, p. 63–92).

18. The tariffs on luxury goods from eastern trade were a major source of income for Rome and much easier to collect than general taxation; see for example McLaughlin (2014, p. 1–17).

19. Luttwak (1976, p. 107).

20. Edwell (2008, p. 63–92).

21. See Frye (2005) for a summary of the sources. One account of his origins is found in *Agathias, The Histories* 2.27.1, which it is claimed derives from Persian royal archives. According to this version Ardashir's legal father was Papak, a seer, but his natural father was a soldier, Sasan. Papak divined that the offspring of Sasan was destined for greatness,

and given that he had no sons himself, he ordered his wife to sleep with Sasan. See also the Sasanian epic the *Kârnâmag î Ardashîr î Babagân*, or *Book of the Deeds of Ardashir son of Babag*; http://www.avesta.org/pahlavi/karname.htm

22. http://www.iranchamber.com/art/articles/art_of_sassanians.php. Confusingly this king is sometimes known as Artabanus IV by an alternative counting scheme; the main thing to know is that he was the same Artabanus who had recently been treacherously attacked by Caracalla at Arbela.

23. See Daryaee (2010, p. 3).

24. For Anahita see Chaumont (1958). For the old religion see Arjomand (1988). For holy water see Ball (2000, p. 433).

25. *Herodian, History of the Empire* VI.2.2-3; *Cassius Dio, Roman History* LXXX.4.1–2; *Zonoras, Extracts of History* XII.15. That Ardashir claimed Achaemenid descent has been disputed by some historians but comes across very clearly in the ancient texts; see discussions in Edwell (2008, p. 156–157) and Dignas and Winter (2007, p. 53–56). For interpretations that reject the testimony of the historical sources and much of the other evidence discussed in this section, see Potter (2004, p. 223), Goldsworthy (2009, p. 91) and Ando (2012, p. 110). It has been suggested that Ardashir's antagonistic attitude towards the Romans was one way he united the Persians under his own rule (Hughes, 2009, p. 10–11). For other ancient sources used in this section see *Herodian, History of the Empire* VI.2.4.; *Cassius Dio, Roman History*, LXXX.3.2, LXXX .4.1–2, LXXX, Fragment 3; *Zonoras, Extracts of History* XII.15; *Agathangelos, History*, 9.

26. Daryaee (2010).

27. The third, China, was by that time in a state of tripartite fragmentation and civil war between the Wei, Shu, and Wu following the collapse of the Han dynasty; see Keay (2008, Chapter 7) for an enthralling account.

Chapter IV: Duke of the Riverbank

1. Hopkins (1976, p. 1–6).

2. Freeman (2009, p. 132).

3. A single inscription survives giving the title. It is from later in the 230s and names one Domitius Pompeianus in the post. The palace, however, dates from two decades earlier.

4. This possibility was proposed by Gilliam (1941); see also Whittaker (1969–1970, Volume II, p. 209), Syme (1971, p. 188), Dodgeon and Lieu (1991, p. 352, note 16) and Weigels (2012, p. 449). The interpretation is based on *Herodian, History of the Empire* VII.8.4. In contrast, a recent detailed discussion of the post of *dux ripae* questions whether it really existed and does not discuss the interesting possibility that is was devised for Alexander's Persian expedition (Edwell, 2008, p. 128–135).

5. Artaxerxes is the Greek transliteration of Ardashir.

6. For milestones see Magie (1950, p. 695). For a list of the milestones and inscriptions from this time see Magie (1950, p. 1560). For Britain see Salway (1993, p. 199). See also the discussion of the forces in Alexander's army by Wiegels (2014). For Herodian see *Herodian, History of the Empire* VI.3.1.

7. *Herodian, History of the Empire* VI.4.4–6 and Gibbon (1776, Ch. 8).

8. Whittaker (1969–1970, Volume II, p. 133, footnote 2). Although plausible in the context of his career, the proposal has been disputed by the majority of commentators, see references in Haegemans (2010, p. 54–55).

9. Whittaker (1969–1970, Volume II, p. 133, footnote 2); see also *Vegetius, Military Institutions* 2.9–10.

10. Whittaker (1969–1970, Volume II, p. 108).

11. See, for example, Luttwak (1976, p. 16) and Le Bohec (1994, p. 33–35).

12. *Epitome De Caesaribus* 157.

13. *Herodian, History of the Empire* VI.5.8

14. Reproduced in Dignas and Winter (2007, p. 63). The *Aethiopica* has been claimed as the world's first full-length adventure novel and is supposed to have influenced the development of the novel in the renaissance.

15. Magie (1924, Volume II, p. 291); see also Brown (1971, p. 160). A more literal but less evocative translation is "oven men" (Haynes, 2013, p. 92). The name *clibanarius* was clearly not resented by the men themselves, because an inscription refers to a *vexillatione eqq(uitum) cat(afractariorum) clib (anariorum)* (see Wiegels, 2014, p. 32). See also Mielczarek (1993) for a general account of heavy cavalry in the ancient world.

16. Simpson (1977).

17. This is according to one chronology, Whittaker (1969–1970). Junius Palmatus is described as a victorious general in Armenia in *Scriptores Historiae Augustae* (Aelius Lampridius), *Alexander Severus* LVIII and Mommsen (1894) seems to have been first to make the connection with this campaign. That the northern column was commanded by Julius (sic) Palmatus is asserted by Dodgeon and Lieu (1991, p. 352, note 14). See also *Cambridge Ancient History*, v. 12. For road repairs see Whittaker (1969–1970, Volume II, p. 108).

18. *Agathangelos, History of the Armenians* 19. Quoted in Dignas and Winter (2007, p. 178).

19. The modern name derives from the Persian for 'Gate of the Alans'.

20. Historians have placed this event in various years but there are strong arguments for thinking that the Armenians would not have attempted a unilateral assault on Ctesiphon so the account fits well as allied support for the great Roman initiative of 232.

21. *Herodian, History of the Empire* VI.5.5. A detailed map of Arsacid Armenia is provided by Khachikyan (2010, opposite p. 88).

22. Whittaker (1969–1970, Volume II, p. 109); Dietz (1980, p. 211). Crispinus's career is discussed by Haegemans (2010, p. 168).

23. *Scriptores Historiae Augustae* (Flavius Vopiscus of Syracuse), *Divus Aurelianus*, XXV.2. For the ruse, see Ensslin (1939, p. 128–129); see also Dodgeon and Lieu (1991, p. 352, note 13).

24. For Palmyra, see Ross (2001). These letters were reproduced by Eusebius of Caesarea in his *Ecclesiastical History*; see also Ross (2001, p. 132).

25. *Herodian, History of the Empire* III.9.2. See also Haynes (2013, p. 66–67).

26. The quotation is from *Vegetius, Epitoma rei militaris* II.2; however see Haynes (2013, p. 285–298) for a more general discussion of ethnic fighting styles. The Mauretanian javelin troops may have travelled from Africa or may have been units previously based on the Danube (see Wiegels, 2014, for discussion). That they were probably part mounted and part foot soldiers is attested by an inscription from this time (CIL VIII 20996) from Caesarea that refers to an officer as *praepositus equitum itemque peditum iuniorum maurorum* (Wiegels 2014, p. 29).

27. For dedication to Alexander see Meissner (2009). For army engineer see Partington (1960, p. 35, note 70) and date see Partington (1960, p. 7). For Bardaisan see Ross (2001, p. 119–123).

28. Origen is himself a fascinating figure. He was an ascetic self-castratee (although modern sources doubt it), inspired by the teaching of Jesus reported in the Gospel of Matthew that "there are those who have made themselves eunuchs for the cause of the Kingdom of Heaven. Whoever can receive it let him receive it." Religious cults that encouraged self-castration for inner peace thrived in the ancient world, especially that of Cybele, the mother goddess of Anatolia, and they even occur today. But nowadays the teaching tends to be interpreted as meaning voluntary abstention from sex, as in the Catholic priesthood, with a softer translation like "and some choose not to marry for the sake of the Kingdom of Heaven. Let anyone accept this who can." Origen and other early Christians seem to have interpreted it literally. Origen toured Christian communities in the east and assembled much of what was later known as the New Testament, but including some texts that were later suppressed as 'apocryphal'. Long after his death he was to be condemned as a heretic, as was Eusebius (a follower of Arius, who held that Jesus was subordinate to God). We do not know to what extent Mamaea or indeed Alexander was influenced by Origen, Julius Africanus, Bardaisan or other Christian teachers they met in the east but church tradition suggests that Christianity had some influence on the imperial household. For Origen see *Eusebius, Ecclesiastical History* VI.21.3 and Freeman (2009) for a sympathetic account of this exceptional man and his teachings. The biblical quote is from Matthew 19:12, *Aramaic Bible in Plain English 2010* translation, http://bible.cc/matthew/19-12.htm. Some members of the infamous 'Heaven's Gate' cult conducted auto-castration and later ritually killed themselves to commune with an alien spaceship that they believed was following behind Comet Hale-Bopp in 1997. For alternative translations see for example, http://bible.cc/matthew/19-12.htm; with many other interpretations of this passage.

29. For roadworks see Whittaker (1969–1970, Volume II, p.109). Singara is modern Sinjar in Iraq, recently a scene of tragedy where the indigenous Yazidi population (an ancient sect with roots in Zoroastrianism) was overrun by fundamentalist Islamist forces. The same organization has systematically destroyed the ancient ruins of Hatra and other important archaeological sites in northern Iraq and Syria.

30. Dodgeon and Lieu (1991, p. 352 note 16).

31. Whittaker (1969–1970, Volume II, p. 109).

32. *Herodian, History of the Empire* VI.5.5. Other information in this section is from *Herodian, History of the Empire* VI.5.7, VI.5.10, VI.5.8.

33. *Jordanes, Getica* XV.88 claims "He fought with marvellous success against the Parthians, under Alexander the son of Mama (*sic*)."

34. It is fair to say that such fears were not unfounded: in later years a Roman emperor, Valerian, and his entire staff were captured by the Persians and the emperor himself ended up dying in captivity.

35. For the donative see *Herodian, History of the Empire* VI.4; the coins included a special issue of coinage showing *liberalitas* (Carson, 1962, p. 206–7). See also Dignas and Winter (2007, p. 76). It is a great loss to us that the early books of the history of the late fourth-century historian Ammianus Marcellinus do not survive. His account of Alexander's campaign would have been a most interesting addition, not least because he himself

knew the same theatre of war as a senior officer in the eastern armies of the emperors Constantius II and Julian in the mid fourth century. Ammianus was also acquainted with the history of Aurelius Victor. But in a preamble to his account of Julian's invasion of Persia of 363 (the main thrust of which followed the same southern, Euphrates, route of Alexander's army) Ammianus provides a list of the successful Roman commanders of the past in the east, namely Trajan, Lucius Verus, Septimius Severus and Gordian. Severus Alexander gets no mention, so it seems fair to infer that Ammianus did not regard this war as a conspicuous success.

36. Carson (1962, p. 82).

37. For the score-draw see Gricourt (1965, p. 319–326) and Dignas and Winter (2007, p. 77). An old but intriguing idea for the lull following the Roman withdrawal is that Ardashir turned his attention to Armenia, which was able to withstand invasion with the support of Roman troops, possibly commanded by Junius Palmatus (Mommsen, 1894). That fighting with Armenia continued seems to be the gist of the account of Agathangelos; see Dignas and Winter (2007, p. 178).

38. However, there is one milestone in Africa that gives him these titles, they do not appear on the coins of 233 or later, which instead display more general themes like *victoria augusti* (Victory of the emperor): see Jardé (1925, p. 81–82).

Chapter V: Empire's Edge

1. For the broad sweep, see the review of Sidebottom (2005). A typical but unsettling view among modern historians is that "we may be able to agree that Roman generals and emperors never sat down and worked out a grand military strategy" (Whittaker, 1994, p. 85). This is reminiscent of J.R. Seeley, who remarked that the British Empire was obtained through "a fit of absence of mind" (Seeley, 1883, p. 10). These may have been the practical effects of vacillating policy and constant regime change, but it does seem unlikely that grand strategy was never discussed. For an account of the development of empires in China, see Barfield (1989).

2. Luttwak (1976).

3. Haynes (2013, p. 77).

4. *Herodian, History of the Empire* VI.6.7. See also Haegemans (2010, p. 58).

5. *Herodian, History of the Empire* VI.7.2 uses the term "Γερμανοί" (Germans), which was the most common Roman term for non-Gallic tribes from the Rhine and to the west, following Caesar and Tacitus. The name probably applied to one particular tribe but was later expanded; it is highly doubtful if the various tribes themselves would have used the term. Haegemans (2010, p. 59) describes the term as "too vague to be of much help in determining which tribes were in revolt". Cassius Dio referred to similar people interchangeably as Germans or Alamanni (e.g. *Cassius Dio, Roman History* LXXVIII.13.30). See also Hummer (1988) and Todd (2004, p. 1–5) for a discussion of these ethnic labels.

6. Birley (1999, p. xxiii).

7. *Tacitus, Germania*, 24.

8. Haynes (2013, p. 90).

9. For Saalburg see http://www.saalburgmuseum.de/english/home_engl.htm and Parker (2009, p. 133–134). For the evidence of destruction see Schönberger (1969); also Whittaker (1969-1970, Volume II, p. 122).

10. See Potter (2004, p. 230) and Mennen (2011, p. 138) for his earlier career.

11. For duplication of the ranks see Whittaker (1970, Volume II, p. 134). For commander of the army see *Scriptores Historiae Augustae* (Julius Capitolinus), *Maximini Duo* VII.1.; also quoted in this section are *Scriptores Historiae Augustae* (Julius Capitolinus), *Maximini Duo* VI.4, VII.2., and XXIX.2-5.

12. The evidence of this inscription and disembarkation at Aquileia was discussed in Whittaker (1969-1970, Volume II, p. 134, 264), although the inscription itself must refer to a later year, when Maximinus was emperor. The inscription was also discussed by Mann (1999) and Weigels (2012, p. 450–451). Haegemans (2010, p. 71) describes this as "actually the only instance of the use of soldiers for road construction in Italy".

13. Reuter (1999)

14. *Tacitus, Germania* 29.

15. *Herodian, History of the Empire* VI.7.8. Also cited in this section are *Herodian, History of the Empire* VI.7.6 and VI.7.7.

16. See Wiegels (2014) for a detailed discussion of which auxiliary units – mounted and foot – and irregular units might have been part of this force.

17. For Caesar see *Caesar, The Gallic War* IV.17. For the medallion see Carson (1962, p. 83).

18. Evidence for this is that the Rhine pontoon bridge had to be rebuilt the following year.

19. See Ezov (1977) for an account of *exploratores* units in the German sector.

20. Analogies can be made with similar situations in more recent times, such as between the United States army and the Plains Indians.

21. For tales of avarice see *Herodian, History of the Empire* VI.1.8, *Epitome De Caesaribus*, 158, and *Zonoras, Extracts of History*. Also quoted in this section are *Herodian, History of the Empire* VI.7.10, VII.1.6; *Scriptores Historiae Augustae* (Julius Capitolinus), *Maximini Duo* VII.6.

22. Carson (1962, p. 209).

23. For the impact of the reforms of Diocletian on Roman strategy see Luttwak (1976, p. 173–178).

24. *Herodian, History of the Empire* VII.1.6.

25. *Scriptores Historiae Augustae* (Julius Capitolinus), *Maximini Duo* VI.6–7.

26. *Scriptores Historiae Augustae* (Julius Capitolinus), *Maximini Duo* VI.1.5.

27. *Aurelius Victor, De Caesaribus* 25.1; *Epitome de Caesaribus* 24.3.

28. Whittaker (1969–1970, Volume II, p. 139). Note that there is no evidence that Maximinus doubled the pay of *all* troops in the empire at this time as indicated by Speidel (1992, p. 88) and followed by Alston, (1994, p. 114), Bland (1996), Prodromídis (2006, p. 26, Chart 1), Haegemans (2010, p. 74, p. 162, p. 236), Haynes (2013, p. 48, albeit with a query), and Speidel (2014). Passerini (1946) seems to have been nearer the mark on this, indicating that such a decision could only have been applicable to the local troops involved in the rebellion. Hence the possible myth that Maximinus doubled army pay in general seems to be at large among modern historians and is factored in to serious analyses of the third century economy, despite it seeming unlikely.

29. *Herodian, History of the Empire* VI.9.1. Also quoted in this section is *Herodian, History of the Empire* VI.9.5.

30. This is all according to Herodian's account (*Herodian, History of the Empire* Book VI). Alternative versions of the assassination of Alexander are given by Zonoras, Aurelius Victor and the *Augustan History*. Zonoras's confused account has both Maximinus and Alexander marching to Rome; the former from Pannonia and the latter from the Rhine, and then Alexander is murdered in the imperial palace in Rome. According to the *Scriptores Historiae Augustae* (Aelius Lampridius), *Alexander Severus* LIX.1–9, the murder took place in a village called Sicilia in Britain, or possibly Gaul, and was not instigated by Maximinus; rather it was the deed of a small group of rogue barbarian soldiers. Both these versions are almost certainly incorrect, given Herodian's much more convincing and internally consistent and contemporaneous account. Interestingly the *Augustan History* does briefly refer to Herodian's version only to dismiss it as pro-Maximinus propaganda, so perhaps there was another, competing version of events now lost to us (possibly by Dexippus). It is not totally impossible that Alexander might have made a brief visit to Britain that winter if trouble had been developing there after the garrison reductions of 231. More likely is that the *Augustan History* presents such a one-sided view of Alexander as the perfect emperor that it seems that widespread disaffection of his army could not be admitted, other than a few barbarians, and this alternative story was concocted. It is intriguing that a similar version of events is given by Aurelius Victor (*De Caesaribus* XXIV.4), who also names Sicilia as a village in Britain. This is easy to explain if Victor derived his information from the *Augustan History*, or vice versa, or both from a common source.

31. Zosimus says both prateorian prefects were killed that year, at least one of which would have been with Alexander at Mogontiacum.

Chapter VI: Soldier-Emperor

1. *Herodian, History of the Empire* VII.1.6.
2. Haegemans (2010, p. 57). Note that Eutropius wrongly claimed that there was no senatorial ratification whereas evidence for senatorial endorsement is widespread; see Haegemans (2010, p. 81), and the testimony of the coinage is incontrovertible
3. Initially, procurator of the province of Bythinia et Pontus (in modern Turkey) and subsequently of Asia (Mennen, 2011, p. 139).
4. That the emperors approved their coinage has been suggested by King (1999) and is discussed by Haegemans (2010, p. 45). For the types see Carson (1962, p. 89).
5. This is the version given by *Herodian, History of the Empire* VII.1.4–8. The *Augustan History* gives a slightly different version of the plot, in which some of the plotters would cross the bridge with the emperor and murder him on the far side: *Scriptores Historiae Augustae* (Julius Capitolinus), *Maximini Duo* X.1–6.
6. *Herodian, History of the Empire* VII.1.4.
7. Discussed by Salway (2011, p. 122, note 27). See also Whittaker (1969-1970, Volume II, p. 152–153, footnote 2).
8. This is also attested by *Scriptores Historiae Augustae* (Julius Capitolinus), *Maximini Duo* X.6.
9. *Scriptores Historiae Augustae* (Julius Capitolinus), *Maximini Duo* X.6.
10. Whittaker (1969–1970, Volume II, p. 157, footnote 3).

11. On army resentment see *Herodian, History of the Empire* VII.9.1 and discussion in Loriot (1975) and Haegemans (2010, p. 95). There is a possibility that having been denuded of its forces, Osrhoene rebelled from Rome in protest. This could explain the lack of coins in the name of Maximinus and some of the diplomatic complexity that is evident in relations between Rome and Osrhoene in later years.

12. A brief mention is made in *Scriptores Historiae Augustae* (Julius Capitolinus), *Maximini Duo* XI.16. The longer account is in *Scriptores Historiae Augustae* (Trebellius Pollio), *Tyranni Triginta* XXXII. See also Haegemans (2010, p. 94).

13. Whittaker (1969–1970) provides detailed references for the standard interpretation of events, as updated by Haegemans (2010, p. 62), but see also the next section.

14. Goessler (1931). The inscriptions are discussed in detail by Weigels (2014) who notes that it is likely these men died in the *expeditio germanica* of Maximinus although the point cannot be proved conclusively. Saluda and Regretho are described as brothers (*fratres*) and the memorial was set up by another brother, Abdetat; it is debated whether this means they were literally brothers or 'brothers-in arms' (see also Haarl, 1996).

15. *Tacitus, Germania* 5.

16. Haegemans (2010, p. 62, 71).

17. Magie (1924, Volume II, p. 336–337, footnote 3) claims that "An inscription of Maximinus, found at Tübingen (in southern Germany), seems to be a relic of his occupation of the country", citing *Corpus Inscriptionum Latinarum* xiii, 9083. However this inscription dates from the end of 236 at the earliest, because it acclaims Maximinus as *dacicus maximus* and *sarmaticus maximus*. Whittaker (1969–1970, Volume II, p. 160, footnote 1) cites this and another inscription as evidence for Maximinus himself being in southern Germany; see also Loriot (1975, p. 675) and Haegemans (2010, p. 62). The reinterpretation of this passage is discussed in the following chapter.

18. Schönberger (1969).

19. As suggested by Casey and Noel (1992) and Casey (1994, p. 37). The idea that Germanic troops taken by Maximinus at this time later formed the bodyguard of Balbinus and Pupienus (Haegemans, 2010, p. 63) seems unlikely. The bodyguard referred to in the historical sources is attached to Pupienus only, and it seems probable that any German recruits enlisted by Maximinus would have been on his side in the civil war, such as those mentioned by *Herodian, History of the Empire* VII.9.1 (see also Whittaker 1970, Volume II, p. 289, footnote 2).

20. This is confirmed by a milestone in Sardinia dating to 235 (Bellezza, 1964).

21. The tradition was started by Manius Valerius after his victory over the Carthaginians in 263 BCE (Mommsen, 1901, Vol. II, p.207). Whittaker (1969–1970, Volume II, p. 166, footnote 1) has suggested that Herodian's narrative of the German expedition derives from, and is structured around, the four hypothetical scenes depicted on these paintings.

22. Haynes (2013, p. 222-223, 376–378). For the coins of Cilicia see Tahberer (2014). An earlier coin showing an emperor in battle was produced by Trajan in 103–107 to celebrate his victory over the Dacians (*Roman Imperial Coinage* II, 536). Rare regional coins of Septimius Severus and Caracalla have a similar design, so it was not entirely new.

23. See Haynes (2013, p. 92) for a discussion of Barsemis Abbei and his interesting career. The Exuperatus stone at Caerleon could either be late second or third century based on the style (notably the complex ligatures). De La Bédoyère (2006, p.210) has suggested that Tadius Exuperatus was "part of a vexillation sent to fight on the German frontier in

the third century." One possibility that has been suggested is the campaign of Caracalla in 214 (Królczyk, 2011, p.208). However, the idea that he was part of the army of Severus Alexander and Maximinus was suggested long ago by Lee (1850, p.22). From what we know now, Maximinus's campaign of 235 is more likely to have gone by the grand title *expeditio germanica* than Caracalla's campaign.

24. *Herodian, History of the Empire* VII.1.3. *Scriptores Historiae Augustae* (Julius Capitolinus), *Maximini Duo* VIII.7.10.

25. *Suetonius, The Twelve Caesars* 55.

26. As recently suggested through the medium of historical fiction (Sidebottom, 2014).

27. Whittaker (1969–1970, Volume II, p. 193); Birley (1988, p. 48); Dietz (1980, p. 178); Haegemans (2010, p. 103).

28. Haegemans (2010, p. 65).

29. Whittaker (1969–1970, Volume II, p. 167). Note that evidence exists for a seventh imperial acclamation, which is only known from milestones in *Hispania* and also the title *parthicus maximus* (greatest victory in Parthia). The few historians that discuss them have dismissed them as aberrations ('a confused stonecutter') (Peachin 1990; Haegemans, 2010, p. 92) but it seems possible that some sort of victory was claimed in Maximinus's name against the Persians in 238 during the confusion of that year. The inscriptions mentioned in this paragraph are from Epigraphic Database Heidelberg HD 018244, HD 032215, HD 057850, and HD 020015.

30. A campaign in this area is indicated by Hekster (2008, p. 18, Map 3 for 235 CE).

Chapter VII: Echoes in Eternity

1. Screenplay by David Franzoni, John Logan and William Nicholson. The final phrase "What we do in life echoes in eternity" is from the *Meditations* of Marcus Aurelius.

2. Lönne and Meyer (2009). Many more finds were found in subsequent years, http://www.roemerschlachtamharzhorn.de/summary-(english).html. The detectorists who found the site are named by Martin (2010).

3. Although it was actually filmed in England.

4. Berger (2010); Wiegels (2014).

5. Whittaker (1969–1970, Volume II, p. 160, footnote 1); Haegemans (2010, p.62).

6. *Herodian, History of the Empire* VII.2.4.

7. The text is from *Scriptores Historiae Augustae* (Julius Capitolinus), *Maximini Duo* XII.1. The version with 30 or 40 miles was preferred in the edition published by Peter (1865) and followed by Magie (1921–1932, Volume II, p. 336, footnotes 1 and 2) and reproduced without comment up to Haegemans (2010, p. 62). Haynes (2013, p. 91) referred only to Maximinus's "operations on the Rhine". The Palatine codex can be viewed online at http://digi.vatlib.it/view/bav_pal_lat899/0425 and was used by early published versions such as that published by Johanis Maire (1632). See the discussion in Lehmann (2011, p. 103) on this point.

8. *Herodian, History of the Empire* VII.2.8.

9. Clunn (2009).

10. Lehmann (2011, p. 109).

11. An alternative version of the tactical situation favoured by some archaeologists is that the valley of the A6 autobahn was in those days too wet and boggy and the main roadway

diverted up the Harzhorn ridge, hence the battle was fought across the main route itself (Lehmann, 2011). Evidence for this is that Roman carts had evidently been on the hillside at some point. However, we should remember that if Herodian is to be believed, the engagement came at the end of a long dry summer. The presence of carts on the ridge could easily be explained as part of the rapid clean-up or for carrying the ballistas.

12. Discussed in Ball (2013).

13. Whittaker (1994, Chapter 4).

14. *Herodian, History of the Empire* VII.2.9; *Scriptores Historiae Augustae* (Julius Capitolinus), *Maximini Duo* XIII.3–4.

15. *Scriptores Historiae Augustae* (Julius Capitolinus), *Marcus Antoninus* XXIV.5: "He wished to make a province of Marcomannia [approximately, Germany] and likewise of Sarmatia and he would have done so had not Avidius Cassius just then raised a rebellion in the East" (c. 175 CE).

16. A close watch on developments is kept by http://adrianmurdoch.typepad.com/my_weblog/battle-on-the-harzhorn/. See also http://arch.rwth-aachen.de/cms/Architektur/Forschung/Forschungsprojekte/Cultural_Heritage/~comx/Roemerschlachtareal_am_Harzhorn/lidx/1/

17. Wiegels *et al.* (2011). In the Third Century it was normal for legions to take the names of successive emperors as epithets (Dixon and Southern, 1992, p. 33).

18. Wiegels (2014, p. 96, note 6). The gravestone could come from another occasion in the third century but the inscription assumes that the reader would know which expedition was being referred to, hence it must have been a significant event.

Chapter VIII: Maximinus Augustus

1. The date at which Maximus was given the title of *caesar* is uncertain. It has been suggested that it was at the former's accession in early 235 (e.g. Sear, 1974, p. 216) but this now seems unlikely as a papyrus from Memphis in Egypt has been discovered that relates to a religious procession organized as part of the celebrations, which are independent of Maximinus' accession (Haegemans 2010, p. 128). It could have been on the occasion of the German victory in late 235 or on the anniversary of his father's elevation in 236 (Ando 2012, p. 104).

2. This is evidence that Maximinus's heavy features and size may have been a pituitary disorder rather than genetic.

3. *Scriptores Historiae Augustae* (Julius Capitolinus), *Maximini Duo* XXIX.8–9.

4. Liggi (1998).

5. Most modern sources suggest that she died before 235, with the deification being posthumous (e.g., Haegemans, 2010, p. 86), but the reason for inferring this is unclear.

6. *Ammianus Marcellinus, Roman History* IV, p. 1–45. There is also a very unlikely tradition that her husband had her put to death. This was the claim of Syncellus and Zonoras (*Zonoras, Extracts of History 12.16*); see also Gibbon (1776–1784).

7. *Corpus Inscriptionum Latinarum* 8.4515. See Haegemans (2010, p. 129).

8. If, as is likely, he personally saw the paintings of Maximinus's victories in Germany as set up before the Senate house, he was probably at Rome in 235/6. It also seems very likely that he was also there in 238, when his history contains many references to scenes he may have witnessed at that time.

9. I have corrected 'stifling' to 'trifling' in this translation.

10. According to *Scriptores Historiae Augustae* (Julius Capitolinus), *Maximini Duo* VII.7.8, he was convinced the throne could not be held except by cruelty.

11. Bersanetti (1940) provided the first list of provincial governors. See also Haegemans (2010, p. 97). For dissolving the cabinet see Haegemans (2010, p. 109).

12. *Herodian, History of the Empire* VII.3.6.

13. Stark (1996, p. 7).

14. *Hippolytus, refutatio omnium haeresium*, p. 35.

15. To pick just one passage from Hippolytus's writings, his account of the early Greek philosopher Anaximander of the sixth century BCE (and hence almost a millennium before Hippolytus) is worth reproducing, as otherwise we would know nothing of that early philosopher: *"Now Anaximander was a hearer of Thales. He was Anaximander of Miletus, son of Praxiades. He said that the beginning of the things that are was a certain nature of the Boundless* [apeiron = infinite, limitless] *form which came into being the heavens and the ordered worlds within them. And that this principle is eternal and grows not old and encompasses all the ordered worlds. And he says time is limited by birth, substance, and death. He said that the Boundless is a principle and element of the things that are and was the first to call it by the name of principle. But that there is an eternal movement towards Him wherein it happens that the heavens are born. And that the earth is a heavenly body supported by nothing, but remaining in its place by reason of its equal distance from everything, And that its form is a watery cylinder like a stone pillar; and that we tread on one of its surfaces, but there is another opposite to it. And that the stars are a circle of fire distinct from the fire of the cosmos, but surrounded by air. And that certain fiery exhalations exist in those places where the stars appear, and by the obstruction of those exhalations come the eclipses. And that the circle of the sun is 27 times greater than that of the moon and that the sun is in the highest place in the heavens and the circles of the fixed stars in the lowest. And that the animals came into being of moisture evaporated by the sun. And that mankind was at the beginning very like another animal, to wit, a fish. And that winds come from the separation and condensation of the subtler atoms of the air and rain from earth giving back under sun's heat what it gets from the clouds and lightning from the severance of the clouds by the winds falling on them. He was born in the 3rd year of the 43rd Olympiad."* (*Hippolytus, refutatio omnium haeresium*.) The date would be 601 BCE.

16. *Eusebius Caesariensis, Historia Ecclesiastica.*

17. Note that this source indicates that Pontian was banished by Alexander, not Maximinus, but this is generally thought to be an error as Alexander and Mamaea apparently supported the Christians.

18. See *Chronography of 354 AD*: Part 12, pp. 71–72, and *Calendarium Romanum 1969*. See http://en.wikipedia.org/wiki/General_Roman_Calendar. The Eastern Orthodox Church did not follow this move, and unsurprisingly, neither saint is celebrated in the various Protestant liturgical calendars.

19. Details can be found in the 1916 English translation of the *Liber Pontificalis*. Different versions record different dates for Anteros, but this is the most logical interpretation of events.

20. He was to suffer torture during the later persecution of Decius in 250, but the inquisitors were careful not to give him the death he apparently wished for.

21. *Cyprian, Epistles* 74.10.

22. Dietz (1980, p. 177).

23. *Sulpicius Severus, Chronicle*. See also Clarke (1966).
24. This arrangement foreshadows the system used by the emperor Constantine who devolved much of the civil administration to praetorian prefects; see, for example, Stephenson (2009).
25. Repairs to the Spanish road system were made by Maximinus' legate Decius, a later Roman emperor (van Sickle 1929, p. 83). See also Haegemans (2010, p. 71).
26. Honoré (1994, p. 114).
27. See Mennen (2011, p. 171) for a brief discussion of this rescript.
28. The edict is recorded under the name of the 'same emperor' as the one that precedes it, that is, Alexander. However, that may be the result of some confusion as Alexander was dead by this time (the confusion may be related to delays in the senatorial ratification of Maximinus' coup). Historians attribute the rescript to Maximinus (Honoré 1994, p. 27).
29. Translation corrected from 'mad'.
30. Indeed the official responsible may have continued working into the reigns of Maximinus's successors, as deduced from his idiosyncrasies of phrasing (Honoré 1994, p. 56).

Chapter IX: Provok'd Rebellion

1. See Goldsworthy (2000) for a lively account of this period. The truth (or lack of it) behind the story of the sowing of salt is discussed by Ridley (1986).
2. *Herodian, History of the Empire* VII.3.5.
3. Kotula (1959/1960).
4. *Herodian, History of the Empire* VII.4.2.
5. *Scriptores Historiae Augustae* (Julius Capitolinus), *Gordiani Tres* VII.2.
6. It was used as backdrop for the spectacular combat scenes in the movie *Gladiator* (2000). Estimates vary of the capacity. Benario (1981) ranks it as fourteenth in the classical world. It has long been speculated that the amphitheatre was being built by the wealthy governor Gordian (Townsend, 1934; Lézine, 1960; Whittaker, 1969–1970, Volume II, p. 183, footnote 1; Bomgardner, 1981) although this has recently been challenged (Haegemans, 2010, p. 133). For the amphitheatre of Carthage see Bomgardner (1989).
7. Haegemans (2010, p. 133).
8. *Scriptores Historiae Augustae* (Julius Capitolinus), *Gordiani Tres* VII.2, and VIII.3.
9. See Potter (2004, p. 258). The authority of this procurator has been discussed at length by various authors and well summarized by Haegemans (2010, p. 134–136).
10. A difficulty arises because a procurator would not normally have authority over private estates. Haegemans (2010, p. 134) has stated that he was raising taxes from them, but this may not have been the case, as the accounts of Herodian indicates that he was bringing about a prosecution, which he could have done as an imperial agent (*Herodian, History of the Empire* VII.4.3). On black magic, see, for example the case of Apuleius discussed in Birley (1988, p. 30–31).
11. For the consulship see the extended discussion in Syme (1971, p. 167–168). There are some years, however, for which the names of one or both consul are not known. See http://en.wikipedia.org/wiki/List_of_Roman_consuls. For important achievements see *Herodian, History of the Empire* VII.5.2. For inscriptional evidence see *Corpus*

Inscriptionum Latinarum VII.1043. See also Haegemans (2010, p. 146). For Achaia see Whittaker (1969–1970, Volume II, p. 181–183).

12. *Scriptores Historiae Augustae* (Julius Capitolinus), *Gordiani Tres* II.3. Modern historians tend to dismiss this claim out of hand (e.g. Syme, 1971, p. 167). However, a link to the Gracchi may be evidenced by his cognomen Sempronianus. It has been suggested by Mullens (1948, p. 69) that this name could have been taken by Gordian at the time of civil war in an attempt to boost his *romanitas* by recalling the famous reforming brothers Tiberius Sempronius Gracchus (c. 169–133 BCE) and Gaius Sempronius Gracchus (c. 160–121 BCE). But that seems wrong because an inscription from earlier in his career records part of the cognomen (*Corpus Inscriptionum Latinarum* VII.1043). The name remained associated with the Gracchi in subsequent centuries (e.g. there was a Sempronius Gracchus who was banished by Augustus for a liaison with his daughter Julia). Hence perhaps the name can be used as evidence in favour of the ancestry claimed in the *Augustan History*.

13. Gibbon (1776–1784) tells us that this house had been taken over from Pompey by Mark Antony during the civil wars of the first century BC; later it had been an imperial palace until sold off to one of Gordian's ancestors by the emperor Trajan.

14. Haegemans (2010, p. 145–146).

15. According to *Herodian, History of the Empire* VII.5.2 and *Scriptores Historiae Augustae* (Julius Capitolinus), *Gordiani Tres* VII.9.1; or 79 according to *Zonoras, Extracts of History* XII.17.

16. *Herodian, History of the Empire* VII.5.7.

17. According to the chronology of Carson (1962, p. 98).

18. *Scriptores Historiae Augustae* (Julius Capitolinus), *Gordiani Tres* XIX.4.

19. Bersanetti (1940).

20. The likely forces present in the province are discussed by Haegemans (2010, p. 139).

21. Suggested by Townsend (1955); see also Carson (1962, p. 96–97). The idea that the plot was hatched in Rome has been dismissed as 'quite fanciful' by Haegemans (2010, p. 10).

Chapter X: The Noble and the Brave

1. *Zosimus, New History* I.14.1.

2. *Herodian, History of the Empire* VII.6.6–9. Whittaker (1969–1970, Volume II, p. 195, footnote2). Note that the *Augustan History* suggests Vitalianus was killed on the order of the senate, but this does not chime with Herodian's account. See *Scriptores Historiae Augustae* (Julius Capitolinus), *Gordiani Tres* X.5.

3. *Scriptores Historiae Augustae* (Julius Capitolinus), *Gordiani Tres* IV.5.

4. Dietz (1980).

5. For Silanus see *Scriptores Historiae Augustae* (Julius Capitolinus), *Maximini Duo* XVI.1–2. However this may be an embellishment because the ordinary consuls for 238 were Fulvius Pius and Pontius Proculus Pontianus and nothing else is known of Julius Silanus. He does not appear in Dietz's (1980) prosopography. The bounty is according to *Scriptores Historiae Augustae* (Julius Capitolinus), *Maximini Duo*, XVI.5. For senate and emperor see Mullens (1948, p. 70). For the secret decree see *Scriptores Historiae Augustae* (Julius Capitolinus), *Gordiani Tres* XII.1 on the authority of Cordus. See also Haegemans (2010).

6. *Scriptores Historiae Augustae* (Julius Capitolinus), *Gordiani Tres* XXIII.2. Note that in that work the eclipse is taken as an omen for the short reign of Gordian III, not Gordian I. But as Carson (1962, p. 98) has argued, the date is too early for Gordian III so, if not a falsification, the *Augustan History* must have got its Gordians confused. Note that Carson (1962, p. 98) also considered the eclipse of 25th September 238 as a possibility, based on the erroneous belief that it was visible in Rome whereas in fact that eclipse was in the southern hemisphere. Bird (1994, p. 172) also was unaware that the September eclipse was not visible from Rome. The eclipse is detailed in Espenak and Meuss (2009) as number 5,345 and was a partial eclipse.

7. See *Scriptores Historiae Augustae* (Julius Capitolinus), *Maximini Duo* XXXII.3, given on the authority of Dexippus; also *Scriptores Historiae Augustae* (Julius Capitolinus), *Gordiani Tres* X.1–2. *Zosimus, New History* describes them as "twenty persons who understood military discipline". An alternative version in the *Augustan History* is that these men were appointed some time later, when news of the death of the Gordians was announced. Historians are divided on which version is most likely, with some (e.g., Haegemans, 2010, p. 165–166) preferring the latter. The first six on this list are included by Dietz (1980). The last was only added from a dedication stone giving his complete career which was discovered in 1994 (Herrmann, 1997). Mullens (1948, p. 47) doubts the inclusion of Crispinus. For the title see *Corpus Inscriptionum Latinarum* 14.3902. See also Haegemans (2010, p. 164).

8. *Herodian, History of the Empire* VII.7.4.

9. For the coins see Carson (1962, p. 97). However according to some more recent evidence the chronology may be incorrect, with the first issue for the Gordians in January 238; but this is more difficult to fit with Herodian's narrative http://classicaleconomies.com/mil_anarchy.shtml. For the die-cutters being in on the plot see Townsend (1955) and Carson (1962, p. 97).

10. An almost certainly fictitious version of this senatorial decree is contained in the *Scriptores Historiae Augustae* (Julius Capitolinus), *Maximini Duo* XV.6–9.

11. http://www.cngcoins.com/Coin.aspx?CoinID=105654

12. As extensively documented by Haegemans (2010, p. 259–276). The inclusion of Britannia Inferior in the pro-Maximinus camp is based on the erasure of Gordian's name on a number of inscriptions (Haegemans, 2010, p. 273) but this seems to beg the question: why was it there in the first place? Also the references to inscriptions in the catalogue of Collingwood and Wright (1965) does not seem to be correct. Decius, the pro-Maximinus governor of Spain prospered in later years and became emperor himself.

13. *Scriptores Historiae Augustae* (Julius Capitolinus), *Gordiani Tres* XV.1. This suggests, perhaps, that he may have served with Maximinus in the past.

14. According to Dando-Collins (2010, p. 495), the third legion was based at Tebessa, south-west of Carthage, but the statement contradicts Herodian and the source for it is not clear. It seems the legion moved from Tebessa to Lambaesis in 128. For *maximiniana* see *Corpus Inscriptionum Latinarum* 8.2675. See Haegemans (2010, p. 162).

15. For *fide punica* see *Scriptores Historiae Augustae* (Julius Capitolinus), *Gordiani Tres* XV.2; see Isaac (2004, p. 329–333) for a discussion of this saying.

16. *Scriptores Historiae Augustae* (Julius Capitolinus), *Gordiani Tres* XVI.2.

17. According to *Vegetius, Epitoma rei militaris*, 1, "a handful of men, inured to war, proceed to certain victory, while on the contrary numerous armies of raw and undisciplined troops are but multitudes of men dragged to defeat".

18. *Scriptores Historiae Augustae* (Julius Capitolinus), *Maximini Duo* XIX.4–5.

19. For reinstated names see *Corpus Inscriptionum Latinarum* 8.10047; *Corpus Inscriptionum Latinarum* 8.757; Whittaker (1969–1970, Volume II, p. 188, footnote 2). For Severinus see *Corpus Inscriptionum Latinarum* 8.2170.

20. The shipwreck story is from *Zosimus, New History*, 1.1.17; the quote is Gibbon (1776, p. 199, footnote 2).

21. *Scriptores Historiae Augustae* (Julius Capitolinus), *Maximini Duo* XIX.5.

22. For the cessation of the mints see Kettenhofen (1982); Edwell (2008, p. 168). For Nisibis and Carrhae see *Zonoras, Extracts of History* 12.18. It is possible that both or either city may have fallen before, in 235/6. The issue is discussed in detail by Haegemans (2010, p. 225–227); conflicting views are taken in two chapters of *The Cambridge Ancient History*, by Drinkwater (2005) and Frye (2005). For Singara see Oates (1968, p. 49); also Edwell (2008, p. 168). However, Ando (2012, p. 104) says the garrison in Singara survived. Note that *Ammianus Marcellinus, The Later Roman Empire* 20.6 later remarked of Singara: "The place had been fortified in days of old as a convenient outpost to obtain advance information of any sudden enemy movement, but in fact it had proved a liability to Rome, because it was taken on several occasions with the loss of its garrison".

23. The name is according to the Arabic historian al-Tabari, reproduced in Dodgeon and Lieu (1991, p. 283); also Edwell (2008, p. 168).

24. See Edwell (2008, p. 168, note 100). Edwell refers to the *Scriptores Historiae Augustae* (Julius Capitolinus), *Maximini Duo* XIII.3 in support of this, but the campaign referred to in that source is against the Sarmatians.

25. Although naval raiding on the Black Sea has been suggested (Ando 2012, p. 108).

26. *Scriptores Historiae Augustae* (Julius Capitolinus), *Maximus et Balbinus* XVI.3.

27. Whittaker (1969–1970, Volume II, p. 205, footnote 3). See Appendix 1 for chronology.

28. For wine see *Scriptores Historiae Augustae* (Julius Capitolinus), *Maximini Duo* XVII.5. For flicker of eyes see *Herodian, History of the Empire* VII.8.2.

29. Two other contrasting versions of this speech can be found in *Scriptores Historiae Augustae* (Julius Capitolinus), *Maximini Duo* XVIII.1–4 and *Scriptores Historiae Augustae* (Julius Capitolinus), *Gordiani Tres* XIV.1–5. As Gibbon (1776, p. 202, footnote) pointed out long ago: "they neither agree with each other nor with the truth." The question of Maximinus' literacy or semi-literacy is discussed in Baldwin (1989).

30. This is the critical evidence that Maximinus had held the post of *dux ripae* (riverbank commander) at Dura Europos.

31. *Scriptores Historiae Augustae* (Julius Capitolinus), *Gordiani Tres* XIV. 6–8. It has been suggested that Maximinus may have raised a new bodyguard at this time, the *ala celerum* (Speidel 1994, p. 70) but the argument seems tenuous.

Chapter XI: Bellum Civile

1. *Herodian, History of the Empire* VII.10.2.

2. Gibbon (1776, p. 197) opined that the arrangements "opened the flattering prospect of the restoration, not only of the civil but even of the republican government". For Herodian, see *Herodian, History of the Empire* VII.10.2. An alternative suggestion is that the election of two emperors may have been an attempt to balance opposing factions in the senate (Mennen, 2011, p. 24) but this is difficult to reconcile with Herodian's

account. In moving away from heredity, the move was similar to that attempted later in the reforms of Diocletian (Potter, 2004). Mullens (1948, p. 71) pointed out that under this system, the office of *augustus* would in effect be the highest appointment of the civil service.

3. That Balbinus and Pupienus were among the 20 is recorded by *Scriptores Historiae Augustae* (Julius Capitolinus), *Maximini Duo* XXIII.3 on the authority of Dexippus.

4. *Scriptores Historiae Augustae* (Julius Capitolinus), *Maximini Duo* XX.1. For Balbinus see Haegemans (2010, p. 171).

5. Mullens (1948, p. 75) suggests that the pro-dyarchy and pro-Gordian factions may have represented a deep split between Italian and African interests in the senate.

6. *Scriptores Historiae Augustae* (Julius Capitolinus), *Maximus et Balbinus* IX.3. This episode has been used to underline the potential power of the Roman populace against the state (Kelly, 2007).

7. *Herodian, History of the Empire* VII.10.7 simply states that he was grandson of Gordian I via his daughter. The name of the father is given in *Scriptores Historiae Augustae* (Julius Capitolinus), *Gordiani Tres* IV.2. An alternative is that Gordian III was the son of Gordian II, as apparently reported by Dexippus (*Scriptores Historiae Augustae* (Julius Capitolinus), *Gordiani Tres* XXIII.1) and repeated in *Zosimus, New History* 1.14.1. For the tall man, see *Scriptores Historiae Augustae* (Julius Capitolinus), *Maximus et Balbinus* IX.4.

8. The story is given in *Herodian, History of the Empire* VII.11.1–5. Herodian's account is clearly that of an eyewitness in the senate and it is one of the strongest indications in his writings that he himself may have been a senator, although the view is out of fashion with modern historians. The altar was one of Rome's notable sites and contained a gold statue of Victory that had been captured from the Greek general Pyrrhus in 272 BC.

9. See Appendix III. The identification of 'Maecenas' with 'Maecianus' has been questioned by Dietz (1980).

10. *Herodian, History of the Empire* VII.7.4 places the death of Sabinus three weeks before, in the orgy of violence that accompanied the initial overthrow of Maximinus and accession of the Gordians, but this is probably an error. The reason for suspecting this is that there is independent evidence from the *Augustan History* that Balbinus and Pupienus appointed a man called Sabinus as urban prefect (*Scriptores Historiae Augustae* (Julius Capitolinus), *Maximini Duo* XV.1 and *Scriptores Historiae Augustae* (Julius Capitolinus), *Gordiani Tres* XIII.7). *Aurelius Victor, De Caesaribus* 26 says that Sabinus died in a riot instigated by one 'Domitius'. If this man is Domitius Gallicanus, the riot is probably the one described in this section. A less likely explanation is that two men called Sabinus, possibly relatives, were both killed in the rioting at different times. See Whittaker (1969-1970), Volume II, p. 201–203, footnote 3, and p. 236, footnote 1. For a general account of mob rule and riots in Rome see Africa (1971).

11. *Scriptores Historiae Augustae* (Julius Capitolinus), *Gordiani Tres* X.3. For the forgery see Carson (1962, p. 32).

12. The charge that Maximinus was slow to advance – for example, not moving for fully four days on hearing of the rebellion according to Herodian – can hardly be used as evidence that he was "not in a hurry" or "underestimating his enemy" (Haegemans, 2010, p. 197, p. 210).

13. *Aurelius Victor, De Caesaribus*, 26. See Gagé (1970).

14. Whittaker (1969–1970, Volume II, p. 240-241, footnote 1).
15. *Vegetius, Epitoma rei militaris*, Book 3.
16. Whittaker (1969–1970, Volume II, p. 240, footnote 1).
17. For the race track see Humphrey (1986).
18. There is an inscription giving his *cursus*; see Mullens (1948, p. 67). See also Haegemans (2010, p. 168). There is a surviving inscription from Aquileia that indicates Crispinus' extraordinary command on behalf of the senate (Whittaker, 1969–1970, Volume II, p. 261, footnote 2).
19. Tavano (1986).
20. Note that in previous centuries the area of northern Italy was known as Cisalpine Gaul; Italia proper began far to the south near the top of the Italian peninsula. Cisalpine Gaul was formally incorporated into *Italia* by the emperor Augustus.
21. As recommended by *Vegetius, Epitoma rei militaris*, for example.
22. *Scriptores Historiae Augustae* (Julius Capitolinus), *Maximini Duo* XXXI.3–4 where it is given on the 'authority' of Cordus. The tale is dismissed without evidence as fabrication by Syme (1968, p. 174).
23. *Vegetius, Epitoma rei militaris*.
24. *Scriptores Historiae Augustae* (Julius Capitolinus), *Maximus et Balbinus* X.5.
25. A later bridge on the same spot was destroyed in 1916 for similar military reasons.
26. According to *Cassius Dio, Roman History* LXXIV.16.5, in 193, Severus reached Ravenna "without striking a blow".
27. For the hydrography see Comici and Bussani (2007). The precise location of the crossing is a little east of the picturesque town of Gradisca d'Isonzo close to where the modern H4 Autostrade crosses the river. Here tumbled Roman masonry still forms an artificial weir, although much of this is no doubt from the bridge rebuilt after the war of 238. For the training of German cavalry to swim rivers, see Speidel (1994, p. 13): various examples of this feat are recorded over several centuries from the campaigns of Caesar, Caligula, Hadrian and Maxentius.
28. *Herodian, History of the Empire* VIII.4.5. Evans (1981, p. 440) describes the destruction of the vineyards as a serious error on the part of Maximinus as it hastened the starvation of his own troops, but the criticism has little to recommend it as the grapes were inedible at that time of year.
29. Campbell (2005).
30. *Herodian, History of the Empire* VII.4.6,VII.8.10.
31. *Vegetius, Epitoma rei militaris*.
32. *Scriptores Historiae Augustae* (Julius Capitolinus), *Maximini Duo* XXXIII.1.
33. *Herodian, History of the Empire* VIII.5.5.
34. *Vegetius, Epitoma rei militaris*.
35. *Herodian, History of the Empire* VIII.3.9. For execution of generals see *Scriptores Historiae Augustae* (Julius Capitolinus), *Maximini Duo* XXIII.1. The account of the siege of Aquileia in this work seems to be a fairly accurate précis from Herodian, but it adds this plausible detail, possibly from the lost history of Dexippus that was also being used.
36. These details are variously from *Zosimus, New History*; *Scriptores Historiae Augustae* (Julius Capitolinus), *Maximini Duo* XXXII.5, where it is given on the authority of Dexippus; and *Epitome De Caesaribus*, Chapter 25. Maximus is cited as being either 18 or 21 at his death; *Scriptores Historiae Augustae* (Julius Capitolinus), *Maximini Duo* XXVII.2.

37. Whittaker (1969–1970, Volume II, p. 284-285, footnote 1).

38. *Scriptores Historiae Augustae* (Julius Capitolinus), *Maximini Duo* XXVIII.9. Characteristically, the tale is dismissed, without evidence, as fabrication by Syme (1968, p. 174).

Chapter XII: A New Start

1. *Herodian, History of the Empire* VIII.6.1. For other references in this section see *Herodian, History of the Empire* VIII.6.3, VII.6.4

2. This episode is reminiscent of the arrival in London of the news of the naval victory on the 'Glorious First of June' in 1794, which interrupted an opera.

3. The evidence is an inscription naming Cuspidius Flaminius Severus, the probable son (http://www.ebooksread.com/authors-eng/archaeological-institute-of-america/papers-of-the-american-school-of-classical-studies-at-athens-volume-v-2-hcr/page-11-papers-of-the-american-school-of-classical-studies-at-athens-volume-v-2-hcr.shtml).

4. *Herodian, History of the Empire* VIII.6. 8.

5. *Scriptores Historiae Augustae* (Julius Capitolinus), *Maximini Duo* XXXI.5

6. See also Haegemans (2010, p. 206).

7. This auxiliary unit had been raised by the emperor Trajan over a hundred years before from Galatia in central Turkey (and still bore his family name, Ulpius). It was probably raised for Trajan's eastern invasion force of 113 CE because it is subsequently known (from other inscriptions) to have been stationed in Syria-Palestine under successive emperors up to the time of Commodus (177–192 CE). From these clues we may suggest that the cohort may have been a component of the eastern army transferred to Aquileia by Maximinus himself a few years earlier but then left in a support role in Aqulieia. http://www.roma-victrix.com/auxilia/auxilia_cohortes_uz.htm. For *praepositus* see Gnoli (2007).

8. See Shaw (1982). *Adiutor* is a military rank (adjutant) but was also commonly used as a boy's name, especially for sons of soldiers. There were probably many men with the name Flavius Adiutor.

9. The coins of Thrace subsequently feature a personification of the province with a lion and a boar, symbols of *legio IIII flavia felix* and *legio VII claudia*, sometimes with their standards raised behind them to emphasize the point. The necessity for this propaganda seems to confirm that these legions were part of the army of Maximinus, and further it can be argued that the *legio IIII* of the legionary *dolabra* found near the Kalefeld battlefield probably relates to this regiment rather than the hypothetical *legio IIII* italicae as some have argued.

10. Speidel (1994b), p. 12–13, p. 26.

11. *Scriptores Historiae Augustae* (Julius Capitolinus), *Maximini Duo* XXV.1. None of the sources mentions a formal triumph.

12. For weights see Carson (1962, p. 104). See also Whittaker (1969-1970, Volume II, p. 300); see discussion in Haegemans (2010, p. 218). The re-introduction of the antoninianus was to drive the denarius out of circulation within a few years. The last denarii were minted in 240 CE. The first had been minted in 187 BCE and would still have been accepted as legal tender 427 years later.

13. *Scriptores Historiae Augustae* (Julius Capitolinus), *Maximini Duo* XXIV.6-7.

14. *Herodian, History of the Empire* VIII.8.4.
15. Dietz (1980, p. 134–136), Mennen (2011).
16. Haegemans (2010, p. 233).
17. *Herodian, History of the Empire* VII.8.1.
18. The older generation would have remembered the disgrace of the praetorians at the time of Septimius Severus. Rioting had occurred in the reign of Elagabalus, and then there had been a wave of disorder in response to Ulpian's attempts to curb their power in the early years of Alexander's rule. See Africa (1971) for a history of the interaction between the people of Rome and the troops stationed there.
19. *Scriptores Historiae Augustae* (Julius Capitolinus), *Maximini Duo* XXI.5.

Chapter XIII: Empire of Fortune

1. *Zosimus, New History* 1.12: The Romans "formed a secret conspiracy against the emperor, instigated by the counsel of Balbinus and Maximus, who incited some of the soldiers against him".
2. Varner (2004, p. 204). It is strange that the altar in Aquileia is defaced in this way; it is very difficult to imagine the men who raised it doing so. Perhaps some detachments of the army of Maximinus were still billeted in Aquileia at the time of the two emperors' deaths and this was their revenge. The other unresolved puzzle of this inscription is that at the end of the expunged part it refers to AVGGG ET M ANTONI GORDIANI... (the three Gs representing three *augusti*). There is no known third *augustus* and it seems simply to be a mistake.
3. Against the general view (e.g. Varner, 2004; Ando, 2012, p. 109) some modern sources say they were damned to the memory: see for example Cascio, (2005). The evidence for this is a number of erased inscriptions and papyri. One is from Aquileia (see previous footnote). Another is from Britain. But these seem to be the exceptions: many other inscriptions and statues survive and it is unlikely that the senate would have damned the memory of the very men they had elected. Unofficial erasures of emperors' names happened in other instances, for example after the defeat of the emperor Trajan Decius later in the century (Potter, 2004, p. 248). The issue is discussed in detail by Haegemans (2010, p. 233) and further ideas are explored in the final chapter of this book.
4. Magie (1924, Volume II, p. 423).
5. Ando (2012, p. 111).
6. This inference is based on the subsequent opening of the gates of Janus (which were only closed if there was peace in the empire).
7. Dietz (1980, p. 39). For more background on the family see Mennen (2011, p. 83–84).
8. Dodgeon and Lieu (1991, p. 32).
9. Dodgeon and Lieu (1991, p. 42). Julius Terentius is depicted in the act of sacrificing to three figures, possibly Pupienus, Balbinus and Gordian III, in a colourful fresco from Dura; see http://romegreeceart.tumblr.com/post/52750373069/a-third-century-roman-fresco-from-dura-europos.
10. Ross (2001, p. 72–77).
11. *Scriptores Historiae Augustae* (Julius Capitolinus), *Gordiani Tres* XXIII.4. A similar account is given by *Zosimus, New History*, I.12.
12. Magie (1924, Volume II, p. 423).

13. Le Bohec (1989). See also Potter (2004, p. 231), Dando-Collins (2010, p. 119) and Ando (2012, p. 110).

14. As a footnote to this failed rebellion, it is interesting that another man called Sabinianus (Caius Vettius Gratus Atticus Sabinianus) was to be consul for 242.

15. Ando (2012, p. 111)

16. See discussion in Ando (2012, p. 118, footnote).

17. Kettenhofen (1982); see Edwell (2008, p. 170).

18. *Ammianus Marcellinus, The Later Roman Empire* XXIII.5.17.

19. Kettenhofen (1982).

20. See also Bird (1978, p. 82).

21. Gibbon (1776, p. 188). That 235 was a watershed event has been repeated many times (up to Haynes, 2013, p.91), but it is also possible to emphasize the continuity of trends that began in the late second century and culminated with full-blown crisis in the mid third century; see for example discussions by Haegemans (2010, p. 235–250) and Weigels (2012, p. 3).

Chapter XIV: The Giant's Legacy

1. For example, when just over a decade later the emperor Decius (who had been appointed as governor of Spain by Maximinus) issued a series of coins in the names of past-deified emperors, Maximinus was not among the honoured (Sviatoslav, 2004). However it is possible that Maximinus's damnation was regarded by some as the act of an illegal regime and subsequently disputed by the guard in Rome and possibly in other parts of the army (see the following chapter).

2. Collingwood and Wright (1965, No. 1553). The list is available online at http://www.roman-britain.org/epigraphy/rib_index.htm. Nothing else is known of Tuccianus (Dietz, 1980; Haegemans, 2010, p. 100).

3. Varner (2004, p. 202); Haegemans (2010, p. 206). The other coin is in the author's collection.

4. The coinage was obviously of prime propaganda value and the emperor would have wanted to present himself and his family in the best possible light. Despite this, it is a curious feature that modern ideals of youth and beauty are not always followed on the Roman coin series as a whole. The portraits actually look like real people and, for the longer-lived emperors, they are usually consistent over decades. Old ladies appear old and even wizened (Julia Maesa is a good example), young boys appear young, and fat individuals such as Balbinus appear quite lifelike in their corpulence too (Bradley, 2011). It is possible to trace the development of Severus Alexander from bare-chinned boy to fluffy youth and finally fully-bearded young adult heroically departing for war in the east, and something similar can be done for the pointy-nosed Gordian III. Moreover the coins generally conform to the statuary and, with a little practice, the features of many of the emperors can be recognized at a glance.

5. Coins were struck from dies made of hardened bronze, in which the designs would have been made in mirror image and inverse relief. Separate dies for the obverse and reverse were made. When struck they could be rotated relative to each other, as the sides are often in random orientation (though often as not they are at 12 o'clock as in modern coins). The dies were cut in stages: a beaded circle and deep outline portrait (for the obverse)

or basic design (for the reverse) were first hammered into the die surface, probably at high temperature. This process has been called 'hubbing' and the initial outline design in positive relief is a 'hub'; and although this process has not been definitively proven, it seems the most likely method of achieving the pleasing deep contours of the surface. The portrait on the die was then finished by a master engraver (*celator*) who added fine details, working in negative relief, possibly working from an actual bust (*imagine*). Of course, with practice the engraving would become second nature, and in some instances in ancient coinage (although not those of Maximinus) experts have been able to spot the repeat handiwork of particular individuals at the mint.

6. Delbrück (1940); Carson (1962); Haegemans (2010, p. 83).
7. Klawans (1982).
8. Varner (2004, p. 201–203); Fittschen (1980). However, Chapter 15 for another possible example.
9. Wood (1986, p. 33).
10. Carson (1962, p. 89); Haegemans (2010, p. 83).
11. Lippold (1991) has argued that Herodian's positive view of Maximinus as military man and negative view as tyrant reflect his use of two sources: one positive, the other negative. This argument robs Herodian of the literary intelligence he so clearly displays. See also Haegemans (2010, p. 48).
12. *Aurelius Victor, De Caesaribus* 26.
13. Moralee (2008).
14. Aubé (1881) dedicated a chapter to Maximinus and the Christians. See also Clarke(1966); Lippold (1975); Barnes (1968).
15. *Zosimus, New History.*
16. Suda online http://www.stoa.org/sol/.
17. The quotes are from Mullens (1948, p. 65), Ando (2012, p. 104) and De la Bédoyere (2006, p. 56). To be fair, more sympathetic opinions were provided by Syme (1971), Speidel (1994) and Haynes (2013). The neurologist Harold Klawans suggested that in his later years, Maximinus may have suffered psychiatric problems and behavioral abnormalities related to his acromegaly. Tumours that initially affect the pituitary and cause growth disorders can eventually affect the hypothalmus, causing episodes of rage and vicious paranoid behaviour (Klawans, 1982, p. 325).
18. See biographies of late great generals Stilicho and Aetius by Hughes (2010) and Hughes (2012).
19. *Jordanes, Getica* XV.
20. Macchiavelli (1513), Chapter XX; McCanles (1982).
21. Macchiavelli (1513), Chapter XX.
22. Altheim (1939).
23. Pringle (2006).
24. Although modern scholars dismiss these ideas it should be remembered that some of it was based on the latest ethnological and linguistic research at the time. For example H.G. Wells' classic *A Short History of the World* (Wells, 1922) has chapters on the Nordic migrations, and implies that Gautama Buddha was of Aryan ancestry (although there is no mention of Atlantis or the more outlandish aspects of the Nazi ideas). This claim is based on the similarities (proven by the 1930s) between Sanskrit, Persian and other

Indo-European languages. Modern scholars think the migration was mostly east to west rather than west to east.

25. Pringle (2006).

26. See the extended account of Altheim's travels by Pringle (2006).

27. Yenne (2010, p. 141).

28. Altheim (1939).

29. Altheim (1942). Ensslin (1942) had denied that Maximinus counted as a German.

30. Quoted in Pringle (2006, p. 129)

31. Pringle (2006).

32. Merkel (1970); see discussion in Pringle (2006, p. 304–305).

33. Aemilius is no doubt entirely fictional, but there was actually a patrician ex-consul from north Italy at the time called Fulvius Aemilianus, descended from a number of great families, namely the Brutii, Gavii, Fulvii, Rufii, Festi, Laelii, Maximi, Barbii, Nummii and Umbrii; see Dietz (1980, p. 357).

34. Tunney (1924).420

35. Home (1760, p. 29).

36. See, for example, Juba the Numidian huntsman played by Djimon Hounsou in *Gladiator* (2000) and Atticus the Gladiator-slave played by Adewale Akinnuoye-Agbaje in *Pompeii* (2014).

37. Sidebottom (2014).

38. Sviatoslav (2004).

39. *Caesar, The Gallic War* IV.14–15.

40. *Suetonius, The Twelve Caesars.*

41. McClynn (2009).

42. de Blois (1984, p. 364).

43. The late story that he had her murdered (Syncellus 680, *Zonoras, Extracts of History* 12, 16) is almost certainly a calumny.

44. *Scriptores Historiae Augustae* (Julius Capitolinus), *Maximini Duo* XII.3. However de Blois (1984, p. 365) goes too far by suggesting that ancient authors criticized Maximinus of risking "the safety of entire armies".

45. See Whittaker (1994, p. 175). Also see the balanced account of Maximinus's strategy in Loriot (1975, p. 688–689) and Haegemans (2010, p. 66–67).

Chapter XV: Postscript: The Ogre in the Met

1. The circumstances of its discovery are discussed in detail by Neverov (1996); Hemingway, McGregor and Smith (2013) and Marlowe (2014).

2. "Two portraits of Trebonianus Gallus". In *Heilbrunn Timeline of Art History*. New York: The Metropolitan Museum of Art. http://www.metmuseum.org/toah/works-of-art/05.30_05.47 (October 2006).

3. For *adlocutio* see Felletti Maj (1958). An alternative explanation for the stance preferred by some modern commentators is that he originally held a lance in his right hand and a sword in his left (Bradley, 2011; Hemingway, McGregor and Smith, 2013). However the fingers of the right hand (which is original, and not restoration) do not look like they gripped a lance; instead the hand resembles a gesture of emphasis described in Quintillian's guide for orators in which three fingers are held under the thumb and the

index finger is extended (see Graf, p. 42). We must also wonder why the lance and sword were not recovered.

4. The quotations are from Marlowe (2014, p. 1) and "Two portraits of Trebonianus Gallus" in Heilbrunn Timeline of Art History, New York: The Metropolitan Museum of Art, http://www.metmuseum.org/toah/works-of-art/05.30_05.47 (October 2006).

5. The 'transitional' form of the statue between classical and Late Antique traditions is considered its main significance in art-history terms, but this has been questioned by Marlowe (2013, 2014) and we are promised more on the subject by that author in an article in preparation. If the statue is lifelike, as suggested here, it gives us another reason not to over-interpret the features in terms of evolving imperial iconography.

6. Quoted in Hemingway, McGregor and Smith (2013, p. 116). Helbig was a well-respected nineteenth century archaeologist but has been accused of repeated fakery in modern times.

7. The cloak (which is probably incorrectly referred to as a *paludamentum*) is not ancient, although he would have had one in a similar place; nor are the genitals, unfortunately. See Hemingway, McGregor and Smith (2013) for details.

8. Like, for example, 'Alexander with the Lance' by Lysippos, with which the pose has been compared (Bradley, 2011; Hemingway, McGregor and Smith, 2013).

9. The story of how the statue made its way from the collection of Auguste Montferrand onto the Paris art market and then to the Metropolitan Museum of Art was described by Mather (1905) and discussed further by Neverov (1996), Hemingway, McGregor and Smith (2013), Marlowe (2014) and by M. Cadario in La Rocca et al. (2015, p. 367–8). Additional details can be gleaned from a report in *Le Figaro* of 1910 where we find that the sale to the Met was the subject of an ongoing court case between a 'Mr Triantaphylos' (presumably the art collector Evangelos Triantaphyllos) and Alphonse Van Branteghem, another well-known art collector, who is described in the article as one of the most curious characters of Parisian society, "like a character from Balzac" (Anonymous, 1910). The article describes how the statue had passed through several hands until being acquired by Triantaphyllos, whereupon he set it up in his garden in the Rue Saint Georges next to a goldfish pond and it started accumulating bird deposits. It was Van Branteghem who valued its true worth and identified it as Trebonianus, apparently writing a pamphlet justifying the identification, which unfortunately I have been unable to trace, and also that he allegedly restored it (a detail to add to the account of its restoration history by Hemingway, McGregor and Smith, 2013). Triantaphyllos sold it for 500,000 francs to the Met, of which Van Branteghem was claiming 100,000 because of breach of contract, something to do with terms agreed when he identified and valued it. We do not know how the case ended. (Note that there is a catalogue entry in the *"Archives des Musées Nationaux Série A : Antiquités grecques et romaines"* for 30 April 1910 of an *"Article de presse : litige entre Triantaphylos et Van Branteghem pour la vente d'une statue en bronze de l'empereur Caius Gallus decouverte a Paris. [1 p.]. "*: presumably a copy of the *Figaro* article or another newspaper report). Another very different version of events comes from an apparently very unreliable newspaper report in the *New York Times* (Anonymous, 1905a) which suggests that the identification as Trebonianus was made "when the statue was moved to the house of Prince Demidoff in St. Petersburg" and that the statue "was dug up 50 years ago" and had been "bought at public auction with other statuary of the Demidoff collection after the Prince's death in 1870", all of which seems to be wrong,

and there is no mention of Montferrand or indeed Triantaphyllos. The claim that the statue had been dug up about 50 years before its acquisition by the Met (i.e. around 1855) was widely repeated at the time. The error was compounded in other sources from that time which relate that the excavation was conducted with permission of Pope Pius IX (1846–1878) near San Giovanni Laterano, as opposed to Pius VII (1800–1823) in Montferrand's account (Anonymous, 1905b): presumably someone noticed that the pope did not fit the date and changed the number.

10. Mather (1905, p. 148) and Fitzgerald (1905). The statue was referred to Julius Caesar as late as 1903 (see Hemingway, McGregor and Smith, 2013, for references).

11. http://en.wikipedia.org/wiki/William_M._Laffan#Artistic_interests.

12. Hemingway, McGregor and Smith (2013). However the information notice beside the statue simply reads (as of 2014) "Bronze statue of the emperor Trebonianus Gallus". The 1970s studies are Bergmann (1977, p. 44–45; who also questioned whether it was necessarily an emperor rather than a private portrait), and Wegner (1979, p. 83–91).

13. The sandals were described and illustrated by Hemingway, McGregor and Smith (2013). Only one is probably original, the other being modelled on it. The closest match to the figure that I have been able to find is a mask of Dionysus, a god originally from Thrace but also popular in other parts of the empire (as Dionysius or Bacchus/Dionysius). See http://www.ancientsculpture.net/Greek-Macedonian-Roman-sculptures/Bacchus-Dionysus-Bacchus-Sculpture-Dionysus. Bacchus was the favourite god of Septimius Severus, Maximinus's supposed mentor (Speidel, 1994b). The difficulty with this is that the face on the sandals seems to be associated with a shell rather than vine leaves and grapes.

14. Kleiner (2010, p. 268).

15. His reign is best documented by late sources such as Zosimus and Zonoras. It is unfortunate his life is missing from the *Augustan History*.

16. http://www.metmuseum.org/toah/works-of-art/05.30_05.47. Some bronze statues survive from antiquity because they were struck by lightning and it was a long-held custom to appease the gods by burying them carefully in the ground, as if in a grave, when that happened. However there is no indication that this happened to the Met statue.

17. Marlowe (2014) refers to a biography in French by Gibert (2008). There is also a biography in Russian by Shuĭskiĭ (2005) which forms the basis of the Wikipedia page. (http://en.wikipedia.org/wiki/Auguste_de_Montferrand#Art_collection).

18. Montferrand (1849) as quoted by Neverov (1996). The English translation is from Marlowe (2014, p. 5). Montferrand's story was repeated by von Köhne (1852).

19. Marlowe (2014). Montferrand was a sculptor as well as architect and it would have been a characteristically nineteenth century conceit and case of inverse snobbery to refer to himself as a mason.

20. For the family tree of the Demidoffs, see Haskell and others (1994). For the art interests of Demidoff's forebears see Neverov (1996). For Demidoff's military exploits see Čerkasova and Mosin (1996, p. 300). For Demidoff in Rome and his appointment as ambassador to Tuscany see Črkasova and Mosin (1996, p. 300) and Bisogni (1996, p. 75). For Demidoff's receptions (twice a week) and comedy theatre see Stendhal (1828).

21. This story is from Stendhal (1828) as reproduced by Pellegrini (1976).

22. Neverov (1996) records excavations in 1822-3 at the Via dei Quattro Cantoni. Elsewhere there were apparently excavations at the villa of Santa Croce (in Campania), and also at

the house of Quinctilius Varus in Tivoli in 1820 (Neverov, 1996) (which had been visited and sketched by J.M.W. Turner in 1819). Certainly statuary was uncovered there around that time and acquired by Demidoff, whether or not he financed the digs directly. More likely, given the timing, is that these excavations gave Demidoff the idea of funding his own.

23. For the record, Marlowe's (2014, p. 8) conclusion is that "interpretations of the Metropolitan statue based on its alleged find spot at the Lateran (such as those that suggest that it was created for the *equites singulares*; and that its military patronage explains its unclassical style; and that this in turn helps us understand the rejection of classicism in favour of increasing abstraction in late Roman art) are houses of cards". She also states "the Metropolitan statue was almost certainly not found in excavations near the Lateran".

24. Josi (1934); See also http://en.wikipedia.org/wiki/Castra_Nova_equitum_singularium. That the statue could have come from the barracks of the *equites* was seemingly first suggested in 1958 by Felletti Maj (quoted by Marlowe, 2014, p. 2 who regarded it as credulous). Note that the new barracks site at the Lateran was first dug in 1713 and 1734 and is described as "magnificently decorated with statues, busts, altars, and works of art of every description" (Lanciani 1897, p. 336; who implies that a marble seat in the Corsini Library came from there).

25. I thank Ian Haynes for making this suggestion. The excavations under the basilica were described by Colini (1944) and are placed in the context of more recent archaeological work by Colli et al. (2009) and Haynes et al. (2012).

26. The map is by Giambattista Nolli and has been turned into an excellent research resource by Jim Tice and Erik Steiner at the University of Oregon in *The Interactive Nolli Map Website* (http://nolli.uoregon.edu/default.asp). The print, showing the Lateran area with its obelisk and square, is by Giovanni Piranesi (www.piranesiselection.com).

27. Lanciani (1885, 1886); Frothingham (1886); Le Blant (1886) who names Maraini; this is possibly the Swiss-Italian architect Otto Maraini (1863–1944) or his father; at any rate the statue of Bacchus was taken to their villa in Lugano, Switzerland; Forbes (1887). Note that Lanciani (1885) promised a second publication with details of the site but that seems never to have appeared. His notebooks have been published by Buonocore (1997–2002).

28. Also quoted by Speidel (1994a, p. 28) and Speidel (1994b, p. 139). The pedestal referred to is Number 11 of Speidel (1994a, p. 45–46). Forbes (1887, p. 241) also adds a few location details and confirms the fragments of statues: "On the right side of the Sancta Scala, parallel with the Via Tasso, the Barracks of the Equites Singulares, or Horse Guards of the Emperors, of the time of Hadrian, were discovered in March 1886 [this should read 1885]. A noble hall 90 feet long, containing many inscriptions, raised by discharged veterans, was discovered; also fragments of statues, and one nearly perfect of the youthful Bacchus, a work that we may class with the school of Praxiteles." The Sancta Scala (Holy Stairs) is a monument outside the front of the Lateran Palace, supposedly the stairway of Pontius Pilate brought to Rome by Helena, the mother of Constantine.

29. The first statue was identified as Mercury by Colini (1944, p. 317); see also Speidel (1994b, p. 140). The building is now dated to Trajan's reign (98–117), not Hadrian's (117–138). The account from Lanciani's article in *The Athenaum* and repeated by Frothingham was not cited by Speidel (1994a). It contains the piece of information that "many fragments"

of other statues were found. The Bacchus is very interesting. The presence of Bacchus, identified with the Thracian god Dionysus, may well be significant, as dedications to Bacchus and the 'Thracian Rider' are also known from the probable *principia* of a third century cavalry unit at Slăveni in Romania (Haynes, 2013, p. 222) so there may be a particular association with the cavalry. The statue of Bacchus was described and illustrated by Visconti (1886, p. 166–169) but no background details of the excavation were reported by him. It was also illustrated by Lanciani (1901) who recorded that it was "now in the Villa Maraini at Lugano". Its present whereabouts are unknown (www.arachne. de). It has been suggested that the statue might date to the time of Septimius Severus, for whom Bacchus was the 'home god' (Speidel 1994b, p. 140).

More details of the excavation are given in another article by Lanciani (1897, p. 336) who says it took place from 1885–1887 "in the grounds of the Villa Giustiniani" on the Via Tasso. The Villa Giustiniani was a grand house built in the seventeenth century and was decorated with many ancient statues found in the grounds long before the alleged excavations of Demidoff (http://it.wikipedia.org/wiki/Villa_Giustiniani_Massimo). Lanciani's sketch map of the excavations was reproduced by Buonocore (1997, p. 61). Additional details seem to have survived and are reproduced in Colli *et al.* (2009) showing the mapping of a series of rooms underneath the Via Tasso itself and on both sides of the modern road, although it is not clear which of the walls may correspond to a hall of the size reported by Lanciani. Note that this map is more detailed and different from that in Speidel (1994b, p. 127) and the ancient road was on a slightly different alignment to the modern Via Tasso; also that the *castra priora* is wrongly labelled as *castra nova* in Colli *et al.* (2009). Part of what appears to be Lanciani's map was reproduced by Speidel (1994a, p. 29) after Colini (1944, p. 315).

30. Speidel (1994b, p. 140).
31. Speidel (1994a).
32. Speidel (1994a) described much of the collection. It may be that some of the 44 (or 45 according to Speidel, 1994a, p. 1) so-called pedestals are in fact altars and did not have statues upon the. See also Speidel (1994b, p. 140). For the recent archaeological discoveries see Colli *et al.* (figure 8).
33. Speidel (1994b, p. 139): hence our statue, hypothetically dating to 235, falls within that range (Trebonianus, on the other hand, came a little later).
34. The rest of the pedestals seem to be altars to various gods dear to the horseguard and may not have had statuary placed atop them (although the distinction between the categories of pedestal and altar are not clear in every case). It is interesting that the gods include both the traditional Roman pantheon and various regional deities, including the Gallic war-god Toutatis as frequently invoked by Asterix the Gaul. See Speidel (1994b, p. 67) and Haynes (2013, p. 231).
35. It may be worth adding that a famous and magnificent equestrian statue of Marcus Aurelius was on display as early as the eighth century in the Lateran area (later to be removed to the Capitoline by none other than Michelangelo, and now in the Capitoline Museum). Even the original of Rome's iconic she-wolf, the *lupa capitolina*, may have been in the Lateran area in the early middle ages. It seems possible, although perhaps unlikely, that these could also somehow have survived Rome's early Christian years by being hidden among the ruins of the forts of the *equites singulares* (cf. Speidel 1994a, p. 1) only to be excavated by a later pope.

36. Anatole was the 'First Prince of St. Donato', for whom the dish "Chicken Demidoff" ("elaborately stuffed, smothered, tied up and garnished") is named. Paul Demidoff was known as a patron of arts and sciences and is described, in a wonderful example of early twentieth century hack writing thus: "Under a skin of satin he had muscles of steel; he was built to resist life and triumph over life... He would call up all his servants, open all the windows, and take a cold bath. He had constantly at his bedside a decanter of iced champagne, of which he drank all night. Nobody, however, ever heard of Paul Demidoff being drunk... He would send for four or five servants, and make them fight together until they had eliminated the victor, who received a handsome gratification" (see "Prince Demidoff and the San Donato Sale" in *The Art Amateur*; http://www.jstor.org/stable/25627067?seq=2).

37. As suggested tentatively by Argenziano (1996, p. 105) and Neverov (1996, p. 159) and also by Marlowe (2014). Note that there is some confusion about what may have happened to the bronze between its initial discovery and it being in the Demidoff collection transferred to St. Petersburg. Neverov (1996) discussed a bronze bust or statue of the emperor Galba that was owned by a Prince Stanislav Poniatowski, nephew of the last king of Poland (of the same name) and may have made its way to the Demidoff collection; however it is not clear (to this writer) that this is the same piece.

38. Marlowe (2014, p. 7). It is important to note, however, that many of the items on those lists certainly do not come from the horseguard barracks: one item is given as having been found in Naples and other pieces came from Demidioff's 1822–3 excavation at the Via dei Quattro Cantoni (which is about 1 kilometre to the northwest of the Via Tasso site) where we know six sculptures were found that match descriptions in the customs lists (Neverov (1996, p. 158). This same story was repeated by M. Cadario in La Rocca et al. (2015, p. 367–8) and seems to be the reason why its discovery is given as 1822 or earlier. At least four of these are given as being from the Esquiline in the Hermitage catalogue. Details of that excavation were published by Visconti (1886) and Lanciani (1902). The excavators interpreted the site as a collapsed workshop, and if so it could even be the workshop that originally supplied the barracks of the *equites* although the Hermitage display notes suggest that the site may have been a workshop from Renaissance times rather than Ancient Rome.

39. This is according to an article on a court case published in *Le Figaro* of 1910 (Anonymous, 1910). The article repeats the claim that the statue was discovered in Rome at the time of Pope Pius VII and had adorned the palace in Florence.

40. The quote is from Shuĭskiĭ (2005). A sepia photograph of the courtyard of Montferrand's home, featuring the big bronze, was reproduced by Hemingway, McGregor and Smith (2013, figure 9.2).

41. The fate of the statues was discussed by Neverov (1996) and Marlowe (2014), who refers to sales in 1863 and 1870. However the 1863 sales do not seem to have included sculptures or marbles according to the list in Haskell and others (1994, p. 115–116). Those that may have done are: Anatole Demidoff's sales of 1–3rd April 1869 at Haro, Paris (12 sculptures); 2–4th March 1870 at Petit, Paris (17 marbles); 22–24th March 1870 at Mannheim, Paris (294 sculptures); 29–31st March 1870 at Mannheim, Paris (247 sculptures); 19–21st April 1870 at Mannheim, Paris (343 bronzes); and Paul Demidoff's sale on 19th December 1891 at Mannheim, Paris (142 various). After the Russian Revolution there was a further sale or resale of 23 Demidoff sculptures on 6th May 1919, at Muller, Amsterdam and some later

auctions with various pieces from the original collections resold. However even the list in Haskell and others (1994) may not be complete because there is notice of another sale of Paul Demidoff (see "Prince Demidoff and the San Donato Sale" in *The Art Amateur*; http://www.jstor.org/stable/25627067?seq=2), described as the "great art event of the spring", although there were no sculptures.

42. Neverov (1996, p. 162): up to 50 pieces were acquired in this sale but these include some modern statues as well as ancient; see also Waldhauer (1928–1936) and Vostchinina (1974) for the Hermitage collection.

43. At least for the pieces catalogued by Speidel (1994a), although there may have been other less important fragments recovered that perhaps still survive in the Museum vaults.

44. Most of the memorials to honourable discharge do not specifically state that they had statues atop them, but as some do, it seems likely they all did. For the record, numbers 14 and 15 also refer to a statue and numbers 38 and 56 are described as 'statue bases' rather than altars (Speidel 1994a).

45. The Antonius Pius in the Hermitage has the accession number A.164. It was not discussed in the catalogues of Waldhauer (1928–1936) but does appear in the list of Vostchinina (1974) which states, with a query mark, that it was found in 1825 near the Lateran Gate. If the excavation took two years, as Montferrand claimed, the it could have started in 1823 following on from the nearby dig at the Via dei Quattro Cantoni on the Esquiline. Conceivably, Demidoff may have been given permission for both digs by Pius VII (who died in August 1823). Unfortunately, despite enquiries at the Vatican and National Museum, I have been unable to find any correspondence between Demidoff and the authorities that relates to these digs. The statue of Antonius Pius appears on the 1828 export license (see Argenziano, 1996, p.103) although the provenance is not given there. If Montferrand's story is essentially correct, and he was in Rome around 1825, then this may have been the time he purchased a statue of Hadrian (see endnote 23). Hence the Hadrian, too, could come from the Via Tasso site.

46. See, for example, Stephenson (2011). For the *equites* at the Milvian Bridge see Speidel (1986).

47. Speidel (1986).

48. Speidel (1994b, p. 116). However recent mapping of the Lateran archaeology shows that the Christian altar was not in fact directly above the *principia* of the guard (I. Haynes, personal communication, 2014).

49. That the old fort (*castra priora*) was demolished at the time of Constantine has been confirmed from the archaeology (e.g., Colli *et al.*, 2009, p. 7).

50. Speidel (1994b, p. 157). Possibly this '45' is a rounding up of the 43 of Lanciani (1886) and 44 of Lanciani (1901).

51. Also, Constantine based his claim for legitimacy on being descended from Claudius II, so arguably his statue would have been recovered at the time of demolition if it had been identified as such.

52. *Herodian, History of the Empire* VIII.8.1.

53. If this seems far-fetched, consider how an ancient sculptor would have depicted an individual like Nikolai Valuev, ex-heavyweight boxer, over 7 feet tall, and now distinguished Russian parliamentarian.

Appendix I: Sources

1. Whittaker (1969–1970).
2. For example, see Syme (1971) and Lippold (1991). The topic is reviewed by Sidebottom (1997) who argued for a late date.
3. Thomson (1976).

Literature Cited

Ancient Sources

Agathangelos, History of the Armenians (Thomson, 1976). Also known as *History of St. Gregory and the Conversion of Armenia*. Available online with commentary at http://www.vehi.net/istoriya/armenia/agathangelos/en/AGATHANGELOS.html

Agathias, The Histories. Extract with introduction: *Agathias and the Persians.* Posted by Warren Soward, Californian State University. Available online at http://www.sasanika.org/wp-content/uploads/AgathiasFinal.pdf

Ammianus Marcellinus, The Later Roman Empire. Selected and translated by Walter Hamilton with an Introduction and Notes by Andrew Wallace-Hadrill (Penguin, London, 1986).

Aurelius Victor, De Caesaribus. Translated by H. W. Bird (Liverpool University Press, 1984).

Caesar, The Gallic War. A new translation by Carolyn Hammond (Oxford University Press, Oxford, 1996).

Cassius Dio, Roman History. Translated by E. Cary, Loeb Classical Library, 9 volumes (Harvard University Press, 1927).

Chronography of 354 AD: Part 12: Commemoration of the Martyrs. *MGH Chronica Minora I* (1892) Available online at http://www.tertullian.org/fathers/chronography_of_354_12_depositions_martyrs.htm.

Codex Iustinianus. Available online at http://www.leges.uni-koeln.de/en/lex/codex-iustinianus/.

Corpus Inscriptionum Latinarum. Available online at http://cil.bbaw.de/cil_en/index_en.html.

Cyprian, Epsistles. Available online at http://www.newadvent.org/fathers/050674.htm.

Epitome De Caesaribus. A booklet about the styles and manners of the *imperatores.* Sometimes attributed to Aurelius Victor. Translated by T. M. Banchich, 2nd edition (Canisius College, New York, 2009).

Eusebius Caesariensis, Historia Ecclesiastica, volume 2, translated by J.E.L. Outon, Loeb Classical Library (Harvard University Press, 1932).

Eutropius, Breviarum. Translated with an introduction and commentary by H. W. Bird. (Liverpool University Press, 1993).

Gildas, De Ecxidio et Conquesto Britanniae. Updated by Robert Vermaat. Available online at http://www.vortigernstudies.org.uk/arthist/vortigernquotesgil.htm

Heliodorus, Aethiopica. Translated by Thomas Underdowne (Anno 1587); Revised and partly rewritten by F. A. Wright, with an introduction (Routledge, London, 1939).

Herodian, History of the Empire. Translated by C. R. Whittaker. Loeb Classical Library, 2 volumes (Harvard University Press, 1967–1969).

Herodotus, The Histories. Translated by Robin Waterfield (Oxford University Press, Oxford, 1988).

Hippolytus, Antipope, ca 170–235 or 6. Refutatio omnium haeresium. Marcovich, M. (de Gruyter, New York, 1986).

Jordanes, Getica (The Gothic History of Jordanes. In English with an Introduction and Commentary). Translated by Charles C. Mierow, 1915. Available online with typographical corrections at http://people.ucalgary.ca/~vandersp/Courses/texts/jordgeti.html#gthird.

Liber Pontificalis. Translated by Louise Ropes Loomis (Columbia University Press, 1916). Available online at https://archive.org/details/bookofpopesliber00loom.

Livius, Ab Urbe Condita Libri. The Latin Library. Available online at http://www.thelatinlibrary.com/liv.html.

Scriptores Historiae Augustae. Historiae Augustae scriptorum minorum latinorum. Lugduni Batavorum. (Ex Officina Joannis Maire, 1632). (An early print edition.)

Scriptores Historiae Augustae (Julius Capitolinus), *Marcus Antoninus.* With an English translation by David Magie. Vol. I, pp. 132–205. Loeb Classical Libraries (Harvard University Press, Cambridge Mass., 1924)

Scriptores Historiae Augustae (Aelius Lampridius), *Commodus Antoninus.* With an English translation by David Magie (1924). Vol. I, pp. 264–313. Loeb Classical Libraries (Harvard University Press, Cambridge Mass., 1924).

Scriptores Historiae Augustae (Aelius Spartianus), *Severus.* With an English translation by David Magie (1924). Vol. I, pp. 371–429. Loeb Classical Libraries. (Harvard University Press, Cambridge Mass., 1924).

Scriptores Historiae Augustae (Aelius Spartianus), *Antoninus Caracalla.* With an English translation by David Magie (1924). Vol. II, pp. 2–31. Loeb Classical Libraries. (Harvard University Press, Cambridge Mass., 1924).

Scriptores Historiae Augustae (Aelius Lampridius), *Antoninus Heliogabalus.* With an English translation by David Magie (1924). Vol. II, pp. 105–177.

Loeb Classical Libraries. (Harvard University Press, Cambridge Mass., 1924).

Scriptores Historiae Augustae (Aelius Lampridius), *Alexander Severus*. With an English translation by David Magie (1924). Vol. II, pp. 178–313. Loeb Classical Libraries. (Harvard University Press, Cambridge Mass., 1924).

Scriptores Historiae Augustae (Julius Capitolinus), *Maximini Duo*. With an English translation by David Magie (1924). Vol. II, pp. 314–379. Loeb Classical Libraries. (Harvard University Press, Cambridge Mass., 1924).

Scriptores Historiae Augustae (Julius Capitolinus), *Gordiani Tres*. With an English translation by David Magie (1924). Vol. II, pp. 380–447. Loeb Classical Libraries: Harvard University Press, Cambridge Mass.

Scriptores Historiae Augustae (Julius Capitolinus), *Maximus et Balbinus*. With an English translation by David Magie (1924). Vol. II, pp. 448–485. Loeb Classical Libraries. (Harvard University Press, Cambridge Mass., 1924).

Scriptores Historiae Augustae (Trebellius Pollio), *Tyranni Triginta*. With an English translation by David Magie (1924). Vol. III, pp. 448–485. Loeb Classical Libraries. (Harvard University Press, Cambridge Mass., 1924).

Scriptores Historiae Augustae (Flavius Vopiscus of Syracuse), *Divus Aurelianus*. With an English translation by David Magie (1924). Vol. III, pp. 193–293. Loeb Classical Libraries. (Harvard University Press, Cambridge Mass., 1924).

Scriptores Historiae Augustae (Trebellius Pollio), *Divus Claudius*. With an English translation by David Magie (1924). Vol. III, pp. 152–191. Loeb Classical Libraries. (Harvard University Press, Cambridge Mass., 1924).

Suetonius, *The Twelve Caesars*. Translated by Robert Graves. Revised with an Introduction and Notes by J. B. Rives. Penguin books, 1957 398 pp. ISBN978-0-140-45516-8.

Sulpicius Severus, Chronicle. Available online at http://www.newadvent.org/fathers/35052.htm.

Tacitus, Annals. Translated by A.J. Church and W. J. Brodribb. Available online at http://classics.mit.edu/Tacitus/annals.html.

Tacitus, Germania. Available online at http://www.geocities.ws/reginheim/germania.html.

Vegetius, Epitoma rei militaris. Edited by M. D. Reeve. Oxford Medieval Texts (Oxford, 2004).

Zonoras, Extracts of History. Available online at https://openlibrary.org/books/OL7040945M/Ioannou_tou_Zonara_Epitome_historio.

Zosimus, New History. Green and Chaplin, London (1814). Available online at http://www.tertullian.org/fathers/zosimus01_book1.htm.

Modern Literature

Abdy, R., 'The Domitian II coin from Chalgrove: a Gallic emperor returns to history' in *Antiquity*, 83 (2009), 751–757.

Africa, T. W., 'Urban violence in Imperial Rome' in *The Journal of Interdisciplinary History*, 2 (1971), 3–21.

Alemany, A., *Sources on the Alans: a critical compilation* (Koninklijke Brill, 2000).

Alston, R., 'Roman military pay from Caesar to Diocletian' in *The Journal of Roman Studies*, 84 (1994), 113–123.

Altheim, F., *Die Soldatenkaiser* (Deutches Ahnenerbe, 1939).

Altheim, F., 'Zum letzen Mal: Maximinus Thrax' in *Rheinisches Museum für Philologie*, 91 (1942), 350–353.

Ando, C., *Imperial Rome AD 193 to 284* (Edinburgh University Press, 2012).

Anonymous, 'Gazette des Tribunaux' in *Le Figaro* (Paris, 13 April, 1910). Available at http://gallica.bnf.fr/ark:/12148/bpt6k2888123/texteBrut (text) and http://gallica.bnf.fr/ark:/12148/bpt6k2888123/f4.image (scan).

Anonymous, 'Statue of a Caesar for the Art Museum' in *New York Times* (August 4, 1905a).

Anonymous, 'Items from the Art Museums' in *Brush and Pencil*, 16, No. 2 (August, 1905b), 47–50.

Argenziano, R., 'Nicola Demidoff e le sue collezioni nei documenti degli archivi di Firenze e di San Pietroburgo' in Tonini, L. S. (ed.) *I Demidoff a Firenze e in Toscana* (Leo S. Olschki, 1996), 89–143.

Arjomand, S. A., 'Artaxerxes, Ardašîr, and Bahman' in *Journal of the American Oriental Society*, 118 (1988), 245–247.

Aubé, B., *Les Chretiens dans l'Empire Romain de la Fin des Antonins au Milieu du IIIe Siècle* (Paris, 1881).

Baldwin, B., 'Illiterate Emperors' in *Historia: Zeitschrift für Alte Geschichte*, 38 (1989), 124–126.

Balil, A., 'C. Iulius Verus Maximinus "Thrax"' in *Boletín de la Real Academia de la Historia*, 157 (1965), 83–171.

Ball, J., 'Small finds and Roman battlefields: the process and impact of post-battle looting' in Platts, H., Pearce, J., Barron, C., Lundock, J., and Yoo, J. (eds.), *TRAC 2013: Proceedings of the Twenty-Third Annual Theoretical Roman Archaeology Conference, King's College London*, 2013 (Oxbow, 2013), 90–104.

Ball, W., *Rome in the East; the Transformation of an Empire* (Routledge, 2000).

Bang, M., 'Die militarische Laufbahn des Kaisers Maximinus' in *Hermes*, 41 (1906), 300–303.

Barfield, T., *Nomadic Empires and China, 221 BC–AD 1757* (Harvard University Press, 1989).

Barnes, T. D., 'Legislation against the Christians' in *Journal of Roman Studies*, 58 (1968), 32–50.

Barnes, T. D., *Sources of the* Historia Augusta (Collection Latomus, v. 155, Bruxelles, 1978).

Bellezza, A., *Massimino il Trace* (Fratelli Pagano, 1964).

Benario, H. W., 'Amphitheatres of the Roman world' in *The Classical Journal*, 81 (1981), 255–259.

Berger, F., 'Die römisch-germanische Auseinandersetzung am Harzhorn (Ldkr. Northeim, Niedersachsen)' in *Germania*, 88 (2010), 313–402.

Bergmann, M., *Studien zum römisch Porträt des 3. Jahrhundert n. Chr* (Rudolf Habelt Verlag GMBH, Bonn, 1977).

Bersanetti, G. M., *Studi sull' imperatore Massimino il Trace* (Rome, 1940).

Bird, H. W., 'S. Aurelius Victor: some Third Century issues' in *The Classical Journal*, 73 (1978), 223–237.

Bird, H. W., *Aurelius Victor: De Caesaribus. Translated with an introduction and commentary by H. W. Bird* (Liverpool University Press, 1994).

Birley, A. R., *Lives of the Later Caesars. Translated with an introduction by A. Birley* (Penguin, 1976).

Birley, A. R., *Septimius Severus: The African Emperor* (Second edition, Batsford, 1988).

Birley, A. R., *Tacitus: Agricola and Germany. A New Translation by A.R. Birley* (Oxford University Press, 1999).

Bisogni, F., 'Note su Nicola Demidoff e la Villa di San Donato' in Tonini, L. S. (ed.) *I Demidoff a Firenze e in Toscana* (Leo S. Olschki, 1996), 69–87.

Bland, R. F., 'The development of gold and silver coin denominations, A.D. 193–253' in C. E. King and D. G. Wigg (eds.), *Coin Finds and Coin Use in the Roman World* (Gebr Mann, 1996), 63–100.

Boardman, J. and Hammond, N. G. L., *The Cambridge Ancient History* (Cambridge University Press, 1982).

Bomgardner, D. L., 'The revolt of the Gordians and the amphitheatre at Thysdrus (El Djem)' in King, A. C. and Henig, M. (eds) *The Roman West in the Third Century. Contributions from Archaeology and History, BAR-IS, Oxford 1981* (Oxford University Press, 1981), 211–214.

Bomgardner, D. L., 'The Carthage amphitheatre: a reappraisal' in *American Journal of Archaeology*, 93 (1989), 85–103.

Bowman, A. K., *Life and Letters on the Roman Frontier: Vindolanda and its People* (The British Museum Press, 1994).

Bradley, M., 'Obesity, corpulence and emaciation in Roman art' in *Papers of the British School at Rome*, 79 (2011), 1–4.

Brown, P., *The World of Late Antiquity* (Thames and Hudson, 1971).

Buckley, R., Morris, M., Appleby, J., King, T., O'Sullivan, D., and Foxhall, L., '"The King in the car park": new light on the death and burial of Richard III in the Grey Friars church, Leicester, in 1485' in *Antiquity*, 87 (2013), 519–538.

Buonocore, M., *Appunti di topografia romana nei Codici Lanciani della Biblioteca Apostolica Vaticana*, I–V (Rome, 1997–2002).

Burian, J., 'Maximinus Thrax. Sein Bild bei Herodian und in der Historia Augusta' in *Philologus*, 132 (1988), 230–244.

Busch, A. W., *Militär in Rom: Militärische und paramilitärische Einheiten im kaiserzeitlichen stadtbild* (Deutsches Archäologisches Institut Rom, 2011).

Campbell, D. B., *Siege Warfare in the Roman World, 146 BC – AD 378* (Osprey, 2005).

Canepa, M. P., *The Two Eyes of the Earth: Art and Ritual Kingship Between Rome and Sasanian Iran* (University of California Press, 2009).

Carson, R. A. G., *Coins of the Roman Empire in the British Museum. Volume VI. Severus Alexander to Balbinus and Pupienus* (British Museum Publications, 1962).

Cascio, E. L., 'The emperor and his administration' in *The Cambridge Ancient History, 2nd edition, Vol XII, The Crisis of Empire, A.D. 193–337* (Cambridge, 2005), 156–169.

Casey, P. J., *The British Usurpers Carausius and Allectus* (Yale University Press, 1994).

Casey, P. J. and Noel, M., 'The Roman fort at Lanchester, Co. Durham: a geophysical survey and discussion of garrisons' in *Archaeological Journal*, 149 (1993), 69–81.

Čerkasova, A. and Mosin, A., 'Le Donazioni del Demidoff in Russia' in Tonini, L. S. (ed.) *I Demidoff a Firenze e in Toscana* (Leo S. Olschki, 1996), 299–313.

Chaumont, M., 'Le Culte d'Anähitä à Staxr et les premiers Sassanides' in *Revu de l'Histoire des Religions*, 153 (1958), 154–175.

Clarke, G. W., 'Some victims of the persecution of Maximinus Thrax' in *Historia: Zeitschrift für Alte Geschichte*, 15 (1966), 445–453.

Clunn, T., *The Quest for the Lost Roman Legions* (Second edition, Savas Beatie, 2009).

Coggan, P., *Paper Promises: Money, Debt, and the New World Order* (Allen Lane, 2011).

Collingwood, R. G. and Wright, R. P., *The Roman Inscriptions of Britain* (Clarendon Press, 1965).

Colini, A. M., *Storia e topografia del Celio nell'antichità* (Atti della Pontificia Accademia Romana di Archeologia: Memorie 7, 1944).

Colli, D., Martines, M. and Palladino, S., Roma. 'Viale Manzoni, Via Emanuele Filberto. L'ammodernamento della linea A della Metropolitana: nuovi spunti per la conoscenza della topografia antica' in *The Journal of Fasti online*, www.fastionline.org/docs/FOLDER-it-2009-154.pdf, 2009).

Comici, C. and Bussani, A., 'Analysis of the River Isonzo discharge (1998–2005)' in *Bolletino di Geofisica Teorica e Applicata*, 48 (2007), 435–454.

Dando-Collins, S. *Legions of Rome: the Definitive History of Every Imperial Legion* (Quercus, 2010).

Daryaee, T., *Sasanian Persia: the Rise and Fall of an Empire* (I. B. Tauris, 2010).

de Blois, L., 'The Third Century Crisis and the Greek Elite in the Roman Empire' in *Historia: Zeitschrift für Alte Geschichte*, 33 (1984), 358–377.

De la Bédoyere, G., *Roman Britain: A New History* (Thames and Hudson, 2006).

Delbrück, R., *Die Münzbildnisse von Maximinus bis Carinus* (*Dar römische Herrscherbild*) (Berlin, 1940).

Den Hengst, D., 'The discussion of authorship' in Burgersdijk, D. W. P. and van Waarden, J. A. (eds), *Emperors and Historiography: Collected Essays on the Literature of the Roman Empire* (Brill, 2010), 177–185.

Dessau, H., 'Über Zeit und Persönlichkeit der Scriptores Historiae Augustae' in *Hermes*, 24 (1889), 337–392.

Dietz, K., *Senatus contra principem: Untersuchungen zur senatorischen Opposition gegen Kaiser Maximinus Thrax* (C. H. Beck'sche Verlagbuchhandlung, 1980).

Dignas, B. and Winter, E., *Rome and Persia in Late Antiquity: Neighbours and Rivals* (Cambridge University Press, 2007).

Dixon, K. R. and Southern, P., *The Roman Cavalry From the First to Third Century A.D.* (Routledge, 1992).

Dodgeon, M. H. and Lieu, N. C., *The Roman Eastern Frontier and the Persian Wars: a Documentary History* (Routledge, 1991).

Drinkwater, J., 2005, 'Maximinus to Diocletian and the "crisis"' in The Cambridge Ancient History (2nd edition, Vol XII, *The Crisis of Empire, A.D. 193–337* (Cambridge, 2005), 28–66.

Edwell, P. M., *Between Rome and Persia: The Middle Euphrates, Mesopotamia and Palmyra Under Roman Control* (Routledge, 2008).

Enmann, A., 'Eine verlorene Geschichte der römischen Kaiser' in *Philologus* (Supp. 4, 1884), 337.

Ensslin, W., 'Sassanid Persia (VI): The Wars with Rome' in *Cambridge Ancient History* 12 (1939), 126–137.

Ensslin, W., 'War Maximinus Thrax ein Germane?' in *Rheinische Museen*, 90 (1941), 1.

Espenak, F. and Meeus, J., *Five Millennium Catalog of Lunar Eclipses: −1999 to +3000 (2000 BCE to 3000 CE)*. NASA Technical Publication TP-2009-214173 (2009): http://ntrs.nasa.gov/archive/nasa/casi.ntrs.nasa.gov/20090028006.pdf.

Evans, J. K., 'Wheat production and its social consequences in the Roman World' in *The Classical Quarterly, New Series*, 31 (1981), 428–442.

Evans, R., *Roman Conquests: Asia Minor, Syria and Armenia* (Pen and Sword, 2011).

Ezov, A., 'The *numeri exploratorum* units in the German provinces and Raetia' in *Klio*, 79 (1997), 161–177.

Ezard, T. H. G., Pearson, P. N. and Purvis, A., 'Algorithmic approaches to aid species' delimitation in multidimensional morphospace' in *BMC Evolutionary Biology*, 10: 175 (2009), http://www.biomedcentral.com/1471-2148/10/175.

Felletti Maj, B. M., *Iconografia Romana Imperiale da Severo Alessandro a M. Aurelio Carino (222–285 d.C)* (Rome, 1958).

Fittschen, K., Ein Bildnis in Privatbesitz. Zum Realismus romischer Portrats der mittleren und spateren Prinzipatzeit. In *Eikones* (P. A. Stucky, ed., Bern, 1980).

Fitzgerald, C. M., 'Bronze statue of Trebonianus Gallus' in *Bulletin of the Metropolitan Museum of Art*, 1 (1905), 12–13.

Forbes, S. R., *Rambles in Rome: An Archaeological and Historical Guide to the Museums, Galleries, Villas, Churches, and Antiquities of Rome and the Campagna. Fifth Edition, Revised and Enlarged; Embracing all the Recent excavations and Discoveries* (Thomas Nelson and Sons, 1887).

Frakes, R. M., 'Cross-references to the Lost Books of Ammianus Marcellinus' in *Phoenix*, 49 (1995), 232–246.

Frank, T., 'Rome and Italy of the Empire' in *An Economic Survey of Ancient Rome, Volume 5* (Frank, T., ed., Johns Hopkins Press, 1936).

Freeman, C., *A New History of Early Christianity* (Yale University Press, 2009).

Frothingham, A. L., 'Archaeological news' in *The American Journal of Archaeology and of the History of the Fine Arts*, 2 (1886), 203–333.

Frye, R.N., 2005, 'The Sassanians' in *The Cambridge Ancient History, 2nd edition, Vol XII, The Crisis of Empire, A.D. 193–337* (Cambridge, 2005), 461–480.

Gagé, J., 'Les organisations de "iuvenes" en Italie et en Afrique du début du IIIe siècle au "bellum Aquileiense" (238 ap. J-C.)' in *Historia: Zetschrift fur Alte Geschichte* (1970), 232–258.

Gibbon, E., *The Decline and Fall of the Roman Empire* (6 volumes; first published 1776–1784; reprinted by Everyman's Library, 1993).

Gilliam, J. F., 'The *Dux Ripae* at Dura' in *Transactions and Proceedings of the American Philological Association*, 72 (1941), 157–175.

Gnoli, T., 'From *Praepositus praetenturae* to *Dux Ripae*. The Roman "Grand Strategy" on the Middle Euphrates (2nd–3rd Cent. AD)', in *The Late Roman Army in the Near East from Diocletian to the Arab Conquest. Proceedings of a Colloquium held at Potenza, Acerenza and Matera, Italy (May 2005)*, Lewin, A.S. (ed.) , (Pellegrini, 2007), 49–55.

Goessler, P., 'Neue römische Funde aus Cannstatt' in *Germania*, 15 (1931), 6–15.

Godbout, L., *GLBTQ, An Encyclopedia of Gay, Lesbian, Bisexual, Transgender, and Queer Culture* (Chicago University Press, 2004).

Goldsworthy, A., *The Fall of Carthage: The Punic Wars 265–146 BC* (Cassell, 2000).

Goldsworthy, A., *The Fall of the West: The Death of the Roman Superpower* (Weidenfield and Nicolson, 2009).

Graf, F., *Gestures and Conventions: the Gestures of Roman Actors and Orators* (Polity Press, 1991).

Gricourt, J., 'Alexandre Sévère "Parthicus Maximus"?' in *Congresso Internationale di Numismatica 11–16 Settembre 1961, Vol II* (Rome, 1965), 319–326.

Gurney, L. W. and Gurney, P. J., 'The *Scriptores Historiae Augustae*: History and Controversy' in *Literary and Linguistic Computing*, 13 (1998a), 105–109.

Gurney, P. J. and Gurney, L. W., 'Authorship attribution of the *Scriptores Historiae Augustae*' in *Literary and Linguistic Computing*, 13 (1998b), 119–131.

Gurney, P. J. and Gurney, L. W., 'Subsets and homogeneity: Authorship attribution of the *Scriptores Historiae Augustae*' in *Literary and Linguistic Computing*, 13 (1998c), 133–140.

Haarl, O., 'Die Kataphraktarier im römischen Heer' in *Panegyrik und Realität, Jahrbuch RGZM*, 43 (2009), 601–627.

Haegemans, K., *Imperial Authority and Dissent: The Roman Empire in AD 235–238*. Studia Hellenistica, No. 47 (Petters, 2010).

Haskell, F., and others, *Anatole Demidoff: Prince of San Donato (1812–70)* (Trustees of the Wallace Collection, 1994).

Haverfield, F., 'The Name Augustus' in *Journal of Roman Studies*, 5 (1915), 249–250.

Haynes, I., *Blood of the Provinces: The Roman Auxilia and the Making of Provincial Society from Augustus to the Severans* (Oxford University Press, 2013).

Haynes, I., Liverani, P., Spinola, G. and Salvatore, P., 'Archaeological fieldwork reports: The Lateran Project' in *Papers of the British School at Rome*, 80 (2012), 369–371.

Heather, P.J., *The Goths* (Blackwell, 1996).

Hedeagar, L., 'Empire, frontier, and the barbarian hinterland: Rome and Northern Europe from AD 1–400' in Kristiansen, K. and Paludan-Müller, D. (eds), *New Directions in Archaeology* (Copenhagan, 1987), 191–261.

Hemingway, S., McGregor, S. and Smith, D., 'The bronze statue of Trebonianus Gallus in the Metropolitan Museum of Art: restoration, technique, and interpretation' in E. Risser and D. Saunders (eds.), *The Restoration of Ancient Bronzes: Naples and Beyond* (Getty, 2013), 113–136.

Hekster, O., *Rome and its Empire, 193–284* (Edinburgh University Press, 2008).

Herrin, J., *Byzantium: The Surprising Life of a Medieval Empire* (Penguin, 2007).

Herrmann, P., 'Die Karriere eines prominenten Juristen aus Thyateira' in *Tyche*, 12 (1997), 111–123.

Holland, T., *In the Shadow of the Sword: The Battle for Global Empire and the End of the Ancient World* (Abacus, 2012).

Holmes, D. I., 'The evolution of stylometry in humanities scholarship' in *Literary and Linguistic Computing*, 13 (1998), 111–117.

Home, J., *The Siege of Aquileia. A Tragedy. As it is Acted at the Theatre Royal in Drury Lane* (G. and E. Ewing, 1760).

Honoré, A. M., *Ulpian: Pioneer of Human Rights* (Second edition, Oxford University Press, 2002).

Hopkins, C., *The Discovery of Dura-Europos* (Yale University Press, 1976).

Honoré, T., *Emperors and Lawyers* (Clarendon Press, 1994).

Hughes, I., *Belisarius: The Last Roman General* (Pen and Sword Military, 2009).

Hughes, I., *Stilicho: The Vandal Who Saved Rome* (Pen and Sword Military, 2010).

Hughes, I., *Aetius: Atilla's Nemesis* (Pen and Sword Military, 2012).

Hummer, H. J., 'The fluidity of barbarian identity: the ethnogenesis of Alemanni and Suebi, AD 200–500' in *Early Medieval Europe*, 7 (1998), 1–27.

Humphrey, J. H., *Roman Circuses, Arenas for Chariot Racing* (University of California Press, 1986).

Isaac, B., *The Invention of Racism in Classical Antiquity* (Princeton University Press, 2004).

Jardé, A., *Études critiques sur la vie et le règne de Sévère Alexandre* (Paris, 1925).

Josi, E., 'Scopertr nella basilica Constantiniana al Laterano ' in *Pontifico Instituto dio Archeologia Cristiana* (1934).

Keay, J., *China: A History* (Harper Collins, 2008).

Kelly, B., 'Riot control and imperial ideology in the Roman empire' in *Phoenix*, 61 (2007), 150–176.

Kettenhoffen, E., *Die Römisch-persischen Kriege des 3. Jahrunderts n. Chr. nach der Inschrift Sahpuhrs I am der Ka' be-ye Zartost* (SKZ) (TAVO, 1982).

Khachikyan, A., *History of Armenia: a Brief Review* (Edit Print, 2010).

King, C. E., 'Roman portraiture: images of power?' in *Roman Coins and Public Life under the Empire*, Paul, G. M. and Lerardi, M. (eds.), Togo Salmon Papers (Ann Arbor, 1999), 123–136.

Klawans, H. L., 'The acromegaly of Maximinus I: the possible influence of a pituitary tumor on the life and death of a Roman Emperor' in *Historical Aspects of the Neuroscience: A Festschrift for Macdonald Critchley*, Rose, F.R. and Bynum, W. F., eds., (Raven Press, 1982), 317–326.

Klebs, E., 'Die *Scriptores Historiae Augustae*' in *Rheinische Museen*, 47 (1892), 1–52, 515–549.

Kleiner, F. S., *A History of Roman Art: Enhanced Edition* (Wadsworth, Cengage Learning , 2010).

Kotula, T., 'L'insurrection des Gordiens et 'Afrique Romain' in *Eos*, 51 (1959/1960), 197–211.

Królczyk, K., 'Der Germanfeldzug des Kaisers Caracalla im lichte der epigraphischen quellen' in Rucinski, S., Balbuza, C., and Królczyk, K. (eds), Studia Lesco Mrozewicz ab amicis et discipulis dedicata (Inttytut Historii UAM, Poznan, 2011).

Lanciani, R. A., 'Gli alloggiamenti degli Equites Singulares' in *Bullettino della Commissione Archeologica Comunale di Roma*, 1885 (1885), 137–156.

Lanciani, R. A., *Gli alloggiamenti degli equites singulares* (R. Accad. dei Lincei, 1886).

Lanciani, R., *New Tales of Old Rome* (Macmillan, 1901).

Lanciani, R. A., *Storia degli scavi di Roma e Notizie Intorno le Collezioni Romane di Anticha* (Volume 1, Ermano Loescher, 1902).

Langford, J., *Maternal Megalomania: Julia Domna and the Imperial Politics of Motherhood* (Johns Hopkins University Press, 2013).

La Rocca, E., Presicce, C.P. and Lo Monaco, A. (eds), *L'Età dell'Angoscia, Roma, Musei Capitolini, 28 gennaio – 4 Ottobre 2015*, (Rome, 2015).

Le Blant, E., 'Lettre au sujet des découvertes nouvellement faites à Rome' in *Comptes Rendus des Séances de l'Académie des Inscriptions et Belles-Lettres, 30e année*, 1 (1886), 38–41.

Le Bohec, Y., *La troisième légion Auguste* (Paris, 1989).

Le Bohec, Y., *The Imperial Roman Army* (Batsford, 1994).

Lee, J.E., *Description of a Roman Building and other Remains Lately Discovered at Caerleon*, (J.R. Smith, 1850).

Lehmann, G. A., *Imperium und Barbaricum* (Osterreichische Akademie der Wissenschaften, 2011).

Lézine, A., 'Notes sur l'amphitheatre de Thysdrusi' in *Cahiers de Tunisie*, 8 (1960), 29–50.

Liggi, I., 'Caecilia Paulina: un destin d'impératrice' in *Etudes de Lettres*, 1 (1998), 131–158.

Lippold, A., 'Maximinus Thrax und die Christen' in *Historia: Zeitschrift fur Alte Geschichte*, 24 (1975), 479–492.

Lippold, A., *Kommentar zur Vita Maximini Duo der Historia Augusta* (Bonn, 1991).

Lönne, P. and Meyer, M., 'Tief im Feindesland. Das römische Schlachtfeld des 3. Jahrhunderts vom Harzhorn, Lkr. Nordheim' in *Programmheft zur Ringvorlesung 2009 Geschichte – Archaologie – Legenden 2000 Jahre Varusschlacht* (Frei Unuiversitat, Berlin, 2009), 20–22.

Loriot, X., 'Les premières années de la grande crise de IIIe siècle. De l'avènement de Maximin le Thrace (235) á la mort de Gordien III (244)' in *ANRW* 2.2 (1975), 657–787.

Luttwak, E. N., *The Grand Strategy of the Roman Empire* (Johns Hopkins University Press, 1976).

Machiavelli, N., *The Prince* (1513, Translated by W. K. Marriott, www.publicliterature.org/pdf/1232.pdf).

Magie, D., *Historia Augusta*, Vols I–III. Translated with Introduction and Notes by D. Magie (Loeb Classical Library, 1921–1932).

Magie, D., *Roman Rule in Asia Minor to the End of the Third Century after Christ* (Two volumes, Princeton University Press, 1950).

Mann, J. C., 'A note on the Legion IV Italica' in *Zeitschrift für Papyrologie une Epigraphik*, 126 (1999), 228.

Marlowe, E., *Shaky Ground: Context, Connoisseurship and the History of Roman Art* (A & C Black, 2013).

Marlowe, E., 'Said to be or said not to be: The findspot of the so-called Trebonianus Gallus statue in the Metropolitan Museum in New York' in *Journal of the History of Collections*, fhu059, doi: 10.1093/jhc/fhu059 (2014).

Marriott, I., 'The authorship of the *Historia Augusta*: two computer studies' in *Journal of Roman Studies*, 69 (1979), 65–67.

Mather, F. J., 'A statue of Trebonianus Gallus' in *The Burlington Magazine for Connoisseurs*, v. 8, no. 32 (November 1905), 148–151.

Martin, R.-P., 'Die Rache der Romer. So besiegten sie die Germanen. Neues Schlachtfeld am Harz entdeckt' in *National Geographic (Deutschland)* (June, 2010), 69–92.

Matthews, J., *The Roman Empire of Ammianus* (Michigan Classical Press, 2007).

McCanles, M., 'Macchiavelli's "Principe" and the textualization of history'. in *MLN*, 97 (1982) 1–18.

McLaughlin, R., *The Roman Empire and the Indian Ocean: The Ancient World Economy and the Kingdoms of Africa, Arabia and India* (Pen and Sword, 2014).

McLynn, F., *Marcus Aurelius: Warrior, Philosopher, Emperor* (Random House, 2009).

Meissner, B., 'Pseudo-Technik und Paratechnik: Technik und Wissenschaft in den *Kestoi* des Julius Africanus' in Wallraff, M. and Mecella, L. (eds.), *Die Kestoi des Julius Africanus und ihre Überlieferung. Texte und Untersuchungen zur Geschichte der altchristlichen Literatur Bd. 165* (Walter de Gruyter, 2009, 17–37).

Mennen, I., *Power and Status in the Roman Empire, AD 193–284* (Brill, 2011).

Merkel, E., 'Bibliographie Franz Altheim' in Stiehl, R. and Stier, H.E. (eds.) *Beiträge zur Alten Geschichte und deren Nachleben* (Walter de Gruyter and Co., 1970), 390–426.

Meyer, C., *Greco-Scythian Art and the Birth of Eurasia: From Classical Antiquity to Russian Modernity* (Oxford Studies in Ancient Culture and Representation, Oxford University Press, 2013).

Mielczarek, M., *Cataphracti and Clibanarii. Studies on the Heavy Armoured Cavalry of the Ancient World* (Lodz, 1993).

Mommsen, T., *Römische Geschichte, Vol. 5. Die Provinzen von Caeasar bis Diokletian* (Berlin, 1894).

Mommsen, T., *The History of Rome* (Macmillan, 1901).

Montferrand, A. de., *Jules César. Statue antique en bronze* (St. Petersburg, 1849).

Moralee, J., 'Maximinus Thrax and the politics of race in late Antiquity' in *Greece and Rome, Second Series*, 55 (2008), 55–82.

Mullens, H. G., 'The Revolt of the Civilians, A. D. 237–8' in *Greece and Rome*, 50 (1948) 65–77.

Neverov, O., 'Le sculture antiche nella collezione Demidoff' in Tonini, L. S. (ed.) *I Demidoff a Firenze e in Toscana* (Leo S. Olschki, 1996), 157–164.

Oates, D., *Studies in the Ancient History of Northern Iraq* (Oxford University Press, 1968).

Parker, P., *The Empire Stops Here: A Journey Along the Frontiers of the Roman World* (Pimlico, 2009).

Partington, J. R., *A History of Greek Fire and Gunpowder* (Johns Hopkins University Press, 1960).

Passerini, A., 'Gli aumenti del soldo militare da Commodo a Maximino' in *Athenaeum*, 24 (1946), 145–159.

Peachin, M., *Roman Imperial Titulature and Chronology A.D. 235–284*. Studia Amstelodamensia ad epigraphicum, ius antiquum et papyrolocicam pertinentia, 29 (Amsterdam, 1990).

Pearce, J. M. S., *Fragments of Neurological History* (Imperial College Press, 2003).

Pellegrini, G., 'Anatolio Demidoff Principe di San Donato' in *Nuova Antologia*, 2105 (1976).

Petraccia Lucernoni, M. F., 'Epigrafi aquileiesi relative al riassetto della vie Annia e Gemina e l'origo di Massimino il Trace' in Mirabella Roberti, M. (ed.), *Aquileia e Roma. Atti della XVII settima di studi aquileieisi, 24–29 aprile 1986* (Udine, 1987), 119–136.

Peter, H., *Historia Augusta* (Two volumes, Teubner, 1865).

Potter, D. S., *The Roman Empire at Bay AD 180–395* (Routledge, 2004).

Pringle, H., *The Master Plan: Himmler's Scholars and the Holocaust* (Hyperion, 2006).

Prodromídis, P. I., *Another view on an old inflation: environment and policies in the Roman empire up to Diocletian's price edict* (Centre of Planning and Economic Research, Athens, 2006). Available online: http://www.kepe.gr/pdf/D.P/dp_85.pdf.

Rathbone, D., 'Monetisation, not price-inflation, in third century AD Egypt?' in King, C. E. and Wigg, D. G. (eds.), *Coin Finds and Coin Use in the Roman World: The Thirteenth Oxford Symposium on Coinage and Monetary History 25–27.3.1993* (Gebr Mann, 1996) 321–339.

Reece, R., *The Later Roman Empire: An Archaeology AD 150–600* (Second edition, Tempus, 2007).

Reuter, M., 'Der Wiederaufbau des obergermanisch-raetischen Limes unter Maximinus Thrax' in Gudea, N. (ed.) *Proceedings of the 17th International Congress of Roman Frontier Studies, Zalau 1999* (1999), 533–537.

Rhodes, P., 'Physical deformity of Richard III' in *British Medical Journal*, 2(6103) (Dec. 24, 1977), 1650–1652.

Ridley, R., 'To be taken with a pinch of salt: the destruction of Carthage' in *Classical Philology*, 81 (1986), 140–146.

Rohrbacher, D., 'The sources of the Historia Augusta re-examined' in *Histos*, 7 (2013), 146–180.

Ross, S. K., *Roman Edessa: Politics and Culture on the Eastern Fringes of the Roman Empire, 114–242 CE* (Routledge, 2001).

Roxan, M., 'Settlement of the veterans of the auxilia: a preliminary study' p. 483–492 in Groenman-van Waateringe et al. (eds), *Roman Frontier Studies 1995: Proceedings of the XVIth Roman Frontier Studies Conference 1995* (Oxbow Monograph 91, 1997).

Rudman, J., 'Non-traditional authorship attribution studies in the *Historia Augusta*: some caveats' in *Literary and Linguistic Computing*, 13 (1998), 151–157.

Salway, P., *A History of Roman Britain* (Oxford University Press, 1993).

Salway, B., 'Prefects, patroni, and decurions: a new perspective on the album of Canusium' in *Bulletin of the Institute of Classical Studies*, 44 (2011), 115–171.

Schönberger, H., 'The Roman Frontier in Germany: an archaeological survey' in *Journal of Roman Studies*, 59 (1969), 144–197.

Sear, D. R., *Roman Coins and Their Values* (Second edition, Seaby Publications, 1974).

Seeley, J. R., *The Expansion of England* (London, 1883).

Shaw, B. D., 'Lamasba: An ancient irrigation community' in *Antiquités Africaines*, 18 (1982), 61–103.

Sheaves, R., 'A history of acromegaly' in *Pituitary*, 2 (1999), 7–28.

Shuĭskiĭ, V.K., 'Auguste de Montferrand: The Story of the Life and Work' [In Russian], (Moscow, 2005). Sidebottom, H., 'The date of composition of Herodian's history' in *L'Antiquité Classique*, 66 (1997), 271–276.

Sidebottom, H., 'Herodian's historical methods and understanding of history' in *ANRW* 234 (1998), 2775–2975.

Sidebottom, H., 'Roman imperialism: the changed outward trajectory of the Roman Empire' in *Historia: Zeitschrift für Alte Geschichte*, 54 (2005.), 315–330.

Sidebottom, H., *Iron and Rust* (Harper Collins, 2014).

Simpson, C. J., 'The date of dedication of the Temple of Mars Ultor' in *The Journal of Roman Studies*, 67 (1977), 91–94.

Smith, W. and Anthon, C., *A New Classical Dictionary of Greek and Roman Biography, Mythology, and Geography partly based upon the Dictionary of Greek and Roman Biography and Mythology* (Harper and Brothers, 1851).

Speidel, M. A., 'Roman army pay scales' in *The Journal of Roman Studies*, 82 (1992), 87–106.

Speidel, M. A., 'Roman army pay scales revisited: responses and answers' in Reddé, M. (ed.), *De l'or pour les braves! Soldes, armées et circulation monétaire dans le monde romain. Actes de la table ronde organisée par l'UMR 8210 (AnHiMa), l'Institut national d'histoire de l'art (12–13 septembre 2013)* (Bordeaux 2014), 53–62.

Speidel, M. P., 'Maxentius and his "Equites Singulares" at the battle of the Milvian Bridge' in *Classical Antiquity*, 5 (1986), 253–262.

Speidel, M. P., 'The army at Aquileia, the Moesiaci Legion, and the shield emblems in the Notitia Dignitatum' in *Saalburg-Jahrbuch*, 45 (1990), 68–72.

Speidel, M. P., *Die Denkmaler der Kaiserreiter Equites Singulares Augusti* (Rheinland-Verlag, 1994a).

Speidel, M. P., *Riding for Caesar: the Roman Emperor's Horse Guards* (Harvard University Press, 1994b).

Spraul, J. E. H., 'Governors of Tingitana' in *Antiquités Africaines*, 30 (1994), 235–260.

Stark, R., *The Rise of Christianity: a Sociologist Reconsiders History* (Princeton, 1996).

Stendhal, H. B., *Promenades en Rome* (Vol. 1, Paris, 1828).

Stephenson, P., *Constantine: Unconquered Emperor, Christian Victor* (Quercus, 2009).

Sutherland, C. H. V., *Roman Coins* (Barrie and Jenkins, 1974).

Sviatolslav, D. '"Good emperors" and emperors of the Third Century' in *Hermes*, 2 (2004), 211–244.

Syme, R., *Ammianus and the* Historia Augusta (Oxford University Press, 1968).

Syme, R., *Emperors and Biography: Studies in the* Historia Augusta (Clarendon Press, 1971).

Syme, R., 'Danubian and Balkan emperors' in *Historia: Zeitschrift für Alte Geschichte*, 22 (1973), 310–316.

Syme, R., 'Controversy abating and credulity curbed?' in *London Review of Books*, 4–17 September, 1980.

Tahberer, B., 'B. *Tahberer Birikimi Antik Kilikia Sikkeleri Derlemesi (Ancient Cilician coins from the collection of B. Tahberer)*' https://www.academia.edu/9189196/SNG_TAHBERER_-_CILICIA_PART_2_CATALOGUE (2014).

Tavano, S., *Aquileia e Grado. Storia – arte – cultura* (Trieste, 1986).

Teuffel, W. S., *Geschichte der Römischen Literatur* (Scientia-Verlag, 1870).

Thomson, R. W., *Agathangelos. History of the Armenians* (Albany, 1976).

Townsend, P. W., *The Administration of Gordian III* (Yale University Press, 1934).

Townsend, P. W., 'The revolution of A.D. 238. The Leaders and their aims' in *Yale Classical Studies*, 14 (1955), 49–105.

Todd, M., *The Early Germans* (2nd edition, Blackwell, 2004).

Trousset, P., 'L'idée de frontière au Sahara et les données archéologiques' in *Enjeux Sahariens*, 47–48 (Table Ronde, CRESM, 1981).

Tse, E. K., Tweedie, F. J. and Frischer, B. D., 'Unravelling the purple thread: function word variability and the *Scriptores Historiae Augustae*' in *Literary and Linguistic Computing*, 13 (1998), 141–149.

Tsonchev, D., *Le Sanctuaire Thrace près du Village de Baktoun* (Impr. de lÉtat, 1941).

Tunney, H. J., 'Home's Douglas' in *Bulletin of the University of Kansas Humanistic Studies*, 3 (1924), 1–100.

Varner, E., *Mutilation and Tranformation: Damnatio Memoriae and Roman Imperial Portraiture* (Leiden, 2004).

van Sickle, C. E., 'The repair of roads in Spain under the Roman Empire' in *Classical Philology*, 24 (1929), 77–78.

Van Slyke, D. G., '*Sacramentum* in ancient non-Christian authors' in *Antiphon*, 9 (2005), 167–206.

Visconti, C. L., 'Trovamenti di oggetti d'art e di antichità figurata' in *Bullettino della Commissione Archeologia Communale di Roma 1886*, 3 (1886), 163–169.

Volkmann, E., *De Herodiani vita, scriptis fideque* (Königsberg, 1859).

von Köhne, B., 'Musée de sculpture antique de Mr. de Montferrand' in *Zeitschrift für Münz-, Siegel- und Wappenkunde*, 6 (1852), 1–97, *Mémoires de la Société Impériale d'Archéologie*, 6 (1852).

Vostchinina, A., *Musee de L'Hermitage. Le Portrait Romain* (Leningrad, 1974).

Waldhauer, O., *Die Antiken Skulpturen der Ermitage* (Three volumes, De Gruyter and Co., 1928–1936).

Webber, C., *The Gods of Battle: The Thracians at War 1500 BC–AD 150* (Pen and Sword, 2011).

Wegner, M., *Das römische Herrscherbild: Gordianus III bis Carinus* (Deutsches Archäologisches Intitut, Gebr. Mann Verlag, 1979), 89–90.

Wells, H. G., *A Short History of the World* (Penguin Classics, 1922; reprinted 2006).

Weitzmann, K., *Age of Spirituality: Late Antique and Early Christian Art, Third to Seventh Century. Catalogue of the Exhibition at the Metropolitan Museum of Art, November 19, 1977 through February 12, 1978* (Princeton University Press, 1979).

White, P., 'The authorship of the *Historia Augusta*' in *The Journal of Roman Studies*, 57 (1967), 115–133.

Whittaker, C. R., *Herodian: History of the Empire (Translated with footnotes)*. 2 vols. (Loeb Classical Library, 1969–1970).

Whittaker, C. R., *Frontiers of the Roman Empire: A Social and Economic Study* (The Johns Hopkins University Press, 1994).

Wiegels, R., Moosbauer, G., Meyer, M., Lönne, P. and Geschwinde, M., 'Eine romische Dolabra mit Inschrift aus dem Umfeld des Schlachtfeldes am Harzhorn (Lkr. Northeim) in Niedersachsen' in *Archäologisches Korrespondenzblatt*, 41 (2011), 561–570.

Wiegels, R. 'Tribunus legionis IIII (Italicae)? Zu einer Notiz in der Historia Augusta und zur Vita des maximinus Thrax vor seiner Kaiserhebung' in *Klio*, 94 (2012), p. 436–461.

Wiegels, R., 'Zu den Herresformationen Roms an Rhein und oberer Donau in der Zeit des Alexander Severus und Maximinus Thrax' in *Klio*, 96 (2014), p. 93–143.

Wood, S. E., *Roman Portrait Sculpture, 217–260 A.D.* (E.J. Brill, 1986).

Yenne, B., *Hitler's Master of the Dark Arts: Himmler's Black Knights and the Occult Origins of the SS* (Zenith, 2010).

Index